AID MEMOIR

AID MEMOIR

Larry Hollingworth

Refuge Press, New York, 2021

Published in the United States by The Refuge Press
Originally published in 1994 by Heinemann
www.refugepress.com
The Refuge Press shares the registered trademark of The Center for International Humanitarian Cooperation, of which it is a part.

ISBN#13: 978-0-8232-9703-0 (Hard Cover)
ISBN#13: 978-0-8232-9702-3 (Paperback)
ISBN#13: 978-0-8232-9704-7 (ePub)
ISBN#13: 978-0-8232-9705-4 (WebPDF)

Cover and book design: Mauro Sarri

Printed in the United States of America.

To Josie, Sarah Jo and Matthew, to the British Army, to UNHCR, and to the people of Bosnia—Serb, Croat and Muslim—for giving me the opportunities which have shaped me and made me what I am.

Acknowledgements

Roger Courtiour. For the idea of the book.
Mark Lucas. For the translation of idea to action.
Tom Weldon. For the translation of action to book.
Ron Redmond. For constant support.
Sylvana Foa. Without whom, no publicity.
Glynne Evans. For wisdom, support, and advice.
Dr. Gary McGrath and New England College. For a "safe haven."
Tony Beard. For help and advice.
Tina West. For technical support.
Vesna Stancic. For Bosnian translation and interpretation.
RAF Lyneham especially the Herc crews.
Colonel Peter Williams and 1 Bn Coldstream Guards.

This book will not explain Bosnia but it may explain what it was like to work in Bosnia with Bosnians. I hope that it will make you laugh; I lament that it may make you cry. I will be proud if it makes you proud, and I am right if it makes you ashamed. The journalists who have covered the war are writing books about the politics and the politicians, soon the historians will write and put the war into context with the previous history of the country and the region. The aim of this book is not to encroach on their territory. This is an account of two years in war-torn Bosnia working as an aid worker. It is a ramble through my mind and my memories. It is how I saw it and as I remember it. Dates may be wrong, names may be wrong, but the events are right.

Could it be that there is not room for all men to live in this wonderful world, under this fathomless starry sky? Is it really possible that in the midst of such natural splendour, feelings of hatred and vengeance, or the passion to destroy one's fellows could reside in the hearts of man?

– Leo Tolstoy, *The Raid.*

Table of Contents

List of Abbreviations

APC Armoured Personnel Carrier

BH Command UNPROFOR Headquarters in Bosnia-Herzegovina

BiH Government of Bosnia-Herzegovina

COR Commission for Refugees

ECMM Monitors under the auspices of the European Commission. Multi-national teams who wore white uniforms and were unarmed.

HDZ Croatian Democratic Union; Bosnian Croat Ruling Party

HVO Croat Defence Council; Bosnian Croat Army

PTT Post and Telecommunications Office. The UNPROFOR Headquarters in Sarajevo and in Srebrenica

RQMS Regimental Queartermaster Seargent

SDA Party for Democratic Action; Bosnian Muslim Ruling Party

SDS Serb Democratic Party; Serb Ruling Party

UN United Nations

UNHCR United Nations High Commissioner for Refugees

UNICEF United Nations Children's Fund

UNPROFOR United Nations Protection Force

WHO World Health Organisation

WFP World Food Programme

Foreword

By Jamie McGoldrick

The release of a second edition of this book is extremely timely. We are given a personal insight into the shaping of the international response and assistance culture when modern humanitarianism was in its infancy. This insight underscores the increasing threats and impediments to humanitarian action today, both ideological and overwhelmingly political. These are seen in shrinking operating space, given counter terrorism legislation that effectively criminalises humanitarian action, and insufficient funding, based more than ever on a geo-political calculus.

In this revised version, Larry's trademark dictum shines through brightly as "to thine own self be true." He lays bare the trials and tribulations during the early years of the Balkans conflict in this personal account of perseverance, humility, and genuine human empathy in one of contemporary history's darkest times.

Larry shepherds the reader through the humanitarian nightmare that had befallen the people of the Balkans in the early 1990s through a hands-on account, which grows darker with each chapter. He writes that he "felt close to the refugees but not close enough to really understand." But what he lacked in understanding he made up for in guile, bravery, and resilience as he battled a conveyor belt of incidents and challenges that tested his resolve as a front-line humanitarian worker.

This is an emotional journey without maps, peppered with belligerent and uncaring people in power, and others showing extraordinary kindness as they tried to help thousands of civilians caught up in the horror and chaos of the conflict.

The wars in the Balkans, Rwanda, and Somalia in the 1990s, changed forever the role of future international humanitarian response. As such, the earlier missionary zeal has now been replaced by a more pragmatic and business-like approach. This book takes us back and captures a period of humanitarian response and helps chart a necessary course through the dominant forces of all things politics ruling our work. The role and interference by States started in earnest during this period. Politicization of aid and exploitation of humanitarian agencies often lead to unprincipled and unprofessional behaviour and heightened the need for reform. Humanitarian principles were stretched with the blurring of lines at the field level. Increasingly, since those early days, it has become the norm for military actors to operate alongside humanitarians, private contractors, political actors, and member states working in the deep field.

Sadly, as a result, conflict resolution and mediation are interwoven in the work of humanitarian response. The substance of humanitarian work increasingly replaces political discourse resulting in inaction or humanitarian action being based solely on political or military imperatives.

As humanitarians, this book should be a reminder to our own conscience. The book reconfirms the criticality of humanitarian principles in action and being close to the people in need. Larry has taken the hard lessons and loss of innocence from his time in the Balkans and set out to improve the humanitarian system. The growth and progress at the International Institute of Humanitarian Affairs at Fordham University, and the thousands of graduates and trained humanitarians who have passed through its doors, are a testament to Larry's mission.

I count myself very fortunate to have worked with him at close quarters and personally benefited from his sage advice and front-line experiences.

One

The Call

I returned to the UK from my tour with Somali refugees, minus my Parker pen which I had had for more than ten years, my UN blue anorak which I had had for five years, and twenty kilos in weight. The pen and anorak were "liberated" by my driver at a halt for a wee on my way to Nairobi airport. The kilos were lost as the result of bugs picked up in "the bush."

My first two weeks at home were dictated by a simple time and distance calculation. At least twice an hour I needed to find a toilet. A time and motions study. Fortunately, the local military medical centre near my home had on its staff a graduate of the School of Hygiene and Tropical Medicine, he cured my loo dependency and I was then ready to move.

The situation in ex-Yugoslavia was the lead story in all the newspapers. UNHCR was the leading aid agency. Jose Maria Mendiluce was the Special Envoy. He and I had worked together in Geneva. A small, broad, urbane, and elegant Spaniard, he is a brilliant linguist with an open charm which hides experience gained as a veteran of tough tours in South America and Kurdistan.

In just over a year, he had seen a lot of history in its making. Slovenia had fought briefly and successfully for its independence, Croatia and Serbia had gone to war. The newly independent, UN-recognised Republic of Bosnia Herzegovina had been pronounced stillborn by the doctor of medicine Radovan Karadzic, who led the Bosnian Serbs. His diagnosis was faulty as was so often to be the case. The infant state was not dead, but, nor was it healthy. Its lifeblood was regrouped and separated; its limbs stretched from their sockets. But it was alive. It was now an incubator state, vulnerable and isolated. Kept alive by infusions of rhetoric and promise and by occasional injections of aid. Sarajevo, its capital and seat of government, was battle scarred and besieged, the population shelled and hungry. To alleviate the suffering, the UN Security Council on the eighth of June had voted to open Sarajevo airport for the delivery of humanitarian aid. The airport was in Bosnian Serb held territory; their tanks and soldiers were on the runway. They protested. On the 28th of June, President Mitterand, in a bold, brave move flew into Sarajevo. The airport was then deemed to be open. The Bosnian Serb forces withdrew under the watchful blue eyes of the newly appointed Commander of Sector Sarajevo, the Canadian General Lewis Mackenzie.

Madame Sadako Ogata, The High Commissioner for Refugees in Geneva, was determined that UNHCR, the organisation she directed, would run the airlift. Jose Maria Mendiluce, her Special Envoy, already had a man on the ground in Sarajevo. The task was to airlift humanitarian aid from Zagreb to Sarajevo to feed the starving blockaded population of 385,000. The decision as to who should operate the airlift lay with the UN Secretary General Boutros Boutros-Ghali. He had an offer from the United States who wished to undertake the task. With hindsight, an amazing offer, and one which, if he had accepted, would have altered the UN involvement and maybe the whole course of the war. The Secretary General gave the task to UNHCR.

A new task needed more staff. I was called to Geneva.

The British Government, very quick off the mark, had agreed to send Wing Commander Angus Morris to set up an air operations cell in the headquarters of UNHCR.

Angus is a dynamic, very switched on, silver haired, handsome RAF officer, with lots of professional charm. He is a Scot. He speaks with little or no accent, in short measured sentences. He is an officer who has perfected the art of giving orders as suggestions.

Angus and I set up an office in a small room adjacent to the UN-HCR communications centre. From there we could contact Zagreb, the UK Ministry of Defence, and the military headquarters of the proposed donor nations. America, France, Italy, as well as the UK had tentatively offered aircraft for the airlift. The Americans sent a team to Geneva to join us headed by Lt. Col. Larry Smith, whom I had worked with previously when getting aid into Turkey.

The whole ex-Yugoslav operation was under the supervision of a senior UNHCR director, Eric Morris, a taciturn American. Bright, direct and reserved. Eric quickly realised that the Geneva end was becoming larger than the sharp end. He therefore decided that I should go to Zagreb and run the airlift. An excellent decision, as I knew the players in Geneva and they would know the man on the ground. It was also a great decision for me, as I am not a "corridor of power" warrior. Eric told me to contact the UNHCR Chief of Operations in Zagreb, Tony Land, an Englishman who had just returned from Afghanistan. In a short, sharp call, Tony made it clear that he was looking for—*a man who will fight for refugees in the most difficult of circumstances. A man who will lie for them, cheat for them, and be a rogue for them. You are ex-army, aren't you?*—he concluded. *You have the right background.* I was not too sure if I was going to like Tony.

I collected a satellite telephone from "comms," a mark one edition, it weighed a tonne, came in an enormous grey box and bore a label demanding to be handled with care. I was given a quick lesson on assembling it and a handbook which was even less clear but had the benefit of being unclear in five different languages. I headed off to Geneva airport where I was to meet up with another recruit for ex-Yugoslavia, a journalist Peter Kessler, who was going out as Public Information Officer. My first minutes with Peter were not too successful. He was waiting for me and was a little irritable. I was late. The check-in desk was closing and we were in great danger of missing the flight. I was short with him. In addition to my own kit, I was struggling with this enormous and heavy satellite phone. The Swiss, to whom time is an obsession, are never happy with late arrivals, the Swiss, to whom money is an obsession, are very happy with excess baggage. Peter and plane left without me.

I took the next flight, changed aircraft at Frankfurt, and sat next to Peter on the flight to Zagreb! Albeit he was cool and calm, I was hot and sticky. In Zagreb, I was briefed by Jose Maria and Tony. They gave me a rundown on the war so far. Jose Maria was anecdotal. He knew all the key players. Tony is like a housemaster who has a good brain but who prefers to run the school sports. He was academic and aggressive. His arms swept over the huge map on the wall. He prodded at place names, followed the course of rivers with his pen. Pointed at Corps headquarters, named Generals. I tried to take notes. But in truth, I knew where Zagreb was only because Angus Morris had pinpointed it on his map. To save my life I could not have placed my finger on Belgrade on this huge map which Tony knew so well.

– *What was the name of that man again?*—I asked.

– *Prlic*—replied Tony.

– *And the General?*

– *Hadzihasanovic.*

– *Can you point out on the map again Biljana Plavsic?*

– *She is Vice President of the Serbska Republika.*

The housemaster was getting irritable. The pupil had not done his homework. I was in danger of getting detention. I decided to nod wisely, pretend to write and ask no more questions.

Head reeling, I left the office and met Anders Levison who had set up the airport operation in Zagreb, met the first aircraft and effectively started the airlift. He is a very tall classic Swede who was eventually to wear himself out by his tireless devotion to the refugees in his charge in Zenica and Tuzla. He reluctantly handed the airlift over to me.

We were operating from an office outside the airport. On the floor below us was Colonel Mark Cook who was in charge of the British military contingent. He was later to retire and to rebuild from its ashes the Children's Home in Lipik, Croatia.

I pestered the airport authorities and they offered us an office co-located with the airport fire brigade. It was on the tarmac, so it was easy to see each aircraft and to ensure that every pilot reported in, after landing. The airport operation was in two parts.

Some aid arrived from donor countries by road and was stored at the airport for loading onto aircraft and flying into Sarajevo. Some aircraft arrived at the beginning of each day with aid loaded at their home airport. They reported into Zagreb, flew on to Sarajevo and then returned to Zagreb for further loads. Other nations parked their aircraft at Zagreb which were loaded from the ground stocks and then flown to Sarajevo.

As the numbers of aircraft built up, so the numbers of sorties per aircraft diminished. Most of the crews were keen to fly and vied with each other for slots into Sarajevo. None were keener than the Brits. They would ensure that their aircraft were loaded faster than others, they would watch like hawks for any delay in another aircraft's take off, and if there was the narrowest window of opportunity, they would rumble along the tarmac, slowly lose contact with the ground, and lumber into the sky. This tactic would throw out the plan and meant another nation losing a trip. The Brits were the worst for excessive zeal but they were not alone. The poor UNHCR representative on the ground would suffer the wrath of the pilot cheated out of his turn.

The enthusiasm of the aircrews was matched only by their bravery. Each and every landing, halt, and take off in Sarajevo was threatened. Many aircraft were to be pockmarked by shrapnel, penetrated by bullets and tracked by missiles. One aircraft, from Italy, was to pay the highest price. It was shot down with the loss of the crew.

After I had spent only a few days in Zagreb, it was decided that I could be replaced and sent to Sarajevo. On my last day in charge at the Zagreb end of the operation Madame Ogata, the High Commissioner for Refugees, arrived on her way to pay her first visit to Sarajevo. As her plane landed from Geneva, President Izetbegovic arrived from Sarajevo. Madame Ogata, whom I had seen in action on many previous occasions was, as usual, bright, incisive and caring. As ever, she knew who we all were and what we were doing.

The President I immediately liked. He looked a kindly but tired man. We talked about the aid, the need and the international response. On the tarmac, a few yards from where he had landed in a British Hercules C 130, was parked the executive jet of President Tudjman of Croatia—a symbol of the trappings of power of a neighbouring President. I wondered if he looked at it and asked himself: "Why me? Why my country?"

I called on the British RAF contingent who were living in a small hangar in the United Nations Protection Force (UNPROFOR) camp adjacent to Zagreb Airport in primitive conditions. The senior Brit was Wing Commander Bryan Warsnap, with longer than regulation length hair, a ruddy lined face, a voice with a gentle burr, the ideal man to send to a front-line task. Unflappable and genuine, able to smooth the feathers of ruffled pilots, to command and control by example, to appear calm almost to the point of being unaware. He was briefing Squadron Leader Steve Potter who was to fly into Sarajevo to liaise with UNHCR and the French. I envied Steve—he was going in a day before me.

My next call was to the Royal Engineers. More specifically to the quartermaster stores.

– *Any chance of the loan of a British Army sleeping bag?*
– *Who are you?*
– *UNHCR.*
– *Where are you going?*
– Sarajevo.
– *OK, but you will have to sign for it.*

The sleeping bag became a close friend. Thank you, RQMS.

The next day I handed over my airport responsibilities to a young UNHCR lawyer who soon handed them over to Mike Aitcheson, a veteran professional airline man. From his arrival onwards, there was no queue jumping by any nation, no disorderly behaviour, no nonsense. The airlift ran smoothly and efficiently.

Bryan Warsnap came to see me off. Steve had contacted him from Sarajevo. *Last night there was heavy firing across the airport*—he said. *Damn*—I thought—*I will arrive and it will be all over.* I hitched a lift with the British plane and had my first Khe Sanh experience. The flight from Zagreb to Sarajevo is dangerous for most of the way. A slow moving fully laden transport aircraft is an easy target to track and hit in a war zone where bored, trigger happy, unaccountable brigands roam the hills. But the descent to land is the most vulnerable manoeuvre. The RAF crews adapted the descent procedure used by the Americans as they landed in Khe Sanh during the Vietnam War. This involves an extremely high approach with tight turns and then an almost vertical angle of descent with a sharp pull out at what seems feet from the runway. It is a spectacular sight to watch from the ground, but to be honoured by the crew with an invitation to travel in the cockpit and to stand behind the pilot's seat during the flight and descent is a truly exhilarating experience. You feel that you can touch the sides of the hills. The navigator indicates that it is time to put on flak jackets. The pilot, Chris Tingay, a Boys Own Paper image of a pilot, bright blue eyes, hero handsome, with a tight tough smile, points out, with his yellow chamois gloved hand, Sarajevo in the valley ahead.

Then the descent begins. Chris pushes the stick forward; the nose goes down. It is as if someone has taken away the floor you are standing on. Your ears block, your blood rushes to your head, your knees buckle. Your stomach, intestines, liver, kidneys, all never before felt, are now individual items and floating within your body. The airport is rushing towards us, surely we will penetrate the runway, not land on it. Chris pulls back on the stick, conversations pass over the headphones, the aircraft levels, the body regroups itself. The aircraft wheels hit the ground, we bounce, Chris and his co-pilot have their hands on the central controls, the aircraft is shaking, vibrating, the noise is deafening and penetrating, the huge tyres again contact the ground, the aircraft races along the centre of the runway, then the engines are reversed, the cargo lurches forward in the hold, straining against the bolts and straps. You, yourself, are holding on, knuckle white to the back of the pilot's seat. The noise and the speed subside. The great overweight bird is now a slow-moving land vehicle controlled by a ridiculously small primitive wheel which is in the corner of the cockpit below the side window. It is parallel to the deck, not angled and is controlled by the left hand of the pilot as if his craft were a trolleybus or a tram. You realise that your eyes are wide open, your face grinning ecstatically. The crew are folding maps, flicking switches, clearing up, closing down. They have entered the most dangerous airport in the world, they have parked their winged chariot on a pockmarked tarmac. They have made themselves the biggest target for miles. They sit and wait whilst they are unloaded, already preparing for an equally spectacular Khe Sanh take-off.

Chris was later awarded the Air Force Cross for his bravery, the first medal to be given for former Yugoslavia. *It's a collective award for all the crews in the operation*—he modestly and generously said on hearing of his award.

I thanked him and his crew, collected my bags, and left the aircraft through the side door and took my first steps in Sarajevo. My initial view was of the damaged Air Traffic Control Tower. Sheets of glass looking as if they would fall to the floor to impale all below. The first person I met was Amra. Red hair, beautiful eyes, and a warm smile. She took me to the UNHCR hangar. Outside were parked two Canadian APCs. The whole of the front of the hangar was open, in the top right-hand corner was the office. It was very make-shift and untidy. The rest of the hangar was either storage space or living accommodation. I walked up to the office area and saw Rick Garlock, UNHCR, American, ex-military and a man whom I had known when he was in Turkey.

– *Hi*—I said. His head was over the laptop computer.

– *What do you want?*—he replied.

– *Nothing.*

– *Well, what are you here for then?*

– *Rick, it's me, Larry.* The length of the beard had thrown him, the constant stream of journalists had tired him. He introduced me to the team. I was told to find myself a place to sleep. I found a large wooden table and placed my sleeping bag underneath it.

Fabrizio Hochschild then arrived. He had been in Sarajevo since before the war began. He was in charge of the office. He and I had last seen each other in Addis Ababa. He is a young, extremely bright Oxbridge graduate, a polyglot, a thinker, and a man deservedly earmarked for the top. He welcomed me, told me to settle in, and outlined my tasks. I was to run the airport and the airlift. He was moving Rick from the airport to the city to supervise the distribution of aid.

The RAF invited me into the area of the hangar that they had curtained off as an officers' mess. Steve Potter shared it with Flight Lieutenant Lee Doherty, a London Irish workhorse. Lee had made himself responsible for the loading and unloading of aircraft. He was unbelievable. He could do every task, from driving the most enormous forklift truck to cleaning his shoes, quicker and better than anyone else. The French, the Canadian, and the Norwegian teams who worked with him were overwhelmed by his energy. His French counterpart was a dozy pudding of a man.

No man was more responsible for establishing the system of loading and unloading the aircraft at sufficient speed to ensure that the aircraft were on the ground for the least possible time and thus least exposed to danger from shell, mortar, and small arms fire, than Lee. He was awarded the MBE for his efforts.

Recently, I met a Sarajevo driver and we talked about Lee. *I remember three things about him*—he said—*hard work, cold showers, and Jack Daniels whisky.* Lee, if ever you are looking for an epitaph that is not a bad one! Ron Bagnolo was the RAF communications king and a general Mr. Fixit, a very open, kind, and courteous man.

The team told me about the previous evening. There had been heavy firing across the airfield as the Serb-held Airport Settlement had fired on Government dominated Dobrinja. The boys told me exciting tales of the sky lit up by tracer fire, they pointed out from where shells had come and where they had landed.

I have to confess that I secretly hoped it would last at least one night more. I hoped that I would see some action myself.

The night was quiet, the firing was subdued. I spent a little time talking to my fellow occupants of the hangar. But I very much felt that I was the new boy, even though no one had been there for more than a week. So I decided that I would wait until the next day before trying to get to know everybody. I went to bed at about nine. I opened out my sleeping bag and discovered a bonus. The previous occupant had left a Maglite torch in it. I had learned that inside the hangar there was one toilet and two washbasins—to be shared between thirty people at night and maybe fifty by day. I established that most people got up at six thirty. I set my alarm for a quarter to six. I wanted to have used the facilities before the others awoke.

I slept well. I was out of the sleeping bag before six. Only one other person was up. Nonjo the cook. Whilst I washed, he made me a cup of tea. The next person up was no surprise. It was Lee.

I went across and talked to Nonjo. He is a tall, heavy, generous man with a warm sincere personality. He is employed as a driver. He is a typical well-educated, streetwise city boy. He has a great sense of humour. Nonjo had as one of his many party pieces a monologue about an old lady learning to drive an armoured vehicle. His timing is as good as Bob Newhart's and the story is as funny with each retelling. Nonjo was to become one of my barometers. I was able to measure the morale of our staff by the mood of Nonjo and their reaction to him.

After breakfast, we were visited by the senior French officer who was in charge of the advance party of the French Marines. Lt. Col. Erik de Stabenrath and I were to become very good friends.

I then was taken to see the commander of Sector Sarajevo, General Lewis Mackenzie. If ever a man looked the part he was playing, it was him. He is a tall, broad, film star handsome man. He is tough physically and cerebrally. A fluent speaker with an enviable vocabulary he was, without a doubt, "in charge." He exuded command and confidence. A brilliant choice. I learned that his hobby is racing cars. If I had to guess his hobby, racing cars would have been alongside sky diving or big game hunting as my first choices for him.

I took my inaugural trip into the city to visit the UNHCR warehouse at the Zetra Olympic stadium and to see the city authorities. It was an opportunity to view the devastation already suffered in the opening days of the war. The newspaper office of Oslobodjenje with the core of its tower still standing, defying the Serb gunners who can see it but whose skills are not sufficient to demolish it and symbolising to the world the spirit of the Oslobodjenje staff bowed, battered but not beaten. Daily, they produce a newspaper, regardless of the intensity of the shelling, the appalling conditions, or even the lack of proper "news." It had a multi-ethnic staff. Sadly, it could not avoid single side propaganda which, on occasions, demeaned its excellence. Next to Oslobodjenje is the garish building, known as the "Rainbow Hotel," built to house old people but taken over by the UN as an accommodation block. The location of one of its first ignominies. It flew the UN flag but was shelled. The UN vehicles in the car park were destroyed, the patches of white on the shattered and burned vehicles were to remind generations of UN soldiers of the first insult. We passed by the PTT building, which was the headquarters of UN-PROFOR, the turning marked by an abandoned tram. On the left is the TV building. A concrete monstrosity which, pre-war, attracted tremendous criticism for its prison-like exterior. In war, it was to prove a gold medal winner. Its windowless walls, its solid exterior, its construction, rejected the Serb calling cards. It became office and studio to many international journalists and home to some.

Our first port of call was to the Municipality, a dark brown stone building next to the Presidency, to pay a courtesy call on Mr. Pamuk the director of the city. His title initially confused me, but he explained that he was the senior civil servant in the city and the district of Sarajevo. A powerful post. He was pleased to see me. My grey hairs pleased him. So far, he had been told how to run his city by men the age of his sons. We had an immediate empathy. I had neither youth nor solution. He is maybe forty-five, on a bad day he looks a little like Brezhnev, on a good day like Lord Healey. He has a craggy face, dark thick hair, prominent eyebrows, eyes which laugh a lot, and a voice honed and trained on rough tobacco. He wears a dark grey party suit. He is a product of the party but has a mind which has easily adapted to the circumstances of today. I liked him, I knew that we could work together. I promised to return later in the week when he would have in his office the committee for the distribution of aid.

We then moved to the Holiday Inn hotel, home of many journalists. We were to meet Minister Martin Raguz who was responsible for Refugee Affairs. The Holiday Inn Hotel is a magnet for Serb shells, in truth its hideous yellow outer walls would be the target of many a brickbat in times of peace. We were driven to the main entrance, made a quick dash to the front door. It was part glass, part fresh air. To the right of the entrance is the reception desk where bored staff deal with tired journalists. A notice board near the door attempts to answer the most routine enquiries. We crossed the reception hall. Our presence was noted by the cabals of media men pocketed about

27

the bar area. We climbed the large but clumsy central staircase and turned to the right. The Minister was waiting for us in a private dining room. Martin Raguz is a young man, perhaps thirty. He is a Croat, tall, dark and presumably attractive to women. As it turned out, he was accompanied by two very attractive secretaries.

We were served a meal. My first meal away from the hangar. It was called *burek*, a pie with meat inside it. They were war economy portions but it was more than I expected. The Holiday Inn survives because of its clientele. The journalists are paid well, many have a generous expense account. They pay in hard currency. The hotel management is therefore able to do deals with checkpoints to bring in food to satisfy customers as voracious at table as they are on the streets.

This meeting was very important to me. It was the first time that I realised the significance of working in Sarajevo. Mr. Pamuk and I had been talking about the needs of Sarajevo. Minister Raguz was talking about the needs of Bosnia Herzegovina (BiH). The UNHCR man in Sarajevo was thus double hatted. Talking to the local authorities on Sarajevo and to the government on BiH. Martin Raguz wanted to talk about aid to his nation. He wanted us to support computer links to the principal towns, he wanted to know how much aid had been delivered to each region, how much was planned. He talked as if there was not a war raging around us, as if communications were normal. I realised that he thought that we, the UN, were better organised than we were. He was presuming that we had a great plan and a system to match. He talked about aid to those areas which were isolated. He mentioned Gorazde, the first time I ever heard the name. He asked if we could send a convoy there urgently. I left the table realising that I had a lot to learn. Feeding Sarajevo looked as if it was only half of the job.

I returned to the airport and sat with the drivers and a map. They showed me where Gorazde was. They explained that it was in Eastern Bosnia. It had been a multi-ethnic town with a Muslim majority but was now surrounded by territory which had fallen into Bosnian Serb hands. They patiently explained that to get there I would need Serb approval and that it was not in the interests of the Serbs to permit aid to enter Gorazde. The Serbs wished to starve the Muslims into submission, then to move them out to Central Bosnia, releasing the whole of Eastern Bosnia to the Serbs. My drivers showed me two other places also besieged, Zepa and Srebrenica. Gorazde was enough for me in one night.

Now that I was aware of the dual role of UNHCR, I needed to know who was who in the government as well as in the city. I began to do battle with the names. The President of Bosnia Herzegovina, Alija Izetbegovic, I could manage. The mayor of Sarajevo, Mr. Kresevljak-ovic was going to take some time.

My second evening was noisy. I stood with the RAF boys and the drivers outside the hangar and watched a battle begin. A tank on the Serb held hill began firing into Butmir. Government-held Dobrinja replied from behind us, Serb held Lukavica joined in over our heads, and Butmir replied. Serb held Airport settlements then fired on But-mir. The rounds flew above our heads, low enough to hear their pas-sage, high enough to avoid frightening us. As darkness fell the tracer rounds flew like rockets across the sky. Following tracer shell is fasci-nating but macabre. The trace disappears at the end of the trajectory of the round, there is a delay, then an increasing rumble, and slowly flames flicker into the sky. It is at first easy to be taken in by the event and to forget the reality of the action. Perhaps at first we see it as we see a movie film. Later, when I was close enough to see the action and to hear the screams, the fascination had gone, replaced by the horror of the result and my hatred of the perpetrators.

On this second night in Sarajevo, we were reminded of our own vulnerability as a rocket exploded close to us. Its multi-head spitting shrapnel close to where we stood. Steve Potter decided that the pri-ority for tomorrow was the building of a bunker. I went to bed tired but excited, my head reeling with "ic's."

Each day started with a conference at seven thirty. It was chaired by the military commander of the airport, a French officer, and attend-ed by the heads of each of the units. UNHCR and UN Civilian Po-lice were the "civilian" units. The runway was swept every morning before the conference by a road sweeper vehicle. The shrapnel, and the rounds, the debris from the previous night's battle were collected and weighed. The weight was solemnly announced at the conference and the more interesting items were handed around. A light night was one sandbag full of malicious metal. The French battalion commander or his deputy, usually my friend Eric, would then brief us on the activity as seen from his positions on the roof aided by infrared night sights and the reports of his sentries and liaison officers.

Whilst we slept, the airport, like the desert and the jungle, came to life. Men, women and children from all sides would attempt to cross the airport to the "safety" of the other side. The majority of the traffic was from the city to Mount Igman. The French who were responsible for the safety and the neutrality of the airport would turn a blind eye to some attempts but were compelled to challenge the majority. The IR or heat-seeking devices would locate a large group elbowing their way across the airport. The searchlight would be switched on and the people invited to stand up. They were then returned to their own side with no further action taken by the UN. Many were escaping never to return; some wore their best clothes. The sister of my driver Zlatan, a prominent psychiatrist, was twice unsuccessful because her high heels stuck in the mud! The UNHCR, boring by comparison, briefed the group on the previous day's deliveries and the proposed schedule.

On my first morning meeting, there were three sacks full of shrapnel and a very concerned Steve Potter who asked the Canadian senior NCO Marty, a small, stocky, blustery man with respect for no one, if he could assist in the building of a bunker.

– *I'll give you some engineers and a container. That should be a start.* He referred to no one. The decision made, he was as good as his word. Before the morning was out, he had delivered a twenty-foot-long container, and "Project Potter" was underway. The RAF team provided the supervision, the Norwegians in the adjacent hangar, under a tall movement controller, Ralph Iveson provided the sweat. The Canadians provided a mechanical digger.

Steve was obviously good with Meccano sets as a child. I'll bet he buys his children Legos. He was determined that "his" bunker would be the Hilton of bunkers. Steve did some reconnaissance for a site. He chose a spot near the perimeter fence, close to a manned observation bunker which could provide covering fire whilst we ran to the bunker. He decided that a seventy-metre dash was the furthest away from the hangar that we could risk. X marked the spot. The digging began, and a hole large enough for the container completed. Then the container was lowered into the ground. Logs were placed over the roof of it. The next task was to cover the logs on the roof with sandbags. Here we had a slight problem; we had no sandbags. The French did, but the platoon commander told us that they needed all they had to cover their own fortification which was beginning to rival the Maginot line. Ron and a senior UNHCR person liberated from the French a large quantity of the much-needed bags. It was my only contribution to "Project Potter."

At the end of the first day, we had protection; by the end of the second, we had protection plus lighting and emergency rations. The RAF Hercules crews decided that we should have a barbecue to celebrate its inauguration. They brought in food and beer from Zagreb.

The Hercules crews deserve a very special mention. They did their job with great courage but always wanted to do more. They had a strict rotation pattern, crews and craft returning to Lyneham after a tour of four weeks. The new crews brought from the UK sufficient meat, sausages and beer for us—both international and local staff—to have a good relaxing party. We never paid for this, they did. They did many other small kindnesses. They made phone calls for refugees, they posted letters, they changed money. I particularly remember Chris Tingay and his crew once finding me looking especially tired. On the next flight he sent up two crates of Pot Noodles, with a little note: "You look weak. Take one twice a day with water." Water we had. They were delicious, nourishing, and restored our strength. We did not always remember to say thanks at the time but a big thanks now may not be too late.

31

Two

Sarchapt

The airlift was increasing by the day. We were soon up to fourteen flights a day. On a rough calculation, we reckoned that we needed to bring in about 4,500 tonnes of food a month for the city to survive. Fourteen flights a day brought in about 160. With a bit of luck, we may be able to win. The calculation, however, did not take into account medicine, fuel, and other essentials. We needed road convoys as well as an airlift. Furthermore, we were not allowed to concentrate solely on Sarajevo, pressure was increasing by the day for a convoy to Gorazde. The Government was whipping up enthusiasm amongst the journalists. They had become excited by the story line: "Large city in the middle of Serb held territory, tens of thousands of people besieged and starving." The story was very similar to Sarajevo, but they had "done" Sarajevo. The Bosnian Government wanted action for the more altruistic reason that their people were dying.

UNHCR was asked to visit President Izetbegovic. I had had the brief meeting at Zagreb airport but this would be my first official visit. The Presidency is in the centre of the city. Normally the entrance is around the back, but for official visits the front door is used. We went by French APC. Vesna Vukovic served as translator. We parked outside the main door on the pavement. The guards checked our identities. Not too difficult in my case, as there were very few Methusaleh look-alikes in Sarajevo.

We were escorted up the wide staircase by the adviser to the President Mr. Somun, whom I felt I knew, as his daughter Leyla worked for us at the airport. She is a graduate in Arabic studies from Sarajevo. Mr. Somun had been an ambassador before the war.

He took us to the great double doors leading to the room where the President met with dignitaries. We were not the only guests. We were ushered in and seated on a huge settee. The reception room was chosen well. It faced the front of the building and had two large windows which were open.

The President arrived. He looked gentle, confused and exhausted.

His daughter Sabine was with him. She acts as secretary and some-times translator. He understands English and in a one to one conver-sation is prepared to use English, but he prefers to use a translator. He sat in the corner of one settee. The shelling began, and there were two loud bangs very close to where we were. The president appeared not to notice them. He never even paused in his speech. He wanted to discuss aid in general and aid to Gorazde in particular. He had with him a senior officer Hadzihasanovic. The Bosnian Government was not strong on military ranks, so it was safest to address them as "commander." Enver Hadzihasanovic I was later to meet in Zenica and again back in Sarajevo. He is one of the ablest Bosnian leaders. Handsome, silver haired, and charming.

We were briefed on the reports coming out of Gorazde. They were horrendous. A hospital with no medicine. A population with no food. The commander discussed the options for getting aid into Gorazde. The Bosnian army had a mule route. But it could take very little and was frequently attacked by the Serbs.

I'll bet it is—I thought to myself. It was an open secret that the mule route took in mainly ammunition for the defenders of the town.

The president was strong—*There is not enough aid for Sarajevo, but Gorazde is of a higher priority.* I could see that it was. Strategically the last thing the president wanted was major towns to fall to the Serbs. Also, he was testing the strength and will of the UN and its agencies. It was a short meeting.

The following day was my return visit to the office of Mr. Pamuk for a meeting with the five to discuss distribution. We had to pass through shelling, which was heavy and dangerously close. It was my first trip at the wheel of the car. Leyla Hrasnica was my translator and guide. She showed to me the "back route," the quieter one. We arrived at the Municipality a few minutes late. The building had tak-en a few hits, and there was machine gun fire bouncing off the walls. As I parked the car under the direction of Leyla, I had two thoughts which I voiced.

– *Leyla, if that was the quiet route, what would the other route have been like?*

— *The shelling would have been a little closer, but...* —she added with a smile—*we would have been a little quicker.*

— *Leyla, just as a point of interest, when are conditions considered to be too bad to cancel a meeting?*

— *When the other side cancels.*

We passed the empty offices and arrived at Mr. Pamuk's. He was there. He had two other people with him. Two of the five. He introduced them to me. One was Professor Kljic, an economist who was to be the architect of the distribution plan after consultation with us.

There was a tremendous bang as a mortar hit the base of the building. We waited a few minutes more for the other three to arrive. The professor and I began to talk. He was hoping that I would have a blueprint for feeding the city. He was not to know that I was as confused and as overwhelmed as he was. I explained that my own experience was with refugee camps where I had been responsible for almost one hundred thousand people—a little exaggeration, but I thought acceptable in the circumstances.

Mr. Pamuk wanted to know for how long the Sarajevo airlift was guaranteed. I was able to answer clearly and truthfully that it had been funded for one month. We began discussing the Berlin Airlift. There was a knock at the door and the secretary to Mr. Pamuk came in, we were not to wait for the others. They had been seriously injured in the shrapnel from the mortar that we had heard explode. I was disturbed by this. But the others were not. They were used to it. I needed more time there before I too accepted the macabre as commonplace.

The professor wanted us to give him the aid which we received as quickly as possible. Furthermore, he wished to sit on it until he had enough to be able to issue a little to everyone or at least a little to everyone in a district, "to issue by rings." The first thoughts of UN-HCR were to keep the aid in our possession until we knew the day of the issue, then to hand it over, so that we could see and monitor the issue. We wanted to see it issued to the most vulnerable, the widows and orphans, the elderly, the homeless. We also wanted to issue it

35

rapidly. The people were starving now and they knew that aid was arriving. Given a little aid their morale would improve. Given no aid they may storm the warehouses.

Not only was there a difference of opinion on method of distribution, there was the age-old shadow boxing between donor and recipient. I hate this mutual mistrust. It happens with every operation. Basically, we believe that the only way to guarantee that all the aid will be distributed to the needy is if you yourself put the spoon into the mouth of the beneficiary. Clearly this we cannot do. We have to trust and use the local agents. Sarajevo was a Central European capital. The professor was a man of honour but I've been ripped off by foreign royalty with degrees from Oxbridge, so I am cautious.

My first thoughts were that he had been told to get the aid quickly because his masters wanted some of it to go to the army. I could understand this. Every resident in Sarajevo was happy to see the defenders of the city fed first. They were their own sons and husbands.

If there was enough aid for everyone, I wanted every person in Sarajevo to get his or her share—be they doctors, dentists, pensioners, nurses, or soldiers. If there was not enough to go around, then I wanted the distribution to be to the most vulnerable, to the children, to the aged, to the homeless.

The professor I learned to like and respect. The job that he had been given was the worst in Sarajevo. He was criticised by everyone. The citizens never appreciated how little we were able to bring in and accused the professor of either stealing it or misappropriating it. The authorities accused him of being too honourable. We accused him of being too slow and weak. His task was Herculean and Solomonic. I was later to visit his home. He had far less than anyone else. His family suffered because of his position. Initially, I gave him a hard time. I did not accord to him the respect he deserved.

At the end of the meeting, whilst we were discussing the terrible plight of Sarajevo, both the professor and Mr. Pamuk requested that we divert aid to Gorazde. *The citizens of Sarajevo who have little, wish to share that little with the citizens of Gorazde who have nothing.* I reassured them that we were negotiating the entry of a convoy. But I knew that Fabrizio was having little success.

Having visited the Government side, it was time for me to see the Serb side, to discuss their needs and their wishes.

Fabrizio Hochschild had set the policy. He knew that aid to one side was morally wrong and practically impossible. There were many thousands of refugees in the Serb held territory around Sarajevo, mainly Serbs, but also some Croats and a few Muslims. All aid coming into Sarajevo passed through Serb territory. There was no way the Serbs would allow aid in to feed the population of Sarajevo without a share going to them. He was put under pressure to choose the suburb of Ilidza as the Serb side delivery and distribution centre but he chose the quieter area of Rajlovac. Hence a percentage of the aid arriving into Sarajevo was to be sent to the Rajlovac depot for distribution by the Serbs to the displaced and vulnerable in those parts of what had been the District of Sarajevo which was now in Serb hands. Both sides referred to these territories by the same names: "free Sarajevo" and "occupied Sarajevo," but to each, of course, it had the opposite meaning.

So I took my first trip across the front line to Rajlovac, which is, as the crow flies, close to Sarajevo airport. The warehouse is next to a huge railway yard and a small aircraft landing strip. I was met at the warehouse by the man responsible for distribution and his assistant. Milivoje Unkovic is an artist by training, a painter by choice. He was wearing an army uniform, but as an artist. It did not restrict him. It was as if a Bohemian was wearing army surplus. He is a neat, gentle, and handsome man. His assistant, Ljerka Jeftic, is the power. She is dark haired with a commanding voice. Polite but firm. Also present was Ljubisa Vladusic, the Commissioner for Refugees for the Serb side, from Pale. He is young, very tall, heavy, with an open friendly face.

Ljerka ensured we wasted no time; we were off to a strong start. The Commissioner began—*The Srpska Republika Government has set up this depot in coordination with the Serbian charity Dobrotvor, the Red Cross and UNHCR to supply aid to the municipalities and to stop its manipulation.* He then added an important line—*This is a civilian task. It has nothing to do with the Army.*

He beamed as I nodded approval. Ljerka then took the floor—*We would like a delivery of aid every two days, we are feeding 200,000 dependents. Forty-five per cent are refugees, women and children.* Very professional. Then from Mr. Vladusic came a very sharp question, asked with no emphasis—*What is the population of Sarajevo at the moment Mr. Larry?* Nice one. I thought.

– *I think they are talking about 340,000.*

– *Then we should get two thirds of what they get.*

– *I am not into numbers yet. I see the parallels and I see the tangents. Sarajevo is of course surrounded, besieged. You have access to rolling plains, open fields, woods, farms. So not all of your people are entirely dependent on what the agencies bring in. Sarajevo is.*

– *Why do you say Sarajevo is besieged?*—Ljerka again.

– *Because the roads to it are blocked by you.*

– *We have opened the airport and a road for you. Also, we have said that if the people want to leave, they can do so.*

Both statements are true, but it is a Bosnian truth. The road was not open to commercial traffic and the airport would never bring in enough to satisfy the total needs of a city. As to her "also," right again. The Serb side were very keen on opening the road out of Sarajevo and permitting the whole population to leave. The Sarajevo Government and UNHCR called this "ethnic cleansing." Sarajevans have the right to live in their own homes in Sarajevo. I went onto the offensive—*The removal of the rightful inhabitants of the city is not an option, nor is 'Stay and starve and be shelled' an option.*

Ljerka ignored this comment. I then carefully and naively explained how I, a recent arrival, saw the situation. Emphasising how the Serbs were receiving a bad press for actions they could put right immediately. They were very polite and patient. Mr. Vladusic and I were to become good friends. I found him always to be fair and honest and professionally cunning.

I returned to the airport wiser.

A few days later we did bring in the first road convoy. It came from

Split in Croatia. A team of British drivers pioneered the route. They were funded by the Overseas Development Administration (ODA). They were recruited and led by John Foster who is the Emergency Planning Officer for the Isle of Man Government who was on loan to ODA. Amongst his drivers was the colourful Peter Milne who arrived wearing his kilt. A character who later helped me to get into Tesanj and Maglaj.

The first deliveries into the city were for those people living in the Bosnian Government dominated area of the city. We were aware of the fact that the district of Grbavica was in Serb held territory and that it had a large population of starving people. Furthermore, it could not be reached by the Serbs themselves from Rajlovac.

I first spoke to Professor Kljic. He agreed that Grbavica needed aid. Painfully he told me that it was the area of the city where he had lived before the war. He had never had any trouble with his neighbours. He certainly felt it right and just that they should receive their share of the aid. This was a good start. He talked to his masters. They agreed. We therefore had approval to take aid out of the city into the Serb territory. We then approached the Serb side via the liaison officers. We agreed a date for a convoy. The Canadians agreed to escort it. It was to be UNHCR vehicles with UNHCR local drivers. At the last minute, the Serbs vetoed this; they would not permit Muslims into their territory. I should have given them an ultimatum—*Aid food, aid drivers*. My Bosnians were prepared to go. But I compromised, which I regret. So we had to borrow drivers from the Canadians.

It was a short trip, and we ended up only a few yards from where we had begun, but on the other side of the river. The organisation for our reception was chaotic. There was a lot of sniper fire from the Bosnian government side. They had approved the convoy but could not resist the chance of taking shots at the reception committee. No one seemed to know where we were going to unload. If in doubt, slivovica out. They plied us with offers of drink whilst they found the location and the keys. Meanwhile, we are parked out in the open with sniper fire only a few metres away. The man with most initiative was a small, feisty priest, Father Vojislav Carkic. He ran the local

Serb charity, was a parish priest, and a military chaplain. He did a little shouting and a shell damaged supermarket was opened. Then came the next crisis, there was no enthusiasm to unload. More words from the priest and a group of men were found. I forbade the Canadians from unloading. It was not a precedent I wished to begin. The recipients of the aid must unload. It is difficult to restrain soldiers especially when they, rightly, want to dump and run in the face of sniper fire.

I had been asked by Professor Klaic if I could see if his precious books were still safe in his flat. I was assured that they were not. With a shortage of electricity, gas, wood, or oil for kitchen stoves, thick, heavy, economics books were especially useful. As we were leaving, Father Carkic gave me a holy picture. *I will give you a different one every time you bring aid. We have started off with the apostles. We need eleven more convoys for you to have your first set.* His toothless mouth stretched into a wide grin. His companions laughed.

With the success of Grbavica, Fabrizio was determined to spread our sphere of influence even further. Dobrinja is a large suburb of Sarajevo very close to the airport. It was cut off from the city, but under the influence of the Bosnian Government. The majority population are Muslim. Fabrizio decided to take aid to Dobrinja. Citing the Grbavica convoy as a precedent, he got Serb approval but took no chances. He took in a small convoy with a one hundred strong Canadian escort. It was successful. The irony of the day was that we succeeded in feeding Dobrinja but failed to get a single convoy into Sarajevo itself. "Somebody" shelled the Canadian barracks.

That evening, Eric de Stabenrath, the French Colonel, came to see me. He was impressed with the convoy to Dobrinja but believed that the key to our safety in the airport was for the combatants on all sides of the airport to see us and to know us and to know that we are impartial. He therefore proposed a "Hearts and Minds" programme. He intended to nominate a Liaison Officer for the peripheral districts of Nedzarici and the Airport Settlements held by the Serbs, and Dobrinja and Butmir held by the Government. The LOs would go into their territory every day and build up a close relationship with the community and its leaders.

– *If they go in, why don't they take in aid?*—asked Eric.

– *Eric, this is music to our ears. We will find the aid. Good luck in getting the approval of the local commanders.* He succeeded and thus began a brilliant and vital programme.

Fabrizio was working non-stop on organising a convoy to Gorazde. Suddenly it seemed to fall into place. The Serbs agreed to give him approval to try, UNPROFOR agreed to provide an escort, UNHCR found the trucks and we diverted the aid from Sarajevo. Fabrizio was exhausted before he left. He had put so much effort into the convoy. Una Sekerez was the interpreter, Major Vanessa Lloyd of the British Royal Army Medical Corps and Sir Donald Acheson of World Health Organisation accompanied it.

It was a gallant attempt. It was mined, it came under fire, it almost reached Gorazde. It lost one APC and one ten-tonne truck. But it failed. On its return journey back to Sarajevo it encountered more gunfire. The team returned safely but some were badly shaken and Una had been lightly wounded.

I stayed behind and followed the progress of the convoy from the operations room. When they returned, I met them at the PTT building. They were so high on adrenaline. Fabrizio was pacing his office like a caged tiger. He wanted and needed a shower but could not relax. Could not stand still. He told me the whole story in short bursts as he paced and turned, paced and turned. Thanks to his debrief, the next attempt would succeed but not without incident.

Fabrizio was called to greater things; he was appointed special assistant to the Special Envoy. He left for Zagreb, and I moved into his office. I was sitting behind his desk when I was visited by Jeremy Brade, an Englishman, an ex-Ghurka officer, the recent head of the European Community Mission Monitors in Sarajevo, and now Lord Carrington's man on the ground in former Yugoslavia. Jeremy knew everybody and everything. He knew the principal players, the splinter groups, the goodies and the baddies, and he knew the geography and the history of the place. By nodding wisely and listening intently, I was able to sketch in whole areas of deficiency in my knowledge.

Jeremy is an excellent mimic. He is an expert at capturing the essence of the mannerisms of those whom he meets. His descriptions are accompanied by mini portrayals.

Before leaving, Jeremy warned me that there were two imminent visits from the UK. One from the Foreign Office and the other from a member of the cabinet. Jeremy ensured that I was part of the itinerary. The first visit was from Dr. Glynne Evans. She was accompanied by Andrew Pringle, a Brigadier, later of the Royal Green Jackets, then working within the cabinet office. Glynne is diminutive in stature, formidable in intellect, and gigantic in drive. Whatever a microchip processor does to a computer, Glynne does it to UN programmes. She is head of the Foreign and Commonwealth Office UN section.

To see her alight from the rear of a Hercules C130 aircraft with flak jacket, high heels and earrings is an experience. She strides across the bullet-scarred tarmac as if it were a military catwalk. She is imperious, compelling, and in charge. Her—*Tell me Larry…* in a clipped crystal-clear aristocratic accent commands undivided attention.

She risked the bullets and the shells to visit the warehouse, and then she left Sarajevo and crossed three front lines to travel to Kiseljak to meet one of the earliest road convoys into Sarajevo.

She fires penetrating, deadly, and accurate questions that demand a rapid response. All delivered with charm. Tricky pauses are defused with a smile and a steely glint from her eyes.

One Glynne story should sum up her abilities.

Larry—she said at the end of the long tiring day—*what would most make life easier for you here in Sarajevo?*" I had no hesitation. I was running into the centre of the city and crossing front lines every day. – *An armoured vehicle of my own. At the moment, I either waste hours begging lifts from a French APC or I risk life and limb in a soft skinned vehicle.*

Right—she said. The following morning she left. Three days later an armoured range rover rolled out of the back of a British Hercules. Glynne had located one in Madrid belonging to the Embassy and persuaded the Ambassador to loan it. She had it driven to London, serviced, and then flown to Sarajevo! And, remember, I am a UN employee, not a member of the Foreign and Commonwealth Office, not even an employee of the ODA.

This was to be only a minor miracle. She was soon to have three thousand British troops on the ground, fully equipped and fully trained.

The cabinet minister proved to be the Foreign Secretary Mr. Douglas Hurd. He arrived on a very hot day. After a short meeting with General Mackenzie he came up to our hangar and had a guided tour. He had been well briefed by Glynne. He knew about the request for the armoured car, and he knew my background. At a lunch in the PTT building hosted by the French, he had a conversation with everyone. When it was my turn, I was, unusually for me, a little tongue tied and we had a "Mutt and Jeff" session. Later when I told my daughter that I could not think of anything to say, she reminded me—*You could have asked him how his son was. He was at Exeter University with me and you met him there.*

Next time!

Having visited President Izetbegovic, I wanted to visit Dr. Karadzic. All negotiation with the Serb side was done through the Serb Liaison officers. There were three. Brane was a professional soldier who had served at the airport prior to the war. He is my height with slightly greying hair, bright, warm, with moist, brown eyes. A neat toothbrush reddish brown moustache, a voice which is deep, friendly, and conspiratorial. A man of charm, humour, and honour. Misha Indjic, slightly smaller, losing his hair, lost some of his "smiley" teeth, eyes like olives, dark and bitter, with a brown moustache. Misha is intolerably Serb and pathologically anti-Muslim. Both men speak excellent English. The third, a professor of geology, Dr. Vlado Lukic. A Balkan intellectual who knows many subjects inside and out but can only argue from one standpoint. Bright but inflexible, a tall heavy man, shy to use his English, he was closest to my age. He was teased mercilessly by Brane. They lived in one room in the PTT building. They slept around the walls. Their job was incredibly difficult. They were four doors away from the Bosnian Government Liaison officers. Whenever there was shelling UNPROFOR would run to the Serb

Liaison officers and demand they stopped it. The LO's would then use an antique field phone to contact their Army headquarters in Lukavica on the outskirts of the airport in Serb held territory. In addition to stopping shelling, all patrols and convoys were cleared through the Liaison officers.

Dr. Lukic was the most conscientious, indeed the most pedantic. He would take ages to get a decision because he would progress the request meticulously. Brane would pressure his masters for an answer. Misha was the most sinister. I reckon he made a lot of the decisions himself. To those he had to refer, he built in a delay factor. Both Brane and Misha spent a lot of time translating for the top generals. They both know too much. Watch your backs boys!

When I eventually left the rigours of the airport for the comfort of the PTT building, I shared for many a month the next room to them. We sank quite a few jars together. Dr. Lukic was later elevated from the floor of the office to the position of Prime Minister of Srpska Republika.

Stopping shelling, clearing convoys and arranging interviews, all legitimate LO tasks. Hence—*Brane, I would like to see your big white chief. Can you fix?* If you asked Brane a rhetorical question, he answered not with words but with a smile.

He fixed me up with an appointment at midday the following Sunday. I have only ever seen photos of Dr. Karadzic, in which he is always wearing a double-breasted suit, so I thought I had better wear mine. When I put it on, the cheeky Leyla wolf-whistled. It was the first and, with only one other exception, the only time they saw me wear it. They cruelly nicknamed it my "Karadzic" suit.

I arrived at Lukavica on time. Serb television cameras were waiting to record the event. Not surprising, as the agency SRNA is a propaganda machine much favoured by the media happy Doctor. I was taken up the stairs and into the end room on the right. Dr. Karadzic was there on his own. There was a buffet type lunch on the table. He is an easy man to be with. He greeted me as if we were old friends. He asked me about the health of Jose Maria. He complained that Mrs. Ogata had recently seen Izetbegovic but not seen him. He asked me where I was from, and through all of this, he is helping himself and me to food.

– *I'm from Liverpool.* The inevitable happened—I get his favourite Liverpool line up. We talked about the Sarajevo football team to whom he was the team doctor.

– *Why do they need a psychiatrist? Do they keep on losing?*—I asked. *Liverpool humour*—he answered.

I gather you are a poet—I said as we ate. I was tucking in heartily. He had more food than we did. This changed the direction of the conversation completely.

– *Do you like poetry?*

– *Very much.*

– *Who is your favourite poet?*

– *Matthew Arnold*—I replied. Actually, it is Kipling, but he is after all a doctor and a president as my mother would have said. She always wanted me to keep up appearances, whatever that meant. He knew Arnold.

– *Who is yours?*

– *Njegos*—he replied. Actually, I thought he had coughed. It was much later that I discovered that Njegos was a famous Montenegrin. He rummaged in his briefcase.

– *I have a copy of one of my books here*—he found one.

– *Do you read Serbian?*

– *No.*

– *Sorry, it is the only copy that I have here. I will send you a copy in English. Who is your favourite author?*

– *It is a toss-up between Dickens and Tolstoy*—I replied, truthfully this time. We talked about books. I watched his mop of hair bob about his forehead. He has prominent eyebrows. At times he looked like Denis Healey.

I was actually enjoying his company. But business is business.

– *Dr. Karadzic. What is your aim for Sarajevo?*

– *Sometimes I believe the Muslims can have it in exchange for other areas. Sometimes I believe it could be an open city. We could have parts of it like Jerusalem.* He is a cartophile. He takes out a map of Sarajevo and shows me the options. He then moved on to other maps, pushing the food out of the way as he spread them out. He does not do this as a general, more as a professor or explorer, a Dr. Challenger. He is not happy with Gorazde, a cancer in his midst. I watch and listen fascinated. I do not need to be there—he is talking to himself, to crowds, to parliament.

– *Do you think it would be possible to stop the shelling of Sarajevo? At least of places like the hospital?*—I ask.

– *It is the Muslims' fault. They place their weapons behind the hospital and fire on us.* Sadly, I know this to be frequently true. So I do not pursue it.

We talked about the opening of the city. He is happy to have corridors. He is happy if all the Muslims leave. He is happy for convoys to move. It is a happy day for Dr. Karadzic. There is a knock on the door. It is his Corps commander from Ilidza.

My time is up. We shake hands. He promises me the book. I return to Sarajevo and put the suit away. Everyone is asking me—*What did he say?* I told them. No one is impressed. They have all heard it on the radio, seen it on the tele, read it in the press. A thousand times. I went to debrief Jeremy Brade. He can do the script and the actions better than Dr. Karadzic.

I never did get the book.

Meanwhile, back in the hangar, we had a reorganisation. Steve was replaced by Squadron Leader Willie Dobson. The French marines arrived in full force, and the Canadians left, which gave us one small problem, the bunker. They wanted their container back. By now it was part of the landscape. I offered to buy it from the battalion. It had a book value of about one thousand dollars, and I could have raised that in Zagreb. But it was administratively too difficult. So the Canadians came and removed it, but not until they had replaced it with a superb 1914 front line trench-type bunker. Steel girders, sandbags, the works. We missed the Canadians. They had read the mandate. They appreciated that they "were in support of humanitarian aid" and acted accordingly. They also appreciated our shortcomings. We had to learn "on the hoof." We made many mistakes. We messed them about a lot. But never deliberately. The Canadians were good at pulling order out of chaos. Above all they were flexible. With the arrival of the French, it was us who had to learn flexibility.

In the hangar reorg, I made myself a super hidey hole. Using pallets of boxes which had just arrived, I built a wall around my bed. It felt safe. It also felt private. I could see no one. No one could see me.

We spent the majority of most nights in our beds in the hangar. If the shelling rattled the walls or exploded close enough for us to hear the whistling shrapnel we moved to the safety of the bunker until events calmed down.

The new bunker was more exclusive than the old container. It was also much more tomb-like and claustrophobic. The civilian drivers, strangers to Blackadder, preferred the open plan of the main airport lounge where the French slept.

Our next visitor is to be Paddy Ashdown. This environment should suit him down to the ground. His office in London asks me if I can arrange for him an interview with the President. I speak to Mr. Somun. The president agrees to meet him.

It is a hot, hot, August day. Mr. Ashdown gets out of the Herc in shirt sleeves and flak jacket. He is to be bundled into a French APC and taken to meet the French commander. Mr. Ashdown is very popular, everyone wants to meet him. He sees me and kindly recognises me.

– *Larry, good to see you. When will we get together?*

– *As soon as you are free.*

– *I would like to stay with you and your men.*

– *No probs.*

After a brief courtesy call, he is back with us. He is delightful company. So easy to be with. I take him to meet General Mackenzie. Mack is in his little office in the control tower. He and Paddy speak the same straight language.

The press are at his heels. He is not pulling any punches.

He is highly critical of the Serbs and wants to lift the arms embargo so that the Bosnian government can be re-armed. Taking him to see President Izetbegovic is going to be easy. Going to Pale is not.

We motored him at speed to the Presidency. Front entrance, up the

47

stairs and into the reception room. The president is waiting to see him. Paddy extends his arm.

– *Hello, Mr. President. Thank you for seeing me.* He could not have predicted Mr. Izetbegovic's reply.

– *Hello, Mr. Ashdown, I am glad to see you. I am told that you are the most handsome politician in the world.* They got on very well. I started the meeting sitting close to Paddy on the same settee. I then saw the Bosnian Sarajevo TV camera and heard Paddy's hard-line defence of Sarajevo, Gorazde, Tuzla, and his forthright condemnation of the Bosnian Serbs. The President was delighted. I was slowly and—I hope—surreptitiously sliding away from Paddy out of the view of the camera. As noble as his views may have been, they were not the UN's, nor UNHCR's, and, in parts, not mine. Furthermore, I was representing impartiality.

After the meeting, he faced the international cameras, and told them exactly what he had said inside.

– *Mr. Ashdown, tomorrow you are going to Pale. Will you be as strong over there?"*

– *Yes*—he replied, not knowing what the result would be.

We returned to the hangar. The shelling was continuous and dangerous. We decided to spend the night in the bunker where we had developed a routine and a system. Lee and Willie had the wall slots. I was piggy in the middle, and Ron slept at the entrance. With Paddy staying, it was going to be a little cosier. I took with me a small hammock, so I gave my bedspace to Paddy and slung the hammock from the supporting girders.

Paddy had brought some refreshments, we provided the mugs. It was a hot sticky night, so we sat huddled around the entrance to the bunker and watched the battle rage between the Airport settlement and Dobrinja. There was a sound and light show to rival Michel Jarre. As usual, we went to bed early. Equally as usual, I was up first. Reminding myself that I was in a hammock, I climbed out slowly, and, in the dark, found my shoes, grabbed my towel and toothbrush—not for me the hassle of razor and brush. I clambered out of the bunker. I paused at the entrance and then made a dash for the hangar, hoping that the snipers were not looking for an early kill.

Nonjo and Ploco were in the hangar but not at the tap. So I washed. As I dried my face, I looked down at my feet. I thought to myself— *That's a fine pair of shoes Larry.* I then realised that the fine pair of shoes were on my feet. They certainly did not belong to me. I raced back to the bunker.

Paddy was still in his sleeping bag. I quietly put his shoes back in place and put on mine. If any of you Liberal Democrats wish to step into Paddy's shoes, I can tell you they are a size eleven.

Today was a Pale day for Paddy. I was to take him to the Serb military headquarters in Lukavica. The Serbs had agreed to take him on to Pale. Paddy always seemed to enjoy the challenge of the Butmir 400, the exposed four hundred metres of front line between the Serb and the Government troops guaranteed to increase the heart rate. The French have raised a memorial at the entrance to it in commemoration of those whom they have lost on its deadly tarmac.

At Lukavica we met Brane, the Serb Liaison officer. They were ready for "the distinguished guest." They had laid on a BMW. The only time I ever saw them do this. They had also laid on an interpreter. We shook hands and Paddy left. The arrangement, confirmed by Brane, was that they would host him, give him an official dinner, and return him the following morning.

Mr. Ashdown was as forthright as he promised the press he would be. Dr. Karadzic had not expected such a strong speech, but he had the last word. When Paddy left the hotel to return to Sarajevo, there was no car and no translator. Paddy, in a none too friendly environment and without an interpreter, had to find a car for himself. This was no challenge to an ex-marine. He found a taxi.

When he eventually returned to Lukavica, I was there to meet him. We returned to Sarajevo. He left for England. I next saw him in Sarajevo a few weeks later. He was to become a regular and very welcome visitor.

The airlift roared and rumbled on. At the end of each month, donor nations pledged their aircraft. More nations joined, some for a token flight, others for the long haul.

The first Saudi Hercules was piloted by a sheikh. I always tried to meet the first flight and to thank the crew on behalf of UNHCR in Sarajevo. I was at the tarmac and could see the Saudi Herc approaching.

– *Larry, there is a phone call from Zagreb!*—shouted Willie over the noise of taxiing aircraft.

– *Damn. Willie, can you do me a favour? Will you meet and greet the Saudi Herc if I am not back?*

– *Sure*—said Willie. I ran to the hangar. It was UNHCR Zagreb. Tony Land.

– *Larry, the Saudi herc will be arriving soon. Can you make a special point of meeting it? It is piloted by a member of the Saudi Royal family.* I ran back to the tarmac. The herc was down, Willie was having his photograph taken with the Sheikh. The Sheikh presented him with a watch!

I met the second Saudi flight. No watch. Being second is never the same as being first!

A few of the flights carried VIP passengers, many carried people who thought they were VIP's. An American herc landed and out tumbled a large US senator who was a senior Member of the Armed Forces committee. He was accompanied by a press team from the Force's newspaper *The Stars and Stripes*. The herc would be on the ground for a maximum of twelve minutes. The Senator saw me and shouted—*Here Sonny, over here. Stand by me, and I'll make you famous!* I am not too sure who was the most embarrassed—the photographer, or me.

Some of the planes had on board the donors of the aid it carried. Most were happy with a photo op on the tarmac. But not all. The first non-government aid to arrive on a Brit herc was accompanied by a small, very insignificant looking fellow, with a little paunch, wispy strands of hair, and weak presence, who had, on his own initiative, touted the sweets and biscuit manufacturers of the UK and asked for misshapen and broken produce. He had been given five tonnes. He arrived with the load on the first Brit herc of the day, having negotiated his return on the last. He explained that he had given his word to the companies that he would return with photographs of the aid delivered in Sarajevo. He had contact numbers of some Catholic nuns who would distribute the goodies to children. He was so plausible, so incongruous, and so unlikely that we took him into the warehouse and took photographs as he handed the aid over directly to the nuns. Back in Reading, they would never ever believe him. But I bet he is not the sort of chap who will ever tell anyone.

The one thousandth flight of the airlift came around quickly. It was the second of September. We were all excited by it, it was touch and go which nation it would be. In Zagreb, there was a lot of friendly rivalry and jockeying for the honour. Mike Aitcheson, the UNHCR airlift coordinator, was refereeing. We had no way of throwing a party, but the event was marked by the boys who made a huge "1000 Flight" banner. When the plane approached, I could see that it was a Brit herc. I was now especially pleased. The herc landed, the crew got out, and we shook hands; it was all a little flat and a little disappointing. Then Mike Aitcheson appeared at the door with promotion hats and banners from the brewery King and Barnes, who, via Mike's local, the Plough at Blackbrook, had donated a lot of English ale to celebrate the occasion. Mike had it with him. The day was suitably celebrated. The local staff were thrilled. Well done Mike and thanks to Robin Squire the landlord of the Plough.

The day ended on a high. The next day ended in disaster.

The airlift was running as usual. Zagreb informed us by satphone of the take-off of the aircraft, the tower in Sarajevo told us of the arrival time. A well-established procedure after more than a thousand flights. Mike informed us of the take-off of the Italian plane and of the flight following it. The later plane arrived first. Unusual, but it had happened before. We waited for the Italian. No news. Both UNHCR and the tower contacted Zagreb. No news. The aircraft was posted as missing. Eerily we kept looking into the sky. But it never came. In the early afternoon, the rumours began that an aircraft had been shot down in the hills close to Sarajevo. Eric de Stabenrath took a group of marines out to investigate. UNHCR sent with him Ed Bishop, our immensely bright and energetic American Programme

Officer whose qualifications included holding a pilot's licence. Tony Land was visiting the Croat headquarters in Kiseljak on his journey back to Zagreb. The Croats told him of the downing of an aircraft and the discovery of wreckage. He set off to find it.

He met Eric and Ed at the crash site. The Hercules was carrying bales of blankets. It came down on a wooded hillside. The wreckage was spread over a small area. It had destroyed trees; small fires were smouldering, the smoke curling up to the roof of trees bedecked in blankets. Blankets were strewn for miles. The bodies of the crew were brought back to Sarajevo. The airlift was suspended. The Italian Government announced that the aircraft had been shot down by a missile. The Croats were unofficially blamed.

The next day, with no airlift, we had little aid to distribute but we decided to empty the stocks at the airport. We chose a bad day. Whilst unloading in the city, heavy shelling began, and our warehouse received seven shells. One vehicle was destroyed, but there were no casualties. We adjourned and returned the following day when fifteen rounds of sniper fire zinged around the trucks.

There was a narrow escape for Ed Bishop in the hangar. I was near my bedspace, Ed was on the satphone and Seyo the driver was standing close to him. One single machine gun round came flying through the hangar window above me on a downward trajectory. It missed Ed by an inch and hit a desk. Splinters from the desk injured the Seyo.

Not a good week.

Three

Gorazde

Returning from the airport to my desk in the PTT, I found the card of M. Bernard Kouchner, the French Minister and founder of MSF. It was he who had accompanied President Mitterand when Sarajevo airport was first opened. He had been brought to my office by Mr. Leon Davico, whom I knew from his UNHCR days when he was head of public information. We had last met in Addis Ababa. The card contained greetings from M. Kouchner and the telephone number of Leon, who was staying at the Holiday Inn. I immediately rang him. Leon is a man of many contacts around the world. He was born in Belgrade where I was certain he would know everyone who was anyone. I explained to him that I wanted to get to Gorazde and asked for his help.

– *No problem*—said Leon. *I know Mrs. Plavsic very well.* This was excellent news for me. She was a Professor of Biology at the University of Sarajevo. She had a flat in Sarajevo, but now as Vice President of the so called Srpska Republika, she lived in Pale and in Belgrade and was responsible for Humanitarian Affairs. Leon arranged for us to meet her, and I drove us both to the Serb army headquarters barracks at Lukavica on the outskirts of Sarajevo. When we arrived, it was obvious we were expected. We were taken upstairs to the main conference room at the end of the corridor. We were offered coffee, and then Mrs. Plavsic arrived. She is a tall, well-built woman with a very strong Slav face. She has a fine head of mouse brown hair. Her English is slow and hesitant but fluent. She was charming. She and Leon greeted each other in their native Serbo Croat. I was introduced, and English became the language of the discussion. Leon had a few messages from Bernard Kouchner.

Whilst we were talking, shelling began. Mrs. Plavsic said that whenever the Muslims saw that Lukavica had a visitor, they shelled. For sure, these were incoming rounds and they were not very far away. Leon introduced my background to Mrs. Plavsic. He told her that we had first met in Addis Ababa, and he outlined my current task—

to provide aid to all sides.

His words were interrupted by an enormous bang. A shell had landed very close. We had heard the whistle, heard the thud, felt the windows rattle and the pressure change. A soldier who was outside the door entered the room and told us to get away from the windows. Mrs. Plavsic, I noted, was unflustered. She picked up her notes and her coffee and moved towards the door. There was another great bang, but this was an outgoing reply to the Muslim intrusion.

The soldier suggested that we find a less exposed room, one with less glass. We moved down the stairs to a tiny room with only a one pane window. It was also at the side of the building.

Mrs. Plavsic took all this in her stolid stride. We resumed our talk. I took the lead and explained that there was tremendous pressure on us to get aid through to Gorazde—*UNHCR, led by Fabrizio Hochschild, whom I know you know well, has tried one attempt, but the convoy lost an APC and a truck in mine explosions.* Mrs. Plavsic confirmed that she knew Fabrizio well. *I had supported the convoy attempt and was sad at its outcome. I have no objection to you trying a convoy, but before you attempt Gorazde, I would like you to try to relieve two other Muslim villages which are cut off and desperate.*

This answer was not what I expected. Her magnanimity took me by surprise. She went on to say that—*there are Serb majority villages, isolated and starving which I should also like you to attempt to reach.* This was good news for me, as I knew that all take and no give would not work in this environment. I showed great enthusiasm to learn the location of all these villages.

She was well prepared for my visit. She called in an army officer and arranged a further meeting for us with some military officers to pinpoint these other locations. She implied that a successful attempt on the easier targets would earn full support for an attempt on Gorazde. At no time did she say—*No*—to an attempt on Gorazde.

I returned to Sarajevo, very grateful to Leon for his introduction and kind words.

I went to see Eric de Stabenrath, the Lieutenant Colonel Operations Officer of the French battalion at the airport. His battalion had rescued the last attempt at Gorazde. Eric and I were determined that we were going to relieve the siege of Gorazde together. Eric's background intrigued me. The name *de Stabenrath* is obviously not French. An ancestor of his had been secretary to one of the Louis' who had ruled France. But Eric's father had commanded the French Foreign Legion at Dien Bien Phu. The parallels between the French position in besieged, surrounded Sarajevo and in Dien Bien Phu were uncanny. Eric's father had died in the closing hours of the battle.

In an unguarded moment, the reserved aristocrat, told me of the time, as a tiny child, when he had told his nanny that he no longer had a father. Long before the news was known, long before it could have travelled, he "knew."

I had another "experience" with Eric. One day we went together to the "Airport Settlement." This was a Serb enclave next to the airport adjoining Muslim majority Dobrinje. The Serb Liaison Officer Major Misha Indic told me that civilians lived there and requested food for them. The Bosnian government told me that only Serb soldiers were there. They demanded that I did not deliver any humanitarian aid there, as it would go only to Serb "fighters."

I asked Eric to investigate. He confirmed that he had been there, with his incredibly brave translator, and visited the settlement and found families. There were women, children, grandmas and grandads living in houses bombed, almost, to dereliction. They needed food.

We decided to take it. A small convoy was organised. Major Indic was our guide. We took in a minimum of food. It was a wild day, lots of shooting and a lot of shelling. In the middle of it all, Indic, who has an impish, nay devilish, sense of humour, took us to a house for coffee. We sat on the floor in the courtyard, the tiny, damaged, house was surrounded by the walls of others. The lady of the house prepared us coffee. In the group was a grandma. Indic knew that she had a reputation for "reading" the coffee cups. As an Englishman, I knew all about "reading" tea leaves. It had never occurred to me that coffee grounds have the same effect.

The old gran offered to read for us. Eric finished his drink first. She told him to swish the dregs around and then hand the cup to her.

55

This he did. The old dear, dressed in black, short of many a tooth, held the tiny cup in her small, surprisingly soft hand. Her daughters were crowded around her, attempting to peek. She called them to order and proceeded, with many twists of the cup, to read... first, Eric's past...

Past and future, his and mine, she told with conviction and passion. I can reveal that she told Eric that there had been two male influences in his life. One strong, but for a short time, the other strong and long. Eric was amazed. Following the death at Dien Bien Phu of his father, his mother had married again; Eric loved, admired, and respected his stepfather.

One other little incident stands out in my mind. During the reading, there was a sudden and accurate outburst of sniper fire from the Muslim side. The bullets bounced off walls close by, the young children who were playing around us during the "reading" quietly moved to the walls of the buildings and stood silently against them during the bursts of fire. A new instinct for children older than their years.

Back to the aftermath of my visit to Mrs. Plavsic. Eric took me in to see his senior, Colonel Patric Sartre. In effect, Eric is the second in command of the Marines, both he and Sartre are small and tough. Interestingly, they both have strawberry birthmarks on their faces; they tell me that it is not a compulsory feature for promotion. We discussed the "Plavsic" proposal. Colonel Sartre requested that he attend my meeting with the military when I would learn about the Serb and Muslim villages.

I returned to the PTT building to see the liaison officers—the government ones to tell them about the progress towards a Gorazde convoy and the Serb ones to arrange a meeting with the military. The following day, Indic gave me the details; Mrs. Plavsic did not hang about!

The meeting was to be at Pale, the capital of the so-called Srpska Republika where Mrs. Plavsic had her Vice President's office.

Sartre picked me up at the airport and we went in his APC. We had with us Svetlana, his outstanding translator. But this day she was nervous, she had not met Mrs. Plavsic and was in awe of her. Before we got to Pale, our APC was stopped by a Serb patrol and we were told that the venue was not to be Pale but Jahorina, the ski resort and famous host of the 1984 Winter Olympics.

We pulled in with our APC at this great resort hotel and were met by Mrs. Plavsic on the steps. We were escorted to the conference room. In attendance were Mrs. Plavsic and some senior army officers. We were told what was expected of us. The villages were Podzieblje and Godzenje. We were given grid references, timings, lunch, and wine. Doing business with Mrs. Vice President Plavsic was a pleasure.

On the way back, Lana admitted that her opening translation passages were a little ragged. I later saw her at much more stressful conferences, and she was never again intimidated.

Armed with the grid references, we planned our movements. Gorazde would be on the following Thursday; the two isolated Muslim villages we would do on the Tuesday. Thursday would be the big event, and Lt. Col. Eric would command the military; Tuesday could be left to a captain.

We set off to do the mini event with lots of confidence. Dragon was my driver. A small very intense Serb with a degree in Agriculture. He was a very loyal, quiet, honest, private man.

LO Brane took the convoy to Lukavica where we were met by a Serb APC. In the turret was a tall intelligent Serb Military Police officer, Nenad Rac, who certainly gave me confidence that all would be well. Sarajevo to Sokalac was no problem, the French APC sat behind the Serb APC, and we were all on auto pilot. After Sokolac, the Serb was a little unsure. I was asked to map-read. I had been at the conference. The turning off the main road was narrow and unexpected. The Serb local residents were surprised at the news that we intended reaching the Muslim villages by this route. As we progressed down it, so was I. We were taking a convoy of ten trucks, one Land Cruiser, and two APC along a woodman's track in a dense forest. What I did not like was the fact that if we came under fire there was no way we could turn or reverse. There being no way to turn or reverse narrows down the options. You have to go on.

On we went. Eventually, we came to a large clearing which should have been on the outskirts of the first village. Our way ahead was blocked by felled trees. The Serb officer told me that there was an alternate route using a path to the left but that we had to be careful of mines and snipers. He therefore suggested that only my UNHCR vehicle went forward; however, he would put in my vehicle an armed escort for my protection. I concurred. His escort jumped in the back. I was sitting in the front, Dragon was driving. We set off.

Suddenly there was the most deafening sound of rifle fire. It awakened the clearing, it reverberated off every tree and bounced off every rock. It was followed by an equally noisy silence.

Dragon asked me how close the shooting was. I knew exactly how close it was. It had whistled past my left ear at a distance of millimetres. Furthermore, it had begun its trajectory not one metre from me. The buggar behind me, my Serb protector, my escort, had accidentally discharged his weapon.

I was not best pleased. I got out of the vehicle, opened the rear passenger door, and dragged him off the seat and threw him out of the vehicle, fully confident that he had no rounds left in his magazine.

With my ears singing, I went to the end of the path where we found this route also blocked by fallen trees.

The Serb officer was now happy. We had done our bit. We had attempted to relieve the villages, but could not get in; Muslims' own fault, blocked themselves in. Time to go home.

This struck me as being a teeny, weeny bit defeatist. I wanted to explore other routes. So we turned the convoy round, which took an age. If you are in strange territory in a war zone, you can only guarantee the path you have travelled along. You cannot believe that the edges are clear or clean, they may be mined. So you reverse in your own tracks, a tedious task.

We returned almost to the end of the woodman's track and found a turning off to the left. The map indicated that this would take us by a circuitous route to the first of the villages. I was happy to take it, but the French captain was not happy about the time. We had about two hours of light left, we were about to proceed along an unknown track, if we were held up for any reason, we would be strung out in perfect ambush formation. He referred his position to his HQ. Colonel Sartre decided that it was too late to attempt a try. I was not happy, as failing with this one could jeopardize Gorazde. Sartre would not budge. I asked him to permit the convoy to laager overnight where we were. He vetoed that on the grounds that we were deep in Serb held territory. Besides, the Serb commander was not happy with this. Reluctantly, I accepted the French "advice," and we left to return to Sarajevo. We arrived at Pale later than we anticipated. There had been shelling in and around Sarajevo, so the captain was told not to attempt to re-enter Sarajevo but to laager overnight deep in Serb held territory!

As we were so close to the Serb headquarters, I, a little cheekily, went to their HQ hotel with my driver Dragon, remember, a Serb. We ordered a meal and amazingly were joined at the table by Mrs. Plavsic. She had heard of the failure of the convoy.

– *I thought that this would be easy, especially for you*—she said in a very disappointed voice.

– *My dear Mrs. Plavsic*—I said—*sadly, I put too much confidence in your escort. I presumed that he would have reconnoitred the route that your military intelligence would have known that the paths were blocked. Having learned my lesson, I will in future rely only on myself.*

– *Very wise*—she replied.

– *Is Gorazde still on?*—I asked her.

– *If you think you can do it.*

Mrs. Plavsic called across one of the hotel staff and Dragon told me that she had ordered rooms for the night for myself, himself and the French officer. I returned to the convoy, explained where I had been, whom I had seen and the offer of a bed for the night. The young officer replied with all the haught (if there is such a noun) as possible—*Non, I stay with my men.*

I stayed with my man in the chalet hotel, each in our own pine clad room.

The following day, back in Sarajevo, I debriefed the French. They were disappointed but ready for Gorazde. I attended their "Orders

Group" where all participants outlined their role. I did my bit which brought back a memory or two. The French were very efficient, this was a battalion with service in Africa's hotspots. Eric, in particular, was very impressive. I came away thinking that we would never have a better chance at making it.

We loaded the convoy the night before we set off. My Sarajevo drivers could not drive their vehicles. The Serbs would have given them too much hassle, and the convoy was too important to risk on principles. If they could not drive, then they were still going to be part of it. They serviced every vehicle, cleaned every vehicle, and loaded every vehicle with care and determination. The drivers would be Ukrainians. I had insisted that they sleep in the hangar the night before the convoy, as they were not renowned for their ability to be on time. I settled into my cosy corner with all the activity continuing around me.

All sorts of thoughts raced through my head and kept me awake. Would we be mined like Fabrizio? Would we get shot at? Would anybody die? Would we get there? Try as I might, I could not drop off to sleep, and when Nonjo came to awaken me at five with a cup of tea, I was wide awake. I got up, washed and then kick-started the drivers. The Ukrainians were stretched out in their coarse uniforms, tall, stocky, peasants, sound asleep. Nonjo then called me over to the table; he, very touchingly, had cooked a special breakfast for me.

My own drivers were putting finishing touches on the vehicles: carefully stacking and loading medicines, vital medicines for a hospital with a daily intake of patients wounded by mortar shells and sniper fire, a hospital carrying out major surgery without anaesthetics.

We lined up the vehicles, and the French escort arrived. It was exhilarating. I felt proud and excited, the adrenaline was running. The dawn was bright, warm and still, Sarajevo was quiet. The local staff wished us every form of luck.

At H-hour we crossed the start line, the runway taxi area outside the hangar. In the convoy was a contingent of the best of the press. Jeremy Bowen of BBC, Kurt Schork of Reuters, the brave Corinne Dufkas (one of the finest photographers in the business who had started her career as an aid worker in South America), and Patrick Rahir of AFP.

At Lukavica, we were met by Brane. Always an honest and good man, he genuinely wished us luck. The tall Serb in the APC swung out of the Serb barracks, moved to the front of the convoy and led the way. I hoped he was not going to take me down any more cul-de-sacs, no matter how scenic.

The road as far as Sokolac was that which we had taken on our unsuccessful trip a few days previous. Looking at it for the second time, it contrasted starkly with poor Sarajevo. The fields were green and full of crops. Houses were complete, windows intact, children played. Materially, these Serbs were untouched by war; mentally, they were scarred by the propaganda pushed out from the TV and Radio stations of Belgrade and Pale. They could not see the suffering that their soldiers were inflicting on innocent civilians in Sarajevo, they could hear only of the alleged impending atrocities about to be committed by "Muslim hordes."

We passed through Podromanje, near Sokolac without stopping; soon the Serbs would establish a checkpoint there to harass and delay our operations. We arrived, still following the Serb APC, at Rogatica. Here, outside a flour mill, the convoy was halted. Here it was to be inspected by the Serbs to ensure that it contained no weapons, no ammunition for Gorazde. The inspection was carried out under the auspices of the Milicija, the police. The Chief of Police of Rogatica who had held the post before the war invited myself, Eric, and some journalists to his office where we drank slivovica and brandy. His office was towards the far end of Rogatica, so we were able to see for the first time the damage done to a front-line town. Before the war, Rogatica had been a majority Muslim town. There had been bitter fighting over it. The Serb army had driven the Muslims out and they had fled into Gorazde. The centre of the town was destroyed, every shop window shattered, most buildings burned. The shopping centre is just one long narrow street. The proximity of one side of the street to the other emphasised the destruction. Literally the damaged buildings leaned over you and hemmed you in. Not a place for a claustrophobic.

The Chief was very friendly, I gave him a bottle of whisky, he assured me that we would have no trouble from the Serb side, but he was certain that the Muslims would attack the convoy and put the blame on the Serbs. He therefore gave to me a formal warning that, as we left Rogatica, the Serbs would no longer guarantee our safety and that we were proceeding at our own risk and against their professional advice. This was the first time I was given this speech, the first of many times. The bizarre, devious events that followed this convoy were an early lesson to me, never to forget the "Balkan" factor.

We returned to the convoy, the inspection was going well.

I briefed the journalists and the drivers—*If we are ambushed, drive on like hell. If we are mortared, keep moving. If a vehicle is hit and the road blocked, get out and seek cover. If you get out in a hurry, look before you leap. At some stretches the road clings to the mountain side with a sheer drop of a hundred or more feet. If we stop and you want to urinate, do it at the roadside, forget modesty, to attempt to find a secluded spot may result in your genitals immodestly spread over the countryside if you stand on a mine. Any questions?*

– *Can you show me where we are going on the map?* Kurt Schork of Reuters wanted my finger to trace the route. I was soon to learn that this was the most innocuous question that Kurt had ever asked. Normally, he and Sean Maguire of Reuters TV deliver the fast ball that dents the ground and smashes the wickets. The Serb APC and the Chief of Police's car escorted us to the boundary of Rogatica, conveniently at the entrance to a gorge. You wave to the Serbs, take a sharp right-hand bend and you are on a wide tarmacked road in a steep sided valley. There are huge rocks on the road which have fallen from above. A peacetime hazard in an eerie area full of wartime, evil potential. Since the outbreak of the war, only Fabrizio's convoy had travelled this far. Somewhere ahead we would find the debris of part of his convoy. We travelled at a slow speed in a strange silence. Birds must have twittered; the river was but yards away but we did not hear it gush and flow.

After a kilometer or so of gorge, the road ran along the valley bed and we saw large houses at generous intervals. They were deserted but hardly damaged. The "normal"—that is in peacetime—way to go from Rogatica to Gorazde is to continue along this good road, our way was to be the mountain route. The Serbs told us that the Muslims had blocked the main road. The Sarajevo Government told us that the Serbs had mined the road. On a later convoy, I was to open up this direct way and find that both were right.

Turning off onto the mountain route, we could see our road ahead. It wound its way up an isolated mountain. Within a few hundred metres, we encountered our first hazard, a rickety wooden bridge with a weight restriction of two tonnes. All of our trucks weighed more than ten tonnes. I decided we would risk it. Eric agreed to send an APC across to secure the other side. The APC is no test of weight for a bridge as their enormous tyres and design specialties distribute their weight more successfully than a truck. I marshalled each vehicle across the bridge individually, they paused about one hundred metres before the bridge, then went at great speed. I waited for the vibrations to stop before sending another. The bridge was obviously grossly underestimated—it eventually took many a convoy.

Soon after the bridge there was a sharp right-hand hairpin bend. It was made negotiable by our trucks because to the left of it extended a rocky plateau at the base of a sheer needle-like mountain. The trucks were able to swing wide onto the plateau. Up at the top of the needle were Muslim forces. It was their outpost—high, safe, and secure. They shared caves with mountain goats whose muffled, plaintive bleats travelled across the still valley. From these observation posts, the Bosnian Army was able to report to Gorazde who was approaching. From their eeries they were also able to snipe at Serb patrols. We passed without incident. One hundred and fifty metres on, there was another bend at which we found a small Serb position, three soldiers in good humour. Just before the next bend (another right hander and exceedingly sharp), we came upon the debris of the APC from Fabrizio's convoy.

I paused whilst I recollected his account of the events after the vehicle hit a mine, lost a wheel and overturned. The explosion triggered off a firefight. They were caught in the middle and took cover in the

63

steep slopes of the hill where they spent a long, confused night. The convoy was accompanied by the former UK Chief Medical Officer Sir Donald Acheson, then Head of WHO (World Health Organisation) for Former Yugoslavia, who kept himself warm wrapped in the WHO flag he had loyally and conveniently brought along with him. In the damaged APC, morale was kept high by Major Vanessa Lloyd Davies of the British Royal Army Medical Corps. The only casualty was Una Sekerez, the UNHCR translator with the convoy. Our translators could always be found at the front, fearless and faithful. Una received only cuts. Vanessa later received an MBE for Gallantry for this and other actions in Bosnia.

We swung past the discarded APC axle, wheel, and other shrapnel and moved to the top of the mountain. We could just see Gorazde, way down in the distance. I was really excited. I still was not sure if we would make it. We could also see a strong Serb military post and behind it the remains of the ten-tonne truck from Fabrizio's convoy which had hit a second mine as he had bravely attempted to continue the morning after the APC explosion. I anticipated trouble from the Serbs, they looked a wild bunch, but they gave me no hassle, and the media some excellent pictures. From their positions on the summit, the Serbs could see the whole panorama of the city of Gorazde. Their guns were trained on the strategic points. They could be in no doubt where their shells were landing. Tenement blocks, the hospital, gathering crowds were all clearly visible. It needed no military skill to land a shell in Gorazde. I was never present on either the hills around Sarajevo or Gorazde when Serb guns were fired. I would like to have seen the faces of those who fired. Did they celebrate, cheer? Did they smile, laugh, slap their thighs when their round landed? I suspect they did. Did any feel sick with sadness or shame? There was a story, which I was never able to prove but which I am sure is true, that busloads of Serbs motored from Belgrade to the outskirts of Gorazde to join the guns and to fire "their" round into Gorazde. Men whose number one sport was hunting swapped their quarry, from boar and bear to Muslims.

The hilltop Serbs let us pass. We had one more checkpoint to go, this, halfway down the road into Gorazde. As we descended this road, you could touch, feel, our excitement. We could see Gorazde, so close, surely, we would reach her. We were stopped at the final checkpoint. The Serbs there were not sure we had approval to advance. We must wait for a military commander.

He arrived, a small grey-haired man, aged about fifty. He confirmed that we had permission but warned me that ahead lay no man's land. He was certain the Muslims had laid mines. Were we certain they were expecting us? They may attack us. He, like his senior counterpart in Rogatica, gave us approval to pass, but at our own risk. We passed his barrier and moved towards our goal. The road was deserted. Bricks, stones, fallen branches littered it. Ahead of me was one APC, then Eric's vehicle. Behind me, the press and the convoy. The first wave of excitement was when we saw the road sign "Gorazde." It was scarred with bullets, but it meant we were there. Just after the sign was a gentle bend to the left, as we came out of it the rooftops of a whole Gorazde street were on our right. Many of the houses were destroyed. There was no sign of life.

I halted the convoy. Eric stopped his vehicle and came over to me.

– *Eric, I think you and I should walk in on our own from here.*

– *My view, exactly*—replied Eric. We set off together. The APC and the convoy, including journalists, halted. God we were excited! It was a mixture of achievement, expectation, and joy. We walked down the hill, on our right there were some large buildings.

– *It seems deserted, Eric.*

– *I think there is some movement in the basement*—he said very quietly. At the bottom of the hill there was a crossroad. There had been traffic lights and streetlamps, but the posts and the wiring hung awry. The shops on the corner were windowless, glass strewn everywhere. We turned right towards where we thought the centre of town may be. We were still alone, but now we were walking along a pavement, and the buildings were within touching distance. *There are people looking out of balcony windows*—said Eric.

Feeling foolish, I shouted in Serbo Croat the only words that I knew.

– *Visoko Kommissariat. United Nations!*

A man appeared. He was in his fifties, plump, jolly and very emotional. He embraced Eric and myself. People now appeared in doorways, mainly women and children. Then balconies filled. The man told us that he was to take us and the convoy to the centre of the town. Eric and I turned to return to the convoy. The journalists were on our tail, cameras thrusting, pencils gliding over notebooks. A wave of the arm was all that was needed for the convoy to move. As it entered the town, people appeared from everywhere, they clapped and cheered and wept and sobbed and hugged us. They placed flowers on the vehicles. We, to a man, were overwhelmed. At the centre of the town we were met by the man responsible for receiving the aid. The centre was a carpet of broken glass. The people of Gorazde could not risk their lives sweeping it up. Your feet crunched as you walked about on it. Part of the aid was to go to the basement of a building in the centre. A chain of men was organised to unload those vehicles which carried baby food. Two more locations were decided upon. They wanted the food dispersed, as they were convinced that the Serbs would watch where we unloaded it and then shell there. They were later proved right. The mayor wanted to see us, and we wanted to see the hospital and deliver the medicines we had brought.

Dragon, my driver, who, as a Serb, had been really afraid about entering Gorazde, had been recognised by old University friends, smothered in kisses, cuddled, presented with flowers, now confident enough to lead, on his own, one of the groups of vehicles to be unloaded. Eric and I went together to the Mayor. His office was hidden in the back streets of the city. In an area comparatively hard to shell. We were led there running across notorious sniper locations. It was a dingy, dark office. For our benefit, the room was lit by a tiny bulb powered by a car battery. Eric handed out the cigarettes. Eyes glowed, there was a clamour to get one. That day I was to learn that if the first convoy into a besieged town only carried cigarettes, it would be welcomed. They were desperate for a cigarette made from tobacco. They had their own made from leaves and rolled in newspaper.

The mayor, Hadzo Efendic, I was eventually to know well. After the tragic death of Mr. Tureljevic, he was to become Vice President of

Bosnia. He welcomed us. Told us the story of the city: the deaths, the deprivations, the despair. He was straight and blunt. He asked why we had taken so long to come to their rescue. When did we anticipate we would be back? I left the diplomatic Eric who patiently and sympathetically explained the limitations of the United Nations troops in Bosnia.

I left for the hospital.

Soon after our arrival, the Serbs had dropped three mortar shells into Gorazde. In fairness to their promise, they had landed them on the far side of the river, well away from us. They missed us, but they did kill and maim some citizens of Gorazde. As we arrived at the hospital while they were being brought in. One victim was a three-year-old girl, her mother was killed outright. The little girl had multiple shrapnel wounds.

I arrived at the same time as Jeremy Bowen of the BBC. We entered the "casualty" department. The hospital had no electricity, the room was dark. The surgeon, Alija Begovic, was digging the shards of metal out of the body of the writhing child, there was no anaesthetic. The small amount we had brought was not yet unloaded. The girl's screams were piercing. Sounds etched on my memory's tape recorder, later to be heard at unguarded moments. The surgeon saw the TV cameraman whose camera had a light attached to it. He called him over, he needed the light to work by, to locate the slivers from where the child was bleeding. We watched as the cameraman closed in on the girl who nurses were holding down.

We, outsiders, were stunned and silent. The Gorazde hospital staff had seen it and done it so many times before. They were able to accept that this was Gorazde in 1992. To me, it was a scene from centuries ago. It was not caused by earthquake or accident. This orphaned child lay bleeding and screaming because some man had fired a mortar bomb into the heart of a city. As we left the room where the girl lay, we passed the other mortar victims waiting for treatment. My heart went out to them. To sit outside a room, to hear that screaming, to know that your turn is next.

I went off to the third location to see how the unloading was going.

It wasn't. Or, at best, it was going very slowly. I started to get angry. *I want this truck unloaded now. I'll give you thirty minutes to unload it or I'll take it back*—I felt guilty because the men were as thin as rakes. God knows how weary and tired they must have been. Opposite where we were unloading was a police station. A policeman came over to me.

– *Mr. Larry, don't get angry. They are not lazy. They are taking their time simply because they do not want you to go. They know that when you go, the shelling will start again and probably worse than before to punish us for your visit.*

I understood their fears, their hunger and their reluctance, but I had an obligation to my convoy. We had told the Serbs we would be out before dark. The road we had come along was bad enough by day. To negotiate it by night would be reckless. Besides, it may by now be mined.

The locals were not interested in my problems, they proceeded at a very slow pace. I was not prepared to compromise, nor was I prepared to take any of the food back as I had threatened.

– *Right. We will dump the sacks straight onto the floor. This will make life more difficult for you. Instead of them going straight onto your shoulder, you will have to pick them up off the floor.*

We began to dump them, in the hope that more people would help with the unloading. They simply called my bluff. We dumped the whole lot on the floor and had emptied the trucks in half an hour.

All three convoy packets met back at the town centre. We had a farewell ceremony with the Mayor. We promised faithfully to be back. Before we left, the French marine Battalion Public Relations Warrant Officer took a photo of a very happy Eric and myself shaking hands. The photo, I saw much later in a magazine when I was in Rwanda. It was captioned: "Bravo Eric. Well done Larry." So far so good. We now had to get the convoy back safely. We left the cheering, clapping crowd and headed back. We were late. We would at least clear the first checkpoint before dark, probably we could get beyond the summit of the hill. We would then need an unhindered run down the twisting road to be back into Rogatica, where we would overnight.

It was a slow haul up the hill. The Serb checkpoints were interested in the conditions inside. The majority seemed genuinely concerned, but I remember one in particular who said—*If the conditions are so bad, why don't they surrender?*

In truth, having the image of the little girl fresh in my mind, I was not in a pro Serb mood. By the time we reached the summit, Eric and I knew that we were going to need a lot of luck if we were to reach Rogatica that night.

– *How far do you think we can go?*—I asked him.

– *We must still aim for Sarajevo*—he replied, then a long pause—*And hope we reach Rogatica.*

We passed again the remains of the ten-tonne truck of Fabrizio's convoy. Now that we had been into Gorazde, we could appreciate just how close they had been to achieving their aim. I silently saluted Fabrizio.

By now, night had fallen and we decided that I would travel in the leading APC, which was commanded by a really bright young French Lieutenant who spoke beautiful English. We started the descent. The APC had a spotlight and the young officer stood in the commanders' hatchway and swept the dirt road with the beam of the light as we motored along at a very steady pace. It was a dark night; the mountain was on our left and the hedge of trees delineated the track and prevented us from falling to the next level on our right. Both the mountain and trees captured the dark and enveloped the convoy. As we approached the sharp hair pin bend which led to the foot of the sheer rise where earlier we had seen the Muslim look out, the Lieutenant slowed the APC down to the pace of an escargot. On our way up, he had fleetingly seen a suspicious pile of stones at the side of the road. The sort of location where a mine could be laid at short notice. As we inched forward, he caught the mound of stones in the beam. He stopped the APC. He slowly traversed the light across the track. In its beam, his sharp eyes saw a wire stretching from the mound of stones to the other side of the track. He was on the radio to Eric, who came forward. I got out of the APC, together we slowly, in my case somewhat clumsily, advanced to the wire. At Eric's order, the Lieutenant held the gaze of the lamp on the pile of stones. There, clearly visible, was a mine, an evil mix of plastic, metal and highly explosive. A few more feet forward and the APC would have set it off. It was so positioned that it would have done most damage to the officer standing in the hatchway. Eric spoke on the radio, and soon we had a small gathering of experts.

– *The end of a long day*—I said to Eric.

– *Non*—said a Warrant Officer—*We can shoot it and set it off. Then proceed.*

I was not happy with this. It may be the "Gung ho Marines" answer, but it was not my recommendation.

– *What happens if it is the first of a number of mines. Do we go down the road shooting at all mounds of rocks? Whoever laid it knows it is there. The side that didn't probably does not. Therefore, if we fire even a single round, let alone set off a mine, we could find ourselves in a firefight*—Eric was in no doubt.

– *We do nothing till dawn*—Sandhurst and St. Cyr were in agreement.

By now, the Press Corps were happy snapping from a distance. For them, the convoy was getting better by the minute. We gathered the drivers together, briefed them and warned everyone to make minimum noise. Mess tins rattled, cans were opened, bottles produced. I particularly remember a good single malt emerging from the bottom of Jeremy Bowen's bag. Whatever the drink, whatever the food, the conversation was the same in every group.

– *Who had laid the mine and why?*

– *The Serbs*—They usually got blamed for everything, so it was natural that someone should start off with them.

– *But why, what have they got to gain? Surely, they would have mined the road on our way in to prevent us reaching Gorazde*—said someone, refreshingly applying logic.

– *Yes, if they had laid it on our way in, the Serbs could easily have said that it was part of the Muslim defence*—added a man with a little more time in the Balkans.

– *It was the Serbs. They did it now, knowing that we would blame the*

Muslims. An old Balkan hand talking.

During the long night, the answer partly became clear. Behind us and above us there was a lot of noise. The French had deployed guards and listening posts. They reported that armed men were moving around us. The Marines knew their mandate. If attacked, they could return fire. If they were not, they sat still and observed. Eric had great faith in their training. It could not have been easy for them. The armed groups were close enough to be heard and seen but far enough away not to be identified.

At first, we feared an ambush. We were in a perfect position. We considered moving the convoy back. But not seriously—there was no room to turn, every vehicle would have to be reversed, in the dark, on a narrow road with a steep drop. Also, had we now been mined behind us? So if you cannot go forward and you cannot go back. You make the best of staying.

At the height of the movement, behind our position, another clue as to who had laid the mine fell into place. A mortar bomb came whooshing through the dark sky and landed amongst the trees about one hundred metres behind us. The trees shielded the flash, the blast, and the splinters. The mortar had undoubtedly come from Serb positions ahead of us in the direction of Rogatica. It was unlikely that the Serbs would fire on Serb troops. I was later to learn that this was not a hard and fast rule. Balkan forces could deliberately fire on their own in order to blame the other side.

But this night, we were convinced that the troops moving around us were Bosnian forces from Gorazde. They had mined us in and were using us as a screen whilst they moved. The mortar was a warning shot from the Serbs who knew what was going on.

– *Eric, do you think the Serbs will fire anymore?*

– *No, I do not think they will risk hitting the convoy. But, if I were you Larry, I would sleep in one of my APC's.*

So saying, Eric stretched out in his flimsy little jeep. But I knew that before long, Eric would be up, out, and at the forward sentry posts. I have to admit that I took his advice and found a corner in an APC. Dragon slept in the back of a truck.

We were awake before dawn. We wanted to see the situation by daylight. Eric and I watched the sun come up. Accompanied by his Lieutenant, we could now clearly see the mine, and the wire. The APC moved back a few metres. We placed a branch across the road. No one was to move further forward of this. This was a necessary precaution as the Lady and gentlemen of the press were dancing around and over the wire. I was worried that one of them might attempt to limbo under it.

Having decided that the mine was laid by the Bosnian side, we agreed that I would go forward with Eric to the clearing and would try to attract the attention of the Bosnian forces in their eerie. This I would do with a United Nations flag attached to a branch from a tree, shouting my favourite words—*Visoko Kommissariat.* I did this, much to the amusement of the soldiers, the joy of the press, and the embarrassment of myself. Whilst I was performing, Eric was looking at the clearing with his professional eye.

– *Larry, there are more mines here. These are anti-tank.* I stopped my "Relief of Mafeking" semaphore act and joined him at the perimeter of a fresh pile of stones clearly covering a large green dish designed to tear the wheels of any of our vehicles.

– *Very well placed*—said Eric—*There is no way the convoy could have avoided it. To swing around the bend, you had to go over the mine. It would have had a more devastating attack on our progress than the first one.*

– *Eric, if we have two, we may have more.*

I returned to my cabaret act but attracted nothing and no one. Eric got on his battalion radio to Sarajevo, by morse, and told them of the latest developments. We were told to sit tight, a meaningful HQ decision, in the circumstances. Sarajevo first asked the Serbs if they would clear the mines. Apparently they said—*Yes*—until they realised where they were. They then said—*NO.*

Sarajevo then decided to send the engineers out from the marines at the airport, from the same battalion who were escorting us. This all took time. We spent the whole day and the whole night in the custody of these mines. It was halfway through the next day when we heard that the marines were in the area. They arrived cautiously and slowly. Which was just as well. At the bridge with the two-tonne limit, they found more mines. It was late in the afternoon before they had made safe the mine with the wire and a little later when they detonated the anti-tank mine in the road.

We were then free to move, forty hours after the sharp-eyed Lieutenant spotted the wire. Incidentally, he was later to receive an award for his professionalism. We returned to Rogatica, where we were met by an extremely agitated Brane.

— *Mr. Larry, get the convoy through here as fast as you can. You are not welcome here. The people may attack your convoy.*

— *Brane, what has happened?*

— *Whilst you were mined in, the Muslims moved their troops using your convoy as a shield. They came into Rogatica, there was a battle, and twelve from the town are dead. This is the largest number of casualties in one battle in this area since the war began. They are very anti-UN, anti-UNHCR, and especially anti-you, Mr. Larry.*

I liaised with Eric and directed the convoy to speed through Rogatica. As I was talking to him, two Serb commanders from Rogatica came up to me. Their faces black with anger. One, Captain Rajic, I would get to know very well. They began to threaten me, to accuse me of having aided a Muslim attack, of having taken ammunition into Gorazde.

— *That is ridiculous. You inspected the trucks. You know they were clean. We have never and will never carry warlike stores for any side.* I was becoming angry. Rajic, in particular, can look very menacing. He is about five foot two, round, podgy face, black straight hair, stained teeth, and unshaven. He is accompanied by a bandoliered bodyguard whom I was to antagonise on many occasions. Being in the company of Rajic was like being an extra in a "spaghetti western," with Rajic playing Zapata.

The other Serb was a reasonable, almost kindly man.

— *The Muslims moved using you as a shield. We fired one mortar, to warn them and to let you know that we knew that they were moving. We could have prevented their attack and wiped them out in the hills but that would have placed you in extreme danger. We had given you our word that you would not be in any danger from us. Our word has cost us lives.*

As we spoke, a small open truck drove by, on it the bodies of eight of the victims of the battle. We were joined by a man who said he was the mayor of Rogatica. He had some very heated words with Brane. It was obvious that the Serbs in Rogatica were identifying Brane with us. Brane, the extremely brave Liaison Officer that he is, had heard the situation developing and raced to Rogatica on his own initiative to assist us. His action was angering his own people.

– *Mr. Larry, they want you and the press to go to a makeshift mortuary and see the bodies unloaded. They want you to see close up what your convoy has done to their people.* This convoy was turning out to be a real media event, a photo call at every phase.

– *What do you think, Brane? Is it wise or not?*—My fears were of meeting either angry soldiers or grieving women.

– *Mr. Larry, I don't think you have an option*—Brane said with a wry smile.

– *Let's go*—I said, knowing that, at least by now, the convoy was clear of the town. I just hoped that Eric had halted it and was waiting for us to catch up. Rogatica was not the place for my Land Rover and two press vehicles! Brane was driving a VW Golf; he followed the Mayor's car, we followed him.

Rogatica is a three road town. We had come from one of them, the convoy was on another, we took the third, the right fork behind the flour mill. We caught up with the truck and formed a macabre procession. The truck turned into a small yard. We swung in after it. The yard was not large enough for more than the truck, my vehicle, and one other. The truck parked in front of a small room with double metal and glass doors. To the left of this room was an office and a workshop. A group of men, some in uniform, some not, started to unload the truck.

I heard Corinne Dufkas say—*My god, some of them are still bleeding*—by which I presumed that she was indicating that they were very "fresh," straight from the battlefield which could not be far

away. Corinne asked me if I could find out if she could take photos.
– *Yes*—said Brane.
Corinne literally raced across to the truck and started snapping, close, bloody, gruesome shots. It's her job. She must have a steady hand, a good eye, and a strong stomach. Taking the lead from Corinne, the TV men moved in. Kurt Schork from Reuters endeared himself to me by saying—*I'm staying right here. I have seen enough dead bodies in my life.*
I had no option. I had not been invited just to stand back. There were eight bodies, the other four were "on their way" from some other location. The bodies were not neatly laid out; they had been thrown on the truck, probably in a hurry near where the battle took place. The initial view was of intertwined limbs. Some bodies faced upwards with open, milky eyes, some lay sprawled across their neighbours, their open-mouthed, lifeless heads supported by blood stained torsos. Some were indeed bleeding. As they were pulled and dragged off the truck, they left red scuff marks on the bodies of their colleagues. Some were very heavy. None of these men had been pro-fessional soldiers. They were men from Rogatica. The heaviest had a large stomach, the men unloading his body had great difficulty. They attempted to lift him by his clothing, but a handful of shirt and trouser leg was never going to support his bulk. They succeeded only in pulling his trousers down, exposing his genitals in an obscene way. I remember clearly thinking—*I hope his wife does not see him now.* The men unloading were forced to take hold of the bodies by their limbs. They sagged under the dead weights.
We were then told to stand back and wait. After a short time, we were told to enter the room where they had been taken. They each lay on the floor, heads to the left, feet to the right. The eighth body was so close to the door that we had to step over his feet to enter the room. I walked the eight paces to the end of the room and stood still. The sun was streaming in through the open door. In the room was myself, the mayor, and Corinne. I slowly looked at each of the dead. Some seemed hardly marked. One had lost half of his head and face, and part of his hand was missing. He must have been close to a mor-

tar round. May even have been hit by a passing shell. Whatever, he was not a pretty sight. The youngest of them was probably thirty; the oldest was maybe fifty. Yesterday they were alive, somebody's father, brother, or boyfriend. Today they were dead. And I was accused of being to blame. I, who had set out with a convoy of food for starving people. Like so much in this war, the facts were correct. Judged by the facts, I was guilty. Judged by the motives, could I be any more innocent?

We left. Brane led us to where the convoy was parked. I was about to chat to Eric, but Brane was in no mood for delay.

— *Mr. Larry, we must move. I want you back in Sarajevo tonight. It will not be safe for you to park the convoy in Srpska Republika tonight.* Eric had done a quick time appreciation and was not happy at us going back the way we had come. One stretch of the road had active gun positions which nightly shelled Sarajevo. He did not want us to pass close to these as they frequently attracted fire as well as delivering it.

— *Leave the route to me*—said Brane. This we did. We moved fast and used a new "tank road." A track carved out of the hill by the Serbs for the safe movement of tanks and heavy artillery.

It was soon dark, but as we were so close to the front line, and as neither sides' front-line troops knew of our presence, we had to travel with convoy lights only; one cowled, measly little bulb in the centre of the rear bumper lights. The going was not easy. It was also not without event. A French APC had broken down and was being towed by the last vehicle in the convoy, the huge, lumbering crane-carrying recovery vehicle. In order to monitor and keep in touch with the progress of our slowest vehicle, I dropped back to escort it. We kept in contact with the convoy, but only just. On a few occasions, the little convoy light of the vehicle in front of me disappeared as it turned a sharp bend or crested a hill. Whenever this happened, there was a moment of panic. Are we driving straight on when everyone else has turned? Are we about to go over a cliff, rapidly followed by a huge recovery vehicle towing an APC? Are they so far ahead that we are lost?

We descended a very steep hill and the convoy came to a halt, itself a tricky movement when you are relying on only convoy lights. We seemed to be moving forward, one vehicle at a time. I got out and advanced towards the front and found the problem. The track we were on was basically a single track, wide enough for a fast-moving ammunition resupply convoy or a troop of tanks or towed guns. In the middle of the dip, at the foot of the hill, was a four-wheel drive vehicle, an ex-German army UNIMOG. It had been part of an ammunition convoy but had broken down. It was facing the opposite way to us and could have been closer to the edge to give us more room to manoeuvre past it. However, the driver had been there some while and had had as his sole companion a one litre bottle of slivovica. Now empty. He was aggressive. I watched the trucks negotiate around him and knew that when it came to my little packet, we were going to have some fun. At last it was time for the recovery vehicle and its APC. No way would it work. I asked politely the drunken driver to get into his cab, and we would gently nudge him closer to the edge. He replied.

– *Dragon, what did he say?*

– *Err, he said no.*

– *No?*

– *Well, the gist of it was NO.*

– *Dragon, you get in his cab and we will push it out of the way.* Dragon, faithful fellow, starts to climb up. The Serb driver lunged at him and pulled him out. It is late, we are so close to Sarajevo, and I am not happy.

– *Dragon, tell him if he does not let you get into that cab, I will drive this recovery vehicle forward and push his vehicle straight over the side. So far over, he will never see it again.* Pause whilst Dragon interprets. The response was unexpected. The driver pulls a hand grenade out of his pocket, puts his finger in the ring, and speaks to Dragon.

– *He says that if you come anywhere near his truck, he will pull the pin and blow us all up.*

– *Dragon, a superfluous translation if ever there was one.*

The commotion we were causing has not gone unnoticed. Eric and

Brane arrive on the scene. Brane talked to the driver, but he was not to be placated. Eric is a long serving marine officer and a very hard man. Calmly and quietly he drew his pistol and placed it at the side of the head of the driver.

– *The grenade. Put it away.*

Another time stopping moment. Which action is quicker, the pulling of the pin or the squeezing of the trigger? Even after one litre of slivo the driver knew that the pistol would win. He actually gave in with a smile. He put the grenade back in his pocket. I then did what I should have done in the first place: I asked Brane to ask him what was wrong with his vehicle. This Brane did. The driver replied.

– *Ovaj Je Sjeban.*

– *What did he say is wrong with it, Brane?* Brane laughed at this.

– *He says it's fucked.* We all laughed. We all felt the same way.

One of the mechanics from the French recovery truck had been with us all the time. I asked him to have a look at it. Brane was back to being agitated and gave us only a few minutes. I watched the French team at work as they tried to start it. But they had no success.

– *What is wrong with it?*—I asked the corporal.

Eric translated—*He says it's fucked.*

Travel broadens the mind and the vocabulary. Dragon persuaded the driver to get into his cab, and we nudged his vehicle to the very edge. We could then pass. At Lukavica we said a heartfelt thanks to Brane.

It was past midnight when we drove onto the tarmac at Sarajevo airport. Outside the UNHCR hangar, all the staff were standing, waiting to greet us. The marvellous Willie Dobson had organised a barbecue. He had kept in touch with our progress through the French ops room. It was a great party. I was called to the phone twice, once to talk to my alma mater BBC World Service and once to talk to the irrepressible, dynamic Deputy High Commissioner of Refugees, Doug Stafford, who was not only a great boss but a good friend. He got me out of many a scrape by his loyal support.

The Sarajevo drivers all wanted to know what it had been like inside Gorazde. Dragon, Serb Dragon, was able to tell it as it was. After a little time at the party, I crept away to my hidey hole. I wanted to be alone. To slowly take in all that we had seen and done.

Four

Rogatica

Convoys are exciting, stimulating and satisfying but a small portion of the aid task. A lot of time was spent in negotiation, listening and learning, attending meeting after meeting.

The conferences between the Government and the aid agencies took place mainly on Tuesdays. They were terrible affairs. We had a representative from all the UN agencies, and other non-UN agencies were invited. The government had a permanent liaison officer for aid, but if the subject or the time warranted it, they would upgun their representation to Vice President level. Initially, the permanent member changed frequently, then for a while, it was a Mr. Beardic who had spent a lot of time in America as a Consul and had the looks, mannerisms and accent of a Godfather. He could be charming but he could also be obstructively rude. After a while, he was replaced by Mr. Mugdim Pasic, an electrical engineer by training but now a diplomat, a skilled negotiator and a genuine person. He understood our problems as he understood those of the government he represented. More importantly he realised that life in war torn Sarajevo was a compromise between the necessary and the possible.

In truth, most of what was demanded of us should have been possible. We, the UN, published and printed a minimum scale of food necessary to preserve life in a Central European environment. We even qualified it further, we stipulated a winter and a summer scale. Then we failed to achieve the minimum by an enormous margin. Sometimes the shortfall was as much as ninety per cent, often it was sixty. Daily we admitted the shortfall. We gave the citizens of Sarajevo, the authorities, and the media a huge stick to beat us with.

Why was it not possible? Most of the time we had the money, most of the time we had the food and the medicines, for a lot of the time we had enough transportation to do most of the job. The simple answer is that we were not allowed to send convoys where they were needed. Who stopped us? For a long time it was mainly Bosnian Serbs, for a while it was Bosnian Serbs and Bosnian Croats. For a brief mad moment, the Sarajevo authorities themselves prevented us from feeding the people of Sarajevo.

Occasionally the conferences produced a flash of humour. High on the agenda of one was "Bull semen for cows in Sarajevo."

The meeting was chaired by the Vice President. Tony Land was leading for UNHCR.

— Mr. Vice President, firstly I have seen only one cow in Sarajevo. Secondly, the transportation of bull semen is not easy, unless you happen to be a bull.

Vice President Lagumdzija replied—*To answer your first point, there are few cows. There will be even less if we do not get semen. To answer your second, it needs to be transported in temperature-controlled containers.*

Tony drew on his chemical engineering degree and his Sarajevo knowledge. *Mr. Lagumdzija, the containers need to be nitrogen cooled. There is no way the Serbs will allow such containers in.*

— There you go—said Lagumdzija petulantly—*back to what the Serbs will allow.*

Tony then said only half in jest—*Maybe we can negotiate that the Serbs have thirty per cent of the semen?*

Back came the vice president's reply—*The Serbs can go and fuck their own cows.*

But more often than not, the conferences were hard work. In January 1993, Vice President Zlatko Lagumdzija came to the meeting in a fighting mood. When we arrived, there were TV cameras set up in the conference room. Always a bad omen.

— Mr. Hollingworth, you are failing in Sarajevo, in Srebrenica, in Zepa, in Gorazde. Let me give you some solutions. Model one: Give us the means to solve the problem ourselves. Model two: Give us airdrops. Model three: You use all necessary means.

This was a good start and left no opportunity for me to get in.

Mr. Hollingworth, are you aware that in Zepa 291 people, including 166 children, have died? You told us that you were going to take a convoy on 21st of December. You said that the Serbs told you it was impossible because of heavy snow. There was no snow. You told us that you would go in on the 6th of January. You said that the Serbs told you it was impossible because of heavy fighting. There was no fighting. Here he paused. He was clearly perplexed and angered by our lack of action. *Mr. Hollingworth, what is the role of UNHCR? What is the role of UNPRO-FOR?*—These were rhetorical questions. He left no time for a reply. *Believing you, we have been promising the people aid. But all of the UN institutions have done nothing…Nothing…*—Another long pause. I thought about interrupting but he continued. *Why do you not adopt the mandate you have been given?*

Oh boy, I am not going to try to answer that one.

– *Negotiating with the Chetniks is a waste of time. Go on, admit that UNHCR and UNPROFOR cannot achieve their aim*—I thought "NO," I will sit this one out—*Mr. Larry, tell the donor governments that it is not possible to provide aid to the enclaves. Tell the governments that hundreds are dying of cold and starvation. Continue the way you are and all will die. The Chetniks started this war to annihilate these locations. They are close to finishing what they started.*

At this stage, the Vice President stopped and amazingly—yes, that is the right word—amazingly, began to cry. These were genuine tears of frustration and emotion. I am sure that they took him by surprise. His emotion devastated some of his colleagues.

I was not prepared for it. I had until the moment of his tears thought that I was listening to a carefully prepared and rehearsed speech.

In the pause a doctor from Zepa whose brother was practising in Zepa stepped in—*Why haven't you reached Zepa? The road is clear today, there is no fighting today. Go now.*

This was not my day. No sooner had he stopped than my friend Murat, the ex-Mayor of Srebrenica, who knew how much effort I had put into attempts at reaching Srebrenica, began.

– *There is no fighting near Srebrenica. Try now*—He caught the "Et tu, Brute?" look in my eye and mellowed—*Try. If you have to return, it is OK. At least they will know you tried.*

These interjections had given Zlatko time to recover and back he came with a vengeance.

– *So we agree we cannot enter anywhere because the Chetniks do not let us. So whatever happens, it is because the other side will not let us. Then let us inform the media that it is the Chetniks' plan to kill all these people. You, the UN, have the mandate to relieve them. You, the UN, are holding cities under siege. At the airport meeting, the Chetniks agreed to allow convoys. They clearly did not mean it. So, UN, with your mandate, there is no solution. We demand airdrops. Please try again this time with adequate air drops. If you cannot respect the UN resolution, we will do something on our own. It will clearly be suicide but we will do it. Mr. Hollingworth, inform Geneva that the people of Bosnia believed in the United Nations. But you have not carried out the mandate it gave to you. We must now do it our way.*

Then he left. No farewell, he just swept out of the room.

Zlatko, if I had been in your shoes, I would have said exactly the same. You were not normally a passionate man—you were on that day and I admired you for it.

I was not too happy with him the next meeting.

– Mr. Hollingworth (a bad sign), *we have received from your office in Zagreb all the paperwork for all the aid that has arrived at the airport. There is a thirty per cent deficiency between that which was put on the aircraft and that which was distributed. Who is eating our food?*

– Mr. Vice President, you cannot eat aircraft pallets.

Zlatko and the Bosnian Government were shouting about Srebrenica and Zepa, but we had promised an early return to Gorazde which, having done it once, seemed easier. We told the Serbs of our plans and they gave approval. Naturally, we told the Bosnian government. They must have told the authorities in Gorazde.

We had a French escort and Egyptian drivers. The drivers were late, and I cursed their ancient ancestors that must have annoyed the Egyptian duty officer. They were late, but the journalists as ever were on time. The first to arrive was one half of the BBC twin legends Kate Adie. She had set off with her team in Sarajevo city. They were the first down the dreaded sniper alley. The duty sniper was alert and delighted to see a single vehicle travelling fast enough to challenge his skills. He fired one round. He was a good shot, he aimed off to compensate for the moving vehicle, his range and distance were correct, but his weapon was firing low. Thank God. The round hit Kate's armoured Land Rover at the base of the panel in front of the passenger door. The round lost velocity as it passed through armoured plate, the footwell of the Land Rover and the boot on the right foot of Kate. Naturally, the crew did not stop. They raced on and arrived at the airport. In the quiet of the morning, we had heard the shot. The Land Rover parked alongside mine and Kate removed her boot. The round had not penetrated the skin, but her foot was sore. As the day progressed, it became a dark blue. She was lucky as she had been in Tien An Men. It was an omen for the day.

The road from Sarajevo to Pale twists and turns, and the final kilometres are down a steep hill. The terrain in Egypt must be flatter. I know this because the Egyptian drivers, each and every one, drove down the hill slowing their ten-tonne vehicles laden with flour using just the brakes. The gear lever was an expensive cab ornament, not even used as an optional extra. I was not aware of this, as I proudly led the convoy waving to the children until the third vehicle burst into flames. The convoy stopped. I walked back to the vehicle, passing vehicles one and two, which smelt of burning rubber. The fire in the third was quickly extinguished. The vehicle was unloaded in Pale. Pleasing the locals and making a virtue out of necessity. The drivers were introduced to the gear lever and we proceeded.

At Rogatica, the inspection team were vicious. But for a good reason. On this very day, the Bosnians had decided to break out of Gorazde, to end the siege. And apparently, they were doing well.

– *It is all your fault*—I was told.

– *Mine? Why mine?*

– *Because you took ammunition in last time*—This was the second time this oft to be repeated accusation was made. I was horrified that they could even think of this. How naive I was.

– *It is not possible that we took in ammunition. Firstly, we are the United Nations. We are totally impartial. Secondly, I would never permit any war material on a convoy. Thirdly, you ransacked the convoy before it went in.*

– *No we didn't, we did a random search. You must have taken in ammu-*

nition. They are using weapons that they have not used before. Weapons and ammunition that they did not have before your last visit.

This actually turned out to be true. But we had not taken it in; it had gone in via the mule route from a little place called Grebac. We later used it to send in food.

The search was long and thorough and may have gone on forever had not the commander who had, on my first visit, insisted that I see the bodies arrive.

– *You have heard of the Muslim attack?* Ah, now it was an attack.

– *Yes, I have and I have been accused of having taken in weapons last time. I am furious and demand an apology.*

He ignored me but continued—*They have ambushed a mobile patrol of ours. We have tried to recover the bodies, but they have a sniper covering them. Will you please go and collect the bodies and bring them here?*

I thought quickly—*I cannot collect them now. The sniper will probably shoot us. I will talk to the commander in Gorazde and ask him to call off the sniper. I will then try to collect the bodies on the way back. OK?*

– *Please, Mr. Larry, the families know that they are dead and lying in the road. They want them back.* I liked this man, he was a good man caught up in an evil war. He agreed that we could go forward but only if I accepted full responsibility. The Egyptian drivers may have been lacking in driving skills, but they were not lacking in courage. They wanted to go forward. The journalists also wanted to go forward, but they were told that Pale had forbidden them to go beyond Rogatica.

Not everyone wanted to go forward. Lovely loyal driver Dragon came to see me.

– *Last time when we went in, they were killing Serbs on our way out. This time they are killing Serbs on the way in. Do you really need me?* On this convoy we had brought three vehicles with aid and medicine for Rogatica.

– *No, my friend, I would much prefer you to distribute the aid here in Rogatica.* I was then without a driver but not for long. A gentleman with previous Hereford skills and current camera expertise volunteered to leap into Dragon's seat. He agreed to pool his resources for the benefit of his less fortunate colleagues. His camera was carefully stowed under my personal possessions, out of sight.

We moved on. In the valley, we found the bodies. It had been a mobile patrol. They had been in a car. All three men were lying in the road. All very dead. It was a very hot day. We had to weave the APC and my vehicle around the bodies, as they almost blocked the road. I stopped my vehicle and discussed with my driver the moving of the bodies. We should have done but we didn't. They were not a pretty sight, and if we handled them there was nowhere to wash our hands. Also, the sniper may not agree. So we drove on but, sickeningly, not all of our trucks could avoid the bodies.

We could hear a lot of gunfire, but we were way up the twisty mountain road before we could positively see the change of fortunes. Near where Fabrizio had lost the APC, a Serb truck had been shot off the road. It had fallen down the side of the mountain and been stopped by a clump of trees. Bodies were strewn over the hill and around the vehicle. They were Serb and all had bullet wounds. The vehicle, probably containing reinforcements, had been ambushed.

On the crest of the hill from where the Serb guns had pounded Gorazde, there was the most remarkable sight, the Bosnian flag was fluttering and a platoon of jubilant Gorazde fighters were sitting out of breath. I was at first disbelieving that they could be government troops, but then, from amongst them emerged the little round civilian who had been the first man Eric and I had seen when we entered Gorazde. He threw his arms around me. I was overwhelmed.

– *When? How?*—I asked, spreading my arms.

He was too emotional to reply. He just hugged me.

I wanted to be in and out of Gorazde within the day. The last night move out of Gorazde had put me off night moves, and now that there was a battle raging, I did not want to be caught up in it.

– *We must move*—I told our friend. He insisted on coming in with us.

We descended down the hill to Gorazde. Government troops were everywhere. Sadly, they were burning houses and bizarrely cutting

87

the throats of pigs which they found in the Serb farms. Muslim symbolism. The pigs were lying in the road squealing and squirming.

Gorazde was chaotic. Last time we had been the star attraction. This time we were a side show. A welcome sideshow. I spoke to Major Bulabasic, the commander and the man responsible for the success of the day. He was tired, but he was not elated. He knew that he had won a battle but that the war was far from over for Gorazde.

We did not unload the trucks where we had on the first occasion. They now had more territory and were able to use the old ammunition depot where it could be stored safely and issued safely. It was weird to use the road to the depot. The previous day, it would have meant certain death from the snipers. Today, it meant low risk, although there was still the odd round coming in. Not all the Serb sites were overrun.

I maintained pressure to get out. There was enthusiasm from the convoy to stay and join in the festivities, but I was worried about a counterattack. If it came, it would be furious. It did eighteen months later and was far more evil than I had expected. It was also a shameful time for the UN. I collected some of the large plastic sheets that wrapped the pallets to collect the bodies in on our return.

We began to leave late in the afternoon. My substitute driver had gone on a walkabout with no intention of returning, so I was behind the wheel. The French APC commander had not been on the first convoy. I had been to Gorazde before. I was in charge. So, I insisted that I lead the way out and took the convoy with flags flying and people frantically waving up a cul-de-sac. That's why they were waving. We had to reverse and there was very little room. So the last became the first, and I became the tail end of the convoy!

So, with the convoy spread out before me, we left. The last APC negotiated the first bend and was hit by a BMW car travelling at great speed having negotiated what it thought was the end of the convoy. There was little damage to the APC, a few flecks of white paint had fallen to the floor; the BMW was a write off. I raced across and was on the scene quicker than the APC crew could dismount. I expected to see tragedy, but four exceedingly drunken Bosnian soldiers tippled

88

out of the car forcing the bent doors open with alcoholic force. I was concerned, they were drunk, they probably had been euphoric. This would not be the way they would wish to end the day. But quite the contrary. They staggered, looked at the BMW, looked at the APC and began to giggle.

By now, I was worrying about exchanging insurance details and thinking of calling for a policeman. The man who had been in the driving seat spoke English. With a "who cares" wave of his hands, he dismissed my apologies and commiserations.

– *Don't worry Mr. Larry, it is a trophy car. We will go and get another.* He had just "liberated" it from the garage of a Serb farmer who had fled. Thank God they had liberated the slivovica as well. Sober, I do not reckon they would have survived the crash. As I motored to catch up with the convoy, I wondered about the car. If farmers in relatively recent capitalist ex-Yugoslavia could run BMW's, what would they drive if they ever join the Common Market?

By the time we entered the valley before Rogatica, it was dark. I spoke to the French commander and asked him to stop at the bodies. He agreed. We were not too sure where the bodies were. Distance is deceptive at night. Also, we were worried about some of the debris on the road. There were the tails of mortar bombs which had not been there on our way out. If any mortars had failed to explode, we did not want to drive over them. We motored very slowly.

It was a night without a moon, but suddenly there was a flash and night became day. The lead vehicle had hit a trip flare. A trip flare without covering fire is useless. A flare on a road usually triggers off an ambush. The French officer was very calm and professional. If I had been the lead vehicle, I would have sped forward with the whole convoy, forget mines, get out of one danger area, worry about the next one if you hit it. He didn't. He quietly ordered his APC's to put their spotlights on, thus illuminating the convoy and showing it to be UN. His APCs had taken up static fire positions and were ready to fire heavy machine gun rounds at anything that opened up.

Nothing opened up. We sat in silence. After a while, I spoke with the French officer. He decided to send the APC ahead to sweep a stretch

89

of road then call us forward. This we did for the next fifteen minutes after which we saw the bodies in the road. They had been moved by the convoy and were more gory. The French officer was not happy to stop and move them. We had had the scare of the flare, moving the bodies may annoy whoever is out there. He then asked,

— *If we stop, who is actually going to do it?*

— *I have some plastic sheets from the pallets. We will just pull their bodies onto them and put them on the trucks.*

— *I will not let the military help. It is a job which needs gloves and masks. I have spoken with Sarajevo. They have said NO.*

I did not want to do it. I could not do it on my own. It was a dirty job and it did have the risk of attracting fire. But I had told the Serb that we would do it. Also, we had damaged the bodies. But at that time of the night, after the day we had had, I was prepared to hide behind a Sarajevo decision.

When we arrived in Rogatica it was absolutely deserted. It took ages to find Dragon. I then went to the house of the commander and explained that I had been unable to collect the bodies. I blamed the flare and the threat of an ambush. He told me that the flare was his and that there had been an ambush section in the hill but that it had seen our convoy. He was not upset that I had failed to bring in the bodies. I offered with no enthusiasm to stay and assist in their recovery the following day.

— *No need, we will have them back before dawn.* He did. By dawn we were back in Sarajevo.

Five

An Indispensable Resource

The local staff who worked for us were, with few exceptions, marvellous. The interpreters were the bravest. They had to represent us in all of our moods. I have tried to describe their role through their presence on the convoys. The drivers are the unsung heroes. Let me at least attempt a chorus on their behalf.

UNHCR Sarajevo began with a fleet of twelve vehicles. They belong to Sweden and were brought into the city by Swedish drivers who had intended to stay and to be the nucleus of the logistic task. The Swedish contingent were from the Swedish Civil Defence, they had brought everything with them to be self-sufficient for three months. Trucks, radio equipment, clothing, food, vehicle spares, even fold up beds. When the heavy shelling began, it was decided in Stockholm that it was too dangerous for the drivers to stay. So the Swedish Government pulled them out. Generously, they left everything behind.

UNHCR then had a fleet of twelve trucks, eight Scanias and four Volvos, and no drivers. So it was decided to recruit local civilians. There were twelve trucks, so twelve drivers were recruited. Two were professional drivers, the rest were university graduates. Two doctors of medicine, one a radiologist, the other a dermatologist, a vet, lawyers, architects, engineers, Serbs, Croats, Muslims, all Bosnians. They could not go home in the evening. The airport road was probably the most dangerous sniper alley in Sarajevo, so they all lived in the hangar which was warehouse to the aid from the aircraft, office to UNHCR, and home for the drivers, the international staff and a few other UN personnel.

The drivers were employed to replace the Swedes and therefore were to drive wherever the Swedes had driven. They had been recruited on a multi-ethnic basis; they were all from Sarajevo.

But the Serbs refused to allow them to deliver on their territory. We argued, but whilst the dispute rumbled on, we asked the Canadians to drive to Rajlovac. This was a mistake on our behalf, mainly on mine. I had told the Serbs that if they wanted aid then they would have to accept the Sarajevo drivers. They said OK, but we cannot accept responsibility for the safety of the drivers. If we took a risk and sent a convoy and a driver was killed, their reply would simply have been "We told you so." I should have said OK, I will not send any aid until you can guarantee their safety. They probably would then have stopped the aid coming into Sarajevo claiming that the distribution was partial. Or would they? I now wish I had called their bluff. So we decided to use the drivers only in the city. The drivers were very disappointed. To a man, they wanted to risk taking aid into Rajlovac. They saw it as part of their city, they also saw it as an opportunity of keeping links open. But it was not to be.

They were to concentrate on taking aid into the city, risking shells and sniper fire every day. They slept at the airport and the risk continued by night.

Towards the end of July, the Ukrainians informed us that they were to receive some new APCs. I did not pay much attention to this information but the Serb Liaison officer came to see me and complained about the imminent arrival.

– *We have not approved of them.*

– *Since when does the UN need your approval?*—I asked, in those days with conviction.

The following day, the APCs arrived. It was late, so they were parked outside our hangar. The RAF boys who knew a thing or two about APCs pointed out that these new arrivals were different from the normal ones. These had an additional dome near the turret.

– *They are artillery locating devices.*

– *Which means?*

– *They can pinpoint from where shells are fired.*

Hence the Serb disapproval. Maybe the UN will locate the position of the Serb guns and knock them out. Maybe the UN will locate the guns and inform the Bosnian government who will take them out. Maybe the UN will accurately pinpoint the weapons and apportion blame correctly after a shelling incident.

Whichever, the arrival of these vehicles and the parking of them outside our hangar was to prove dangerous and expensive. That evening when the convoys returned, the drivers parked their vehicles outside the hangar, parallel to it and in one long line. They were slightly further away from the hangar than usual because of the Ukrainian APCs.

Ploco, our architect turned cook, designed the evening meal. There was a battle brewing outside. The rounds were zipping around the hangar. We decided that it was not safe to sit outside even though it was oppressively hot in the hangar.

We went to our respective beds early. The night got noisier. I heard a group of the drivers decide to race to the French hangar. The rounds were certainly close. I heard Ron set off for the bunker. Willie then told me that he was off and suggested that I came with him. I was comfortable and felt safe. He went. I sensed that I was alone in the hangar. The noise seemed to increase. "It's because I am on my own." I reassured myself. But as a concession to my feelings I pulled on my trousers without lifting my body a centimetre off the bed. I heard a bullet fly through the hangar. Then there was an enormous bang. I heard Willie's voice.

– *Larry, it's time to go*—He had come back to get me out.

I heard Ron's urgent voice—*Come on Larry.*

The action was very close. I could hear rounds close enough to touch them. Willie and Ron were checking that everyone else was out. I picked up my sleeping bag and ran. At the door I saw Willie and Ron. *You OK?*—Willie asked.

– *Yes.*

– *Let's run… NOW!*

As we ran, there was a terrific thunderous boom with a great flash of light. We would have beaten any Olympic sprinter to the bunker. Shrapnel was whanging through the air. I could smell burning. We reached the bunker breathless but elated. I located my spot and climbed back into my sleeping bag.

– *Goodnight guys, and thanks.*

Sleep was slow to come. The night continued as it had begun. The earth shook as round after round thudded in; we could hear metal on metal as bullets ricocheted above the bunker. The bunker felt good, strong and womb-like. I felt really safe and was able to listen to the battle as if it were a soundtrack on a film.

The following morning, I was up first. It was quiet. I ran onto the tarmac. Our vehicles had taken a hammering. Five were badly damaged. They sat on the tarmac with their tyres punctured by shrapnel, their windscreens shattered by blast. They lay in a pool of their oil spilt as their engines were hit. Shells had bounced off the APCs. I picked up the tails of nine mortar bombs. I walked into the hangar and around our bed spaces. There was no damage to them but we had lost a few more windows during the night. As I stood at my own bed, as undamaged as it was, I was glad that Willie had come back for me.

The excitement was not over. The Ukrainians came to look at their APCs. At least one was going no further. Various militaries came to view and to pronounce. None came to remove the offending APCs. So, at about nine in the morning the shelling began again. This time, it was much easier for the Serbs. It was daylight and last night they had zeroed in. We were quick off the mark. At the first loud bang, we ordered everyone into the shelters. Willie and I did a quick check of the hangar and were on our way back to the bunker when the Serbs put one shell straight through the roof of our hangar, our home. We had to wait more than an hour before it was calm enough to go back.

Shrapnel had shredded many of the bed spaces of the drivers. There was a large hole in the roof. There was shrapnel and what looked like cotton wool everywhere. The "cotton wool" itself was a health hazard—it was asbestos used to line the roof.

Some of the drivers moved permanently into the main airport lounge where the French soldiers slept. Ironically, of those that did, three "lost" their beds whilst they were out driving. Something that never happened in our hangar. Three of the drivers, Dominko, Franjo, and Veseljko came to see me.

– *From the five vehicles that are damaged, if you will agree to us cannibalising, we reckon that we can get two back on the road.*

I had reported the damage and the spares required to Zagreb. They told me that they would get the spares needed as quickly as possible. Within hours they were asking:

— *Do you want an xyz1235 or an xyz1234?* I could see that this would run forever. Logisticians with catalogues are like trainspotters.

— *Dominiko, cannibalise.* It took them more than two weeks, but they did it. What I marvelled at was their enthusiasm and their ability to get dirty. They were covered in oil and grease. It did not help that we had no water. We did have some excellent liquid soap. A fact I discovered by accident.

A few days prior to the hole in the hangar saga, it had been a disturbing night but mainly with small arms and machine gun fire. At one stage, a few rounds had passed through the hangar. This had caused a thinning out of the residents, but some of us stayed. I reckoned that I was OK, as it seemed to be passing up the centre of the hangar. I fell asleep. The battle must have stopped, but before dawn they started again. I heard the whistle of a round and a thud which I knew was inches from my head. Most rounds flew through the building at about three metres high. Meaning that it was safe even for basketball players, of whom there are many in Yugoslavia and we proudly had our fair share. This last round was either fired from a weapon which was pointing in the wrong direction or from a weapon so far away that the bullet was at the end of its trajectory. Either of these possibilities could be repeated, so I decided to move.

I pulled myself out of the sleeping bag and put my bare feet on the floor. The floor was sticky. I put my finger in the sticky and brought it before my short-sighted eyes. The sticky was red.

— *Oh my God*—I thought—*Is it me? Where am I hit? No it can't be me. Ugh, there may be someone sleeping on the other side of my bed space. Journalists often did.* I got up and trudged through the sticky around the other side of my bed. There was no one there. I was now much bolder. I was almost standing up. Then I saw the source of the sticky. It was pouring out of a box. The box contained "Hibiscrub," a medical liquid soap. The box said, "Hibiscrub saves lives." The box stopped the bullet at the height of my head as I was awaking. The bullet had been slowed down as it passed through six containers of the stuff.

"Hibiscrub saves lives." It saved mine. Five litres of it cleaned up our mechanics.

The following night, some enterprising thief stole the radios and speakers out of the damaged trucks. Five sets neatly done, wiring and all. It really annoyed me. I went to the morning conference and gravely announced the loss, adding the pompous words—*The enemy is outside the perimeter, not within.* My colleagues were unable to work up any enthusiasm for the loss of five radios from bomb damaged vehicles.

In late October, the drivers had a bad day. Most of the convoys into the city were escorted with an APC at the front and at the back. The convoys moved slowly and children would gather at the side of the road, especially at corners and junctions where the convoys were at a walking pace. The children would beg for "bon bons," which shows which army was first involved. The soldiers threw sweets or biscuits or any surplus food, sometimes even tins, to the children. There would then be a mad scramble as the children rushed to gather up the donations. Often standing behind the children and encouraging them would be their parents. I was against the practice for two reasons. First, the children were not starving. I have often seen African children beg. They indicate their hunger by moving their hands to their open mouths. This they do slowly if they are really hungry. The effort is a strain to a really weak body. In Bosnia the gesture was always vigorous and energetic. The children on these junctions were there every day, getting extras from every convoy. They looked well fed and healthy. Incidentally, my rule has exceptions. I have seen some Oscar winning performances in places like Addis Ababa, hand slowly raised, eyes misted, little mouth opening—moving me to donate generously. The recipient then races away like a whippet so as not to share my extravagance with his fellow "sufferers." The second reason I do not like the practice is that if some of the sweets or packets bounce along the road, the children pursue them. They get dangerously close to the vehicles.

On this tragic day, the group of children included a little toddler of about three. Sweets were thrown, the children pushed and pulled each other. The little one chased one sweet which bounced as it hit the road. It bounced back into the road, and the toddler followed it under the rear wheel of our first truck. The driver, whom I dare not name, heard the crunch as the wheel passed over the infant. He knew exactly what had happened. He stopped the truck and felt sick. The driver of our escort Toyota vehicle was Sejo, the brother of Nonjo. The driver of the second truck, who had seen only the closing moments of the accident, was Zlatan, the doctor of medicine. They raced out of their vehicles and approached the child. Zlatan could see that the child was dead. The truck was laden with flour. The little child had gone under a wheel. By now, Svabo the convoy leader and the driver were by the wheel. But so were the child's parents and a group of neighbours. A minute ago, they were cheering and clapping the convoy as the escort threw sweets. Now their mood had changed. They were violent. They kicked Zlatan away from the child, they stoned the vehicles, they beat up the driver of the truck which had hit the child. A very brave Sejo picked up the messy body of the child and carried it to his vehicle. He then sped away, first to the nearest First Aid post and then to the police. The driver was badly cut and bruised. We were never able to use him again on city convoys. The practice of throwing "bon bons" never stopped.

Despite the good work that they did and the risks that they took, the drivers were not liked by everybody. To many of the men of Sarajevo who were in uniform, our drivers were draft dodgers. To the Serbs, our Serb drivers were traitors, our "Muslim spies" and our "Croat lackies." Many of the citizens of Sarajevo saw them as opportunists, capitalists. Some believed that they were part of the black market. One or two of them may have been. We did dismiss some. Undoubtedly, they took food home. Food from the kitchen in the hangar. Our food, their food, my food.

When, after a couple of months, the Swedish food ran out, the UN-HCR Logistic Officer approached the French and negotiated two meals a day for our staff. It was not a happy arrangement. The Sarajevo drivers were not used to eating in a military dining room. If they saw a friend, they joined him at a table. If the friend was a French officer, they saw no problem. The French dining room was however segregated. A portion for the officers and the senior NCOs and one for the rest. We were part of the rest. The drivers took some time to get used to this protocol.

To the French, even in the field, meal times are special, ritualistic. To our drivers, it was fuel time for their physical engines. What the French had on offer was beyond the wildest dreams of the citizens of Sarajevo. The drivers could have fed blocks of apartments on the contents of the swill bins.

Little surprise then that my drivers took a slice of bread for themselves and one for their family. Little surprise that they scooped pats of margarine into paper to take home. Little surprise that they stuffed their pockets with fruit, sugar, and jam.

It was wrong. But it was understandable, except to some of the French. The first complaint was about the table manners of my drivers. They did eat as if in competition with each other. That was true. Then came the complaint that they were dirty, then that they were smelly. Both true. This was curable. The French had showers with hot water. Allocate a session to us and we will smell better.

Some of the French saw the drivers as local peasants. They treated them as they have locals all around the world. My drivers resented this. Many were professional men, better educated than most of those with whom they dined. They were victims of the war; most had lost homes, clothes, friends and relatives—and manners.

By their attitude in the restaurant, they were not biting the hand that fed them, surely, they were being fed by the hand that came to feed them. They could have learned "manners" and "etiquette." Perhaps the time was not right. Perhaps some of the French could have learned tolerance.

The life of the drivers changed drastically with the arrival of a Norwegian Army officer on loan to UNHCR. Dag Espeland was a captain in Norway. A tall, lumbering man with a heavy boxer's face. His hair never looked combed. Dag was not a man for the front rank on a big parade. But he is the finest logistician I have ever come across. He does all his calculations with a pencil on a dog-eared pad. He writes simple notes in a primitive hand. But he can see the centre of a problem and come up with a solution faster than anyone I know. He reorganised the warehouse, the distribution programme and the amount of aid coming in. Delivering aid in Sarajevo was dangerous but easy. The problem was the amount of aid we received. Dag hit on the idea of sending the Sarajevo drivers out of the city to Croatia to collect more aid. More convoys, more aid.

To my surprise, the drivers were delighted. They were prepared to risk the Serb checkpoints as they both departed and entered the city and to risk motoring unescorted along damaged roads close to front lines. A risky enough task with an empty vehicle in a war zone where banditry and hijackings are commonplace events. A heroic task when the trucks are filled with highly desirable food worth a fortune on the black market.

Dag divided the convoys into two, one to be led by Svabo whose hair is very fair and the other to be led by Milan whose hair is jet black. Thus the convoys became known throughout Bosnia as "Boss White" and "Boss Black."

Ever cautious Dag led a trial convoy out of Sarajevo to the warehouse at Vitez. The Serbs were clearly told that more convoys meant more food for them. The first convoy had no trouble at the Serb checkpoint. Three days later, Dag decided it was solo time, and the "Boss White" convoy set off to Vitez on its own. It succeeded. The drivers were teased by the Serbs but not hassled.

Meanwhile, I made my first attempt at breaking the siege of Srebrenica. The reports from the amateur radio were describing a horrendous scene. The town was overcrowded, its population doubled, there was no food, little water, heavy shelling, and no medicine.

The Government had made Srebrenica its top priority. The ex-Mayor of Srebrenica, Murat Effendic, was a tireless worker on behalf of the town. His sister and brother in law lived there. He visited us almost every day. He attended every conference. At each conference, he raised the subject of Srebrenica. I spoke to Eric. Could we use the same team that we had used for Gorazde and get into Srebrenica? He was very enthusiastic, but Colonel Sartre wanted the senior French officer to be much more junior. A Captain was chosen to be escort commander.

To get Serb approval, I went to see Brane, the liaison officer in Lukavica who had helped so much with Gorazde. Again he was enthusiastic.

— But to get into Srebrenica you will need the approval of General Mladic. That is, the renowned leader of the army of the so-called Srpska Republika.

— Great, how do I get that?

— You will have to see him face to face and ask him.

— And how do I do that?

— By following me.

I followed Brane up the stairs, we turned right, went down the corridor to the offices at the end and were stopped by a Serb lady in uniform. Brane left me, knocked on the door and entered. After a few minutes he came out—*He will see you.*

In I went. Sitting at the table parallel to the window with his back to it was General Mladic. Unmistakable General Ratko Mladic. He was not wearing his *shapka*, his hat, which was on the table.

He stood up. We shook hands.

— General, I wish to thank you for the honour of this interview. I very much appreciate you seeing me without an appointment. I would like in your presence to thank your Liaison Officer Brane for the tremendous help he gave to UNHCR on our convoy to and from Gorazde.

— Because of your convoy many of our soldiers were killed. This is the man I had heard about, blunt.

— I know, I saw their bodies. And I was fair to you, I reported to the World what had happened.

— Now you want to go to Srebrenica?

— Yes.

— Are you aware that the Muslim forces in Srebrenica are killing our people?

— I believe, Sir, they are killing your people because they are either trying to break out or trying to prevent your people from breaking in. Not a reply he expected. But one he turned to his advantage.

– They do not have to break out. We will let them go. All of them.
Do I tell him that for most of them Srebrenica is their home? If I get
into an argument with him, I am not likely to change his mind, but
I will antagonise him and jeopardise the convoy.
– I will tell them when I get there.
– Yes—and tell them to stop killing Serbs. A hint of agreement.
– So you will not prevent a convoy?
*– No. But I cannot guarantee that you will get there. If the Muslims at-
tack us, then we will attack them. If there is fighting, you cannot enter. I
am responsible for your safety on our territory.*
Get out whilst the going is good, Larry.
*– General, thank you for seeing me. Thank you for approval. You are a
very busy man, and I have taken enough of your time. May I progress
this with Brane?* He calmly agreed, and we shook hands while staring
into each other's eyes.
Outside, I spoke to Brane—*Thanks, my friend. For the opportunity
and the result.*
The end result was a week of frustration.
Srebrenica can be entered from three different routes. The main one
is via the large town of Bratunac, the second is through the tiny village of Skelani, the third, the most difficult, by a little village called
Milici. Because it is an active and disputed area, most of the roads are
blocked. Therefore, reaching Bratunac and Skelani involves leaving
the so-called Srpska Republika at the bridge in Zvornik, entering the
Serbia proper of Milosevic, and using this border road to approach
the bridges across the River Drina back into Srpska Republika. The
Serbs in Pale had chosen the Milici route for our convoy. It is across
rugged country, a route for hunters and hikers.
We arrived there late in the afternoon with a convoy of ten vehicles.
Dragon is my driver; the French are escorting. There was a checkpoint about one hundred metres from the town which was hidden
by woods. They stopped us but were not surprised to see us. They
must have had us in their sights for at least the last ten barren kilometers. One of their soldiers jumped into our vehicle and we moved
forward, turning right over a bridge spanning the Zeleni Jadar. The

101

military headquarters is in the village square and the military commander was waiting at the steps to greet us. He was very welcoming. He called us into his headquarters, produced slivovica and denied that he had been told of the arrival of the convoy. He would be very pleased to help us; the problem was that the road from Milici to Srebrenica was mined. First, on his side, by him, and he presumed, after that, by the Muslims.

– *Can you remove those on your side?* I asked sincerely.

– *Of course. But it will take forty-eight hours. But why wait, I am told that they are expecting you in Bratunac? That is the route that is cleared for you. Why they sent you here I do not know. Stay the night here, leave early. You will be in Bratunac for early morning and in Srebrenica by midday.* Oh, innocent abroad Larry believed all this.

– *If you agree*—he continued—*just sit here and I will contact Bratunac to confirm they are expecting you.*

I agreed and he left the room. Whilst we are waiting, the commander's deputy—whom I do not like—gets the conversation around to the "ethnicity" of Dragon who most enthusiastically confirms that he is from the longest line of Serbs ever, even pre-dating Adam and Eve. The number two jokes about the purity of Serbs and mixed marriages and Serb Serbs and half Serbs. I do not like this and I can see that Dragon is very worried. The deputy then asks Dragon to follow him outside.

– *Stay Dragon*—I say.

– *No, it is OK*—he replies.

The number two and Dragon are followed by a number of soldiers with lots of nudging and winking. Soon they all return and there is lots of laughter.

The commander then returned and told me—*It is fixed. They are expecting you tomorrow.*

We parked up for the night and arranged an early start. Back in the vehicle I asked Dragon—*Why did they take you outside?*

– *They made me drop my trousers. They thought that I might be a Muslim. They wanted to see if I was circumcised or not.*

– *You passed the test?*

– I'm still here.
– Dragon, as a point of interest, who is what?
He laughed—*Serbs are not. Muslims are.*
– Bloody hell!—I said—*In Balkan logic that makes me a Muslim.*
The following morning we left at the first shafts of dawn. I could not find the Commander, but I spoke to the number two.
– If we have any trouble with Bratunac then we will return here and wait whilst you clear the mines. Alright?
– Of course.
We left and motored to Bratunac, which is about twenty kilometres east of Milici as the crow flies. We had to go west twenty kilometres, then north twenty kilometres and then south thirty kilometres— the last thirty in the Serbia of Milosevic. We were at the bridge just before eight. There was a slight delay before we were met by the military commander of Bratunac. Whilst I now know that the Milici commander was taking me for a ride, I believe that the Bratunac commander is an honourable man. Before the war, he was a Nuclear Physicist at the University of Sarajevo. His family, his wife and children, still lived in Dobrinja, the suburb of Sarajevo. He confirmed that he was happy for us to attempt to enter Srebrenica via Bratunac, but he warned me that there were many women who had lost husbands and sons who were opposed to convoys for Srebrenica.
– Also, I must inspect the convoy. There is rumour that your convoy to Gorazde took in ammunition.
– No problem—we have nothing to hide.
He quickly organised an inspection team. They must have been waiting in the wings. The inspection went well. Whilst it was taking place, the commander and I talked about the war, when it would end, what the result would be. He was a pessimist on all counts. He longed to see his family, he had had little contact with them since the war began. I promised to go and see them.
When the inspection of the cargo on the trucks had ended, the commander asked in a very embarrassed manner if we would object to the number of rounds on the APCs being counted. We replied that we would. The commander then asked me to line up the convoy

103

which he would escort into Bratunac. After I had lined it up, he disappeared for a few minutes, then returned.

– *Everything is ready.* I remember his words clearly. We set off into the town and drove straight into a huge demonstration of women spanning the road. They were shouting and waving. We were at least one hundred metres away from them. The APC was stopped immediately behind the car of the commander which was nose-to-nose with the women. I initially stayed in my vehicle. I sent Dragon down to listen and to report back confident in the knowledge that in addition to the right language, he had the right shaped genitalia.

Apparently, the major did try to persuade them to let the convoy through, but they shouted him down. He appealed to the women as mothers to let food go into Srebrenica, but they refused. After facing them for about ten minutes, he came back to me to discuss tactics.

– *Why don't we offer them half of the convoy?*—he asked.

– *No I do not agree with that.*

– *Then I do not think that you will get through.*

I gathered together a small group and told them of the proposal. All were enthusiastic. Except me. I called the major over.

– *I do not agree with dividing the load. This is my reason, and you as a nuclear physicist can assist me. To get this far with this convoy, I have gone through seven checkpoints. If I leave half of the load here I, Mr. Larry, the UNHCR, all of us of the UN, will then have a reputation for giving away half the load when challenged at a checkpoint. So, if I am to bring ten trucks for Srebrenica, and I use this route again, I will have to start out with 640 trucks. Am I right?*

– *Mathematically*—he replied.

– *Morally?*

– *Depends how important it is to get food into Srebrenica.*

I went and faced the women and tried my power of persuasion. I was jeered and booed.

– *OK. Let us go back to Milici and wait whilst that nice Major there removes his mines.*

We motored back to Milici, still only twenty kilometres away, but to be reached only by thirty kilometres north, twenty kilometres south and twenty kilometres east. Once again, we were stopped at the checkpoint one kilometre from the town. The officer waiting for us told us there would be a slight delay. We waited about an hour, then we were led forward.

On the bridge, the only way into the town, all the women and children of Milici were waiting for us. They surrounded the leading vehicles including men and, using a tannoy, they harangued us. Little children were pushed forward to squeak—*Go home UN.* Older children used digital language to signify their dislike.

One woman in Serb army uniform was the leader. She rallied her troops and led the chanting. The nice major refused to see us. We turned the convoy around and left. The Serbs had found a new cheap and plentiful weapon.

I was to make one more unsuccessful attempt at Srebrenica before getting in. I was given approval to enter via Bratunac. On the Serbia side of the Bratunac bridge, the convoy was stopped by police. I was told to park the convoy and proceed alone. On the Bratunac side, I was met by the Mayor of Bratunac who told me that the ladies of Bratunac were waiting for me. He was exceedingly worried for my safety. His name is Mr. Simic, as I later learned, quite a common name. He convinced me that he had genuine sympathy for the people of Srebrenica. As Mayor of neighbouring Bratunac he knew many of them, they were old neighbours, schoolfriends, colleagues.

It sickened him that the women and children were starving. He wanted the convoy to succeed, but the women who were leading the blocking of the convoys had all recently lost husbands or sons or both. He told me that at least one or two of them were unhinged by the tragedy, were irrational and certainly unreasonable.

– *I would like to see them myself.*

– *I do not recommend it.*

– *I insist. Please ask them to see me.*

– *OK, I will arrange a meeting. Come back at five.*

– *May I bring some journalists? Then the ladies can explain not only to me but to the world what the problem is.*

– *Good idea.*

I came back over at five with one carload of journalists. The military on the bridge were not cooperative, but Mr. Simic, who showed great courage over the coming hours, smoothed our way in. He had arranged a meeting in the Civic hall with the leaders of the women. We had one hiccup—Joel Brand, an American student of journalism, who decided that studying journalism is only second to being a journalist. Who has now become the Hemingway, the Flynn, of the Bosnian Conflict. He gave up college and arrived at Sarajevo with some of the most spurious accreditations I have seen. This tall, tough tyro had come on the convoy without any credentials, as if he had come from the moon or were royalty. Fortunately, the Chief of Police of Bratunac arrived. He had come from the centre of the town. The road to the Civic hall was blocked by angry women. He insisted that I should travel with him in his car. This left my car and driver free. A haven was found for Mr. Brand.

We set off in the police car, it was now dark. In the back of the car was the BBC Belgrade correspondent Jane Howard. The policeman set off with confidence. He began to slow down when he saw how the crowd had swelled. There were perhaps two hundred women in the street. As we approached them, he slowed almost to a halt. They began shouting.

I have been caught in the middle of a mob on a few occasions, and I now know that you can get the sense of a crowd very quickly and assess the likely outcome. Usually they are being led and the majority of the participants are a little embarrassed. You can see that some are smiling nervously and non-aggressively. They are interacting with each other, sharing the experience. If you look directly at one of them, they look away. If you smile at them, they smile back. Sometimes, if you wave at them, they will wave back. There was no sense of fun or embarrassment about this crowd. They meant business. There were some very angry, contorted faces in the crowd. Some of the women were carrying sticks. This was a wall of angry women. I cannot remember seeing any young children. The police car was a Golf and therefore was low. I wished I had brought the Land Cruiser. You sit above the crowd. You feel more in command and much safer.

We had our windows wound down as we tried to talk to the women, but they started to bang on the car. I wound mine up almost to the top. An old woman put her hand on it to prevent me completely closing the window. The police chief was either very brave, very foolish, or very sure of the outcome. He began to move the car forward. This incited the crowd. Those in front of us were pushed back by the car, they in turn knocked into those behind them who pushed them back against the bonnet. They began to drum their fists on the side of the car. But the worst result of moving forward was that we were now surrounded by the crowd. They began to rock the car. The policeman stalled the engine. We are now becalmed in a sea of foaming women. A tall, thin woman dressed all in black with a severe, sharp, hatchet face begins to bang on the car with a heavy stick.

I was glad that I was not in my vehicle.

Amazingly, I then see the diminutive mayor who was in the car behind us forcing his way through the crowd on my side of the vehicle. They are kicking him, tearing at his clothes. He is trying to reason with them, they are shouting him down. He shouts to me that we should go. The policeman starts the car and begins to reverse. He has to inch back for fear of driving someone under the rear wheels. The crowd is now cheering and jeering. They know that they have won. We break clear of the crowd and reverse into the nearest clear space. The crowd is moving towards us, the policeman engages forward gear and inevitably stalls the engine. This breaks the tension in the car, and we all laugh. He then speeds away back to the bridge, where we find Joel Brand interviewing the soldiers!

The journalists gather around us. The telling of the story relieves some of the tension. The hero of the day, the mayor, then arrives.

– *Mr. Mayor, you were very brave.* This pleases him.

– *I am sorry Mr. Larry. There is no more we could do. I tried.*

– *You were fantastic. The police chief was excellent too. Please thank him.*

– *Thank you. You will go back now?*—he asks with relief in his voice.

– *No my friend. I am sorry, but I must ask you to do me one more favour. So far, I have faced these women and been beaten by them. I have not had a chance to reason with them.*

— But that is what we were trying to do, Mr. Larry. The leaders were waiting for you, but we could not reach them. What more can we do?
— My friend, if I cannot get to the leaders, can you get the leaders to me?
— Where?
— Can you arrange for them to cross over into Serbia? There is a hotel on the other side of the bridge. I can meet them there. I will buy them a meal and we can talk and they can meet the press. The mayor is one hundred per cent genuine. He agrees to go and try.

Thirty minutes later he is back.

— Yes, they will meet you in the hotel in one hour.
— Brilliant.

They came. Twelve of them. I noted that they included the hatchet-faced woman. She had not been waiting for us in the Civic hall. In a large dark reception room seated around a huge conference table, drinking coffee, I told them why I was there: to deliver aid to all sides. I told them of the aid we had brought in. Where it had gone. To all sides. I read them some of the reports we had had from Srebrenica. I appealed to them as mothers and sisters to allow food into Srebrenica to feed the innocent. Some were moved. Some wavered in their opinion. All at one stage or another cried. But the majority opinion was to stop the convoy. They asked me to go with them and see where their beloved ones are buried.

— The convoy will have to pass their graves. We cannot insult them. We cannot let you take aid to those who murdered them.

There was hatred in the eyes of some. There was bigotry in the voices of others. There was ignorance in the minds of a few.

Collectively, they were dangerous. They were all genuine individuals. These were not women put up to stop the convoy by others. This was the early days of the war. Will war weariness mellow their hearts, will propaganda and prolonged aggression harden their hearts? Will reasonable, sane, Mayor Simic ever be able to sit side by side with his Srebrenica neighbours? I at least want them to know that you tried hard, Sir.

The result of my first Srebrenica expedition was unexpected. It was a failure, so I returned to Sarajevo depressed. There my depression increased. Both UNPROFOR and UNHCR were not happy with me. UNHCR because in my enthusiasm, I had apparently not informed Zagreb of my intention to take a convoy to Srebrenica. UNPROFOR because I had changed the aim of the convoy. I had approval for an attempt via Milici which was loosely in the working domain of Sector Sarajevo. I had then added Bratunac and a return to Milici both involving stepping into a country, Serbia, where we had no approval to operate.

I was summoned to Zagreb to take a rap on the knuckles. I was replaced in Sarajevo by Izumi Nakamitsu.

I was very unhappy with this.

In Zagreb, I was given a convoy to take to Bihac where a good friend of mine, Jacques Franquin, was King. He lived in Velika Kladusa in a small hotel. He was known and respected by everyone. He introduced me to Fikret Abdic, the leading politician and businessman. Part of my brief was to hire from Mr. Abdic a fleet of vehicles to bring more aid into that region. This was an easy task.

Back in Zagreb, I met up with Jeremy Brade. Lord Carrington had given up the task of peace broker and handed it over to Lord Owen who wanted his own staff. Jeremy was therefore offered to UNHCR by the Foreign and Commonwealth Office. He was holding preliminary talks with the Special Envoy Jose Maria Mendiluce who decided to put him in charge of the Sarajevo office! I was told to visit our office in Slovenia, to which Jeremy knew the way, so we went together. I took from the office a neat, quite new Golf which I kept for six months.

Back in Sarajevo, the proposal by Dag to increase the tonnage into the city by using the local drivers had gone well. They had successfully done the Vitez route. They now wanted to do Sarajevo-Split. The problem was that the road was closed. The crucial bit of Capljina-Mostar-Jablanica was in Bosnian Croat hands who at that time supported the Bosnian Government, though the Serbs, who in effect held the East bank of the road, regularly shelled the road and even more regularly shelled Mostar. I was told to open an office in Mostar and to negotiate locally the freedom of the road for our convoys.

We first needed the support of the Bosnian Croat leadership.

I was delighted to find that in charge of the UNHCR Split office was Fabrizio Hochshildt. He arranged a conference in Mostar with Dr. Prlic, who was number two in the Bosnian Croat hierarchy. For the meeting, we were joined by top gun Jose Maria Mendiluce. He said to me—*The Croats will want something for their help. The best we can offer them is money to repair the roads. I have got approval for $100,000. But do not tell them that. We will just say that we are leaving you in charge of the programme and that you will have an unspecified sum. OK?*

– OK.

We went into the conference which was held in the ground floor reception room of what had been before the war a super residential house in the centre of Mostar. We were met by Dr. Prlic, Mr. Stojic, the Minister of Defence, and Mr. Puljic, the spokesman on refugees. Dr. Prlic began—*We are honoured to see you here. We hear that you are going to open an office. It is overdue but still welcome.* He then went straight to the heart of the problem—*You want to make the corridor safe. You want to bring in more aid. We have 200,000 refugees, we have 420 kilometres of front line. So you can see that we too want more aid and that we too want a safe corridor. Our aims are compatible.*

Jose Maria warmed to this and began—*Excellent, we will open the office immediately. Mr. Hollingworth will stay. He will negotiate with the Serbs. He will inform you when the convoys will begin and how many vehicles will be in them. He will need extra vehicles from you. We will need a warehouse.*

Dr. Prlic interjected—*Will there be any money for the repair of roads?*

I opened my mouth to reply with my rehearsed answer and heard Jose Maria beat me to it.

– Yes, Mr. Hollingworth has $100,000 available for road repairs. The conference was over. Dr. Prlic had heard all that he needed.

In truth, it was a fraction of what has been spent on the vital task of keeping the road open. Placing it on the table made my task easier.

Fabrizio and Jose Maria left, and I looked for a place to sleep in Mostar. I discovered that the town was shelled regularly twice a day, once in the morning and once in the evening and occasionally sporadically throughout the day. Being a new arrival, I had the advantage over the occupants. I could choose a place in an area with the best record for safety. I discovered that the International Committee for Red Cross had an office which was close to the headquarters of the Ministry. I went to see them. They pointed out where they were living and reckoned it was as safe as anywhere.

I then went to see Minister Stojic. I told him of my accommodation plans.

– *You have just come from Sarajevo, haven't you?*

– *Yes.*

– *Do you like shelling?*

– *No.*

– *Then do not live in Mostar.*

– *But we have just told Dr. Prlic that we are opening an office in Mostar.*

– *Mate Boban, Dr. Prlic, and myself all have offices in Mostar but we do not live in Mostar. Let me recommend a place to you. My cousin has a great hotel in Medjugorje. Here is his card. He will find accommodation for you.*

I went to Medjugorje, famous for being the place where the Blessed Virgin Mary has appeared to several young children. A Yugoslav Lourdes or Fatima. I sometimes worry about what heaven is going to be like. The Holy Family seems to hang around some terrible places. If heaven is as dull and as dismal as Medjugorje, I shall be very disappointed. Furthermore, I hope Heaven is not full of cheap souvenir shops run by relatives of the apostles selling rubbish blessed by one of the many resident popes.

I lived in the hotel of the cousin of the Minister and travelled daily to Mostar. On my own, in the Golf, without a translator.

I got a lot of help from the ECMM at Grude from Geoff Beaumont, a fastidious fixer. A Brit ex-Army officer, he had a wide network of contacts and put me in touch with the Croat HVO commander and, more importantly, the Serb commander at the Serb headquarters in Nevesinje, who commanded all the gunners firing the shells into Mostar and onto the road.

I discovered that the problem on the road was not just shelling. There was also a fair number of Croat soldiers who were freelancing, setting up spurious checkpoints and ambushing passing vehicles. Sometimes loads disappeared, sometimes trucks, and sometimes people. I therefore liaised with the local warlords. This exercise involved my motoring back out of Bosnian Croat territory, the so called Herceg-Bosna, into Croatia proper. At the border post there was a duty-free shop where I could buy alcohol. I think that I can honestly say that I took a bottle to every checkpoint on the exposed area of the road. Etiquette demanded that I partook in at least one swig. Often my hospitality was reciprocated. The tasks I do for UNHCR!

Medjugorje is to the southwest of Mostar and the Neretva River. The checkpoints and the Split Sarajevo road are to the east. To cross from East Mostar to West Mostar was a personal test of courage. For me, it was the only test which you could take and retake to assess the state of your own courage.

You could motor down to Capljina and cross by the bridge. This was safe but took forty-five minutes. Or you could use the only bridge in Mostar still standing, that over the dam. The dam bridge was in clear view from the hills. It was littered with cars that had been hit with shells from the hills. The rumour was that the Serb gunners would bet on whether they hit the front bumper or the rear bumper of a moving car. There were no takers on whether they would hit the car. That was a foregone conclusion. The approach to the bridge from the West bank was along a narrow road which went only to the dam. It was highly visible to the hill. Even the doziest Serb gunner could see the car approaching and say to himself: "It is either going only to the dam or it is going to cross the bridge."

They knew by sight those that went to the dam only. The final approach to the dam is through a gate, then a sharp right-hand turn, then over a hump, then a mad dash across the bridge, slow down, hump, turn right, fifty metre dash, then turn left and, at the Croat checkpoint, breathe a sigh of relief.

The most vulnerable spot is the first right turn—you cannot do a handbrake turn, as the track is blocked with cars that have failed—

after which you have to slow down for the humps, and for the cars that have failed. The hump and the right hand turn on the Eastern end of the bridge are not as attractive to the Serbs. There are less wrecks there. The return trip had the hazards in reverse.

I developed my own system. I motored leisurely along the dam approach road. In the village before the dam I stopped the car in an open area. I took out the huge UNHCR flag, which I carried on the back seat, and placed it in its holder welded onto the rear wing by a moron in Zagreb so that it prevented the hatch from opening. Then I slowly put on my flak jacket, made myself comfortable in it, placed on my head my trusty helmet—white and emblazoned with the UNHCR letters. I then pulled the flag out to its maximum extension so that even an illiterate in the hills could make out the odd letter. I then turned to the hills and waved both my arms. Then I went like a rocket.

If in my dotage I am found wandering around the hills trying to attach my handkerchief to the aerials of stationary cars…

It worked for me at that time. Unfurling a UN flag in the sights of Serb gunners after the air strikes would have been less effective.

I crossed the dam bridge many times. Once I got as far as the open space in the village and found that I could not do it. I sat in the car and argued with myself.

– *Do you really want to go the long way around?*

– *No.*

– *Then get out and put the flag up.*

– *I do not want to.* And I didn't. No, I couldn't. The next day I was OK. I crossed and headed for Split.

Now it was time to put all the negotiations to the test. The British laid on a convoy and we set off for Sarajevo, which we reached with very little incident. The Brits returned from Sarajevo to Split with eight extra vehicles. Boss White and Boss Black were in the long haul business.

The road that we had opened was not direct Split-Sarajevo. At the village of Tarcin, twenty kilometres from Sarajevo, the road was blocked. Tarcin was in Bosnian government hands, Hadzici, the next village along, was in the hands of the Serbs. Hence, the convoys had to turn left at Tarcin and take the unmade mountain road to Kresevo and thence to Kiseljak and then in to Sarajevo via the most infamous checkpoint, Sierra One, the last serious Serb checkpoint before entering Sarajevo, notorious for the ruthless, drunken thieving, and thuggish men in uniform who usually manned it. This diversion added seventy kilometres onto the route, tore the heart out of the trucks, and was a strain on drivers at the end of a long journey. It also meant going from Bosnian Government dominated territory to Croat dominated territory and finally into Serb dominated territory. We decided to negotiate the opening of this stretch of the route. I went, first, to see the government side. I subtly placed myself back inside Sarajevo at least for a week.

– *Are you in favour of us attempting to open the Tarcin-Sarajevo road?*
– *Yes, but the Serbs will not allow it. They are frightened that the Bosnian army will advance along it and break the siege.*
– *OK, if I get approval from the other side you are happy?*
– *Yes.*—Jolly good. Next to the Serb side.
– *Are you in favour of us attempting to open the Tarcin-Sarajevo road?*
– *Yes, but the Muslims will not allow it. They are frightened that we will advance into Sarajevo.*
– *OK, now if I get approval from the other side you are happy?*
– *Yes.*

UNHCR and UNPROFOR arranged a reconnaissance. We informed the Serb side—*Impossible, there is a huge hole in the road.*
We informed the Bosnian side—*There is no hole in the road at the moment, but if you call the bluff of the Serbs, they will soon make one.*
At this point, General Morillon steps in. He sends for Colonel Sartre, the French Marine Commander, and myself—*Go and do a recce.*
Colonel Sartre arranged two APCs, and his flimsy jeep. I went with my Land Cruiser. Sartre decided to carry out the recce from the Serb side. We set out and went through Ilidza. Just before the terrible, shudder-inspiring, Sierra One checkpoint, we turn left at Blazuj and report into the Serb checkpoint that, "there is fighting in Hadzici." There obviously is, we can hear it loud and clear. The question is, has

it been initiated to prevent our recce? We sit and wait. In Colonel Sartre's lead APC, he has his tough Samoan sergeant.

We wait and chat. Colonel Sartre is not a patient man.

– *We have approval for this recce.*

– *But there is fighting.*

– *Then stop it.*

– *But it is a battle.*

– *If one side stops, it ceases to be a battle. You tell your side to stop.*

He then turned to me—*We go, OK?*

– *We go.*

We line up, one APC, one jeep, one Land Cruiser, one APC. We move off at a sedate pace. The closer we get to Hadzici the louder the noise of battle. Soon we can tell that the Serbs are on the left firing south. The Bosnians are on the right firing north.

Now French arrogance in the kitchen I do not like, but this I love. This is what the French are good at. Sartre has done this in a dozen African countries. He keeps the same pace, neither looks left nor right, and advances into the middle of the battle.

The shooting stops. We do not. We pass through the centre of Hadzici and on to the Bosnian front line at the far end. A pathetic little front line held by a small group of men as old as myself. They are ill equipped but determined. There is a hole in the road which prevents us going on to Tarcin, so we turn about and pass back through a silent, bemused Hadzici. Later the French repaired the hole and complicated plans were drawn up to use Ukrainian APCs to man UN checkpoints to open the road and preserve its integrity. But sadly, in my time it came to nothing.

Boss White and Boss Black continued to do well but not without event. I moved back to Mostar and arranged to meet the Boss White convoy at Mostar outside the dam on its return from Split. There had been heavy firing on the road and the Croat commander was refusing to allow them to proceed. They were all parked up facing north. Svabo and I went off to see the Croat in his headquarters. He was a young man and after a little persuasion he agreed that the convoy could travel back to Sarajevo through his patch of the road.

We returned, triumphant, just as a Serb shell exploded near the convoy. Parked in the open, it had been too inviting a target. Shrapnel from the shell shattered the windows of the vehicle nearest to its explosion point and peppered the sides of other vehicles. We were lucky the shell had landed on the soft verge. The earth had absorbed most of the blast and a lot of the shrapnel. Had it hit the hard road surface, there would have been serious casualties. As it was, the morale of the team sunk. I decided that even though we had approval to go forward, the drivers would not feel safe. I would have to leave them after about twenty kilometres. They would then be on their own in the dark having had one near miss. I sent them back to the warehouse. Their faces were like sunflowers.

That evening, I went the long way back to Mostar, and my lone Golf, with lone Englishman, met one lone British Land Rover with two ODA stalwarts, Jack Jones and the Honourable Gilbert Greenall. They were on their way to Zenica.

Not long after this, I met again Boss White in Mostar and travelled with it to Sarajevo and learned a little lesson. We were coming up over the mountain road from Tarcin, the terrible dirt track. The convoy took ages. I was in radio contact with Sarajevo and Kiseljak. We came off the mountain and down the narrow track heading into Kresevo, which was about two kilometers ahead. I looked behind me on one of the bends and all seemed to be going well. I could see all the vehicles. I was bored, so for something to do I radioed in—*Boss White through Kresevo*. Back came the reply from Sarajevo and Kiseljak—*Boss White through Kresevo*.

I then looked behind me and discovered that I was leading a convoy of one. We turned around and headed back up the hill, where I met Svabo coming towards me. *Stop, Mr. Larry—One of our trucks has slipped off the road and into the river."*
– *Is the driver OK?*
– *We think so.*
It was difficult to get to the point where the truck had left the road, as the convoy was blocking the entire road. When I got there, I could see that the driver had driven onto the verge of the road, which had

given way, and it and the truck had plunged down ten metres into the river. The truck had done a complete sideways turn but was now upright in the stream. The driver, an ace Bosnian basketball player, was complaining of back and neck injuries. It was not easy to get down to the truck, but they got him out and away to a hospital from where he was discharged one week later. Lucky man. The truck we were in had great difficulty recovering. The only way out was across the garden of the house of a man who lived at the edge of the water. A garden in which he had a swimming pool! The only swimming pool for miles, and he had to build it where we needed to tow our truck. He was asking for compensation money before we had even started. A good advert for Volvo—the truck started with the turn of the key. We used it for months but only on short distances, as the chassis was so buckled it had the tendency to go around in circles. It was like driving a crab.

After all the excitement, I got back into my vehicle and heard an exasperated Kiseljak asking where we were. *Boss White through Kresevo*—I replied, this time truthfully.

Boss White and Boss Black continued to have eventful days. Their first trips through the Serb checkpoint Sierra One were relatively incident free. But the aggression against them began to build up. Not only were our drivers considered to be pro-Government and therefore anti-Serb because they lived in Sarajevo, but also the Serbs at the checkpoint were jealous that the drivers had the opportunity to travel away from the war zone to places where there were normal shops. Also, they resented the fact that they themselves were in uniform earning nothing and our drivers were earning money. They asked our drivers for favours. Some they were able to do, like buy cigarettes or coffee, in small amounts. Everyone in Sarajevo wanted the drivers to bring in something. This one checkpoint could have been amenable, but it was greedy and temperamental. The UNHCR rule to the drivers was categoric—*You bring in nothing. If you are caught jeopardising the reputation or the neutrality of UNHCR, you are out.*

But naturally, they brought in sugar, meat, and butter for their own families, with some sort of negotiation with the Serbs.

117

The Serbs at Sierra One, and later at Sierra Two, were notorious for drinking. One huge thug in particular was often drunk. His colleagues were wary of him. Initially, he would be amusing when drunk. Fine if you were prepared to be crudely insulted. Then, he would become violent when drunk. Looking for any pretext to confiscate, to shove, to push, to punch. Then he would be maudlin drunk and want to cry. A very dangerous man. Sadly, his weaker colleagues would humour him. I never saw anyone challenge him. He robbed journalists, humiliated the UN, and frequently assaulted my drivers.

This particular day, they were coming into Sarajevo and were escorted by a Ukrainian APC. The Serbs were drunk and aggressive. The big bastard was there. The Ukrainians were disinterested or afraid. The Serbs decided to rob the drivers. Plain and simple theft. They stole their watches, their wallets, their loose money, and their flak jackets (their UN flak jackets, that is). Little Skroba, our vet turned driver, was petulant. He did not like being robbed so he protested and was slapped and beaten up. The Ukrainians were too busy collecting apples from a nearby tree to intervene.

I saw the drivers when they returned. They were very frightened but all confirmed that they would risk returning the following day, all except Skroba. He refused. He desperately needed the job, but he would give it up if it meant such humiliation. I gave him a job in the hangar stacking boxes.

We reported the incident to the Serbs, but they did little. Mladic was always complaining that we wrongly accused his soldiers of drunkenness. In this instance, he was apprised of their drunkenness, their robbery of personnel and UN property, and their assault on a UN employee. Nothing happened.

The following day Skroba, watched as his colleagues left and wished them luck. Relieved, he set to work in the hangar. There was a sudden burst of sniper fire and Skroba and others instinctively hit the deck. Skroba landed badly and broke his arm!

A radio message was passed to his convoy—*The Chetniks have got Skroba again.*

The Serb authorities were either unwilling or unable to control the behaviour of their checkpoint troops, so UNHCR took its own measures to enhance the safety of the drivers and their loads. A change of personnel was the catalyst.

Dag had the extra convoys that he needed. He next suggested a quicker turn-around of convoys. The logistic officer in Zagreb, Ian Henderson, produced the solution. He moved the aid from the warehouse in Split, Croatia to a warehouse in Metkovic, Croatian Bosnia, thus reducing the convoy turn-around time by four hours. He also had a stroke of genius—he moved Dag from Sarajevo to Metkovic to set it up and run it.

Marc Vachon, a colourful French Canadian, replaced him in Sarajevo. A tall, tough, tattooed muscular man. He spoke English with a heavy accent and a limited number of adjectives. Marc was an erratic but sound logistician. More importantly, he had found his niche. Sleeping rough in the hangar, mixing with the drivers, integrating with the community, barracking the French soldiers, squaring up to the Serbs. This was his scene. He was slightly mad, slightly bad, and could be very dangerous. Nonjo had a guard dog at home and we were losing kit from the hangar, so Nonjo brought the dog to guard the hangar. The dog bit Marc, and Marc personally killed the dog!

Marc decided to visit the checkpoints daily. He got to know every Serb. They got to know him. They were wary of him. He was far more streetwise than any of them. I think they may also have been scared of him. They respected him. On his birthday, they presented him with a cake. There was never any trouble at a checkpoint if Marc was there. He was a better value than any Ukrainian APC. He was not easy to work with, even less easy to command. But he was the right man for restoring the confidence of the drivers.

Marc had his moment and moved on. He was replaced by Mike Challenger, a Welshman equally as colourful. Silver haired, rosy cheeked, blue eyed, and when he arrived, overweight. He was an ex-soldier and an ex-businessman. He had an arrogant walk but a big smile. He began his day by visiting the checkpoints. He became part of the checkpoints. When Mike was around, the drivers were safe. Being much older than Marc, he was more of a father figure to

119

many of the drivers. Despite the fact that we had a rigid set of radio callsigns, Mike Challenger insisted on being "Mike Charlie." Mike Charlie got many a driver out of a scrape.

Marc and Mike were able to protect the drivers in and around Sarajevo, but once they were out on the road, they were on their own. They were particularly at risk after January 1993 when the warring factions were realigned. Put simply, the Croats abandoned the Bosnian government and allied with the Serb side. This meant that the convoys, with their ethnic mix, were now at risk in three territories, not just two.

Prozor is a Croat stronghold. A garrison town. Until October 1992, it was a peaceful place with one third of its population Muslim. They were driven out in a vicious wave of violence. It now has pro Croatian slogans daubed on the walls. There is almost a palpable evil arrogance about the place. Unfortunately, it is on the route from Metkovic to Sarajevo. It is the scene of many horror stories.

The Sarajevo convoy was moving towards its home base in May of '93. As it approached Prozor, the drivers could see smoke. Each driver in his own vehicle felt the early warning feeling of fear. There was that extra sharpness of perception that forces one to sit up straight, to touch the flak jacket and helmet, to know it is there. For the convoy commander of Boss White, there is the added tension of responsibility; one questions oneself incessantly—*Should I stop the convoy? Have the other drivers the same premonition as me? Am I scared for no reason?* Once in the main street, Boss White was in no doubt. The smoke was from burning houses. He could see Croat soldiers. They were kicking in doors.

– *Shall I stop the convoy and reverse it before they see us?* He knew that was impossible.

– *Keep them close together. Get through as quickly as possible.*

– *Please don't let them turn around and see us.*

Too late. The soldiers saw the convoy. They stopped what they were doing. Some ran into the road.

– *Shall I accelerate around him?* A mad momentary thought—*I may make it, but the others will not.*

He stopped. The convoy stopped behind him. Every driver felt sick. They knew that they were witnessing "cleansing" and looting. The Croats would not want witnesses to this action. But look what had fallen into their hands. An unarmed, unescorted, fully laden convoy worth a fortune on the black market. Soldiers surrounded and stopped Boss White's vehicle. The convoy halted behind him.

One Croat soldier was in charge.

– *Get out. Get out*—he shouted to the drivers indicating with his weapon that they were to leave their cabs. Only the drivers at the front of the convoy could see this, so other soldiers ran along the convoy ordering them out. They were bundled from their trucks and lined up in the street—all except thin, tall, and bearded Zoran, ironically a Croat. He had locked the doors of his cab on entering Prozor. He lay across the seat and could not be seen from the road.

– *What is in the truck and who is it for?* asked a soldier.

– *Food for the people of Sarajevo*—said Sejo the florist, who was standing by his own truck.

– *Food for Muslims?*—spat the Croat slapping Sejo.

– *What is in the cab?*—the soldier asked, opening the cab door. Next to his seat, Sejo had a leather bag with a handle. The soldier grabbed it and commenced beating Sejo about the face with it. The handle hit him in the eye. The other soldiers laughed and joined in slapping the other drivers. The soldier with the bag turned his attention to the smallest driver and began beating him about the neck and back. It was poor Skroba the vet, who had overcome his fear and joined the convoy again. Nonjo's brother, Sejo the architect, attempted to defend himself as he was beaten with the same bag. A Croat drew his pistol and put it to Sejo's head. Then there was silence. The other Croats were not sure whether their comrade would pull the trigger. Zoran the Croat driver was watching this from his cab. He shouted:

– *I am a Croat. Leave them, they are my friends.*

The soldier with the pistol was not impressed.

– *Get out of that cab!*—he shouted. Zoran did not move. *Get out! Get out!*—shouted the soldier and fired his pistol into the truck. The shattering of the silence with the pistol shot terrified the driv-

121

ers. They each thought that it would signal a frenzy of murder. But the soldier returned to Sejo and struck him across the face with his pistol. He then shouted to Zoran—*You are next!*

Then, like an apparition from heaven, a British army patrol arrived. Any other military patrol may have passed by not questioning why a convoy was stopped. Not this one. It stopped, had the courage to get involved, and stayed. It escorted the convoy to its base at Gornji Vakuf. Sejo the florist was lucky not to lose his eye. Sejo the architect had stitches in his head. Skroba, poor accident prone Skroba, was hospitalised for one month with injuries to his spine. When visited by Sejo the florist, he asked—*Sejo, what did you have in the bloody bag, stones?*

The days of Boss White and Boss Black were over. It was too dangerous. Even for them.

Six

Sniper Fire, "Friendly" Fire

We were looking for an assistant to work with Leyla in the new warehouse. She recommended Suad, a friend who before the war was a croupier. He is a dark, oily, handsome man. A meeter and greeter oozing charm. Speaks excellent English. We took him down to the old warehouse in Zetra. No one was on the streets. There was no shelling, but a strong foreboding of danger sharpened a torpid day. We left the centre of the city and headed out to Zetra. We were the only car moving. We were in the unarmoured Land Cruiser, clearly marked "UNHCR" on the doors and the roof. We could sense that the Serbs in the hills were watching us. I had a feeling that perhaps we should not go. It was not absolutely vital. But tomorrow may be no better. Life must go on.

I was driving and conscious that we were alone. There were no pedestrians, no other cars. We reached Zetra, and I turned right, swung across the road, and entered the stadium. The huge steel door to the tunnel road where the storehouses were located under the stadium bowl was closed. Those inside were taking no chances. I hooted on the car horn and stopped at the steel door. I heard someone approach the door. I asked Leyla to shout out that we were UNHCR. I felt very exposed. I kept the car engine running.

The heavy door began to open. One guard was pulling it from right to left. I shouted "Good day" to him. He smiled. Suddenly there was one huge bang. It felt as if it was on top of us. There was pressure on my ears. We were enveloped in a cloud of grey brown smoke. Through it, I could see that the door was open probably wide enough to get through. I gunned the engine and sped through. A second bang louder than the first reverberated to our right. A second shell had exploded on hitting the outside wall. It sounded louder because it was echoing off the walls of the underground tunnel we had entered.

I did not stop the car until I was deep inside the tunnel road. We got out and all smiled at each other. Ten minutes ago, Suad was a new outsider, now he was part of the team. Leyla, not yet twenty-one, was ice cool and calm. We walked back to near the entrance. A shell had smashed through the top left-hand corner of the door, then bounced off the concrete wall. The guards were attempting to clear up the debris of glass and wood and metal. The door was buckled, the guard room was raked with shrapnel which had knocked out the security camera monitors and console.

The man opening the door was dead. Shrapnel had hit him in the chest. We stayed for an hour or more whilst I psyched myself up to risk driving the car out through the same door we had come in.

A few days later, I was motoring into the centre of the city again with Leyla, but this time Dragon was driving. It was one of our first trips in the newly arrived armoured Range Rover. We were approaching the entrance to the barracks of the Ukrainians when a shell hit the road no more than fifty metres ahead of us. It left a small crater in the road. It baptised the Range Rover.

I was always happy to be out with Leyla. Lucky Leyla. So young, so wise, so brave. She hated being out with me.

The sniper fire along the airport road was considered too severe to risk my return to the hangar, so I decided to stay the night in the PTT building. I had heard that General Morillon was in the building. I was looking forward to the opportunity of meeting him. It was obvious that others knew he was there as well. In the middle of the evening, heavy shelling began. It drew closer to the building and then one round hit the entrance, slightly wounding a French soldier. The alarm was sounded, and people began to make their way to the cellar when a second round slammed into the room occupied by the UNPROFOR police.

No one was in the room. The last man had just left. The room was destroyed. Girders were bent, large chunks of masonry from the outer wall thudded against the inner walls, and as the mortar had exploded, fragments of the shell case—from splinter sized slivers to ashtray sized slabs—had pock mocked the walls and tore through the woodwork.

Two rooms were wrecked and one badly damaged. The occupants of the rooms were on the landing and on the stairs outside their rooms when the shell landed. The explosion at the entrance and the scream of the wounded Frenchman had caused them to leave their rooms to see what assistance they could give. Their sense of duty saved their lives. They lost their possessions but not their lives.

Down in the basement, at the foot of the stairs, I had my first view of General Morillon. He was in his grey fatigue uniform. He was wearing his blue beret, which was shrunk to fit his head, a trick learned early in service by all soldiers. If you do not shrink them, they flop on your head like a cow pat. Beneath the line of his beret, I could see his distinguished, close-cropped silver hair.

The General was smoking. He is a walking advert for Davidoff cigars. If ever the company does "Rolex-type" adverts, then they must feature General Morillon. Not only was he smoking, but he was pacing up and down the confined space of the basement stairwell like a caged tiger. A few paces, then a quick turn. He was accompanied by Colonel Davout, the acting Sector Commander. Tall, angular, straight-backed Davout, an aircraft pilot, although, how he ever fitted into a cockpit, I will never know.

I watched the tiger. He should have returned to his headquarters, but he was caged here. Was he prevented from moving by "aggressor" Serb provocation, as the Bosnian government would want him to believe? Or had his return to the city initiated a touch of Balkan intrigue? Was the shelling of the building done by Government troops, attempting to make General Morillon believe that the Serbs were antagonising him?

Whatever. I had watched enough; it was time to make his acquaintance. I introduced myself directly. He was instantly charming. He exuded calm command. As he talks to you, he squares off to face you. His voice is unmistakable. Every word begins in his throat and swirls over the back of his tongue, reaching his lips as a growl. He is every inch the professional soldier. He has served in the most illustrious of French Regiments, including the Spahis, and he has commanded the Foreign Legion.

We had only the shortest of conversations, but I knew that I was going to get on well with him. After a while, Colonel Davout decided that everyone could return to their rooms and offices. I went back to the HCR office. Una and Leyla slept in the outer office, on mattresses on the floor. I slept in the inner office on a mattress against the wall furthest from the entrance door. There was a communicating door between the girls' office and mine.

I was tired, so I went straight to bed. Outside in the corridor, I could hear people discussing the extent of the damage done by the shells. With these conversations in my ears, I fell asleep.

I am a very light sleeper. I heard my office door open. I looked up and saw a soldier enter. He was tall and thin. Because of the association of the last conversation I had heard before I went to sleep, I thought that he must be checking the rooms for damage. I closed my eyes. However, he moved from my room to where the girls were sleeping. I still thought that he was inspecting the rooms. He made little noise. I suddenly realised that it was far too late for anyone to be inspecting anything.

I leapt out of my sleeping bag—I was wearing only my underpants. I entered the girls' room. The soldier was standing over the girls who were fast asleep. He had not heard me. I watched him as he began to undress. I moved quickly across the room, grabbed him and forced him towards the door of the girls' room. He was a wiry man, taller than me, but he offered little resistance. I pushed him out of the room and into the corridor. I yelled at him and shoved him out through the double doors onto the staircase.

I thought he was French. I had shouted at him in English anyway. He had not spoken to me, not a word. I thought perhaps he was drunk, but I could smell no alcohol on his breath and, far from being unsteady, he gave the impression of being rigid and isolated.

I returned via the girls' room. Leyla murmured to me. I told her everything was OK and went to my room. I went back to my mattress, thinking that it had been a busy day and making a mental note to tell the girls to lock their door at night. I was soon asleep.

I heard footsteps in the corridor. They stopped outside my door. I unzipped my sleeping bag. I heard my door handle turn; I saw the door slowly open. The soldier entered my room. He came straight towards where I was lying. He was carrying in his hand a bayonet.

I was on my feet in a flash. I met him halfway across the room and bundled him back to the door. I was trying to hold down his hand which held the bayonet. As I got him against the wall, I realised two facts. First, that the bayonet is very long and a most unwieldy weapon. Second, that he was much stronger than me. I pride myself in being strong. I am not running fit, but I am able to shove and push as good as the next man. This fellow was not the next man.

Up against him, I was able to better assess him. He was maybe twenty-nine. He had an angular face, tanned light brown, with a pointed nose and mean, thin lips. I think his eyes were brown. His breathing was imperceptible. I felt that mine was like a steam train by contrast. Most significant was that he never uttered a word.

I was about to lose this contest. It was taking all my effort to keep his bayonet hand pinned to his side. If he had been carrying a knife with a shorter blade, then I would have been in big trouble. Discretion is the better part of valour, so casting my pride to the wind, I yelled out—*Girls! Girls!* This diversion spurred on my assailant, and he very nearly put me through the door. To me it was vital that I hung on to him. I continued—*Girls! Girls!* I heard no response, heard no movement, but suddenly was joined by my good friend, WHO doctor Nedim Jaganjac, who, apparently, short of a mattress, was sleeping in the outer office near the girls. He was a little sleepy eyed, but he saw the struggle and the bayonet. He bear-hugged the soldier thus pinning his arms and the bayonet to his side.

I then had a brilliant idea. I would knee the soldier in the genitals. In films, it always seems to drop the assailant to the floor. I expected that it would, at least, make this fellow's eyes water. What actually happened was, as I drove my knee into his groin, I drove my toe onto the pinned down bayonet. We both winced. But he dropped the bayonet. He then seemed to lose the will to fight.

One of the girls went to the duty operations room which was only forty metres down the corridor. Nedim went upstairs to the damaged rooms to get Sergeant Jim Hull, the Canadian RCMP, who was the

Sector Commander of the Civilian Police in Sarajevo. I bundled the man out into the corridor, for the second time this evening. He resisted but in a non-violent way. I was able to shove him along whenever he stopped.

As we were close to the ops room door, he stopped and we scuffled. From his pocket, a pistol fell to the floor. I went cold.

By then there were other people about. He was taken over by them. Then Jim arrived. Jim is the man who should have dealt with him. He is not your tall, handsome, moustachioed "Mountie" from the posters, who can yodel, ride horses and lance pegs. Jim is a balding, stocky, streetwise muscle man, in the image of Yul Brynner. The soldier would have met his match with Jim, without "girls, girls."

Jim arrested him. I returned to my room, still in my underpants and incidentally asked God that, if I had to go hand to hand again, please may I be wearing my trousers and shoes.

Traumatologist Dr. Nedim looked at my bleeding toe with little interest and even less sympathy. The girls were fast asleep. On the violence scale of Sarajevo, this had been for them a very minor incident.

The irony of the evening was that the soldier was a Ukrainian and a policeman. He worked for Jim. He was one of the occupants of the room destroyed by the shell earlier in the evening. The theory is that the closeness of the event shocked and numbed his mind. Hence his strength and his behaviour. He was sent home. Which pleased me.

What did not please me was the departure of the RAF team who were given their marching orders. They had to return to the UK. A great loss.

I then had the bunker to myself. I was very happy there, but the summer ended, the weather broke, and the rain came. One night, as it was pouring down, I was stretched out on the floor about to go to sleep when I heard a creaking and a cracking. The metal support bars were bending under the weight of the now rain sodden sandbags. The last straw was a rumour of a possible invasion across the airport by the Serbs using tanks. If they came, they may not see my lone, solitary bunker. If it was not holding up to the pressure of wet sandbags, it may not take too kindly to the weight of a tank. Enwombed I liked—entombed I didn't. I moved to the PTT, a French colony. We in UNHCR had been in the PTT before the French arrived. Fabrizio had laid claim to quarters befitting his station. When I arrived, the French were drawing up new borders. We in UNHCR were to move from the first floor to the ground floor. All civilians were to be in the one corner. Civilians meant UNHCR, UNICEF, WHO and the local liaison officers.

Now, I had this strange idea that the military were in support of the humanitarian agencies. An idea encouraged by the mandate written in New York. The French, however, considered civilians to be a nuisance. They were to be put in a corner where an eye could be kept on them—on the ground floor near the exit as a constant reminder. Furthermore, the French insisted that civilians—national and international—must produce proof of identity on entering the building and must submit themselves to a body search and their bags and envelopes to a rummaging by a French conscript. Military of any shade or hue were exempt from this inconvenience. There were no more than thirty of us civilians, and no more than ten internationals, but exempting us from this humiliation was beyond the wit, the power, or the inclination of the French. I was body searched up to thirty times a day. I appealed to the better nature of the senior French officer, only to discover that he did not have one.

On one memorable occasion, I was returning to Sarajevo from Zagreb where I had collected for a member of my staff her suitcase. It was full of her clothing and her intimate purchases. I arrived at the front door of the PTT having forgotten about the insult about to hit me. The French conscript advanced towards me and the suitcase—I remembered its contents. I stopped and waited for a military man to enter the building.

– *Would you be so kind as to take this suitcase through for me?*—I enquired.

– *Of course*—was the polite reply. The conscript watched with anger as the suitcase eluded his itchy fingers.

I had the smaller office, the girls the larger. We worked, slept, and played in them. By day they housed nine or ten, by night they slept

129

four or five. The whole building heaved with humanity. If there was water, we washed. If there was no water, we didn't. The greatest inconvenience was the conveniences. No water and they stank. Jerrycans of water were placed in them daily. But as often as not, the jerrycans were empty and the toilet bowls full.

Living cheek by jowl, everyone together, was fun. It created a team spirit amongst those who were clubbable and madness in those who were not. Despite living on top of one another, there was the opportunity for living on top of one another. Liaisons were formed and relationships flourished. Where there's a will there's a way!

Seven

Rajlovac

Once again, we had trouble with the delivery of aid to the Serb held territories surrounding Sarajevo. The Bosnian Government forces were preventing our convoy from delivering to the Serb warehouse at Rajlovac. They refused to accept that our charter was to feed all sides. More importantly, they refused to accept the reality that if we did not give aid to the Serbs, then the Serbs would prevent anything from entering the city by road and could disrupt the airlift.

The first sign of this round of trouble was a convoy sent back at the last Bosnian checkpoint. The reason given was "the Serbs are fighting on the road." The fact that you could hear no shooting and that the Serbs wanted the food belied this. I complained and was assured that the next convoy would go through without a hitch. It did not. It was sent back because "it had no approval."

Meanwhile, we had a convoy en route from Metkovic, due to arrive at the final Serb checkpoint outside Sarajevo, "Sierra One," the following day. I went to the Bosnian Liaison Office, explained my case and then went to see our Government link, the delightful, charming, Mugdim Pasic. The army had given him the party line. Sarajevo was besieged by Serbs. The Serbs were not besieged. Why did we give any food to the "aggressor" Serbs? Was the UN a party to bribing the Serbs? Did the world know what was going on? Each line was given to me as if it were fresh and new.

– *My dear friend, no more rhetoric. Does my convoy go through or not?*
– *Not*—was the answer. So I had to go to the Serb Liaison Officer and get myself an appointment with the Serb hierarchy to try to keep them sweet, so that they would let the Metkovic convoy move.

The meeting was arranged for the following day. I reported back to Mugdim who promised to make sure that I had no difficulty getting to Rajlovac. To test the system, I organised a convoy to attempt to enter Rajlovac prior to my visit. It failed! It was a noisy day, there was a lot of activity in the city. When the convoy reached the Bosnian checkpoint, they just sent it back.

131

I had arranged to leave Sarajevo at one o'clock for the meeting at two. I left with my driver Pepe, a Bosnian Sarajevo Serb, my faithful translator Meliha Hadzic, a Bosnian Sarajevo Muslim, and two visitors from Zagreb—an African protection officer with a great sense of humour, which was about to come in handy, and Boi Lan Van Chau, the Vietnamese born American, whom I first met in Geneva. We left the airport, travelled down the infamous sniper alley, crossed the flyover, and then turned left for Rajlovac. At the Bosnian checkpoint we normally find a soldier or two manning the barrier, but there was nobody there. We drove slowly forward, and thirty or forty metres beyond the barrier, we heard a shout from a house on our left. Pepe stopped the car, he and I got out and walked towards the voice. A Bosnian soldier appeared at the shattered window and called us into the house. He said that they had taken cover to avoid heavy sniper fire from the Serb side. There were a group of soldiers in the house, which was strewn with the remains of some poor family's furniture. War billeted soldiers make pretty poor tenants.

We explained to the soldiers that we were going to Rajlovac to see the Serbs to try to ensure that our convoy due in from Metkovic could pass through Serb territory and to explain why we were unable to get a convoy through to them. The Bosnian soldiers were not happy, they gave me all the usual hassle, but because they knew me well, they agreed that we could go through.

We set off from the Bosnian checkpoint, slowly, slowly, towards the Serb checkpoint. This also was not manned but we could see a soldier who waved us on.

At Rajlovac depot, we were met by Ljerka, the Serb Liaison Officer, a woman whom I knew well from early days, when she was the deputy in charge of the depot. She took us into the conference room, where a large group of people waited for us. This included the Mayor of Ilidza, the Military Commander, various civilian dignitaries, and some local aid workers from Red Cross and the Serb charity Dobrotvor. Around the table there were about twelve; on the table there was slivovica; it was going to be a long hard session.

My radio crackled and Sarajevo asked if I could send Pepe back as they were short of vehicles and drivers. I was guaranteed that he would be away no more than two hours. Foolishly, I said—*OK.* As we were on Serb territory, I did not feel unhappy about sending Serb Pepe back alone, and he was quite happy to go.

The meeting was as tedious as I expected. The military commander, a very difficult man, began by accusing me of—*favouring the Muslims*—and—*delivering low percentages to the Serb side*—and the usual, but always infuriating—*and you smuggled ammunition into Sarajevo.* I refuted the wrong accusations and tried to explain the accurate ones. The commander would not listen. I tried to be patient. He tried my patience, I raised my voice, he his. It was a well-tested formula. The Mayor, a gentle and wise man, did his best to keep the bile and venom down.

Ljerka and the Serb humanitarian workers then came in with another old chestnut. When we were able to get a convoy to them, could it also bring in the contents of the convoys that had failed to arrive? This argument I have heard wherever I have served. My answer is always the same—*You cannot eat yesterday's food.*

As a compromise, I promised that in the first convoy, I would deliver the best protein that I could; tins of beef and fish as well as flour. By four o'clock, I was worn out and they were not too happy. We shook hands with them all, left the conference room, and discovered no vehicle. I got onto the radio—*Where is Pepe?*

– *Don't know*—was the reply—*he did not return.* I was not happy—*...then you have two problems; find Pepe and find me a vehicle.* We had a problem ourselves, as there was shooting and shelling not too far away.

So it was back into the building and back into the conference room. It is always embarrassing to say farewell, shake hands, and then reappear. Ljerka took us to an outer office, her conference continued and we waited. After about five minutes, I was back onto the Sarajevo office. They said that they thought they knew where Pepe was. He had been arrested at the Bosnian checkpoint. Some of the soldiers had recognised him and knew that he was a Serb. He was now in prison and no-one knew where the vehicle was. However, they would try to find one for us. Meanwhile Ljerka's meeting had ended, more handshakes, off they all went leaving Ljerka and us.

I was back on the radio—*What the hell is going on?*

– *There is a vehicle on its way. Be with you in five minutes.*

– *Ljerka, is it inconvenient if we stay here until our vehicle arrives?* She was honest; it was. If she did not leave in the next few minutes, she would not be able to get home that evening, and at home she had two children. I got back onto the radio and was assured that the vehicle was approaching me, so I made a decision—*Right folks, we will leave Ljerka, so that she can get away, and we will walk to the warehouse gate by which time our vehicle will have arrived.* Ljerka was pleased and away she went. We walked towards the depot gate with the distant rumbling of shells in our ears. Ljerka's car overtook us. At the gate the guard waved us through, then locked the gate and he too set off for home.

It was a fairly strange feeling to be alone in Serb territory with the sounds of war in the distance. I began to feel that I had not made the right decision and I got back on the radio—*Any news about the car?*

– *It should be with you now*—was the reply. There were two choices open to me: stand outside the locked exposed depot or walk along the road where the car would come. I chose the latter. The first hundred or so metres were fine, behind us was the depot. Then we turned into the main Sarajevo road, it looked lonely and the light was now beginning to fade. I tried the radio, my voice was not as demanding as before. I needed them.

– *Definitely on its way, should be able to see it from where you are.* More decisions! We were wearing our flak jackets and our helmets; it was obvious who we were. I decided that we would walk along the main road, twenty paces between each of us and we would make as much noise as we could. The distance was in case we were mortared; better to lose one of us than to lose all of us. The noise was to ensure that we did not suddenly startle any guards or checkpoints. Off we went—*The vehicle will be with us very soon.*

I was not happy, I have to confess, I was not happy at all. I consoled myself that having made one bad decision, that of leaving the depot, my decision to move was better than standing still. When we got very close to the Serb front line, we were opposite the entrance to a barracks. We were walking single file, as high profile as possible. Suddenly all hell broke loose. Bang, bang, bang, rounds flew over our heads. The sentries on the front line did not know who the hell we were. In the failing light we could have been anything or anybody, so they opened up.

Time stood still. I was at the back of the line. I saw the tall, beautiful, elegant Meliha trying to get into a ditch in a ladylike way, trying not to get her overcoat dirty. My African friend turned to me, his eyes bright and white. Calm Boi Lan asked me—*What do we do?* – *Down, down!*—I shouted, somewhat unnecessarily, as I was the only person standing.

I turned and walked towards where the shooting was coming from. I had my hands above my head and shouted—*Visoki komesarijat! Humanitarian Aid! HCR! United Nations!* The shooting continued, but I had by now realised that it was above our heads and not at us. As I walked towards the barracks, I could see a man of about fifty. I shouted to him—*Stop shooting!* He shouted something back at me. I was then very close to him. He turned to his troops and, I think, gave the order for the shooting to stop. I called my group forward and they began to run towards the barrack entrance.

Then we had a complication, the outgoing Serb fire caused a response from the Muslims in the hills and they started to fire into the Serb barracks. Not surprisingly, the Serbs returned fire. We were now in the middle of a firefight. I was yelling in English at the Serb to stop his firing. He understood not a word and was otherwise preoccupied. My little group needed no more leadership from me. They raced towards the guard room. The Serbs let us in, and the shooting stopped. Meliha then explained to the Serb soldiers why we had been walking along the main road. They were incredulous. They accused me of being reckless. I do not want to absolve myself, but the whole episode did stem from innocence.

In the guardroom, Meliha was very worried. Meliha is Muslim. Meliha is a very Muslim name. All the soldiers in the guardroom, who

135

had been firing at the Muslim troops and indeed, at us, were Serbs. Young Serb boys. Meliha quietly asked me what she should say if they asked her name. *Meliha*—I said—*Let's play it by ear.* I then realised that I had called her "Meliha" quite openly. I also realised that my priority was to ensure the Sarajevo knew that we were now in Serb Army hands. I contacted Sarajevo very publicly—*What the hell is going on? Where is my car?*

Fortunately, Tony Land was now back in the office. Tony never panics and always thinks logically. I felt a lot better when his voice came up. Tony explained the situation—*Pepe was recognised as a Serb. On his way out he was arrested at the Bosnian Checkpoint, he is in jail.*

He continued—*The second car we sent was refused entry by the same Muslims who arrested Pepe. We have now sent a United Nations armoured personnel carrier to get you out. In it is Captain Jan Segers. It is held up at the checkpoint because there has been a mini battle in the Serb lines which you obviously caused.* He concluded by stating, firmly—*Stay where you are*—A totally unnecessary piece of advice. We were now happy. Well, happier. I was certainly pleased that Jan was involved. He is a Belgian officer whom I have had many dealings with, he is a bulldog. He never gives up on a problem and never lets go.

A young Serb officer then arrived and demanded that I go with him to be interviewed by his commander. To divide our group would have been a great mistake. So I declined the "invitation" and sent the reply that I would be delighted to see the commander in the guard room where I was waiting for my APC to pick us up. This reply did not go down very well.

Whilst we waited, we handed out some cigarettes. One of the soldiers asked Meliha where she came from. She replied—*Sarajevo.* He asked her—*Where?*

She answered, very reluctantly, as she comes from a fairly strong Muslim area. The Serb soldier brightened up—*I don't live very far from there*—he said—*tell me have you seen...*—They then began to discuss neighbours, school friends, university friends. The heat was taken out of the situation as far as Meliha was concerned. She relaxed enormously and a smile came to her face. They chatted as if they were, what they really were, twenty-five-year-olds swapping stories about friends and neighbours.

Meanwhile, I was back on the radio to Tony. We could hear the APC. We could also hear the shooting. Every time it moved forward it was fired upon. It received direct hits. The tough little Irish APC driver from the French Foreign Legion did his best—no doubt encouraged by Jan. They were persistent and brave. But they could not get through.

Throughout this, I was on the radio to Tony and the inevitable happened. The radio battery died. We were then incommunicado but able to hear the progress of the APC and watch the tracer bullets bouncing near it. It was now pitch dark. We heard the receding noise of the APC. I then had to plan the night. So I asked if the commander would be so kind and come and see me. I did not think that he would, but he did. He was not friendly. He told me that we would stay in the guardroom until it was considered safe to move us to Ilidza where we would be taken to the Sector commander. My adversary of the afternoon.

Meliha was happy, she was the centre of attention—gossiping forth, a fount of knowledge. Giving some of these men the first news of their homes and their relatives. We others were cold, bored, and hungry. After a couple of hours, we were collected and taken outside into the bitter cold night. We were told to follow our guide keeping close to the buildings. It was a very dark but quiet night. There were distant rumblings but nothing in our vicinity. Eventually, we came to a dirty old blue van which took us along a bumpy track. We had no idea how safe the route was. We did not ask; we were not told. Eventually, we arrived in Ilidza, at the municipal office buildings. We were taken up to the Mayor's office and met by a man I knew from a previous experience. The sinister, silent detective who had arrested me in Ilidza the day the bus drivers disappeared. I was not too sure what sort of reception we would get. Soon the door opened and in came the Mayor with the military commander, who had given me such a hard time earlier and whose hands I had already shaken farewell twice. They had great beams on their faces and the Mayor said to me—*What were you doing walking through Rajlovac?* They were amused. They told us that they had informed the UN where we were and how we were. After very welcome slivovica, for we were freezing cold, they told us that they would accommodate us for the night. What they did was to open up the Hotel Ilidza, which had been closed since the beginning of the war.

They brought some staff in, and by candlelight, we were shown to two rooms. The place was freezing, so we took the blankets off the beds and wrapped ourselves up in them. They then took us to a room where the military commander had an office. We were given more slivo. They then produced a bottle of wine, some hot soup and a good meat meal. We were so happy. After the meal, we went back to the two rooms allocated to us. The Serb accompanying us said—*Look, there is only one double bed in each room. You will be much warmer if you are mixed.*

He got a withering look from the women, and so that was that.

– *Why do I always end up with the ugly one?*—I asked.

We then got the giggles. We giggled away the tension of the day. We slept little. It was too cold. We left the hotel at six and were taken to a place where we would be picked up by a French APC. It was late. We were starving, cold, and in a fairly dangerous spot. Eventually, it arrived and we were taken to the airport. All our UNHCR colleagues were present. I had forgotten that it was the day of the visit of Madame Ogata.

The majority were pleased to see us. Karen Landgren, the Chief of Mission, was not. She came across to me with her ice-cold blue eyes and an ice-cold manner and informed me that I had been totally irresponsible and had hazarded the lives of her staff.

In the circumstances, I think her remark was unfair. It was neither the right moment nor the right place to say it. I also do not think it was true. On the tarmac I saw Pepe. Tony had managed to get him out of jail. He was none the worse for his experience.

Eight

Students and Their Kit

The pressure to get "Third Country National Students" out of Sarajevo was increasing. Every day a delegation was in the office with some tale of woe. The majority of them were Arabs and they had enlisted the support of the Head of Civil Affairs in Sarajevo Adnan Al Razak. He is a Palestinian, so he is well qualified to understand refugee problems. He is also a hell of a nice guy, very efficient at his job, and most supportive of HCR.

The majority of the students were from the medical faculty of Sarajevo University. In fairness to them, they were not going to learn a lot in the classrooms. If they wanted to be hands on medical workers, then a Ph.D. of experience was at their disposal. In truth, the majority did not see this as their war and wanted out. A bright young Sudani was their principal spokesman; whenever one of his fellow students was wounded or killed, he was banging on my door demanding that we get the students out.

Adnan and I decided to try to do something. Adnan promised to organise a bus. I was to smooth their exit with both parties. After a lot of effort, a lot of hassle, and many false starts we were in a position to say "GO." The Bosnian government agreed to release them. The Serbs agreed to them transiting through their territory. The Croats agreed to their entry into Croatia as long as they had the means to move on and did not stay.

The number of students had swollen to eighty-nine. Adnan laid on three buses. It was a bright sunny day. We arranged to be at the PTT building at seven a.m. The buses would arrive, with all the students. We would check their passports, ascertain that they were self-sufficient, and away they would go, escorted as far as Kiseljak by one UNPROFOR APC under the command of an UNPROFOR military policeman, who turned out to be from Poland. Warrant Officer Andrzej Buler, a short, stocky, smiling cube of a man, with a great sense of humour and, as the day was to prove, a lot of courage. Jim O'Neil, the Head of Office of UNICEF in Sarajevo, a good friend and a great supporter of UNHCR, would also accompany the convoy. I would monitor its progress from the Serb HQ at Ilidza.

Contrary to the arrangements, the students started arriving at the PTT building at about six a.m. As ever, this taxed the thin patience of the French guards, who in the main were conscripts, and did not want to be in the army and certainly did not want to be in Bosnia.

The buses arrived at seven. Adnan and I went out to meet the crowd. My task was to ensure that they were all "foreign" nationals, all students, all eligible to go and that they all had the means to get themselves home. We had given to the Serb liaison officers their names, and Momcilo was in attendance with me. Right from the start, it was obvious it was not going to be easy. There were far more than eighty-seven. Some of the students had local wives, girlfriends, or associates, and despite all the warnings, they had brought them along to try to get them out. I understood it but did not appreciate it.

So, task one was to separate those who could go from those who could not. This meant tears, breaking down luggage, farewells, and hassle that I could do without. Task two was to line up everybody who could go and to check passport and holder. This also proved to be fun.

Many of the students had not renewed their passports, and they were out of date. A very good question, which they put to me, was how could they renew their passports when their embassies were in either Zagreb or Belgrade and they could not get out of Sarajevo? Momcilo, the Serb LO, thought that out of date passports would be OK as long as the students had arrived originally with a valid one.

As I walked along the ranks of the students checking their passports, I rapidly realised that many of them were "professional" students. One or two had birth dates as old as mine. They were "Economics" or "Social Studies" students, on their third degree. Quite a few looked nothing like their passports. Two were eliminated because there was no way, even with the passage of time, that they could be the person in the passport.

Some of the passports were written only in Arabic. I could see the Serb checkpoint enjoying these. The compliant Momcilo thought they would be "OK." Momcilo just wanted the show on the road. He had no idea what would be accepted at the checkpoint. It would depend on the whim, the fancy, the mood of the soldiers who, I suspected, had spent all night drawing lots for the fun of ransacking this exclusively Muslim convoy.

To pass the means test, many of the students had letters from their embassies. All told me that they had money. Eighty-seven passed the test and were motioned forward to join the buses. I went over to see the drivers; they were in good humour. The buses, however, were a typical Sarajevo scene. They were battle scarred, ramshackled, creaking, groaning hulks on shattered springs and bald tyres. The chances of them reaching Split were zero. The drivers assured me that the buses were the best in the city. My impression was that the drivers did not give a damn how far they got as long as they themselves got clear of Sarajevo. Two of them were young men, and one was middle aged.

We got everyone on board, I stood by the door of each bus and counted them on. The APC growled into life, the Polish policeman stood in the turret, and away they went. Adnan and I shook hands and breathed a sigh of relief. We now had eighty-seven less problems. I arranged to motor to the Serb headquarters with Momcilo, to be on hand when the convoy went through the checkpoint. We went in my armoured Range Rover, which I noticed was short of fuel. It was petrol driven and petrol was forever in short supply.

Momcilo, "Momo," is a tall, very serious man. He looks and acts like a public schoolmaster on secondment to a London comprehensive. He was as bewildered by the circumstances of the war-torn Bosnia as we were. He longed for a return to the orderliness of his pre-war business and domestic scene. "Momo" was without malice and unable to be devious. Two serious character deficiencies in a Balkan political environment.

We went to the Military Police headquarters in the centre of Ilidza. It was in a side street and protected by a tank which had a rubber skirt attached to its sides, presumably to deflect light anti-tank weapons. It always looked to me like the front cover of an immediate post-war era Berlin "kinky" magazine. It had that grotesque, bizarre imagery, metal, rubber, and violence. Whenever I arrived at any headquarters, I tried to ignore the guard. To walk past them, to look as if I was there by right. I knew my way into this complex and was about to breeze through, but my guide, the self-effacing Momo, was explaining to the guard who I was, who I wanted to see, and the guard was explaining to him that we would have to wait outside the barrier until he cleared our arrival. Whilst we were clearing up this difference of opinion, a car exited the barracks. In it was the commander I had come to see. I recognised him, he recognised me, he stopped the car, we hugged and exchanged news. He spoke to Momo and then he left. Momo was impressed, but his news was depressing. There was trouble at the checkpoint. The soldiers would not allow the Sarajevo drivers to proceed. The Serbs were doing a deal with the Croats whereby three Serb soldiers would drive the buses to Kiseljak, offload the students, and then return.

I realised it was going to be a long day. I further realised that I was going to have to motor to Kiseljak at some stage. The vehicle did not have enough fuel to take me to Kiseljak, so I got on the radio and spoke to Dag. He was at the airport, there was an acute shortage of petrol, but the other Range Rover, the one that I had loaded for my aborted attempt to Gorazde, was full. He would come into Ilidza, and we could swap vehicles. I concurred, better a ten-minute delay now than hours later.

I got onto the radio to HCR in the PTT. The latest news from the checkpoint was not good. In addition to the driver problem, there was a dispute over how many students there were. Dag arrived in record time. We swapped vehicles, and Momo and I set off for the checkpoint.

It was manned by a particularly unruly, drunken bunch. One of them I knew very well, a giant with the rustic looks, the ruddy complexion, and the enormous hands of a farm labourer. He was well fuelled, swaying and giggling, taunting and mocking with that unpredictability of the man of limited intelligence, violent tendencies, and local power. His fellow Serbs were humouring him, a bad sign.

They too were frightened of him.

The situation was grim. Some of the Serb soldiers claimed to have seen one of the bus drivers, a Muslim, fighting in the front line against them. Another Serb then claimed that the bus driver was a known murderer and furthermore was responsible for the death of his brother. All three drivers had been taken to the building where we had left. One under arrest, the other two under investigation. Apparently, the Polish policeman and Jim O'Neil of UNICEF had fought hard under a lot of pressure and threats for the release of the drivers but without success. The Serbs had provided three Serb bus drivers who were to drive the students to Kiseljak, where they would be unloaded, and the buses would then return to Ilidza. They claimed that it was reckless to risk those buses on a trip to Split. I noted that they said that the buses would return to Ilidza, not to Sarajevo. The Serbs would therefore gain three buses. The Serbs then harangued me about the numbers—there were eighty-eight, not eighty-seven students. I was adamant that eighty-seven had left the PTT building. I explained that I had counted them on. I volunteered that it was possible that the bus had stopped outside the PTT and that someone could have jumped on, but I doubted it. The Serbs were insistent that eighty-eight had left the PTT. The more I insisted, the more they insisted. Just before I went into my usual anger overdrive, I sensed that their anger was as "staged" as mine, that I was being set up. Momo was no help, they clearly regarded him as "Uncle Tom" at a Ku Klux Klan party.

The Serb female interpreter was called across. She was a Sarajevan girl and, for a while, the girlfriend of my first driver Dragon. We knew each other but by sight only. She could have stayed in Sarajevo but opted for the Serb cause. She is an excellent translator and scrupulously fair in her dealings with UNPROFOR. She confirmed eighty-eight students but with a big smile. I was then let in on the story.

The three buses arrived at Sierra One, the Serb checkpoint.

They were halted and checked bus by bus. The drivers were told to report to the checkpoint control room. A dirty, sparse and spartan room in what had been a roadside shop. Two soldiers and the girl got

143

onto the first bus and checked the passports of each student. The students were, at first, subdued. They had left Sarajevo on a high, they were escaping, fleeing from the shelling, the sniper fire, the hunger, the deprivation. Here for the first time since the war began, they were face-to-face with what the Sarajevo government was calling "the aggressor." The majority of them were Arabs and some were viewed by the Serbs as mercenaries, as "Mujahideen."

It was a hot day. The first bus was crowded with twenty-nine students. In the hold of the bus was the bulk of their kit, spread around them on their seats were their more valuable and their more personal possessions, including the compulsory one radio per person without which students from the Middle East seem unable to travel. There was not a lot of room for the Serbs to move but they did their job. They frightened some students, they awed others; the majority were too high on the imminence of their freedom to be intimidated.

The students in the second bus were a little more fractious. They had had a longer time in the sun to bake and were apprehensive. They had watched some problems develop with the drivers. The girl got on. The passport check was carried out. The soldiers rummaged through some of the bags. Relations were strained between the Serbs and a couple of the older students. There was some accusation of them being "Turks," although none held Turkish passports.

The third bus was the most over-crowded. The Serb team was cantankerous. There was kit everywhere and Arab students everywhere. The coach was hot, sticky, and smelly. The girl, by now, knew how many students were on the other two coaches so it was a cumulative count. She worked her way from the front of the bus to the rear seat, checking passports, adding the total. She was quicker than in the other two coaches because this one stank. As she and the soldiers reached the end of the coach, they counted the last two students, eighty-six and eighty-seven.

Next to these two, lying on the rear bench seat, was a large cardboard box.

– *What is in the box?*—one of the soldiers asked.

– *My friend*—the Arab student replied. Student number eighty-eight had died three weeks before. His fellow countrymen, believing that they were close to leaving, had decided that he was to go home with them and be buried in his homeland. They wrapped him up and kept him in their room. They had put him on the bus without the drivers' knowledge. I had happily inspected passports, counted them all on, but had not inspected the empty vehicle. The Serbs were right. There were eighty-eight students.

One of the Serb soldiers could verify this. He had insisted that the Arab opened the box. The interpreter had attempted to intervene. Her nose told her what her eyes did not need to see. Big brave Serb managed to hold his vomit until he had left the coach. The Serb commander summarised my problem. I needed to get to Kiseljak quickly. I had to find three coaches and arrange for the transportation of eighty-eight students, eighty-seven living and one dead, from Kiseljak to Split. The circus of the early morning had moved to comic opera.

Kiseljak was in Bosnian Government hands. Momo was not brave or foolish enough to come with me. Only the special Brane risked his life crossing front lines with me.

I therefore moved off to Kiseljak. In doing so, I made a great error of judgement. My mind was on the students. Time was precious. I needed to hire drivers, coaches, and get the students away before dark if I was not to have the problem of trying to accommodate eighty-eight Arabs in Kiseljak. In my haste, I left behind the three drivers—three Muslim drivers, one of whom was accused of the murder of the brother of a Serb soldier. I left them behind in a Serb stronghold. So simply are nightmares foaled.

I arranged for the Sarajevo coaches to stop at the warehouse in Kiseljak used by UNHCR. When I arrived, the students were all standing around their coaches. As I got out of my vehicle, quite unexpectedly, they broke into a great round of applause. Many came across and hugged me. They felt free and safe. This threw me a little, as we had only fought half the battle. I called together a group of the student leaders. I asked them about the extra passenger. They were not at all contrite. They felt they had a duty to take him home. I explained to them that I would try to arrange other coaches. I almost said fresh coaches.

145

This proved to be a challenge. I went to the bus company and saw the manager. Kiseljak is a small town. He knew the story, but not all the story. He knew that he had a captive audience. He wanted two hundred dollars a coach. If I agreed quickly, he could find drivers and they could leave this evening. I did not have that sort of money. I promised him that I would return the next day with the cash, but he was adamant—cash now. I understood, he had to buy fuel and pay the drivers, and in a war zone, everyone wants money "up front," as they say.

I went back to the leaders and explained that we needed money. They were incensed. They had paid in Sarajevo, and they could see no reason why they should pay twice. At times, refugee work can be unrewarding. I patiently explained that without money, they were going nowhere. One of the leaders was most reasonable. He explained to me that many of the students genuinely did not have any money. They intended throwing themselves on the mercy of the embassies when in Split. So much for their assurances earlier in the day. I lined them all up. Told them that I needed two hundred dollars a coach. After a debate, it was agreed that we could squeeze everyone on two coaches. So, the demand was for four hundred dollars. I led the way, I put in all I had, a mere twenty dollars, an emergency note I had in my back pocket in case I came upon any shops selling wine. After a lot of murmuring, we raised just under three hundred and sixty dollars.

I went back to the bus company. The manager agreed to do it with two coaches for three hundred and sixty, providing I would do him a favour. His family was in Sarajevo, and he wished me to take a parcel of food to them. I agreed, and still knew something he did not know. One of the passengers needed more room than the others. We agreed that the coaches would arrive at five. I returned to the students. They were very happy. We unloaded all the bags and the box and waited.

When the two Croat coaches arrived, I met the drivers. They wanted an UNPROFOR escort to Split. I explained that this was impossible. I agreed to contact both UNPROFOR and the European Monitors ECMM and warn them that they were on their way. It was then load-up time. I asked the students' leaders to put their recumbent colleague in the luggage hold. This we managed to do unobtrusively without the driver being aware. However, when the rest of the students came to put their kit in the hold there was not enough room. So out he came. I was standing next to the driver when opera comique became opera bouffe. The students were struggling with the box trying to get it up the steps and into the coach.

– *What the hell is that?*—asked the driver.

Everyone looked at me. *A box*—I replied. Then he caught the smell of it.

– *It stinks*—he said. *What is in it?*

Riddle time—*What is six-foot long, two feet wide, and stinks?*—Riddles do not translate easily.

– *I am not taking that*—said the driver—*Get it off*—Off it went. I told the driver that I would go and sort things out with the manager. At his office, I met him heartily and asked him if he had the parcel ready for me. He did. It was an enormous box; tins, fresh fruit and vegetables, cooked meats and three or four bottles of spirits. We loaded it into my car. There was a letter with it. I took the precaution of taking the letter out of the box and put it in my pocket.

As I was leaving, I asked him if he would come around to the coaches as one of his drivers was refusing to take one of the passengers. He came immediately, and I watched as he began to remonstrate with his driver. After a second or two he turned and looked in my direction and laughed and laughed and laughed. I had a Croat with a sense of humour. The driver was still not happy. I asked the manager if he had any other suggestions. If the driver refused to take the body with him, did he have any ideas as to what he could with it? Was there a "left luggage" office or anywhere we could leave it? The driver now began to see the funny side and eventually agreed to take it.

The students insisted that he travel in the coach on the back seat. By this time, I was fed up with the whole saga. I told the students that when they got to Split, the late student would travel in the aircraft hold back to his home. He would not be permitted to travel on the bloody aircraft seats. The driver also had had enough. He wanted to

147

get away. The box travelled passenger class.

I took my farewell of the students and was impressed that they were all very concerned for the safety of the drivers who had been arrested by the Serbs.

Throughout most of the afternoon, Jim O'Neil had been around and about giving support and assistance. He could easily have left me on my own and returned early to Sarajevo, but that is not Jim's style. Despite the delays, the confusion, and the chaos, Jim was determined that we see the whole task through together. I really appreciated this and we set off for Sarajevo together. Me in the lead in my armoured Range Rover, Jim following in his soft skinned Land Cruiser. My own troubles were just about to begin.

At the Croat checkpoint we were very rarely stopped and checked. This evening we were. I was confident, I opened the back, they hardly looked in. But I realised that, in addition to the bus manager's parcel, by swapping vehicles because of the shortage of fuel, I now had with me all my kit for Gorazde. I was going to need a bit of luck at the Serb checkpoint.

The Croat's gave Jim's vehicle a going over. He had boxes of UNI-CEF children's clothing, T-shirts, hats, and the like. Jim gave the usual reply that they were for the children of Sarajevo regardless of race, class or creed, and on we went.

We arrived back at the Serb checkpoint. Momo was waiting for me where I had left him. So were many of his colleagues. Two in particular. I recognised them as Ministry of the Interior—hoods, threatening hoods. They were waiting for me. They demanded to search the vehicle. I told them "NO." They could look in but they were not rummaging through my possessions. Often, I was bloody minded for the sake of the principle, today I was genuinely concerned. By having swapped vehicles I had no idea what was in mine.

I called Momo over and reminded him that we had come into Serb territory to facilitate the passage of the convoy, which they had agreed that I had left Serb territory at their request to organise the coaches. The contents of the vehicles were as at this morning. I had no intention of permitting a search of the vehicle.

148

Jim watched fascinated as I did a little war dance. They lost interest in his vehicle. One of the Ministry of the Interior men pushed me away from my vehicle and a soldier removed the bus manager's box. Their eyes lit up with this. I was now genuinely furious. I pulled away my vehicle from the Secret policeman—a little runt of a man. I slammed the doors of the car. The contrast between white beard and red cheeks must have been alarming. I felt that I was close to bursting a blood vessel. One soldier removed my briefcase from the far side of the car and was about to remove letters from it when I assaulted him. At this stage, they decided that I was under arrest. The Sarajevan translator was embarrassed at the hassle I was giving. She advised me to quietly agree to follow their car to the police station—*Either that or they will throw you in theirs.*

I got into my car with Momo, locked the doors and the windows, and followed the police car. Momo was very upset and ashamed. I noticed that the ever-faithful Jim followed. They were happy for him to return to Sarajevo but he would not.

Whilst we were stopped at the checkpoint, we heard a lot of shells falling on Ilidza. When we arrived at the police station there was a lot of noise. The shells were landing not too far away.

I thought about not leaving the car. This would certainly embarrass them. They would have a hell of a job trying to break in. However, I had Momo inside with me. Locking him in with me would be a real test to his Serb loyalty. So I let him out, got out myself, locked the car, and followed my escort. I shouted to Jim that because of the shelling he should go on to Sarajevo. He replied that he would wait.

And wait he did. I followed the girl into the police station, and was led through the door, down to the area of the cells. There we awaited the arrival of an investigator. He was a tall, gaunt, pre-war professional. He spoke exceedingly quietly. I had to strain to hear him. He was courteous and determined. He told me that in my briefcase there were letters addressed to Gorazde. He wanted them.

He was right. Before I attempt to enter any besieged area, I let it be known that I am prepared to take in mail. If I am successful, the

149

news I bring in is often the first for many months. The morale boost by exchanging mail is immeasurable. The mail in my briefcase was however special in that it had been given to me to hand to the Mayor of Gorazde. In my opinion, he was as entitled to mail as anyone. All mail that we take in we examine carefully. We do not take parcels, we do not even accept bulky letters.

Back to the investigation. I had in my briefcase mail for the Mayor of Gorazde. All I had to do was hand it over, and I could go. I politely told the investigator that if he had mail for anyone in Gorazde, I would happily take it and that rest assured, once he gave it to me, it would be either delivered or returned. He smiled.

Meanwhile, outside, the shelling intensified. Poor Jim was still sitting in his soft skinned vehicle, his ears ringing and the ground shaking. Jim decided on action. He marched up to the desk and asked if he too could be arrested. He reckoned that it would be safer than sitting outside. His request was turned down.

Inside, I am told that the investigator has to leave. If I give him the mail then I may leave. If I do not, I remain. I asked them to prepare a place for the night, but I remind them that I am a UN official and that a formal complaint will be made. The quiet investigator reminds me that I am a neutral UN official, not a Muslim postman.

Touché!

He left the room. The girl is not sure what is going to happen next. We sit and wait. The investigator returns. He is sorry, but I have to hand over the mail. If the mail is innocent, then I will be released immediately. If it is not, I may be held as a spy.

Ouch!

I have an idea. I propose to him that I return to Sarajevo with Momo and the mail and that we take it to the Bosnian Muslim Liaison Officer together. There, it is opened in our presence. If it contains anything nefarious, then Momo reports it and the Serbs report me to the UN, and I am labelled whatever they believe is appropriate. The girl thinks that this is a great idea. The investigator thinks it is childish. He leaves the room.

I am once again fed up. When he returns it is contrasting colour time. Red face on white beard. The investigator is genuinely shocked by this outburst. He attempts to reason with me in a voice quieter than before. I actually am genuinely annoyed, mainly with myself.

He may have guessed this because he then summarised the day's events and outlined my failings. I had attempted to smuggle a body out of Sarajevo. I had attempted to smuggle food and drink into Sarajevo. I had attempted to smuggle mail into Gorazde. I was a senior representative of a United Nations Agency. Was this the conduct they could expect from me?

This man was twisting the blade.

He then said that I could go. No more mention of mail, no nothing, just go. Outside it is dark. It is very noisy. Jim is sitting patiently in his soft skinned vehicle. He tells me that he is glad to see me. He is not half as glad to see me as I am to see him. We have a quick debate. Shall we ask the Serbs for accommodation or do we risk a quick dash back to Sarajevo. There would be a certain pleasure in demanding a bed for the night on my terms, but to be frank, I am at a low ebb and whenever that is the case, there is no bed like home, wherever home is and however so humble.

Momo, by now thoroughly embarrassed, sits in with me, and with Jim on our tail, we set off for Sarajevo at breakneck speed, no lights, no stopping. Ten breathless minutes later we are back in the PTT. My arrival is reported to General Razak. He asks me to give him a full briefing. The Bosnian Government is furious about the arrest of the drivers. He has Adnan with him. I recount the day. The General promises to see Dr. Karadzic the following day to obtain the release of the drivers.

But the circus turned to tragedy. The drivers were never seen again.

Nine

Spoils of War, Casualties of Peace

"It's a small world" is a trite expression, but it is often proved to be true. Enesa and Aris Sparavalo had a beautiful daughter, Ana. When the baby was very young, she was diagnosed as having a heart problem. In the very early days of the war, Enesa got herself and Ana away, first to Slovenia and then to England. They were sent by the immigration authorities to Bourne End in Berkshire, where they lived next door to the parents of one of my closest friends. It was impossible for Enesa to keep in touch with her husband. The normal telephone lines between Sarajevo and the rest of the world were down. My friend is a man of great initiative and large heart. He contacted my wife in Salisbury. She was able to contact me by satellite phone. She asked me if I knew how to contact a family called the Sparavalos. Standing next to me in the office was Amira, she saw me writing the name down and said—*I know the Sparavalos, they are friends of mine.*

Two coincidences. Small world.

My wife passed messages to me. I gave them to Amira, she passed them on to Aris. The news was always good. Ana was happy and strong. Enesa lived with a wonderful family. The man of the house idolised Ana, and Ana looked upon him as her grandfather. Ana was awaiting an operation at the Royal Brompton Hospital.

The demand for fuel for Sarajevo, be it coal, diesel, wood, or whatever else burns and produces energy, was a constant nightmare. The media could never understand why we were not able to bring in at least sufficient fuel for the generators in the hospitals.

The answer was simple—the Serbs refused. They believed that if fuel was brought in, it would be used by the Government to support the war machine. They very carefully monitored the amount of fuel brought in by UNPROFOR for its own use. We, the civilian arm of the UN, were the poor relations. We had to beg from the UN military for our domestic fuel. The military did allocate a small amount of its fuel to the Bosnian Government hospitals. I discussed with my masters in Zagreb and with the Bosnian Serbs ways of funding and transporting sufficient fuel to keep the vital functions going.

The Bosnian Serb attitude was simple.

"If you bring in fuel for the Muslims, you must bring in fuel for us." This sounded fair until you looked at it. Firstly, the Bosnian Serbs were getting plenty of fuel from Serbia, which itself was blockaded but with sieve-like barriers. Secondly, no Bosnian Serb town was besieged. UNHCR was therefore very reluctant to spend money on fuel for Bosnian Serbs as a bribe to permit vital humanitarian fuel into Sarajevo. There was a justifiable element of "What will the donor nations say? What will the media say?"

To make matters worse, the Croat community in Sarajevo were offered fuel by their fellow Croats in Croatia. Tanker loads of it, in Split, and all that was needed was approval to bring it in. The Croats were clever—they knew that an offer of fuel for Croats only in a besieged multi-ethnic city would not go down well with the city fathers and would also alienate the other communities. So the Croats sent Anton Rill, the son of a famous Croat family, a well-respected man in his own right, to ask if I could negotiate into Sarajevo "fuel for aged priests and the hospitals." The first reaction of the Government was—*How can you do this for the Croats when you cannot do it for us? – Look, this is an exploratory request*—I replied—*If I pull it off, will you let it in and let the aged priests have at least some of it? – Maybe.*

I then went to see the Serbs. As usual, their answer was predictable— *What is in it for us?* Anticipating this, Anton and I had discussed the "availability" of ten per cent for "aged Serb priests and Serb hospitals." With a number of "ifs" and "maybes" still outstanding, Anton began to order a tanker load of fuel. But this tanker, if it arrived, would be a drop in the ocean of the needs of Sarajevo.

Meanwhile, the Bosnian Government exerted extreme pressure on UNHCR to produce fuel. On almost a daily basis they contacted the UNHCR office to inform us how many patients had died on the operating table because of a lack of fuel, especially for lighting the operating theatre after periods of heavy shelling. They demanded that we provide fuel for them. I knew that it would only be a matter of time before they came up with a Croat type proposal, so I quietly started to do my homework.

The Bosnian Minister responsible for fuel and energy was Rusmir Mahmutcehajic. In addition to his jaw cracking name, he had the strange title of Minister for Energetics. He is a small dark man who possesses a formidable intellect. He has a fiery temper and a short fuse. He has a serious problem with his eyesight which he hides well. It is obvious only when greeting him. You extend your hand, he extends his, but you have to find his as he cannot see yours. His secretary is his eyes. She is also his ears. She sits in an outer office where visitors wait and where she understands English, especially indiscreet comments. Her total loyalty to the Minister is unquestionable. She is his wife.

I was first summoned to see the Minister on a very cold day. The ministry is in the centre of town in a narrow street. I drove myself and had Meliha with me. We parked on the corner of the street and walked to the office entrance in an old building. There was a policeman outside with the inevitable gun. The building was freezing cold. We went up the stairs, turned right, and we could smell the warmth. Unbelievably, this little corner of the building was heated. Not excessively, but enough to be able to stay and work in.

I met Mrs. Mahmutcehajic, and the deputy to the minister whom I had previously seen in my office. They asked me to wait, as the Minister was on the phone. The phones rarely worked, so when they did, he was taking full advantage. Through the wall I could hear him, he was not happy with whoever was on the other end. With each sentence his voice raised. His voice was deep and resonant. He was warming the ears of someone. *Would you like me to come back?*—I politely asked his wife. She is a fair haired and attractive woman with a pale face, bright eyes, and a friendly smile.

– *No. No*—She then entered his office, without knocking.

– *Meliha, what is the conversation about?*

– *I can only hear half of it. He is angry.*

Sometimes I wondered why I had an interpreter. But before I could probe further, the door opened and the Minister was gently guided towards me by his wife. She is taller than him. He welcomed me profusely. He had a conversation with Meliha, I am certain in order to establish how open he could be with me. Old habits die hard. He took his seat at the desk, which was at the head of a long conference table. He began immediately and brusquely.

— *Mr. Larry, we have many tonnes of fuel in Split in Croatia. I want you to bring it into Sarajevo*—This had the tone of déjà écouté.

— *Minister, your request should be simple, but unfortunately the Serbs will not allow the fuel in*—This triggered a tirade. The minister gave me a lecture on the charter of the United Nations, the sovereignty of Bosnia-Herzegovina, the mandate of UNPROFOR, and the needs of the people.

— *Fully understood, Minister. But no Serb approval, no fuel.*

— *Why does it depend on the Serbs?*—he asked in a menacing tone.

— *Because minister, so far, they have won the war. You are not besieging Pale, they are besieging Sarajevo.* The minister did not like this. But I continued—*So if you want fuel in, you, or more accurately, we, have to do some deal with the Serbs.* I expected apoplexy. But Rusmir Mahmutcehajic is a solver of problems.

— *What do you think they will want?*

— *I know exactly what they want. They want forty per cent. They will permit a convoy of five vehicles, three for Sarajevo, two for them*—My homework visit to Pale was beginning to pay off.

— *That is too much. We cannot agree to give them that much of our fuel.*

— *Dr. Lukic who, as you know, believes that he is the Prime Minister of Srpska Republika, tells me that the fuel in Split was paid for with money which belongs to Serbs as well as Croats and dare I say it, Muslims. He says it is Bosnian money and a share of anything it purchases must go to the Serbs.*

— *If we agree*—said the minister—*how does the fuel get here and what happens to it when it arrives?* Two crucial and complicated questions.

— *Well minister, UNHCR is prepared to hire a tanker, and we have the strong possibility of the loan of a fuel tanker from the British Army contingent in Split.*

156

– *We also have tankers in Sarajevo and in Split*—said the minister—*I offer them to you.*

– *Excellent. Are they fit for the journey and can we paint them white?*

– *No problem, we can also provide drivers. What about my second question, the distribution of the fuel?*

– *Minister, when the fuel leaves Split it will become UNHCR property, it will come into the city, be stored and distributed under our auspices.*

– *Where will you store it?*

– *We will park the tankers at the airport in a secure location*—We both smiled. He knew that UNHCR had lost at least half a dozen trucks to shellfire at the airport. A fully laden tanker would surely earn a Serb mortarman bonus points.

– *We have underground fuel tanks in the city, why can you not store it there?*

– *Because if it is not under our direct control you will issue it to the Army.*

– *You do not trust us?*

– *Correct*—I then added—*Correct, Sir*—for courtesy. At this, he looked at me coldly.

– *To whom will it be issued?*—The correctness of "to whom" suddenly made me realise that so far this conversation had been held in English.

– *We will issue it according to priorities drawn up by you. We would hope that the hospital and the bakery will be the top priority.*

– *And any fuel that goes to the Serbs. How do you control that?*

– *Easy. We insist that the fuel comes into the airport from where we issue their share. Same priorities*—The minister had heard enough.

– *OK. I will speak to Split. My deputy will liaise with you. Thank you for your cooperation.* That was the end of the subject of fuel for the day. He then changed topics—*Mr. Larry, I have heard that you are keen on art. Do you know the work of Dzevad Hozo?*

– *The lithographer*—I replied. Rusmir was pleased.

– *Yes. Have you met him?*

– *No.*

– *Then I will arrange a meeting.* I found his hand, shook it, and we left. Both of us had much work to do if this conversation was to lead

157

to the arrival of fuel in Sarajevo.

The Brits had indeed offered a tanker and more.

On the most recent of her frequent visits, Glynne Evans, realising how understaffed UNHCR was, suggested that she speak with the British contingent commander, Brigadier Alastair Cumming, to see if he could assist. As ever, with Glynne, within days of the conversation, there was action.

The Commanding Officer of the Logistic Battalion Lt. Col. Malcolm Wood, an old friend of mine, arrived in Sarajevo from his headquarters in Tomislavgrad in Central Bosnia. He listened to my tale of woe and promised the use of a tanker and, more importantly, the loan of a logistic team.

At this time, the only Brit in uniform in Sarajevo was the Chief of the United Nations Military Observers. The Brits had their own sector, with bases in Split, Tomislavgrad, and Vitez. Sarajevo was not part of it. So, although a team was promised, there were a number of turf problems to be sorted out. Would the French, whose sector Sarajevo was, allow Brits to operate in the city? Who would "command" the Brits? There were also a few UNHCR questions. Will they be in uniform? Will they be armed? Who will they report to?

The team arrived on reconnaissance, in uniform and with weapons. Malcolm Wood, as expected, has chosen the best. An interesting team, commanded by Captain Peter Jones, included Don Hodgson, a Warrant Officer from the REME, Alan Knight, a Staff Sergeant from RLC, and surprise, surprise, a woman from the Adjutant General's Corps, Caroline Cove.

In a quiet efficient way, they were to transform our operation. It was agreed that Don would run fuel, Caroline and Alan, the warehouse. Peter would keep an eye on both tasks but would concentrate on the distribution of aid. I briefed "Don the Fuel" on my talks with the Minister and took him to meet his deputy.

Rusmir Mahmutcehajic was pleased with the speed of response. True, there was no fuel, but he could see that we had a fuel expert on the ground. He invited myself and Meliha to have tea with him, his wife, and the artist Dzevad Hozo. The venue was to be the artist's house. We agreed to meet outside the Presidential building.

We arrived a little late. Despite the danger from shelling, the minister was waiting in his car. His wife was with him, and he was driven by his bodyguard.

The artist lives in a house on a very attractive small estate on one of the hills in Sarajevo. The road is narrow and the artist's house is at the top. We arrived as darkness was falling. The minister left his car quickly, and his bodyguard ushered him rapidly to the house. I could see as I parked the UNHCR vehicle that the front of the house was overlooked by a hill which must have been in Serb hands. Hence the speed and caution.

There were cars parked in the road. Some looked OK, others had been victims of the war. I parked off the road facing the hill and noted that we would have to go back the way we had arrived. The top of the hill went nowhere.

The artist and his wife were marvellous hosts. I was always embarrassed when people who had so little were so generous.

The house was small, crowded, and very much an artist's home. The room used for entertainment was up a flight of stairs and was lit by candles. We had a super evening. Good food and wide ranging, provocative conversation. I also had the pleasure of seeing a lot of the work of the artist. In particular, he was assembling a book about art which was in the proof stage before the war began. The project was shelved until life could return to normal when paper, ink, printers, and publishers would be available.

With great reluctance, at around nine, Meliha and I said our farewells. I had to take her home and then get myself back to the PTT building. Dzevad kindly gave me a book about his art. Rusmir and his bodyguard escorted us down the stairs. The bodyguard opened the door, and Rusmir and I were about to shake hands when there was a burst of gunfire in our direction. The bodyguard bundled the minister back up the stairs. Meliha and I followed.

The bodyguard explained that a sniper had seen us arrive, recognised the minister, and had waited for him to reappear.

– *Just wait a minute or two, then try again, but without the minister.*

– *OK*—I agreed. After a few minutes standing in the dark behind the door the bodyguard opened it, wished us luck and out we went.
– *Move quickly and with no lights*—he said, unnecessarily.
Meliha and I moved very quickly out into the dark night and across to the car. I opened the doors. Meliha jumped in. I got in, put the key in the ignition, and paused. So far, no shooting.
I was used to driving at night in Sarajevo. Move fast. Stop. Move fast. Stop. I had parked the car off the road. The road was narrow, I did not know the road, it was very dark and there seemed to be parked cars everywhere. I sat in the car and waited. If anyone had seen us move, they would now be up in the aiming position. Wait a while, they may come out of it. After a couple of minutes, I turned the key. The engine sprang to life. I engaged reverse and the reversing light, bright and white, lit up the street.
– *Jesus, Lord!* I quickly disengaged, the light went out, and a burst of gunfire whistled over our heads. I sat and thought. My first thought was the most ridiculous—*I will get out and remove the bulb.* My second thought was to drive forward and swing around in front of the parked cars, but this was the side of a hill—the edge of which I could not see. My third thought was to see if the car would roll back. It would not. I engaged reverse, swung back like a car on a movie set and hammered off down the hill.
There were no more shots. On reflection, I believe that the sniper was after the minister. When my illuminated vehicle reversed, he fired, but then realised that it was a UN vehicle and decided against further action. I tried to persuade Meliha to return to the PTT building, where she had a bed, but she had promised her dad that she would be home. If she did not return, he would worry all night. So I took her to the end of the road near her house. It was not possible to drive her to the door. Furthermore, there was a Bosnian army checkpoint she had to pass through. At this checkpoint I asked one of the soldiers to escort her to the door. This he did whilst I waited in the vehicle to see that she got there safely. The other guard said to me—*Switch the engine off, there has been some shooting up the hill.*
– *Tell me about it*—I said.

By ten I was in bed with my new book.

Rusmir wanted fuel. Kosova Hospital in Sarajevo was forever plead-ing with us to bring in cylinders of oxygen. There were a number of problems with the request. Driving a truckload of any sort of aid in a war zone is a risky business. Driving a truckload of highly explosive cylinders of oxygen is highly risky. There are more uses for a cylinder of oxygen than just medical. It took a lot of negotiation with the Serb side before they would agree. Their terms were that oxygen cylinders must be provided for their hospitals as well. Simon Mardell of the World Health Organisation decided on the quantity needed and the split between the two sides. There was the usual hassle. The Bosnian government provided empty cylinders. The Serbs said that they did not have any. The Bosnian government refused to loan cylinders to the Serbs. The Bosnian government paid for the refilling of the cyl-inders in Zenica. They refused to pay for the filling of the Serb cyl-inders. This was all sorted out. The Serbs had the checkpoint. They dipped into the trucks and took what Simon had allocated. It took at least a month of negotiation to get the first convoy moving. Subse-quent convoys were infrequent and demanded almost as much effort as the initial one. The drivers were very brave. There was a constant demand from the doctors to increase the frequency of the convoys and the number of bottles.

The transportation of the oxygen was a small success but we were proud of it, especially as it was for the hospital.

Well, so we thought! Tony and I were in the office, Tony was sum-moned to the operations room. We had a convoy blocked at the Serb checkpoint. It contained the truck of oxygen bottles and the oxygen bottles contained gunpowder!

Tony was taken to the checkpoint. The Serbs were not annoyed but ecstatic. Since the beginning of the war they had accused us of smug-gling weapons and ammunition on behalf of the "Muslims." Now they had proof. Tony had taken with him UNPROFOR policemen. Together they were shown oxygen cylinders which, when the top was unscrewed, revealed a black powder which the Serbs said was gunpowder. They were right. In Tony's presence other cylinders were

161

opened—they too contained gunpowder.

We were furious and lost faith in a number of people. We delivered the cylinders directly to the hospital, so some of the doctors must have known what some of them contained. The pressure that they put us under to bring in more must partly have been motivated by the demand for more gunpowder. We felt betrayed. It put our reputation at risk. It put our drivers at enormous risk. Not only were they carrying oxygen through active front lines but oxygen and gunpowder. Furthermore, they could have been arrested by the Serbs.

This incident gave to the Serbs a big stick with which to beat us. It was followed by an increase in their vehicle search techniques and the constant gibe that we had smuggled ammunition to the Muslims. An accusation we could not deny.

The gunpowder plot was not the only time we knew we had been used.

The delivery of food to the areas around the airport was progressing brilliantly under the supervision of the French Battalion. In order to minimise the unloading time, which was often accompanied by shelling, the French containerised the aid, took the container on a trailer to the recipients' warehouse, and left the container and trailer to be collected on the next run. They did this in the Muslim areas of Butmir and Dobrinja and the Serb area of the airport settlements. The trucks and the containers were not specific to each area. The Muslims in Butmir who had access to ammunition from the Bosnian army quickly realised that there was a space between the base of the container and the platform of the trailer. This they filled with ammunition, mainly Kalashnikov rounds, and waited; sooner or later the trailer would end up in Dobrinja. There the container would be lifted up and the ammunition removed. If the container and trailer went to the Serb side, it made no difference. They did not know about the space, and never looked for it until one night. Tony was called again to be shown the evidence of our treachery. This time, it was the turn of the French to be furious. They were quite prepared to stop delivering aid. We persuaded them to carry on, but they were never as enthusiastic. The French liaison officers in the Muslim sectors who had risked their lives by identifying closely with their sectors particularly felt the betrayal of trust.

These were scams which were discovered. God knows what took place without us finding out. Journalists were in and out of the office. Many had with them a local translator who not only knew the language but knew who would give interviews, who wouldn't, and how to get to those that would.

Amira is an outstanding translator. Diminutive, full of energy, and with a wide circle of influential friends, she is a favourite with journalists, especially those from the international cerebral broadsheets.

The first time I met her, I did not know who she was. She breezed into my office with two Spanish reporters. Her English was excellent. All three sat in the available chairs and fired questions at me. There was an equality amongst them. I presumed that she was an international journalist.

I had just come from the dining room and had collected an apple and an orange. They were on the sandbagged windowsill behind me. As the interview came to an end the girl said—*Is the orange yours?*

– *Yes.*

– *May I have it?*

I was a little cold. I thought that she was a journalist. She would be here for a few days and then move on. We rarely had fruit. I was about to say—*No.* When I noticed that the two males were a little uncomfortable. I suddenly realised that the girl was not an international.

– *Are you Bosnian?*—I asked.

– *Yes.*

– *OK*—I said very ungraciously, and to my shame I turned, picked up the apple and the orange, and threw them towards her. She caught them and with a big smile put them in her coat pocket. Still seated, I said goodbye to them. When they had left, I thought over the incident. My attitude and action had been arrogant and ignorant. I tried to find Amira's telephone number to ring and apologise, but the phones were down.

The incident bugged and niggled me for the remainder of the day.

It was a month later before I saw her again.

– *Remember me?*—she asked.

– *Oh yes. And I owe you an apology.*

– *Let me tell you about the orange*—she said, riding straight over my reply—*I took it home and gave it to my mother. She longed for fruit. She was dying. It gave me so much pleasure to find fresh fruit for her.*

– *Look, I want to apologise for throwing the fruit at you. I should have got up and handed it to you. I'm sorry. I thought you were a cheeky, greedy, journalist.*

– *And not a starving Bosnian?*

I blushed—*How is your mother now?*

– *She died. That is why the fruit was so special. It was the last treat that I was able to provide for her.*

I have two other fond memories of Amira. I went with her to the office of Colonel Divijak, the incredibly brave Bosnian Serb who has served with the Government forces throughout the conflict. He is a pre-war officer, an outstanding leader, and a very courageous man. If the supporters of Mladic ever overrun Sarajevo, he will be one of the first men they will seek. Despite this, Colonel Divijak is a front-line leader. He is to be found in the trenches often within metres of men who would happily skin him. On this visit, we were with John F. Burns of the New York Times who is a friend of the Colonel. The vivacity of Amira and her disarming manner allowed me to bring up the subject of the oxygen bottles containing gunpowder and to express at the right level and in a civilised way my annoyance.

On the other occasion, I invited Amira—or she invited me—to the production of the musical *Hair*. The performance days depended on the density of the shelling and on the availability of sufficient electricity. It was done in a small room in the centre of Sarajevo. The cast were from the Sarajevo Theatre Company. The colours, the vibrancy, and the sheer defiance of the cast made it one of the memorable theatre events of my life. In the audience the day we went was Joan Baez, who joined the cast for a couple of numbers and Susan Sonntag, who went on to produce Waiting for Godot, an apt choice for Sarajevo. At the end of the musical, the cast invited the audience to come up and dance. Little Amira was first up and danced frenetically. The radiance of her smile and her energy could have lit and powered a second performance of the musical.

The battle for the Sarajevo suburb of Otes lit the sky day and night for four days. The drama was intense and vicious. In four days, the two square kilometres were hit with more than 14,500 shells. For four days and much of four nights, the ground shook as shell after shell pounded in. A shell every thirty seconds! The families who lived in this pretty, modern village which had the misfortune to become a strategic target, first took to the basements of their buildings. When it became clear to them that they were locked into a battle unto death and destruction, many husbands persuaded their families to attempt an escape into Sarajevo.

Many of the women, children, and elderly left by night and crossed the icy water of the River Bosna. Most survived, though some drowned. Meanwhile, their men fought on. There were many deaths. Whilst the battle raged, we in UNHCR, frequently attempted to gain access to the area to assess and to assist. We visited the Serb Army Corps headquarters in Ilidza. It was located in a large old house down a magnificent boulevard designed in the days of the Austro-Hungarian Empire, lined with huge poplar trees, which reached to the sky. In better times, carriages drawn by horses had trotted tourists up and down its length viewing the splendid houses of an earlier era, whilst en route to the nearby source of the River Bosna. More recently, it was a venue for weekend cyclists. Now the road was scratched and scarred by tank tracks and the country homes scuffed and stained by the boots of soldiers.

The Corps commander, himself a tall thin figure, handed us on to his sector commander, a long, lank, battle weary professional soldier. His eyes were rimmed with grey-black circles caused by the lack of sleep. His neck was bandaged, wounded in a recent battle. His office had been a small bedroom. The bed had gone but the heavy furniture ingrained with polish applied by generations of maidservants remained. He had recently been visited by the French battalion commander, his calling card, a box of six bottles of red wine, stood on the side table.

– *What do you want?*—he asked.

– *To enter Otes*—translated Vesna.

– *What is your name?*—he asked her. She told him—*Vesna Stancic.* Both her Christian and surname are Serb. *Where are you from? Who was your father?*—He wanted to know if she was Serb—*What was the maiden name of your mother?*—He wanted to know how Serb she was. Satisfied that she is Serb-Serb, he relaxed—*What does he want to go to Otes for?*

– *To see if he can help the families in there.*

– *Does he think the war will stop for him?*

– *No.*

– *Come back tomorrow—the battle will be over.*

That night the noise eased. The following morning we returned. Three of us. Myself, Vesna and the Chief of the UN Military Observers, Lt. Col. Richard Maule, a British Army officer who had taken the job over from a gung ho, exceedingly brave and excessively caring New Zealander, Lt. Col. Richard Grey. The Brit led equally as successfully but by calm example.

The sector commander agreed to see us. I placed my single Johnny Walker card next to the still untouched box of wine. The commander had with him an officer, a small, sincere, chubby faced pre-war schoolteacher with warm, soft brown eyes—*He will be your guide*— The conversation was over.

As I rose to leave, I looked carefully at him. The war had turned him into a professional officer. The battle was over, he had won. But there was no elation, swagger, or bravado. He had gained ground but lost men, and the war was not over. Before we could leave, he shouted something to our guide. *What did he say?*—I asked Vesna and then looked at her for the answer. The blood had drained from her face. He said—*Do not let them see the bodies.*

We took the guide in our car from Ilidza to Otes. As we passed under the bridge which had separated the two districts, we met a large group of soldiers. They were returning from looting the houses. They had boxes, bundles, prams full of household items, televisions, videos, and pictures. One stopped and hung up on the wall of the bridge a magnificent head of a wild boar.

They were not embarrassed by our presence. These were the spoils of war. Our guide, however, was.

– *Look at them. Look at that one.* He pointed to a young man with a pigtail—*He thinks he is Rambo, but he is a tourist.*

– *A tourist?*—I asked.

– *Look at his eyes. Look at mine. He has not been here fighting over the past days.* I looked. The eyes of Rambo were bright, alert and laughing. Our guides' were sad. Deep pools of sadness.

– *Did you lose many troops?*

– *Too many. We underestimated their ability and their resolve. I think we lost more than they did.*

We left the car at the entrance of the village and walked. We first saw a small block of apartments. The ground floor had shops. The walls, windows, and doors had been shattered by heavy gunfire and the stock stripped by looters. The floors above were like a doll's house. The outer wall—the complete front wall of the building—had fallen away, pulverised by tank shells. The rooms were open to view. Beds with linen, tables with cloths, and chairs with cushions stood open to the elements. Water gushed from wash basins and toilets and fractured pipes.

Our guide let us wander. We went down a street of small detached houses. There were groups of civilians, mainly older couples, going from house to house, looting.

– *What is going on here?*—I asked.

– *These are people who have returned to collect their possessions from their damaged homes.* Our guide replied inventively. The civilian looters did look guilty as we watched them. I suspect they were the parents of the front-line troops and were getting the first pick of this war harvest.

We wandered along the interconnecting network of trenches built by the defenders. Deep, narrow burrows leading from street to street. Bodies lay where they had fallen. Some from each side not yet collected. One was close to where we stood—a young man. He was lying against the wall of the trench as if he were standing. His face was turned towards us, his eyes were open, his skin was a strange dark green. I hate looking at bodies when I know that the next of kin have not been informed of the death. The knowledge alienates you from them and in some strange way allies you with the body. I dwelt too long for Vesna. She gently tugged on my sleeve.

— *Where are the civilians?*—I asked.

— *Gone.*

— *Gone where?*

— *Some left during the fighting. Others have left now. Some to Sarajevo, others to Kiseljak.*

— *Where are the bodies you are not allowed to show us?*

— *They are in different corners.*

— *Are they civilians?*

— *Yes.*

— *Why can we not see them?*

— *Because the commander said 'No'.*

— *But why? Are they mutilated?*

— *No, they are just bodies.*

— *Women and children?*

— *Some.*

We walked back to our vehicle. I was not going to press this man to see bodies. They had cleaned the area up. They had gathered together the bodies. My seeing them was not going to alter the world. *Come and look in the Bosnian army headquarters*—said our guide. We went into a ground floor room of a well-protected building. It had been a military headquarters. Maps, pencils, manuals, and UNHCR aid stacked to the ceiling.

— *That is what happens to your aid. It goes to the army.*

— *I am sorry my weary friend, but I do not buy your self-righteousness. When we issue aid to your side in Rajlovac, it is stored in a military warehouse. It is distributed on military trucks.*

Back at the car, I took a last look at Otes. It was a bright, crisp December day. This time last year it had been Otes with Christmas in the air. Now, it was still, almost silent Otes, just the sounds of trickling water, and creaking, squeaking carts laden with goods stolen from the dead and the dispossessed. We passed the bridge under the beaded eye of the boar's head. Dropped off our host, thanked the commander, and left. I slowly realised that I had no animosity towards them. I knew that if Otes had defeated Ilidza the carts would have tumbled in the opposite direction.

I received a message to meet the Brit Hercules. There are some parcels on board for me. I am very excited. Even more so when the plane lands. There is a large box and four sacks. The box is wrapped in Harrods paper. Like a squirrel, I collect my goodies and race back to my bed space. I open the box. It contains a Father Christmas outfit, minus the beard. The sacks are full of toys. It is all from Harrods. The Al Fayed brothers have donated them to be given to children at Christmas. A really spontaneous and generous gesture. Peter Kessler and I hand them out over Christmas to the children's wards in the hospitals. Well done, Harrods. By the way, I still have your suit.

From England, I received news that little Ana was now in the Royal Brompton Hospital which had agreed to waive the fourteen thousand pounds cost of the operation normally charged to overseas patients. As is the custom of this outstanding hospital, Enesa was allowed to stay close to her daughter. Aris eagerly awaited news. Little Ana had the operation and began to recover. Being a very pretty little Bosnian refugee, she was the darling of the ward. The surgeons were pleased with her progress.

I then received a phone call.

– *Larry, I have just had a phone call from Enesa. Ana is dead.* My eyes filled with tears. I felt numb and cold. I had never met Enesa. I had never met Ana and I hardly knew Aris. But I felt part of the family.

I asked Amira to send a car to the flat of Aris and to bring him in to see me. I rang the hospital and was put through to the children's ward. The sister was very pleased to hear me. They were at a loss. Enesa was alone. There were many private questions to be answered. They had asked Enesa where her husband was and where she wanted to go. "Sarajevo," was the answer to both.

There were many practical questions. What was to happen to the body of Ana?

– Let me talk to Enesa—I asked. She came to the phone. I was her link with home in this her loneliest hour.

– Enesa. I am so sorry about Ana. I have sent a car for Aris. He will be here soon. When he arrives, I will tell him what has happened, and then I will ring you and you and he can speak.

A soft, stunned—*Thank you.*

– Enesa, you need people around you now. Have you informed the couple with whom you live?

– Yes. They are coming here.

Then thinking very clearly and bravely she asked me—*What will happen now to Ana and myself?* The question had already run through my mind.

– Enesa, I am sure that I could arrange for you and Ana to fly back to Sarajevo. I do not think that would be right. I am sure that I can arrange for Aris to come to England so that you may...—I fumbled for a word —*...look after Ana together. Just think about it and discuss it with Aris when he arrives.*

– Thank you.

Aris arrived. He had not been told. I met him in the corridor of the busy, scruffy, chaotic PTT building. He looked so vulnerable. His face was grey, his eyes tired. He looked at me as if I had a way of influencing the news that he was about to hear. As if I could make the news better.

Amira translated for me. I put my arms around him and held him to me as he sobbed. I left him with Amira for a few minutes so that she could console him in his own language. Then I returned.

– Aris, I am going to ring England now and put you in touch with Enesa. You must be very strong. She is there alone. She will want to know what is happening to herself and to Ana. I must therefore ask you some insensitive questions so that we can help Enesa.

– I understand. I confirmed that he would want Ana to be buried and I explained to him my thoughts on where.

– Aris, I believe that you should go to England. You have suffered enough here. Think it over whilst I ring England.

170

I rang the hospital and put them in touch with each other. Amira kept everyone else out of the office. They spoke for a long time. From where I stood, it was obvious that Enesa was the stronger of the two. But Aris had endured six more months of war. Aris finished the conversation and we then spoke.

– *I would like to go to England.*

– No problem—I replied, lying heavily. I rang the British Ambassador in Zagreb, Mr. Sparrow, and explained the situation. He was marvellous. Understanding, kind and considerate, he promised to have a visa for England waiting at Zagreb airport for Aris.

So far, so good.

I rang the hospital to see how things were and to keep them in the picture. The Bourne End family had arrived and were with Enesa. I spoke to them. We talked about the arrangements so far. I then spoke again to Enesa. She is emotionally very strong.

– *I have one worry*—she said—*the funeral will be expensive. We have no money.*

– *Leave that to me*—I replied. I asked to speak to the Bourne End family and we discussed the cost of funerals. The cost of dying in the Stockbroker belt is as expensive as the cost of living.

I then had a brilliant idea. Jeremy Bowen, the BBC journalist who was with me, had returned to London. His producer Vin Ray had gone back with him. I rang the Beeb. Jeremy was out, but Vin was in. I explained the problem. *Leave it to me*—he said. UNHCR got Aris on the next British Hercules to Zagreb where he was met by Mike Aitcheson, the UNHCR airlift chief, and a man from the British Embassy. Aris was given a visa and moved on to England.

Little Ana was buried in a plot provided free by the Wooburn Green cemetery. The funeral was paid for by F. G. Pymm and Son of Maidenhead—a remarkable company whose policy is not to charge for the funerals of children under sixteen.

At Sarajevo airport today, we have confusion with fatal results. There is a Turkish Hercules arriving. We have had them before, they are always a provocation to the Serbs, who are convinced they carry Turkish soldiers, or Mujahideen, or ammunition, or all three. When this one lands, there really is trouble. The rear door opens and twelve Turkish military rush out and form a ring of steel around the aircraft. The Hercules contains members of the Turkish Government who have come to meet members of the Bosnian Government. The Serb liaison officer is turning cartwheels. His first thoughts are that it is a Turkish invasion, he is calmed down by the Norwegian movement controllers. He complains he has not been informed. It is a provocation. It is an outrage. There is no way he can guarantee the safety of the Turks. He must inform his masters in Lukavica. We understand all of this. We have no intention of permitting the Turks to leave the airport. We contact the Bosnian Government and they know of the arrival of the aircraft. They are annoyed that the Turkish contingent cannot travel to the centre of the city. After a great debate, they agree to send vice president Dr. Hakija Turaljic to the airport to greet them and to negotiate with them. This in itself gives UNPROFOR a headache, but they agree and provide an APC from the French Marines Battalion. Dr. Turaljic, whom I know well, is a straight, upright, grey-haired engineer and a man of immense courage. He agrees to go to the airport where he meets and discusses with the Turks. There is a small piece of Bosnian skulduggery. At the airport, there is a disabled person who manages to get on board the Turkish aircraft. When Dr. Turaljic has finished talking to the Turks and the aircraft takes off, he gets back into the APC and sets off for Sarajevo along sniper alley, the most dangerous road in the city, part of which is in Serb territory. Near the turning to Ilidza on the left and Nedzarici on the right the APC is stopped by a strong Serb military presence. They have been tipped off from the airport. They say they believe that the APC contains Turks. Inside the APC is Dr. Turaljic and one French soldier. They are both worried. Travelling behind the French APC is the British Captain Peter Jones with a British armoured vehicle. He stops and offers the French robust support. Colonel Sartre, the commander of the French Marines, arrives. He talks to Dr. Turaljic and restores his confidence. He refuses the offer of assistance from Peter Jones with the rather heavy-handed reply—*This is a French show.* With great reluctance, Peter leaves with his team. The Serbs simmer down. Colonel Sartre and the Serb officer appear to have defused the situation. Somehow, someway, for some reason, the door of the APC is opened. A lone Serb soldier sprays the corner of the APC with Kalashnikov rounds. Dr. Turaljic receives many hits. The Serb officer is stunned. It was not part of the plan. He waves on the APC which races to the PTT. When I heard of the incident, I went to the French hospital in the basement. Because I know Dr. Turaljic, I push my way to the front of the gathering crowd and speak to the French surgeon. He takes me inside the basement room, which is the general ward. There I see the body of Dr. Turaljic, he has been hit by many rounds.

There is a silence in the PTT building. We are all embarrassed. How could it have happened? The Government cannot believe it. The press has a field day. The Serbs arrest the soldier and put him in jail. The General gives a press conference with Colonel Sartre in attendance. The French soldier in the APC is posted back to France. He is physically well but is better away from questioning tongues. The bloodstained APC is washed down and transferred out of Sarajevo. It is jinxed. No one wants to sit in it.

Ten

Zepa, the Long Way Round

Of all the convoys that I did, the one that gave me the most satisfaction was to the small, intimate village of Zepa.

Zepa is a village at the bottom of a steep valley. The valley is dotted with small groups of houses all dependent on Zepa for direction and support. The nearest town is Rogatica, the nearest city Gorazde. Zepa is almost unique in ex-Yugoslavia. Because of its location and the tenacity of its occupants, it alone during the Second World War managed to keep the invading Germans out. Not a single German soldier entered Zepa. Convoys and patrols often entered the valley, but their vehicles were blocked on the narrow twisting roads by obstacles natural and unnatural, and they were easily and accurately picked off by sniper fire as they attempted to recover their vehicles.

As the Bosnian war progressed, Muslims from Rogatica fled to Zepa or Gorazde and Serbs from Zepa and Gorazde to Rogatica. Blood was spilt on both sides. Outlying and isolated groups of houses were attacked and burned. The Zepa valley was encircled, Serb forces prevented the access of vehicles and more than ten thousand people were besieged.

The Tuesday meetings with the Sarajevo government described an ever increasingly depressing scene within Zepa. The media had heard a rumour that conditions were so desperate, some had turned to cannibalism to survive. I was determined to get there. I bombarded Pale with requests. I pleaded with all my Serb friends.

– *Come on, what difference does it make to your great war plan if I get one convoy into Zepa? I'll just take medicine. Just one convoy, once.*

After the usual delays and rejections, I eventually got a tentative—*Yes*. HCR Zagreb, Tony Land, and UNPROFOR all swung into action. The escort was to be Ukrainian, the drivers from the joint Belgian Netherlands battalion base in Pancevo near Belgrade. Risto Tervahauta from the World Health Organisation would accompany me. Risto, a world expert on cold weather survival, also ran his own hospital in Finland. Coughs, colds, haemorrhoids, piles, heart attacks, and major and minor surgery were all his daily fare. A good man to take to a clinic performing major war operations without anaesthetic.

As the roads were covered in snow and ice, the French volunteered a recovery truck and a heavy vehicle with a snow plough blade, which I was delighted to accept. My driver and interpreter was to be an engineering graduate, Predrag Blagojevic—Pepe—a quiet, polite, tall, handsome, and laconic Serb, who I am convinced was cured of a stutter as a child by speaking to the beat of a metronome. His conversations were preceded with a pause as he tensioned his stomach muscles, he would then fire off staccato sentences, like the chatter of a hot machine gun. When translating, he would never look in the eye of either party. He bowed his head, paused, shifted his weight from foot to foot, appeared to balance word against word and then delivered his translation, like a philosophy don or a divorce lawyer.

The press were interested. The dean of the corps on this trip was John F. Burns of the New York Times.

We left the PTT building at quarter of seven on Friday the 15th of January and arrived there for a seven thirty start. The French were lined up and ready to go by seven. The Ukrainian escort was nowhere to be seen. I used the French ops room to contact them. They had not left their barracks. I spoke to the Ukrainian duty officer in the PTT. He was not as concerned as I felt he should be, so I quietly reminded him of the UN mandate and the reason why he was there—to support the humanitarian effort. Fifteen minutes later, I informed his senior that this particular convoy was to attempt to relieve an area besieged for ten months. Finally, I spoke to the Commanding Officer, an old Afghan hand, who was later to be wounded in Sarajevo.

– *Colonel, I have no doubt that you know that your troops are to escort the convoy to Zepa, which has been besieged for ten months. I am aware that, as the occupants of Zepa have waited ten months, another hour or two makes little difference. However, as I have the press corps with me, I wonder if you could be so kind as to tell me what time your idle troops will arrive, so that I may inform the media.*

I then relayed the same message to the Chief of Staff of BH command, the Ukrainian Colonel Bezrouchenko, an outstanding officer. The unprofessional escort eventually arrived at a quarter to nine, and we left immediately after I had berated the officer in charge through the second in command, Captain Boris, who spoke excellent English. Why the hell we ever feared these people for forty years I will never know.

At Pale, we met with the convoy, which had arrived the night before from Belgrade. The commander was a small and thin Belgian captain. He looked like a young boy, but in a quiet way, he had the total respect of his soldiers. We moved on to Rogatica and arrived there at midday.

The Serb military commander for Rogatica is Major Radomir Furtula. He is an ex-Yugoslav National Army regular officer. He is about thirty-eight, open faced, dark haired, and slightly portly. He is a decent man and probably an honourable man, but he is caught up amongst soldiers of fortune, profiteers, and gangsters. Examining his conscience later in life may be a bitter experience for him. His home village is just outside Gorazde, so he is a local boy. He went to school with the leaders of the community in Zepa and in Gorazde. His home is in Muslim hands, and he worries if it still stands, who lives in it, or if he will ever see it again. And, because he is a sensitive man, he worries whether his old neighbours will understand what he is doing now. I like Furtula.

Our convoy contains two truckloads of medicine. The local doctor, Radomir Bojovic, a civilian now in uniform, is to inspect the medicine. I know him from Gorazde convoys. A doctor of the hypocritic oath—a medical pretender—he is small, officious, and bumptious. He is also a man with a nervous giggle. I have long ago learned to beware of men who giggle under pressure. He begins with the first vehicle. I am hoping that he will accept the vehicle manifest, which states the number of cartons of medicine. Not this practitioner of medicine, he wishes to open the cartons.

— *What the hell are you doing?*—I ask him as politely as I can in the circumstances.

— *Firstly, ensuring that there is only medicine in the cartons and, sec-*

ondly, that the box contains only that which is on the manifest.

– Doc, each box contains medicine for Zepa, for a clinic which has grown into a hospital, which has no drugs. I wanted to add—*because you have besieged it*—but it is, as yet, too early in the proceedings for me to be rude. I must keep some powder dry for a possible final volley. The doc and his henchmen, some brutish soldiers whom I have clashed with before and whom are storing up their scorecard, waiting for the day when they can collect, ignore me.

WHO Dr. Risto gets the task of supervising the "medical inspection." The task stretches his faith in fellow doctors but then he has not been tainted, nay, discoloured, no, stained, by racism. It goes badly. The doctor finds some boxes which have more tablets than they should have, even some boxes which contain items substituted for brand names not available at the time of dispatch. Sadly, initiative in the medical warehouse in Copenhagen is not appreciated by this warrior doctor in Rogatica. His eyes gleam, his giggle increases. He wants to confiscate the non-manifested items. Now, I want to make it clear here that I am not being anti-Serb or excessively cynical but this is a deliberate attempt to hinder the passage of vital life-saving drugs to a desperate medical team serving a hideously deprived community. I know that the people of Rogatica are short of medicine. I know that this doctor is short of medicine himself. I approach him—

Doc, I have given you medicine. On every trip through here I have told you, if you want medicine, I will bring you what I can, based on needs, not on desire. At no price will I go along with your covetous eyes. More importantly, I will not be robbed by you.

Poor Pepe, his verbal machine gun jams.

– Mr. Larry, do you really want me to translate "I will not be robbed by you?" They will not like it.

– Pepe—My eyebrows are raised, my voice stentorian. Pepe concentrates on his diaphragm and translates. He is right. They do not like it.

For revenge, they open every box and put the excesses and the substitutes to one side for confiscation.

After much hassle and a large waste of valuable daylight, the paper qualified healer clears the convoy for Zepa. Patient Risto negotiates a division of the spoils: some for Zepa, some for Rogatica, and some to be collected on the way out. If the Serb medicine man ever applies for post grad training in generous Finland, I suspect Risto will have him blackballed.

Furtula has hidden during this blot on Serb humanity.

With the convoy now ready to roll, nothing untoward having been discovered during the inspection of the food carrying vehicles, he reappears. There is a small dispute over the two French vehicles, especially the one with the snow blade. Neither are on the convoy list approved by Pale, but Furtula agrees to let them go. He provides an escort vehicle to the Serb front line at Borike. I am feeling confident. Pepe is not—*Mr. Larry, the Serb soldiers are looking forward to you meeting Captain Kusic in Borike.*

The road to Borike twists and turns, the steep, steely blue mountain is on the left and the deep valley on the right. We pass isolated houses, some burned, some shell damaged, some untouched. After a few kilometres, we round a bend and the road is blocked by a barrier. To the right of the barrier, there is a small hut. I stop the convoy. It is late in the afternoon, if I am to proceed with any safety, I need no delay here. The escort vehicle disappears. I get out of my vehicle with Pepe. The man on the barrier is a simple soldier, aged about fifty. He looks at us as if we have come from the moon.

– *Convoy for Zepa.*

– *For where?*

– *For Zepa.*

– *Zepa?*—he says, unbelievingly.

– *Tell him to get his commander*—I wearily ask Pepe. The poor soldier is now surrounded by the press.

– *What is the score Larry?*—Reuters TV asks me. For a brief moment, I wonder if I should say—*I do not know. I have just arrived here myself*—But I do not. *This gentleman is going to get his commander to lift the barrier so that we can proceed*—I lie.

Pepe tells the poor, hapless soldier that he had better get Captain Kusic. The soldier disappeared into the little hut, which I now notice

179

has a chimney puffing dark grey smoke which indicates a stove and maybe hot water, even a cup of coffee.

– *Pepe, come with me.*

The hut was small and contained one bed and two chairs but was dominated by a stove with a faulty joint radiating heat and billowing curling smoke. There are three soldiers in the hut. They are local men, in for the duration of the war. Our arrival has thrown them, and they are worried. They do not welcome us in the hut, as they want to have a conversation on the phone without us being present. They ask us to wait outside. I pause before I agree, my first thoughts are—*I wonder what would happen if I just lift the barrier and wave the convoy through. These guys are scared. They do not know what to do. I am sure that they would not fire on us.* Caution then overtakes my thoughts—*Is the road ahead mined? Are there more alert, better led troops in the hills or the village ahead of us?* Then the cop-out—*When the local commander comes, he will wave us through anyway, we have approval.*

The journalists are milling around the barrier.

– *Do you think we will get through, Larry?*

– *I'm sure we will.*

– *No, not you, us journalists?*

– *Ah, that my friends, I do not know. But we will, all, stick to the same story. We all have permission from Mladic. It is good PR for the Serb side.*

A green Yugoslav army jeep arrives from a village on the other side of the barrier. It stops at the barrier and the first man out is a small, round, unshaven man with a Zapata moustache. I recognise him as the Borike commander Captain Rajko Kusic. He is carrying a weapon, but he probably doesn't need it, for he is quickly followed out of the vehicle by two bodyguards. One looks normal, the other is the classic image of a Chetnik—the Serb mountain fighter.

He is medium height with long, dark, straight hair and a raven black full beard. On his head he wears one of those upturned boat keel shaped hats, the Shapka. His eyes are like shiny black olives. He is carrying a heavy machine gun and crossed over his square chest are two bandoliers of brass cased bullets. He wears a thick leather belt from which hangs a long sheathed knife. He moves to the side of his leader. The soldier who was initially at the barrier, quickly briefs Zapata. I move forward to introduce myself and my task. I have to force my way through journalists who believe it is their show.

– *Commander. It is good to see you*—I have my hand outstretched.

– *Mr. Larry*—He replies with a slight smile, as he shakes my hand. His eyes are bright.

– *Hello*—I say to the walking armoury who is by his side. I offer my hand. He moves half a pace forward, takes my hand in his and attempts to crush it with a vice-like grip. Fortunately, I have a firm grip myself and I have been caught out by these macho masonic-like competitions before, so when I offer my hand I widen my palm and try to lock my thumb against his thumb. If these hand crushers can take just your fingers or, worse still, the lower joints of your fingers, they can drop you to your knees. We square off. I look not just into his eyes but into his soul. I am slightly taller than him. Our faces are separated by no more than ten inches. I can smell him. Peripherally, I can see the shining bullets and I am aware that, in order to shake hands, he has transferred the heavy machine gun into his left hand and has the butt pressed against his side by his elbow and forearm. I hold my gaze until he breaks eye contact. This he accompanies with a slight body shuffle. I can see that I have an enemy. Kusic and the other bodyguard sense the outcome of the confrontation and seem to be amused. Pepe, I can tell, is worried.

I release the hood's hand and turn to Kusic—*Commander, I have brought the convoy for Zepa. As you know, it has been inspected in Ro-gatica. It is getting late. I want to move before it is dark. Please have your men remove the barrier and guide us on the road to Zepa.* Kusic looks pained, as if he has a naughty child in front of him.

– *The way to Zepa is dangerous. There are reports of fighting on the road. At the moment, it is not safe for you to go there.*

– *Commander, the convoy has approval, it has been inspected, we were permitted to leave Rogatica. I intend taking the convoy there tonight.* Poor Pepe. He recognises the anger in my voice and attempts to convey the message and the tone. Rambo, the bodyguard, repeats the al-

181

most imperceptible body shuffle. It is a twitch, a tremor in his upper body. It is enough to make Pepe move back slightly. Kusic is crafty. He changes the subject.

– *Who are all these people?*—he asks pointing to the notebooks, the pencils, the cameras, both still and TV.

– *John Burns, New York Times*—says the Pulitzer prize winner seizing the initiative from his unruly colleagues. *Can the convoy go forward?*—he continues.

– *Who gave the journalists permission to be here?*—Kusic asks me. A clever way of changing the subject and attempting to make me feel guilty.

– *We have approval from Pale*—says Burns, pulling from beneath his coat an accreditation card. This is like a signal from the Chairman of the Magic Circle, accreditation cards are produced with a flourish from the pockets, the chests, the necks, of his acolytes. Most correspondents have their cards on a chain around their necks, these ID discs are the dog tags of journalists. The cards are therefore extended only for a quick viewing. Just as well, as many are out of date, many forged, and some very spurious. Why fashion magazines and canine newspapers should have a Bosnia correspondent I never could work out. Kusic has achieved his aim. More of my time and, more importantly, daylight time, is being wasted. The journalists are keen to impress him. They know that only he stands between them and Zepa. There is a babel of sound as their translators vie for the ear of the Commander. They are a Press corps, but a corps of individuals with an eggshell thin veneer of loyalty to each other.

– *Please Captain Kusic, let us all go through, if we can't, then at least let me. Nice, kind, friendly, insistent me*—seems to be the message. This show is slipping away from me. Time for a little initiative.

– *Commander may we go to the office?*—I ask pointing to the hut near the barrier. Kusic agrees. Pepe, myself, the Commander and Rambo head for the hut. It is crowded. The Ukrainian officers have been much quicker off the mark. They are crowded around the stove. They are handing around slices from a huge sausage they have brought, and in return they have been given a bottle of slivovica. I would be pleased if I knew that this initiative was to win over the locals in order to further our immediate advancement, but I am certain that the Ukrainians have decided that it is too late to move forward and are negotiating the best option for the night. Kusic is delighted to see them. There is a rapport between the Serbs and the Ukrainians. They have enough common words to keep a conversation going, and they share the same attitudes to communism and orthodoxy. I am now attempting to run a three-ring circus. The convoy, the press and the escort. The hut is too crowded, so I steer Kusic outside.

– *I want this convoy moving now.*

– *There is no approval for the press*—replies Kusic very calmly—*They must leave.*

– *It is the convoy that is important, but I think you are making a mistake. If you send away some of the best reporters in the world, you will receive bad publicity. If you let them accompany the convoy, you will get good publicity for letting them go forward. If they find that conditions in Zepa have been exaggerated by the amateur radio, the Bosnian cause will receive adverse publicity.*

Like many local commanders, his reply was simple—*We do not care what the press say.*

– *Why don't you just allow a pool of reporters? Or just one to represent them all?*

Then another standard local commander statement—*The orders are no press*—I have my own battles to fight and I'm fed up with this one.

– *So do I go forward or not?*

– *I am waiting for orders.* I left him and briefed the press. They were upon him in seconds, each pleading their cause. The interpreter with a TV company thought he had been clever; he asked the Ukrainians to negotiate on his behalf.

The light was failing fast. Kusic was both flattered and irritated by the attention he was receiving. He was surrounded by the press when I asked once again to raise the barrier.

– *The convoy cannot go forward tonight.*

Ah. "Tonight." A key word. That meant hope for tomorrow. And once again, as it was dark and the unknown lay before me, I was

183

in truth happy to park up and begin again at dawn. Then came the punch line.

– *So you will have to leave here and go back and return tomorrow.*

– *I am sorry commander. The convoy cannot return. It is too late*— Rajko Kusic then upped the stakes.

– *You cannot stay here. There are bandits. I cannot guarantee your safety.*

– *Too right there are bandits*—I thought to myself—*and you sir are the leader of them.* But, on an isolated hill, with the shared responsibility for a fair number of lives, I felt that the truth may be just a little too provocative.

– *Then let me go forward.*

– *Impossible*—It is now dark. So let us add a new ingredient.

– *Commander, the road is very narrow. I cannot turn the convoy round. It must stay here.* I am determined that the convoy will stay. If I agree to go back, where do we go back to? Me to Sarajevo? The trucks to Belgrade? What happens tomorrow, a new inspection? The approval for the convoy is for today. Tomorrow they can tell us we have no approval.

– *It cannot stay here.*

– *Then it must go forward.*

– *It has no permission to go forward.*

– *Then it must stay here.*

– *It cannot stay here.* This could go on all night, which would at least achieve my aim. But Pepe, reading the vibes, quietly tells me that I have gone too far.

– *Commander, I cannot go forward, you are right* (this is said with great sincerity). *I cannot go back* (pause). *I cannot stay here* (resignation). *Tell me, Commander, what can I do?* Over to you Pepe. At this moment, I also catch the eye of John Burns. He is close to laughter which may not help matters.

– *The press must leave now*—says the good Captain. Which implies that the rest of us may stay. An admirable face-saving non-decision. Well done, Captain.

– *Thank you, Commander*—I say, losing not a moment to cement the agreement.

184

– Sorry boys—I said to the press, then over to brief Dirk. *We are here for the night.* Next the Ukrainian commander—he already has his boots and socks off and is preparing for the night.

The press stay and plead their cause until they have totally exhausted the patience of Kusic. The great John F. Burns is one of the last to leave.

– I am off to Pale to get approval. See you tomorrow. Good luck.

Kusic then came to see me.

– I want all the drivers and crews to stand by their vehicles and to show me their identity cards.

– OK.

Dirk gave the order and his men lined up. Kusic and his soldiers then walked the length of the convoy checking each soldier. They looked at the identity card, at the face of the soldier, and at the list approved by Pale. My first thoughts were that he was just making sure that all the journalists had gone. Poor naive me. He reached the last two vehicles—the French recovery vehicle and the truck with the snow plough. They are not on the approved convoy list. They were offered as a bonus and I had gratefully accepted them.

– Mr. Larry, what are these vehicles?

– Snow plough and recovery vehicle, Commander.

– But they are not on the list!

– Quite right. I offer my humblest apologies. They were included at the last minute because of the road conditions.

– But they are not on the list—Kusic is using his "Got you by the testicles" voice. Rambo is twitching, imperceptibly but ecstatically.

We have reached yet again the part I hate. The temptation is to say—

Look, you little pillock, I have here a convoy which has to go through ice and snow on tracks not used for months. I need a snow plough and a recovery vehicle. I need one. I have one. And I am taking them with me. But he knows all of this. He is there to stop or at least delay the convoy. His credibility, in the eyes of both his seniors and his subordinates, is at stake. Furthermore, in the old communist days, if you turned up without the correct paperwork, you were sent back. So it is: grin and bear it.

— *Commander, you are once again right. The vehicles are not on the convoy paperwork but (time for a little fib) they are approved. When it was realised that the roads were so bad, we contacted Pale and asked for approval. They gave it verbally. If you can contact Pale, they will tell you that they are approved.* Kusic shakes his head.

— *They must go back.*

Stalling tactics time—*OK, but it is too late now. They can return tomorrow.*

— *OK.*

The French who are fired with enthusiasm for reaching Zepa are delighted. I am optimistic that Kusic will allow them to go, Pepe is not. As we walked back to the barrier Kusic began a strange conversation.

— *The Muslim commander in Zepa is an old colleague of mine. I was his pupil on a military course. His name is Avdo. He is a good man. I want you to give him a message from me. Tell him that I will not attack Zepa. In return, he must not attack us.*

— *Commander, why not write him a letter and I will deliver it personally to him?*

— *Good idea*—This was a different Kusic. Reflective, deep, and sincere. At the barrier he smiled, we shook hands, and he went into the hut.

I returned to my vehicle to prepare for the night.

In the good old days of touristy Yugoslavia, the bleak but rolling hills around the village of Borike were an attraction for horse riders. Some visitors may well have pitched their tents or parked their caravans where we were now laagered. But today, we were near a front line. It was isolated. We were in a Serb stronghold, the home of Rambo and his friends, and we had a convoy with attractive items destined for the very Muslims whom local propaganda blamed for a catalogue of evil. The Ukrainians, our escort, did not fill me with confidence. But they were cavorting with the local troops, which is better than antagonising them. Dirk briefed his boys for minimum movement and posted sentries, correctly assessing our "escort." It was a black, moonless night, and the nearby hilltop loomed like a dark monster. Sleep would bring security.

What followed was a bitter cold night—minus seventeen degrees Celsius. After a quick tour of the convoy and a little sip with the Ukrainians, it was time for a wee. Another case of grin and bear it, then into the vehicle and, removing only my boots, into the sleeping bag. Sleep came slowly and in snatches. The night was long, quiet, and very cold.

As dawn broke, Dirk had his soldiers up and about. We had to wait until eight before Kusic returned. The bastard was adamant that the French vehicles had to go back. Arguing with him was delaying the start. So, most reluctantly, I agreed. The French were very unhappy and disappointed with me.

I asked Kusic to provide me with an escort or guide up to the Zepa road, but he refused. He ordered the barrier to be raised and the convoy moved forward.

– OK Pepe?—I asked. There was a pensive pause before he replied.

– OK, Mr. Larry—was the apprehensive reply. I never give the bravery of these translators enough credit. I have been pushing and stretching the courage of Pepe with the Serbs. That in itself is a test. The Serbs do not like what I ask him to do and say, they do not like the fact that a Serb works for the UN.

Now I am about to stretch his courage further. I am about to take Serb Pepe into ten-month besieged Zepa, a Bosnian Muslim enclave. They cannot know that Pepe is a Yugoslav, a Bosnian. They may see him as one of those Serbs who have held them up, shelled them, raped them, and murdered them. I looked at Pepe—pensive, apprehensive Pepe—and I gently touched his arm. Sometimes the best sentences contain no words.

I hope he realised how much I admired him.

The road from Borike to Zepa is well defined on the map but not clear on the ground, especially when it is, in fact, a track and is carpeted white with snow. We moved down the hill to deserted Borike Village and swung left. The map indicated a few kilometres before we took a right turn. There were some Serbs in the wooded hill rising to our left. I could see no one ahead or to our right. The convoy was moving very slowly. The track was no wider than one vehicle.

187

In the Ukrainian lead APC, the commander was looking back to me for direction. To the right of the road, at a distance of about one hundred metres and running parallel to it, there was a snow and ice-covered riverbed. Beyond this rose a steep sided hill. After moving for about ten minutes, I could see many of the convoy vehicles stretched out behind me. My vehicle passed the hill to our right. The track was then bordered by a small open plain rising to more hills in the middle distance. Suddenly, there was a burst of machine gun fire. The Ukrainian APC stopped. The whole convoy came to a halt. The machine gun was joined by the "crack crack" of individual rifle fire.

As the convoy had just started, out and I knew that we were some distance from Zepa and still in Serb territory, I was not as alert as I should have been. I got out of my vehicle and took cover behind it. Risto was quicker than me. He was out but assessing the situation.

It's outgoing—he said, meaning that the rounds were not coming in our direction. Dirk had left his vehicle and joined me. I now switched on and realised that four of our vehicles were exposed—two trucks, Dirk's vehicle, and mine—and that Risto was right. There was a lot of noise. Many rounds were flying but not in our direction.

Just then, Kusic arrived in his vehicle. He swung in front of mine. He was furious. Pepe translated.

– *You idiot!*—he said to me—*What are you doing here?*

– *I...*

– *You are killing my soldiers and risking your own!*

I was still crouched behind my vehicle when I replied—*You let me move along this road. It's the road to Zepa.*

– *It is not the road you have approval for. You have missed the turn, and the Muslims are attacking.*

– *Where is the turning off then?*

– *Too late, too late, you must now go back. Some of my men are dead. You cannot go forward.* The gunfire increased. Kusic continued to hassle me.

– *Just leave us alone*—I said to Kusic.

– *Larry, I must get my vehicles into cover*—said Dirk. The track was too narrow for a vehicle to turn on. The snow was so deep it was not possible to delineate the sides. Nor was it possible to reverse rapidly. Ahead, about fifty metres into the firing zone, was a track to the left. Dirk spoke to each of his drivers in the two trucks which were exposed.

He calmly walked in front of the first truck, guided it around his and my vehicle and led it to the highly exposed track junction. Here he supervised the reversing of the truck. This brave action he repeated with the leading four trucks thus giving his second in command time and space to reverse and turn the others under cover. During this action, the sound of gunfire intensified. It was impossible to know if the Serbs were firing at nothing just to scare us or whether they had located a party from Zepa and were keeping them away from us. This lack of knowledge made the brave actions of Dirk even more courageous.

Eventually, the convoy was facing Borike, from where we had set out. Kusic was alongside my vehicle and shouting that we must go back to Rogatica—...*until the Muslim attack is over.*

I was not buying this suggestion at all.

—*Where should we have gone, which track should we have taken?* He pointed to a narrow track off to the left. A small vehicle had recently disturbed the snow and left its tyre marks. The track seemed to cross a stream and then rise quite steeply for fifty or so metres. It then disappeared around to the left of the hill.

— *OK*—I said to Kusic—*I am taking this track.* He argued but not as forcefully as I expected. I realised that he had either received orders to let us advance or he had a surprise waiting for us somewhere on route.

The track was extremely narrow, the snow was deep, and there was ice. The APC, my vehicle, and Dirk's swung around the turn to the left with ease, but we were then into a sharp "S" bend and on a steep slope. Our wheels spun and the vehicles slewed, but we made it to the brow of the hill. Not so the first truck. It spun its wheels deep into the snow and ice on the "S" bend.

Dirk and I left our vehicles and went back. Dirk ordered chains on tyres for all those vehicles which carried them. Fitting chains to any vehicle is not easy, and fitting them to trucks up to their axles in snow and ice is time consuming, skin scraping, oath-issuing work. The heavy chains are taken out of the coarse sacks, laid on the ground near the wheels, and then the struggle commences. The vehicle is moved either back or forward so that the tyre moves onto the chain. Not easy when the wheels are spinning, the vehicle is sliding, and the hands are numbed with cold. Once on, the chains must be pulled tight, a job demanding brute force and determination, as spinning wheels shed loose chains with speed and anger. A chain thrown by a wheel can stun or maim.

Even with chains, the ascent up this, the first incline of our journey, was slow. Kusic could well wave us on, and he must have enjoyed it. I cursed him for not letting us have the snow plough. I cursed myself for not fighting him over it. I wanted to save minutes, now I was likely to waste hours.

At the brow of the hill I was surprised to find a crossroads with a few houses. The houses were inhabited by Serbs, as we were still in Serb territory. Kusic could have escorted us this far if he had wanted. The occupants of the houses were old and friendly. They waved and smiled.

Beyond the houses, the track dropped away down a long persistent decline. There was nothing on either side of the track, the wind pushed and sucked snow from the hills on one side and deposited it on the other. The descent was fun. The APC slipped and slid, but the little military jeep was fine, and my Land Cruiser covered large sections without any guidance from Pepe. The trucks made progress, sometimes bunched together as one came to sudden halt, sometimes hundreds of metres apart. I left the progress of the convoy to Dirk, who, I am sure, cursed both Kusic and myself for the loss of the snow plough.

After a couple of kilometres, we came to another sharp bend with a clearly visible but unused track off to the right. Was this the way to Zepa?

We stopped. It was eerily calm and quiet. Risto and I decided to walk and follow the track to the left before we explored the turning to the right. We were deep in snow, and ahead the track disappeared. On our right was the beginning of a dense pine wood. Huge, slim pine trees, with pencil point tops and circular bases. The branches ended a metre or two from the snow line, the whole cone of the branches of the tree laden with fresh, pure snow.

There were no vehicle tracks, no footprints. Were there mines or trip wires under the virgin snow? There was no way of telling. The convoy arrived vehicle by vehicle and parked behind the APC. Risto, Pepe, and I decided to check the track to the left. We walked into the woods in a single file. We found a set of footprints which wove their way in and out the trees and never led onto the track. These we followed. They led to a huge barrier. Felled trees blocked the track. We carefully walked to the edges of the barrier and found wires leading into the snow. Wires do not grow in woods. They led somewhere, probably to anti-personnel mines.

We retraced our steps back to the vehicle where I radioed in to Tony Land in Sarajevo. I told him about the tree felled barrier and the mines. There was a pause from his end.

– *Larry, are the trees Serb trees or Muslim trees?* Risto and Pepe laughed.

– *Tony, am I now some sort of ethnic dendrologist?*

Tony praised the intelligence of my backside and asked directly—*Are you in Serb or Bosnian territory?*

In truth, Tony had hit on my number one problem. From the moment that we had turned left after turning the convoy around, we were not able to follow the map. The track we had used was not on the map. I could not therefore pinpoint our position. I did not know where we were.

– *Tony, we are on the front line*—I said positively. A reply vague enough to permit Tony to brief the press.

Risto and I walked into the wood. There were no tracks, there was no sign of anyone. The snow was so thick its carpet could cover all sorts of hazards. Do we go ahead, left, right? Go back? The Serbs would love that, for us to return voluntarily and unsuccessfully. I felt really down. We had come this far, right through the Serb lines, and could not find Zepa. I felt lonely and panicky.

— Come on Larry—I said to myself. I quietly cursed the Bosnians for not being here to meet me. *Risto, where the hell are we?*

Risto, in addition to being a doctor and a cold weather expert, is a Finn and therefore an ace orienteer.

— Larry, I think we are here—he said pointing to a spot on the map.

— Think we are here or know we are here?

— Larry, give me the map. I will return in half an hour and tell you exactly where we are. He then set off alone in no man's land and raced up to high spots and took bearings. Within the half hour he was back. *We are here*—he pointed out on the map. *No question. This is Boksanica wood.* Then, just to clinch his certainty—*We are now at an altitude of 1100 metres. Zepa is at five hudrend metres.*

If Risto was right, then we were half a kilometre from the track to Zepa. Somewhere ahead of us in the woods was a path which would take us to the track we would have been on if we had not been re-routed by the shooting. This path had to be wide enough and safe enough to take the convoy.

The Ukrainians, Dirk, Risto, and myself set off to find the path.

It was now the middle of the afternoon. Our first indication that Risto was right came from the Serbs. They landed a mortar bomb in the woods to our left. One lone noisy round. Its shrapnel was contained by the branches of the trees. Its only effect was to scar a few pine trees and to confirm that we were on the right track.

In case there were more rounds, we pulled back out of the clearing and, to my surprise, bumped into a three-man Serb patrol. They were hatless and lightly armed. They looked as if they were out for a stroll. They were led by a very charming man, aged about thirty. He greeted us warmly and Pepe translated—*We have been sent by Captain Kusic to ask you to withdraw. You are in great danger. The Muslims have started to shell you.* Then he came out with a lovely line—*We can no longer guarantee your safety.* At this, I have to confess, I laughed and he had the good grace to smile.

I got the map out and showed him where Risto said we were. He confirmed that Risto was right. I asked where the track was to the Zepa road.

– Just weave your way through the trees, you will hit the track.

– Is it safe?—I asked. *Are there likely to be any mines?*

– I do not know. We have never tried to go in that way. So that was why we had been sent this way—to trailblaze for a future Serb assault. If there were mines, we would find them. If we met up with the people from Zepa they would have to remove their barriers to let us in.

– How far am I from Zepa?

– If you could fly, maybe four kilometres, but by road, you are still about twenty kilometres away. But from the first Muslim village, you can only be one or two kilometres.

– If it is so close my friend, what are you doing here?

– I live around here. This is my home. I will know them, they will know me.

– Aren't you afraid they may capture you?

– Not with you here. I was touched by his confidence.

– Mr. Larry, please return to Borika and try again tomorrow. It is not safe here.

– I will discuss it with my colleagues—I rounded up the principal players.

– We are in the right place. We have made enough noise for the people of Zepa to know that we are here. If we try to advance into the woods without a Bosnian escort, we may be in trouble. Also, we have no more than ninety minutes of light left. So there are two alternatives. One. Stay the night here in no man's land and hope the Bosnians make contact. Two. Return to Borike and try again tomorrow. Comments?

The Ukrainians wanted to return to Borike. Dirk was not happy with the trucks stuck out in the open but was even more reluctant to move them under the cover of the woods because of the danger of mines. I was alone in wanting to stay. My reasons being that I hate going back, the Serbs may not let us return, and darkness would be an ally to the forces from Zepa who would find it easier to contact us in the night. In fairness, I pointed out the snag in this scenario. If the Bosnians do appear, the Serbs may attack them, and we could be stuck in the middle. I obviously painted this picture too graphically, as it produced a strong consensus to return to Borike. No sooner had we finished our pow wow than a Serb vehicle appeared with my favourite heavies. Our discussion had been purely academic, they were here to turn us round and take us back.

Turning the convoy took an age, the journey back even longer.

By the time we arrived at the outskirts of Borike, it was almost dark. There was a reception committee awaiting us. Major Furtula, Captain Kusic, the captain from Podromanija, and a number of Milicija vehicles. I stayed in my vehicle but wound the window down to speak to them.

Furtula spoke first—*You did not meet with the Muslims?*

— No.

— That is very strange.

— I will try again tomorrow.

— Yes, you can, but tonight you must return to Podromanija.

— Podromanija?! You are joking Major. I am going no further than here. We park where we parked last night, and I move off at dawn. Pepe obviously translated well as the usually calm and charming Furtula suddenly became furious. Maybe I was insulting him in front of his colleagues, maybe he felt he was losing face.

— You will do as you are told!—Now this is something I have never been very good at.

— Major, I do not like your attitude or your tone.

— You will follow these Milicija vehicles, which will escort you to Podromanija.

— I will not.

— Then I will arrest you—said Furtula. At this, Rambo moved towards my door.

— Major, I will immediately inform Geneva of your threat. A blatant lie if ever there was one. There were times when the radio could not even contact the vehicle behind me, let alone Geneva. I picked up the handset and called Sarajevo. Miraculously, Tony, through the trees, was able to receive us. I briefed him of Furtula's proposal and threat.

— OK, just sit tight. I will speak with BH command.—I looked Furtula in the eye.

— Geneva is contacting New York. Rambo was kicking our tyres. He had obviously done the short mechanics course.

194

– *Stop that at once!*—I commanded. Poor Pepe translated, making, I am sure, a mental note to emigrate as soon as possible. Rambo stopped. He spoke to Pepe.

– *What did he say?*—I asked.

– *He said that one day he wants to get you in the sights of his weapon.* Furtula then approached again.

– *Move this convoy NOW!*

– *I am awaiting instructions.*

– *I will put you under arrest.*

– *My friend, me, or all of us?*

– *All of you.* Just then the radio came to life. It was Tony.

– *It has been agreed you go to Podromanija. They are guaranteeing that you can try again tomorrow.*

– *Tony that is not the answer I wished to hear.*

– *Send me a postcard from Podromanija.* I got out of my vehicle and approached Furtula who was with his fellow officers.

– *Major, the United Nations agrees for this convoy to go to Podromanija. The Serb authorities in Pale have given their solemn word that it returns here at dawn.* We fell in behind the Serb escort and motored back through Rogatica to Podromanija. I do not know what the views were of the rest of the convoy, but as we travelled along the dark isolated roads, following the rotating blue lights of the escort vehicles, I was convinced that we would enter Zepa the next day.

At Podromanija, we were parked by the Serb police. They were very efficient. The Podromanija captain, a straight, honest man, re-affirmed that we would leave there at seven. He also told me that the Serbs could not understand why I had not met with the Muslims from Zepa. They were convinced that I would have been in Zepa tonight. *The convoy has maximum Serb cooperation*—he concluded.

I briefed the leaders and returned to my vehicle. Pepe was with two relatives from nearby Sokolac. They had recognised him on our outward journey, heard that the convoy had returned, and come to take him to their house. I was not happy and overruled it, much to Pepe's delight. He had no desire to bump into Rambo on this very dark night.

A reporter came up to me and told me that he had heard on BBC World Service that the convoy had been returned to Podromanija but would make a further attempt tomorrow. Well done Tony Land, keep the pressure on!

That night I slept very little. At first, I accepted the captain's statement that the convoy had had maximum Serb cooperation and that I had failed to get it in. I then remembered that maximum cooperation had included a little shooting and a little shelling.

What was keeping me awake was the prospect of returning to the same place tomorrow, not finding any Bosnians, and having to find a route through the snow in the woods, which was twenty kilometres from Zepa, the Serb patrol had said. I could flounder around in those woods for days. My poor little brain swirled and reeled as I held conversations with myself. If only I had the vehicle with the snow plough. I will ask for it. It is now back in Sarajevo. It will take hours to get it up here. I have made a song and dance about leaving at dawn. Better to wait and have success than go early and fail. But the Bosnians may be there. Concurrent activity. Ask Tony to get the thing on the way as early as possible, to join us en route. Rubbish, it would not arrive here before early evening, by then I am either in or back here.

Dawn broke. The Serbs were as good as their word. The convoy lined up and we left with a police escort at seven a.m. They took us to the barrier just before Borike. To Kusic's kingdom. He insisted that the convoy stopped, that all drivers stood by their vehicles and produced their identity cards. The vehicles were cursorily inspected, the barrier raised, and we were off again. This time along a road we, at least, knew. However, knowing the road did not improve the conditions.

We reached the mouth of the woods at about ten thirty. The convoy was lined up behind me. I got out of my vehicle and began to walk up the snowy slope, Risto and Pepe behind me. I said a quick prayer—*Please God, let there be some Bosnians here.*

Yesterday the woods felt empty. Today I knew they were not. There was an electric feeling. My whole body was alert and tingling. Pepe whispered—*There is someone by the tree on the left.*

I looked up and saw a stocky figure in uniform. I smiled and shouted out that we were United Nations. He stepped out into the open. I saw the blue Bosnian badge with the fleur de lys on his sleeve. He was a Bosnian. We had made contact. We looked at each other from a distance of about fifty metres. I could see that he was smiling. My own smile was warm enough to melt the snow. I felt lightheaded. Exhilarated, I moved towards him with my arm out to shake his hand. I don't know if we ran or walked to each other. We did not shake hands, he threw his arms around me, kissed me, and cried. I remember his cold, stubbly beard and his warm tears. I am sure he will remember mine. He was a great, barrel chested bear of a man. We hugged and laughed and cried.

As I came out of his embrace, I saw others stepping from behind trees. Some in uniform, most in civilian clothes. Soon there were ten or more of them. Risto, Pepe, Francois, each had his own group around him.

I took the "Bear" to my vehicle and informed Tony. I could tell that he was as excited as I was. I gave a bottle of whisky and a packet of cigarettes to the "Bear." He was like a child at Christmas. We both had a swig from the bottle, and he then put it in his trouser pocket. For the rest of the day, I saw him sharing his bottle and his cigarettes with his special friends. Whenever our eyes met his face beamed.

More and more people arrived. They had left Zepa at dawn and walked the whole way to meet us. Some had been in the woods yesterday but arrived too late to make contact with us. They were bitterly disappointed, as they thought that we would not return. But back in Zepa, they heard on the radio that we were to try again. Well done Tony for keeping the media informed!

After so long without contact, they were happy to chat and to smoke. They had had no commercial cigarettes for months. We offered cigarettes, they took them, lit them, puffed on them, and passed them around. I think they would have been happy to stay there all day, but the convoy was still twenty kilometres from the centre of Zepa.

I spoke with the "Bear." He told me that there were ten sets of barricades on the road to Zepa. All huge felled trees. The Ukrainians

197

were now in their element. They used the APCs to winch, push, and shove. Our aim was to clear a path wide enough for the convoy. Branches had to be cut, snow shovelled away. Once again, I cursed Kusic for the loss of the plough and the heavy recovery vehicle.

The main work force for this mammoth physical task had to be the men from Zepa—men who had been besieged for ten months. God bless them, they were like rakes. They were enthusiastic but so weak. It was cold, and many were in flimsy clothes. Few had boots.

Their weapons were pathetic. We had left Rambo, who looked like an arms manufacturer's Christmas tree, and joined "Dad's Army." There were hunting rifles, First World War rifles, and homemade weapons.

The military commander arrived, Avdo, the colleague of Kusic. He is a gentle, innocent man. He is unarmed and has no bodyguards. I gave him the letter from Kusic. He was really touched. It brought a little humanity to the war. He promised me that he would write a reply.

Avdo may be the commander of the troops but the true protector of Zepa is its terrain. The track is narrow and these primitive barriers, if protected by even the lightest of covering fire, would delay a Serb advance.

It takes hours to clear the route. The fitter UN soldiers and their vehicles end up doing most of the work. Reinforcement labour from Zepa continues to arrive. I marvel at their spirit. They want the convoy in for their families as quickly as possible. Their desire to assist exceeds their ability.

Amongst the new arrivals is the Mayor of Zepa. He has with him the best English speaker in Zepa, a young girl. The mayor is Benjamin Kulovac, a doctor of medicine who is the son of the doctor who is in charge of the Zepa hospital.

Benjamin has had the responsibility for the preservation of life and morale in Zepa during the ten months of the siege. He is tall and thin, painfully thin. He is bearded and has tired but bright eyes. He wants to know what we have brought. He tells me that he has 29,000 people to feed.

– Sir, I have brought ten trucks, maybe eighty tonnes. I am embarrassed. The men from Zepa are breaking down their barricades, making way for a convoy which will provide a maximum of two kilos of flour to each person after ten months of siege.

– We will give what you bring to the most vulnerable—says Benjamin with a genuine, honest smile and a warmth in his voice.

– You being here is more important than the food. He then asked about medicine and Risto is able to brief him. When he hears that we have brought anaesthetics, his eyes well up with tears. To appreciate the full significance of this I have to wait until we reach Zepa hospital.

Benjamin's translator is a beautiful girl. Her name is Denisa Kulovac, probably a relative of Benjamin. Her English is good, but she is tired and is relieved to see Pepe and give the translation task to him. She has lovely eyes and a very gentle voice, but she is weak and her face is very white, milky white. The younger women in the besieged areas often have ashen complexions. Because they menstruate, they lose blood. In a normal world this is no problem, but when food is scarce and vitamins scarcer, they soon lose their rosy cheeks. Eventually, they stop menstruating, which is traumatic for differing reasons. Some falsely believe they are pregnant; others fear they may never be pregnant.

One of the men from Zepa has brought a chainsaw. It has not worked for almost a year, as they have no fuel. We syphon some fuel from a truck and the woods are soon filled with a buzzing and a burping as this resurrected machine trims branches and cuts through tree trunks.

Eventually, we have a path through the five obstacles. The convoy sets off for our goal, Zepa itself. In my vehicle, we take with us Benjamin, his interpreter, and the "Bear" who, God bless him, is now high with excitement and awash with whisky.

The APC leads the way with at least fifteen passengers sitting on top of it. I hope that the Ukrainian officer has explained to them where the exhaust pipe is, as it is highly visible, highly touchable, and very tempting to hold onto. If they touch it, they will get a nasty burn. At night, it can glow with heat.

199

Soon we clear the woods and are on the main track. We have travelled no more than one hundred metres when we meet the first hairpin bend. The twenty-four-foot-long APC has to have two goes at getting around it. During its manoeuvring, one of the men from Zepa falls off the APC, while another, in attempting to grab him, accidentally pulls the trigger of his rifle. A lone bullet whistles through the air as the one who fell off is hauled back up. He seems none the worse for the experience. Both incidents provoke only laughter.

As we round the bend, we see a small group of houses. All the occupants are standing outside and wave and cheer as we motor past. This is the first of the forty-eight villages dotted around the Zepa valley. The view beyond the houses is spectacular and frightening. To my right and above, I can see back up the track where the first of our trucks is shunting around the bend, to my left and below, way below, is the River Zepa.

The icy road twisted and turned in a series after series of hairy bends. When halfway down, I was able to look back and see the whole convoy, each vehicle clearly pinpointed, some travelling from left to right, others from right to left. It was easy to see how Zepa kept the Germans at bay.

I am very pleased that the Ukrainian APC has wheels and is not tracked. If the Brits were escorting us, their magnificent tracked machines on this surface could easily have become thirty tonne sleds. Not a pretty sight to follow, a nightmare if they are behind you.

At long last we reached the bottom of the valley. We crossed a small bridge, then saw Zepa itself. It is a tiny one street village. First you pass the graveyard on the left, then the hospital on the right. The narrow main street was lined with the whole population. The road is so narrow we were in danger of running over their feet. The convoy was to unload at a group of buildings which stand at the end of the main street at the top of an unbelievably steep slope which was a sheet of ice. Only one vehicle at a time could unload, and then only after it had negotiated the slope. It was impossible to walk up the slope. I tried and ended up on my bottom, much to the amusement of the assembled crowd. I therefore left the marshalling and unloading to Dirk and Francois and went back to the hospital where I had dropped off Risto and Benjamin. They had already manoeuvred the medicine vehicle out of the convoy to the side of the hospital. When I arrived, Benjamin was waiting for me with his father, who before the war was the medical technician at the hospital. With them was Dr. Ibrahim Heljic whose brother, another doctor, I had met in Sarajevo. The amateur radio had broadcast horrendous reports about the hospital, and both Risto and I wanted to see for ourselves how bad it really was.

The hospital was never built as a hospital. It was a clinic. In days gone by, if anyone from Zepa was ill, it was Zepa for diagnosis and Rogatica or Gorazde for treatment.

We entered the hospital by a small door which led into a corridor, and where there used to be consulting rooms there are now wards. Outside, it was very cold, inside, it was oppressively hot. What they lacked in drugs they were trying to compensate with heat. I have learned in Bosnia a little formula, a scientific equation: Heat plus Trauma Hospitals equals Gagging Smell. Each ward contained more beds than space. Each ward had a stove—a wood burning stove—with pipes and funnels leading to ill-fitting holes in window frames. Smoke, heat haze, and the smell of putrefaction mixed and swirled and assaulted the air. The bouquet of death and fear and despair attacked the nostrils of the visitor. If under pressure, ATTACK. Anything to take your mind off the sickness lying on the stomach waiting to be thrown up, to embarrass and to shame.

– *Benjamin, how many people have died since the war began?*

– *We keep very accurate records Mr. Larry. Nine hundred and one have died in the last ten months.*

– *All from the war?*

– *No no. There is both war and civilian trauma.*

Benjamin's father, the Director of the hospital, maybe my age, handsome, fit, lined and war weary, interjected—*We have lost four hundred who have died from hunger and cold. Four hundred and thirty who have died from war trauma, war wounds, and seventy-one from diseases.*

Armed with these facts, we walk from "ward" to "ward." Images of bent and broken and bloodied people flash across my vision. Risto is a professional. He is interested. He is asking the right questions. Technical jargon, medical mumbo jumbo is being exchanged. Words I cannot distinguish. I am hanging on, hanging in..... just.

It is now dark, and in these cubicles, so speciously termed wards, lights are being lit. I am suddenly fascinated and nauseated. Fascinated because the lights are some sort of wax held in a glass container, nauseated because the pungent smell of the burning fat adds to the already noxious cocktail, which I am forced to swallow. We move to a small room. It is dominated by an old kitchen table.

– *This is our operating theatre*—says Benjamin with pride.

Attack, Larry, Attack.

– *We have heard that you have had no anaesthetics for months. Is this true?*

– *We have carried out thirty-six amputations without anaesthesia.* Oh my God!

– *Twenty-seven were major. Twenty-two legs and five arms.* I imagine myself on this table. But he has not finished.

– *Seven were children, of whom three died. We also had to try to operate on two patients with stomach complications. But we lost both of them.*

– *Show him our instruments*—says Benjamin's father.

– *OK*—says Benjamin. Whilst he got them out, his father spoke.

– *There are three doctors in the hospital, none of whom are surgeons. None of us have done any surgery since medical school. There were no medical instruments here. This is what we have.*

His son produced two scalpels and, I swear on the Bible, a carpenter's saw. A wooden handled, serrated edge saw. These instruments had carried out thirty-six operations without anaesthetics. In the nineteen nineties, a two-hour flight from London.

– *How did you calm the patient during the operation?*—Risto asked Benjamin's father.

– *It depended on the patient. If they were male, we made them drink as much alcohol as possible, mainly slivovica, if they were women, we gave them the option to have alcohol. If they were children, we gave them no alcohol.* He then added so poignantly—*That is why we lost three of the seven.*

Perhaps I dwell too much.

— Benjamin, what are your thoughts, what are the patients' thoughts, when you begin to saw? Do they scream, do they keep still?—These questions, I am sure, would have been Benjamin's ten months ago. But now, thirty-six operations down the line, he answers them a little wearily.

— We encourage the patient to shout out prayers or to scream. We have helpers who hold the patient down. We work as quickly as we can. I am stunned—speechless and stunned. I can hear the echoes of the screams which are embedded in these very walls. I can feel the first cut, the scratch, the scrape, the ripping, and the rasping.

Benjamin, sensitive Benjamin, can feel my shock, my horror.

— Mr. Larry, we do not like doing it. That is why we are so pleased that you have brought anaesthetics. Let me show you a man who must be operated on soon, a man who, if you had not arrived, would tomorrow have lay here without anaesthetic.

We left the "operating theatre" and returned to a ward. We had seen the man before, but I had made him a blur. He lay in bed with a gangrenous leg. A leg which, I am sorry, looked hideous and smelt nauseous. It was explained to him that he would be the first operation for months with anaesthetic. He looked at us and thanked us. I wondered what had given him the greater loss of sleep. The smell and the pain from his leg or the thought of the amputation.

We had spent time with the living, they now wished us to spend some time with the dead. The majority of the war victims were not buried in the graveyard near the hospital but were in a cemetery on the banks of the River Drina at a place called Slap. We motored in my vehicle ten or so kilometres. Slap is a tiny village situated where the River Zepa joins the Drina, which at this point is wide and deep bottle green.

The history of burying citizens of the Zepa valley at Slap is recent, mystic, and symbolic. The burial site is exclusively for victims of war. They are buried at the banks of the Drina in the hope that the great river will wash away from the valley the shame and the pain and the anguish of such an ignominious and unnecessary cause of death.

We arrived at dusk. We were taken to a house, or perhaps a water authorities building, where we met two civilians and a soldier. The river flowed directly past the building. One of the group pointed out his home on the water's edge a few metres away.

Slap by day is idyllic—a beauty spot, a tourist's dream, a fisherman's haven. The steep sides of the Zepa valley rise out of the dark brown banks of the deep green river. But when visiting graves on a cold winter evening, with the fading light casting long dark shadows on the rippling shimmering waves, Slap is melancholy and haunting.

There is no path to the graves. We scrambled along the narrow undulating bank of the river. At one, point centimetres from the icy water. At another, it was metres below us. The bank was slippery, our guide sure footed, though my boots were not gripping the surface. I fell behind the others and worried about sliding into the river. When I caught up with them, they were at the graves. It was like a Trappist cemetery. The path, bordered by the almost vertical hillside, had little room to spare for resting souls. The graves lay parallel to the river. Two or three side by side with little space between them. They were fresh graves. The bodies were not buried deep, a mound of moist earth covered each of them. They were there to be purified by the Drina. It could not have been closer to them. I have no doubt that tiny tributaries of this ancient river were seeping through the soil and offering nature's condolence for man's aggression.

We stayed only a few minutes—several long, soul searching minutes. Then we struggled back to the vehicle. I took one last look at this mythic place. The emerging moon was silvering the surface of the river, I half expected to see a hand rise from its depth. There are too few knights in shining armour and too many Excaliburs.

We returned to Zepa and were invited to the home of Benjamin's father which adjoined the hospital. We climbed a cement staircase and came to the front door of the flat. Everyone removed their shoes and we were invited in where we met Benjamin's mother, his fiancé Selma, who is a vivacious dentist practising as a doctor for the duration of the war, and another doctor colleague, Nijaz Stitkovac, who is with his wife and children.

Our host produced a bottle of slivovica, our hostess some bread. There was no flour in Zepa. She had made it from the floor sweepings of the barn. Offering it to us was a great honour.

It looked dark brown and wholesome; I could see ears of corn, and stalks of grass. I drank the slivo with no difficulty. I, who have eaten snails, slugs, raw fish, insects, beetles, all in the service of Her Majesty, failed to eat the bread. I took it in my mouth but could not swallow it. I gagged on it. I admitted defeat. My hostess was not surprised but nor was she amused.

– It is what I give to the children as a treat—she said gently rebuking me.

–I am sorry. But I cannot eat it. I must spit it out—And I did. Fortunately, I had brought a small stock of food, which included chocolate and whisky and, most importantly, cigarettes. We handed them over. Benjamin's father called me out of the room and onto the balcony where he had, hanging by skewers in a wire cage, long, fat slivers of dried meat. He chose a choice piece and we returned to the table. I knew that I should raise the subject of cannibalism. It would be high on the agenda of questions when I returned. My host was offering hunks of dried meat from a large stock, surely now might be the time to ask. But it is not exactly a subject which trips off the tongue.

– Ah doctor, tell me, do you eat people? Or even a light-hearted—*Doctor, there is a silly rumour that there has been some cannibalism in Zepa. Haha ha.* Instead, I settled for a very lame—*What meat is this then Benjamin?*

– Lamb—he replied.

End of subject. But just in case, I ate very little.

The star of the evening was Pepe. Shy, worried, Serb Pepe was the source of all knowledge on the war, the situation in Sarajevo and the world in general. He was delightful company.

Midway through the evening, the doctors rigged up a car battery to a radio and we listened to the nine o'clock news. World Service announced that the siege of Zepa was over and that a UN convoy was in the town.

We clinked glasses and hugged and kissed. I can honestly say it was one of the proudest and most emotional moments in my life. It brings tears to my eyes as I write.

By ten o'clock, I could take no more slivo. I told them that I was off to bed. They were most insistent that I should stay and sleep in the house, but I could see that it was already overcrowded and that there was a shortage of beds. Risto needed no persuasion. Pepe was offered accommodation with a friend. But I firmly refused, and I tottered back to the convoy. In truth, my head was spinning. Whether it was the slivo, the bread, the hospital or the anti-climax, I do not know, but I was up most of the night and was as sick as a dog. Thank God I had not accepted their hospitality. All around me there were sounds of fraternisation as the people of Zepa celebrated our arrival.

The following morning, Benjamin collected me for breakfast. Risto was looking particularly bright and chirpy. Breakfast was tea. Risto did a final tour of the hospital, gave advice on how to remove the gangrenous leg using the anaesthesia we had brought, and made a list of medicines and medical instruments needed. The doctors request-ed a book on surgery in Serbo-Croat. Risto went to a lot of trouble to get them all that they needed. I spoke to a woman who was one of thirty who had had an abortion last June. She had been raped in the early days of the war. A doctor had walked from Srebrenica with the medical instruments, assisted with the abortions and walked back.

Our final task was to syphon from the vehicles some fuel. They des-perately needed fuel for the hospital, and they had one vehicle which they used as an ambulance. The sick and the wounded from the thirty-three remaining villages were brought down to the hospital by horse and cart. One of the doctors did village calls on horseback to respond to emergencies.

Because we had been forced to leave our vehicle jerrycans in Rogatica and because of the road conditions, we were able to spare very little. Commander Avdo gave me two letters, one for Kusic and one for Furtula. With hugs and kisses and promises to return soon, we left. Back at Borike we were met by Kusic. He seemed genuinely pleased that we had been to Zepa, and he was concerned about the condi-tion of the people. He invited Risto and myself into the smoky hut.

He read the reply. It was an exchange of greetings and the assurance from Avdo that he commanded only citizens. Men who had no intention of attacking but who would defend to the last man.

In Rogatica, the convoy halted whilst we recovered the medicine and the jerrycans that the Serbs had removed. Major Furtula came and sat in our vehicle, we gave him the letter. He read it and was silent. His eyes were moist. He gently shook his head and sighed. Apparently, it was a letter from a friend to a friend. No bitterness, no blame, just a wish for peace and a return to former times.

Eleven

Interview with a General

Srebrenica, Srebrenica, Srebrenica. Every conference, every meeting, every discussion was punctuated with demands for a convoy to Srebrenica. The latest reports from the amateur radio station were quoted. They were sickening. Starvation, severe cold, lack of doctors and medicine, heavy shelling. We kept on applying to the Serbs. They refused blaming the Muslims for attacking Serb positions from within Srebrenica. General Morillon, fed up with travelling from Sarajevo to Pale, called for a meeting between General Mladic and his Bosnian counterpart General Sefer Hallilovic to discuss a cease fire. A cease fire at least long enough to permit a convoy of humanitarian aid into Srebrenica. It was to be in the conference room of the French battalion at the airport. The French battalion were the hosts. General Morillon to be in the chair. Victor Andreev the Chief of Civil Affairs on Morillon's staff to attend.

Tony Land and myself represented UNHCR. The conference was to begin at twelve. We were there by eleven forty-five. The room was laid out with four long tables forming a square. We entered the room and sat at the table on the far left. Behind us on the wall was a detailed map of Sarajevo. Petite Vesna was next to arrive, her red hair was drawn back tightly to her head. She was to translate. She was very nervous. She had not met Mladic before.

Mladic arrived on time with Misha Indic. General Morillon and Victor Andreev met him at the door. There was no sign of Hallilovic. General Mladic sat opposite us. On the wall behind him were detailed blown up photographs of the various checkpoints and French positions. Mladic removed his hat, we exchanged greetings across the table. General Morillon, Victor and Vesna sat at the table nearest to the door between our table and that of the Serb contingent. Behind them was a map of the whole of Bosnia. For fifteen minutes, we sat and drank coffee. Aides whispered messages into the ear of Morillon. There was a problem. Hallilovic was refusing to come. He wanted to send his deputy Colonel Siber. General Morillon explained to

Mladic the situation. Mladic stood up as if to leave.
- *I am a General and a commander. You are a General and a commander. We will deal with their General and their commander.* General Morillon agreed that he was right and persuaded him to sit down again. Victor Andreev left to sort it out, leaving us with Mladic. I decided on some small talk.
- *General who is your favourite author?*
- *Clausewitz, then Sun Tzu.*
- *Ah, what about generals then, who are your favourites?*
- *I have many. Some you will know, some you will not. I like Rommel and Montgomery*—he smiled. He had given me the easy ones. Next came—*the Russian Marshalls Suvarov and Zhukov. There are many.* He then turned the tables. *We have seen each other before. I have been on many military courses. Where did we meet?* I ran through my career which includes neither Staff nor War colleges. He was not impressed. But it did give me the chance to observe him. He sat at the centre of the table. His distinctive peaked hat to his right. He was square to the table. He is a broad bull of a man. His face is slightly too fleshy to be handsome. It is ruddy and moist with sweat. He has piercing steel blue eyes. His mouth is small but too full lipped to be mean. His hair is greying and en brosse, exposing two deep peaks of brown tanned scalp. His hands are small with fat fingers.
I asked him who was the most important influence in his life and his reply surprised me—*My mother. She brought me up. My father was murdered by the Ustasha. She cared for us and gave us our values.*
Whilst talking, he took an orange from a fruit bowl placed in front of him by a French soldier. Then in silence he took from his pocket a clasp knife, opened it, and began to peel the orange. He started with a surgically precise insertion at the top and ran the blade along the circumference of the skin. The orange peel came cleanly away as one long crinkly snake. I watched fascinated. I expected the orange to bleed. I realised that he had mesmerized us with this action. The room was silent and electric. I looked at Vesna. Her mouth was open and her eyes were wide. Wide with fear. Mladic went on the attack.
- *Do you like Hemingway?*—he asked me.

– *Yes, I do.*

– *You look like him.*

– *I hope I do not end up the way he did. Committing suicide at six-ty-three.* Mladic held the knife in his hand. He stared straight into my eyes.

– *You will not have to worry about that if you stay here much longer.* He closed the knife with a loud click and then laughed as his words were translated by Indic.

Hallilovic did not have the courage to face Mladic. The conference was postponed but not before we had the chance to discuss a convoy to Srebrenica.

– *General, we need to send a convoy to Srebrenica. We have discussed this before. I have tried and failed. I wish to try again.*

– *You always want to try to reach Muslims. Have you ever thought about giving aid to Serbs?*

– *That is unfair, General. We deliver aid regularly to Raylovac, to Banja Luka and to many other Serb dominated areas.*

– *But you specialise in convoys. Tell me where you have taken a convoy to a Serb town?*

– *Grbavica, Rogatica.*

– *En route to Muslim towns!* I began to notice Mladic's attitude to Vesna. At the end of a reply he looked directly at her and just percep-tibly nodded his head. When he was making the point, he concluded with "mala" which is a diminutive "little girl" of maybe "lass." But she was the instrument by which he was conversing, not the person through whom he was conversing. As his steel blue gaze fixed her, you could see her shrink away from the table. Like a mouse in the gaze of a cat.

– *OK General, tell me where there are besieged Serbs.*

– *I will tell you where you must do convoys before you enter Srebrenica.*

– *OK.*

– *You must do three convoys, the first to Slovici-Vlasenica-Han Piesak-Milici.*

I really liked that one. Han Piesak is the Serb Aldershot. Milici is where the Major made Dragon drop his trousers and made me careen around the country.

– *The second to Bratunac-Skelani-Srebrenica.* That I was happy to do.

—*The third to Kalinovik-Miljevina-Neversenje.* Another beauty. Kalinovik is the birthplace of Mladic, Neversenje, a corps headquarters.

– *Thank you General, may we do the second first?*

– *No.*

By now he had had enough. Indic was given the sign. They were on their feet. Hands were shaken. They left. The last word belonged to Tony.

– *Orange anyone?*

Vesna shuddered.

Gordana is probably thirty-eight. She lives with her father and her son in a flat very close to the Presidency. Shells fired at the Presidency which drop short of their target frequently explode close to her building. The front entrance of the block of flats is in the trajectory of one of the most dangerous sniper lanes. She is a widow; her husband was a famous television actor. She has an excellent knowledge of English. She is full of nervous energy which can be irritating to some in a city as volatile as Sarajevo. I like her. We spent a lot of time together talking about pre-war Yugoslavia, the stage and life in general.

The girls in the PTT building lived in the so-called "tower," in the offices off the main staircase. She lived in one of the top rooms, which she shared with three or four other girls. The PTT building has been hit on many occasions. Every floor has received at least one hit. The top floor has received the most.

The Ukrainian officer for whom Gordana worked was going into the city. Gordana would go with him—that would give her the chance to see her son and visit her home for a few minutes. She went to her room to put into her bag a few luxuries to take to her father and her son. Food which she had saved, for them, from her own plate.

She had just entered the room when the shell hit the base of the window frame of her room. Some of the blast went up the outer wall scorching it brown. The round tore through the wall, flew across the room and embedded itself in the wall near the door. Flying wood, glass and concrete mixed with the choking smoke. Two of the girls who lived in the next room ran in panic out of their room onto the staircase where they saw Gordana. Swaying, shocked, white and bleeding. As they ran to her, she fell. She had shrapnel in her thigh, her ankle, her wrist, and her hand. Two French legionnaires carried her down to the basement, to the French hospital.

I had heard the shell and was at the base of the stairs as they carried her down. I followed her to the casualty area. There were a lot of people. This French MASH was outstandingly efficient. Surgeons and anaesthetists were around her, so were nurses, friends, soldiers, reporters and me. The nurse removed her jeans. She was wearing tights underneath. The nurse began to remove these. Gordana was in great pain, and in shock, but she was not revealing her pants before this crowd. She looked imploringly in my direction. She clutched with her bleeding wrist the top of her tights. She resisted the nurse's attempt to remove them. A French male medic saw her actions and appreciated her position. He roughly pushed the onlookers away, including myself, and pulled screens around her.

She was operated on. Two days later she was evacuated to the American MASH in Zagreb. It could have been her ticket to freedom, but she returned to Sarajevo, to her son and her father, with a limp which may always be with her.

The father of Zlatan, my driver, had put his life savings into an attractive house in the country between Kiseljak and Visoko, not too far from Sarajevo. The house was built to his own design. There was a bedroom for each of his own children and their partner and a bedroom for his grandchildren. It was built with retirement in mind. His children and his grandchildren loved it. It was second base for them all. For Zlatan and his wife, it was a weekend escape from the rigours of the busy hospital where they were both doctors.

When old Mr. Oruc bought the plot for the house, he bought it for its beauty. It never occurred to him that Kiseljak had more Croats than Muslims or that Visoko had more Muslims than Croats. When the Bosnian war first broke out, his house was comparatively safe. It

was within range of Serb machine gun fire, but there were no artillery guns or mortars to threaten its substance. But as the conflict spilt
over and pitched Croat against Muslim, his retirement haven became
a front-line target. It lay equidistant between the land dominated by
the Croats fighting out of Kiseljak and the Muslims out of Visoko.
The Serb machine gun became a side show. Mr. Oruc fled ahead of
the heaviest fighting. He and his wife could take little with them.
The road was full of fighting patrols ready to strip and loot and rob.
He had some money in the house and was tempted to take it with
him. His wife said—*No. If we are stopped, we will lose it. We may be
killed for it.* The calm grandad crept out to his patio, lifted a paving
stone and dug the money deep into the ground. One quick tour of
the house, a peep into the bedrooms, a flood of memories. They then
left, passing the orchard so carefully planted, the trees beginning to
fruit. Muslims by name, they turned right for Visoko.

Months later, we were asked to send a small convoy from Sarajevo to
Visoko via Kiseljak. Within minutes of the request, I had a volunteer
driver, Zlatan. Nonjo agreed to go with him. The convoy passed,
with only a little hassle, through the Croat checkpoint and sped towards Visoko. It made an unscheduled halt midway between the two
towns. Zlatan and Nonjo ran through the orchard. The house was
destroyed. There was no time to linger over that. Together they lifted
the paving stone and dug away the earth. The money was where the
old man had hastily placed it. Zlatan recovered it and together they
sped back to their trucks.

A few days later, I needed to go to Visoko. I took Zlatan. Just the two
of us and the Land Cruiser. We tucked the vehicle into the gateway
of the orchard and made a more leisurely tour of the remains of his
father's dream. There was no roof to any part of the house, the central
staircase still stood. The ground floor was an uneven jagged carpet of
shattered tiles and burnt beams. We carefully picked our way up the
staircase. Zlatan pointed to where each room had been. He cursorily
searched through the debris, looking perhaps for teddy bears, photo
albums, favourite pieces. But he and his family will have to rely on
their memories. There was nothing recognisable. We went out onto

the patio to see his father's improvised but reliable safe. Machine gun bullets whistled past us. We had woken up the Serb gunner. We left. Zlatan, on behalf of the family, had exorcised the ghost.

Later, I was to find out that the house had been burned to the ground, not by Croats seeking to drive out Muslims, but by a group of Visoko bandits who had looted the house and wished to lay blame on the Croats. A bitter pill for Dr. Zlatan to swallow.

The Sparavalo family have invited me to lunch at their flat in central Sarajevo. Sasha of the Agency is to be my guide and interpreter. – *Please Mr. Larry, if you say you will go, you cannot cancel*—he warned me. We arrived at the block of flats where the Sparavalos live. The family are at the front entrance waiting to greet us.

Mr. Vjelko Sparavalo is a famous TV and stage actor. He looks the part. He is wearing an immaculate pair of slacks with a knife edge crease, a tailor-made blazer and an elegant cravat. He is tall, very handsome, with a neat moustache. Quite debonair. His wife Kira is an attractive lady, slightly taller than he is, she has close cropped hair and a neat elegant appearance. Their younger son is a student of music, tall and gangly. He looks seventeen but is twenty-two.

They are embarrassingly effusive with their welcome. We climbed the stairs to their flat. On entering, I can see that they have gone to enormous trouble. There is nothing in Sarajevo, but they have laid a table which creaks and groans with food. *I am sorry, but I could find no wine*—says Mr. Sparavalo.

I have brought with me a selection of the food available to me, it includes wine. We are all delighted. The meal and the hospitality were outstanding. Young Denis played the guitar brilliantly. I had great pleasure at looking through a photo album of the most notable performances of my host. He is desperate for the war to end so that he can return to the stage. We toasted Enesa and Aris, and then I left having had a super time.

During the Second World War, the British government issued a poster warning servicemen against discussing military affairs in public.

The slogan was "Loose talk costs lives." The peace negotiations in Bosnia were going very badly. Every five minutes, Lord Owen was heard on the radio, seen on the television with his maps of ethnic majority cantons. His proposal was rejected by the Bosnian Government, supported and rejected by the US Government, and killed by General Mladic imposing his iron will on the Pale Government.

The media wanted a comment on the post Pale situation. I was very busy but was tracked down by the BBC. In the middle of a "What is the aid situation" type interview, the smooth measured tones asked—
Apropos the rejection of the Vance Owen plan, what do you think Lord Owen should do now?

— I think he should get himself a new colouring book and a new set of crayons—I replied, surprising myself with spontaneous wit.

The BBC repeated it on the hour every hour for what seemed like days. If I walked into a room, it was always news time and there it was. If I sat in a car with someone, and they had the radio on, it was news time. An unfair remark became a trite remark. It did not please Lord Owen and it did not please my masters. I was rebuked soundly by Mr. Stoltenberg. Loose talk almost cost my UN life.

Twelve

Thoroughly Decent People, Indecent Times

Srebrenica was becoming a fixation. The nightly reports from the amateur radio were unfolding a horror story, even allowing for the inevitable and understandable exaggeration of the operator.

I had tried the two direct routes and failed. The Bosnian Government were putting tremendous pressure on us. They told us that the villages of Kamenica, Cerska and Konjevici Polje, which were to the north of Srebrenica, were in danger of falling and that if they did, their populations would move to Srebrenica, thus swelling an already intolerable situation. We therefore decided to attempt a convoy to Cerska. If at all possible, we would drop off some aid at a small village called Kamenica, if we were really lucky, we would attempt a reconnaissance into Srebrenica.

There was a grave shortage of food in Sarajevo, so the trucks and drivers would come from Belgrade from the Dutch/Belgian battalion. The French Foreign Legion was to be my escort. The press interest was confined to the intrepid Jeremy Bowen and his BBC crew, Ian Dabbs on sound, Allan on camera, and Diana—a Slovenian born, Canadian passport carrying translator. Pepe was my translator and driver. The Finnish WHO doctor Risto Tervahauta, who guided me into Zepa, was our medical expert and companion.

We were scheduled to leave Sarajevo at midday on Saturday, the thirteenth of February, but there was a fire fight between the Serbs and the government troops across the airport which delayed our departure for two hours. We did not get far. After half a kilometre, we were stopped at the first Serb checkpoint as the battle recommenced. We parked in the open for an hour as the battle raged over our heads. In Jahorina, at a crossroads near the principal site of the Sarajevo Winter Olympics, we met up with the escort and together moved on to Pale. When we arrived there, it was too late to go any further so the French parked up in a secure, fenced compound near the Serb administrative buildings. We moved on to a small "pension" recommended to us by Brane the Serb liaison officer. It is a large three-story

house owned by a fascinating two-story owner. The place has sufficient parking space at the side to permit small convoys to overnight
in safety.

The entrance is up a set of concrete stairs. The door is wood and glass
and leads to a steep staircase also concrete and uncarpeted. At the
top of the stairs there is a mini mountain of shoes, reminding the
visitor to take off his muddy footwear and put on slippers from the
stack of all shapes and sizes. This house is run by Novka Savic, a lady
who likes cleanliness. Her husband Nenad is obviously a hunter, as
the walls are covered in trophy heads and stuffed birds. He is of medium height, but barrel chested and with huge forearms, wide wrists,
massive palms and a crunching handshake. It must be part of the
curriculum at school for Bosnian boys. His open, handsome, rugged
face carries a war wound. He has lost his sight in one eye.

– *Welcome Mr. Larry, Brane has told us about you.*
– *And I have heard all about you my friend. They tell me that you are
one of the most famous hunters in the whole of ex-Yugoslavia.*
– *I used to hunt with Marshall Tito. Come with me.* He took us out
of the dining room past the shoe mountain to a staircase leading to
the bedrooms. On each of the walls on either side of the staircase was
stretched the skin of a bear. The one on the left wall was big, but the
brute on the right was enormous. He pointed to it—*The second largest bear ever shot in Yugoslavia. Shot by me.* He showed me a photo of
Tito standing over the fallen carcass of a bear—*That was the largest
ever. Shot by Tito, after we had hunted it down together.*
He produced an array of weapons, one of which had robbed the
bears of their lives. He patted the head of the larger bear and stroked
its paws which had long, thick, slate grey nails—*We came very close
to this one. It was on all fours near a bush. I took aim, pulled the trigger and hit it here.* The gun barrel touched the still visible hole in the
skin—*It reared up on its hind legs and screamed and then fell with a
thud.* The words were accompanied by the actions. The weapon was
raised, his cheek rested on the butt and the sight aligned with his eye,
the now blind eye. He copied the action of the stricken bear drawing
himself to his height and extending his arms, he mimicked its cry

and dropped his arms as the bear, vivid in his memory, collapsed to the ground.

Next to the smaller bear was the skin of some rare civet-like cat. The demise of this silver furred creature, with a thin face and pointy ears with tufts of hair sprouting from them, had taken great tracking skill. The killing was swift and silent.

Our hostess, an outstanding country style cook, produced a great spread of home cooking: soup, hams, and cakes. Our host provided bottles of slivovica. Local visitors came to see our hosts and we were joined by Jeremy Bowen and his crew. We all shared in what to us, direct from Sarajevo, was a feast. We had heard the story of the bear, there was still one more story to hear

– *Nenad, how did you lose your eye?*—I asked. He was sitting, squat and powerful, to my left at the dining table, his wife was standing behind him, she lightly placed her hand on his left shoulder, his right hand moved and covered the tips of her fingers. Mummy bear and Daddy bear.

– *Last summer, we Serbs organised a food convoy into Zepa. We had negotiated it with the Muslims. I was a driver of one of the trucks. Because we were on a humanitarian mission, I was not armed. We had just a few guards with us. It was a hot day, the windows were wound down in the cab, and even though we had negotiated approval, we knew from the moment that we entered the valley that things could go wrong. We were all tense and alert. Deep in the valley, as the convoy was spread out by the twists in the road and at its most vulnerable, the firing began. Some of the vehicles were destroyed, there was noise, flames, and screams. I got out of the vehicle to find cover. I could see our attackers; they were so close. They could see me. The bullet hit me in the face. I ran and ran. There were bodies everywhere. Fifty-nine Serbs died that day. I hid. I could hear the Muslims around me—hear them in the vehicles, hear them killing. As night fell, they left. I was bleeding, and I knew that I had been hit in the eye. In my aiming eye. Fortunately, the bleeding stopped. The pain didn't.* The hunter survived. For four days, he used his special skills to avoid capture and to move back into Serb territory.

Meanwhile, the world heard of the "massacre." All of those who had not managed to escape were presumed dead. One of the survivors who escaped had seen the hunter hit in the face and fall to the ground.

– *So you thought he was dead?*—I said to his wife.

– *Yes. There was a memorial service for them, which I attended. His death was announced on the radio and the television.* Her eyes were moist—*Then he just came back through the door. Back from the dead.* I looked at him and his eyes were moist, one bright and moist, the other dull. Later, he told Risto that he had had treatment in a Moscow hospital. He told me that he was learning to shoot left-handed. He reckoned that he was now as good a shot as the average man with his left eye. He accepted that he will never be the great hunter that he was.

In one of the bedrooms, the son of the hunter was sleeping. He was ill. Risto was asked to do a house call. He diagnosed tonsillitis and dispensed antibiotics. Baby bear.

We from Sarajevo took advantage of the bathroom, the flush loo, and the shower. I slept well.

Even though we left before seven, our hosts insisted on giving us a good breakfast. They became good friends, and I stayed with them often. They never resented our convoys to Muslim populations. They took care of us on our way into and on our way back from trips to "enemy" territory. The hunter guaranteed that our vehicles would not be touched whilst parked outside his house. They are thoroughly decent people behaving decently in bad times. I once asked them— *Do you hate Muslims?*

Novka was horrified by the question—*Not at all. We had neighbours who were Muslims, not Muslims who were neighbours.*

His reply was a little different—*Only the one.*

We joined the escort and the BBC at seven and left to meet the convoy at Zvornik. We passed through all my least favourite places, Podromanje, Sokolac, Han Piesak and through the "Valley of Death," where the danger was from wild bands of Bosnian soldiers up in the hills who sniped on anything that passed through the valley. Civilian traffic risking this route waited at either end of the valley for a

Bosnian Serb army escort, which was a bizarre vehicle, a truck armoured by welding massive steel plates onto its chassis. The truck had painted on its leading armour plate a "Skull and Crossbones"—the crew were real cowboys. They enjoyed leading the convoys down the valley. They were comparatively safe in their vehicle, though the soft skinned vehicles they escorted were much more exposed. I used the valley often but was never shot at, so I had no knowledge about how they would perform under fire. Badly I suspect—they looked a group of posers.

This day was no exception. We arrived at two o'clock without incident at the Karakaj checkpoint on the outskirts of Zvornik. We parked our vehicles just before the bridge which spans the River Drina and separates Karadzic's so called Srpska Republika from Milosovic's Serbia. The bridge is controlled by Major Vlado Dakcic, the king of the bridge, a reservist lawyer, a very tall, heavy, chubby faced man with a drooping moustache. A blubberous walrus responsible to the local authorities for the heavy traffic crossing the bridge. He controlled a police post, a customs detachment, and liaised with his true masters, the army.

I called in on his office, a tatty hut containing two desks, a telephone, one comfortable chair, and a few rickety typists' chairs.

– *Mr. Larry*—said the major, rising from the comfortable chair—*How are you? Going to Belgrade?*

– *No, my friend I am here to meet the convoy from Belgrade.*

– *There is no convoy from Belgrade here*—he said looking for approval from his colleagues, who dutifully laughed.

– *There soon will be my friend. We are on our way to Kamenica*—This seemed to bring the house down.

– *Ah, the Kamenica convoy. There is a convoy from Belgrade on the other side of the bridge Mr. Larry, perhaps it thinks it's for Kamenica*—More laughter.

The game had begun.

I always hated this bit. At the beginning, you never know how tough to be. Too tough and you blow it. They just disappear. You cannot find anyone to answer anything. Too weak and they send you away.

But it is bloody hard to smile and to shake hands and to laugh when it is all at your expense.

— *I'll go across and see if the convoy has arrived and return later.*

— *Sorry Mr. Larry, but you cannot do that.*

— *Why?*

— *You have no approval to enter Serbia, and if they refuse to let you in, you have no approval to come back into Srpska Republika, you may have to live on the bridge.* More laughter accompanied this threat. This was going to be a difficult mission. However, the immediate problem was solved by the arrival of the single jeep of the Belgian commander. I went across to meet him.

— *Captain Dirk Van Bruck*—he said. I knew immediately that I liked him. Tall, broad, fair, excellent English, and a big smile. He turned out to be an ace leader and an excellent companion. He had a visa to enter Srpska Republika so he could come across as often as he liked. He had parked his convoy facing Zvornik, fifty metres from the bridge, which was causing chaos with the traffic, but he refused to move. He meant business.

I introduced him to the French escort commander who was not happy with parking the escort so close to the bridge. The road is close to a barracks with soldiers constantly passing by. Also we were parked opposite the town's main cemetery. Zvornik at war is a spooky enough place without having its dead as your neighbours. So we decided to move back to the checkpoint at the entrance to Zvornik. I told Dakcic what I intended to do. He then showed traditional Serb hospitality which is so often at odds with the situation. He sent a man with us, by the time we reached the checkpoint, a civilian was waiting to direct us to a nearby office block where at least some of the escort could sleep. There was a toilet, and a couple of the rooms had wood burning stoves. Dirk returned to spend the night with the convoy on the other side of the bridge. Risto, Pepe, and myself slept on the floor in the office block. We chose one of the rooms with a stove. The overcrowding, the fumes, the smoke, and the aroma from the much-used sleeping bags soon filled the room with a funk and a smell that even pigs would reject. I decided that another day, another location.

We were up and out at dawn. We moved off to the bridge. The Major was nowhere to be seen. Some European Community Military Mission observers were looking for him, they could not find him. The French escort lined up by the bridge, and the BBC had set up its camera for the grand entrance of the convoy. After a lot of hassle, I found the king of the bridge. He was in a very jovial mood.

– *There is no approval for the convoy. Therefore, it cannot enter Srpska Republika.*

– *There is approval. We have approval from Pale, from General Mladic himself.*

– *He has not told us. If you have approval, be our guest. Just wait until we are informed, then you can go.*

I made many calls to Sarajevo. Tony Land visited Pale. Sarajevo made calls to Geneva, Geneva to New York. The temperature was minus five. We were back parked alongside the cemetery, which, as a result of the war, had extended beyond its fence. Three lines of graves had advanced towards the roadside. We watched as a grave digger took many hours to pick and shovel and spade ice cold clods of earth from the frozen ground. Today was the funeral for a young boy who had accidentally killed himself using his father's weapon. His classmates led the funeral procession, weeping parents and silent relatives followed. The rites at the graveside took ages. Then the mourners dispersed, the children recovering more quickly—they were chatting and bantering before they left the cemetery. The adults were ashen faced as they passed our intrusive convoy. Some scowled, some shook fists, others acknowledged our silent sharing of their grief.

As the day progressed it became colder and more bleak. Dr. Risto decided to light a fire at the side of the road. He asked a young boy who was watching the convoy from a discreet distance from where he could buy wood. The boy raced away to his home, the house nearest to the bridge, and adjacent to the cemetery. He returned with a wheelbarrow of firewood.

Once Risto had taken the initiative everybody wanted to join in, including a BBC cameraman, French soldiers, and Pepe. But Risto is a Finn, a cold weather expert, and a solitary fire maker. He has a system. With his trusty Finn sheath knife, he took branches and lightly slivered the surface, the white strips of wood curled like watch springs, still attached to the branch. These were the first twigs to be lit. The fire grew, slowly, slowly. Larger branches put on only when smaller pieces were ablaze. The Brits and the Bosnians were impatient and wanted to throw logs on it at the first sign of flame, but Risto treated the fire as his baby and was possessive. His ritual and success drew an admiring audience, amongst whom was the young Serb boy who had provided the wood. Pepe talked to him, found out that his name was Milenko. Jeremy Bowen shared some sweets with him. Soon the boy was joined by his grandfather, Slavko Sikimic. We talked about our task. He pointed out his house from where a large black flag was flying. His eldest grandson had recently been killed whilst on a Serb action near Cerska, the very place we were hoping to reach.

The man invited us to his house for coffee. UNHCR and BBC went together. His wife Bojka was lovely. She had been very beautiful, but she now looked much older than her husband. She gave us coffee. There was no venom in her voice as she explained to us what had happened to her grandson.

– *He was my favourite. He went out on a patrol to Kamenica, there was one single sniper shot. It hit him and killed him instantly. The only casualty on that patrol.* We talked a lot about the war.

– *What do you feel about us wanting to reach Kamenica where your grandson was killed?*

– *The people there are like us—they need food, we understand that. It is not their fault.* They were joined by their other son, the father of the young boy and his mother. They told us that they had applied to go to Australia. They would soon be away.

They asked where we were sleeping. When we told them—*in the vehicles*—they offered to accommodate and feed us in their house. There were only two extra rooms and two extra beds, but we were welcome. The offer was spontaneous, the hospitality was free.

Jeremy knew that they had little and that we could easily outstay our welcome, so he insisted on us staying, only if they would take some payment, at least for our food. They reluctantly agreed.

The day passed without any positive news from Sarajevo. I occasionally saw the major whose bonhomie was wearing really thin. I tried to see the local military commander Major Pandorovic but was told he was out "at the front." He eventually arrived for a brief visit with a group of soldiers.

– *Major I am here to take a convoy to Cerska.* The Major was polite but off hand.

– *There is no approval. When approval comes, you can go.* Pandorovic left as abruptly as he had arrived but not before one of his soldiers infuriated me. There was an outbreak of laughter from amongst them.

– *What was that about Pepe?*

– *One said that if the convoy gets through, they will be killing fat Muslims—if not, then it will have to be thin Muslims.*

By dark, we had achieved nothing. The escort went back to their overnight laager, where they had made good friends with the locals. They soon had a large fire blazing, without using the Tervahauta method. Jeremy Bowen, great professional that he is, was filming campfire and fraternisation footage. His experience told him that this was the best he was going to get this day.

Dirk returned into Serbia and briefed his convoy. He himself was sleeping in the tiny confines of his soft skinned canvas topped jeep. It meant that he could keep in contact by the vehicle radio with Belgrade. He had chosen his driver well. A man with a sense of humour and a sense of priority. The vehicle had enough food in it for a fortnight. He also had a copy of this month's *Playboy*, which guaranteed him a steady flow of visitors.

We went straight to the house of Milenko; the BBC crew were already well installed. The family had cooked us an excellent meal. During the meal, Dakcic, the king of the bridge, arrived. I hoped that it was not to intimidate our hosts. It wasn't, it was more Serb paradox. He wanted to offer his apologies for not being able to accommodate us himself and to pass on the order from Pandorovic that we were not welcome, and we were to leave Zvornik and return to Sarajevo in the morning.

– *What are you going to do?*—asked Jeremy.

– *Stay*—I replied. Jeremy and his crew filed their "UN convoy ordered back" piece.

We returned to the table and drank a few glasses of our hosts' slivovica punctuated with a few nips from Jeremy's whisky bottle. Unlike at Gorazde, this was a blended bottle. The BBC must have cut down on his allowances. We were next disturbed by shooting close to the house. We had tucked in, by the side of the house, both of our vehicles, but they could still be seen from the road. After a sensible pause, we went out to investigate and found no damage, but the source was still there. Some drunken Serb soldiers were weaving their way home and firing into the air.

We returned inside the house, had a nightcap, and reluctantly left the warm living room for the morgue cold bedrooms. Being the oldest, I qualified for one of the beds. Being the most handsome, and because he was paying, Bowen qualified for the other. Our fellow teammates slept on the floor, all of us wrapped up in our sleeping bags with only our noses peeping out.

The next day was no better. Dakcic was very unhappy when I refused to move. He ordered Dirk to return the convoy to Belgrade. Dirk refused to cross back over the bridge into Serbia, knowing that if he did, he may not be permitted to return. Despite Serb intimidation, the convoy remained on the Serbian side, close to and facing the bridge.

To show aggression and to prove our determination, we again lined up near the cemetery facing the direction of Cerska. Milenko played truant from school and attached himself to Pepe and Risto.

Tony Land was constantly in touch with us. Apparently General Morillon was trying to arrange a cease fire around Cerska. Madame Ogata was putting pressure on New York, which was squeezing Milosovic. At midday, a Swedish convoy from Belgrade was permitted to cross from Serbia. We watched as Dakcic and his men inspected it. It was waved through. Its destination was Sarajevo. Sarajevo was OK. Cerska wasn't.

We spent a fair portion of the day chasing Pandorovic. We went

226

down to the barracks, which was out of bounds, and infuriated everyone. We saw the arrival of a convoy of fresh troops; sadly, some of them had sleeping bags with them, which we had issued as humanitarian aid to refugees.

Our persistence paid off. Pandorovic came to see us. He was more amenable than the previous day and stayed longer, which gave me time to assess him. He is an ex-regular Yugoslav army officer. He is about five foot ten, stocky with ginger hair and freckles. He has green eyes and is about thirty-eight. He stands square, looks fit and decisive. I would guess that he is a good leader.

— Major, why can't we proceed? We have approval from your masters in Pale. You know that. If we had not, we would not have got this far.

— I have received no orders to let you go through. Besides, there is heavy fighting in Kamenica. Can you not hear the shelling from here? This was true, the distant, muffled rumble of artillery was ominously audible.

— But surely Major, if there is shelling, you must be doing it. Kamenica is a small village. There are no heavy weapons there. I suspect that you are delaying us here whilst you take Kamenica.

— You can think what you like. Why should I let you into an enemy position to feed them?

— Because, Major, you are mainly besieging women and children, starving women and children. At every checkpoint, I had to have, at some time or other, this same conversation. This was slightly different because Pandorovic may not have had the power to let me proceed, but he certainly had the power of life or death over those people I was trying to reach.

— If there are only starving women and children there, then starving women and children are killing my soldiers.

— Major, I just want you to know that I am not taking this convoy back. I am taking it forward to Konjevici via Kamenica via Cerska.

— Then I will meet you in Kamenica—he replied cockily. His entourage roared with laughter. He turned to go, but I was determined to achieve something.

— Can you give approval for the convoy to cross the bridge? I would like to have both convoy and escort here. This was actually very important

to me. A favourite tactic of mine in a deadlock situation is to move the convoy forward and to see what happens. Moving forward with the escort and no convoy was a real empty gesture.

– *We will discuss that tomorrow*—he said. He then bizarrely told me that he had ordered sandwiches and tea for the escort, the BBC, and ourselves. He left, and sure enough, within a few minutes, a Serb vehicle arrived with urns of tea and doorstep-sized sandwiches containing meat. By six, it was dark and cold. Reluctantly, we had to admit that there was nothing else we could do. Dirk went back to the convoy, the French to their fires, and we to Milenko's.

More hospitality, more slivo, more subdued.

Major Dakcic then surprised me; he suggested that I host a meal for Pandorovic in Loznica. I asked him to arrange it. This he did, and we hosted Dakcic and Pandorovic and a number of hangers-on to a meal. Pandorovic was very late. I had almost given up on him coming. Loznica is in Serbia, but he arrived in uniform with his bodyguard. The meal was very interesting. He understands English but is shy to speak it. He told me about his wife and children, about life in the Yugoslav army, about the great country it had recently been. I listened to yesterday but was more interested in today.

– *Am I going to get into Cerska?*—I asked him.

– *Not before me*—he replied.

– *Konjevici?*

– *Maybe.*

– *Srebrenica?*

– *Never!*—he emphatically replied.

– *What about the women and the children?*

– *They are not my problem. If the Muslims want to save their women and children, they can lay down their arms and surrender.*

– *How can you shell villages and towns where the majority of occupants are women and children cowering in the basements of their homes?*

– *Their men are firing at us.*

– *But Major, they are firing at you, because they are being attacked by you. They are defending their homes.* He responded with the litany of the few villages and towns where the Muslims had fired on innocent Serbs.

– Major, you are a professional army officer, are you not afraid of being branded a war criminal? His reply to this amazed me.

– I have never killed anyone. I do not even carry a weapon. All this whilst people ate, drank, and a band played. My last memory of the evening was of Pandorovic dancing in one of these Yugoslav folk dances where people dance and bob in a huge circle around the tables.

He danced elegantly.

After a wickedly cold night, we were up at dawn. Before joining the escort, I sat in the vehicle at the side of Milenko's house and contacted Sarajevo. I was told that there was intense activity on the political front. Having the BBC with us had kept the story in the public eye. Their presence had attracted other journalists. Madame Ogata, who was about to leave for a tour of Africa was contacting New York and Belgrade, demanding progress for the convoy. General Morillon was in Pale, berating Karadzic and Mladic.

Although cold and weary, I felt that all we had to do was stick it out. Dirk and his drivers were cold but never miserable; they were as determined as we were to get through. Unfortunately, the noise of shelling was more intense. We were racing against time for Kamenica. A lot of military trucks obviously carrying ammunition raced past our position. The Serbs, realising they were under pressure, were determined to take Kamenica before world pressure allowed our convoy to proceed. The king of the bridge became cockier as the day advanced. He was getting news from the front. We were getting little or no good news from the rear echelons.

UNHCR convoys crossed the bridge for Tuzla, Sarajevo, and Gorazde, but ours was blocked. Dakcic requested my presence at his office. I went in an aggressive mood. *Soldiers of the Srpska Republic have captured Kamencia*—he told me with a huge smile. I left his scruffy office deeply depressed and briefed Dirk, the escort commander and the BBC.

Kamenica had fallen. Whilst we had waited so close, the Serbs had overrun the village. Homes were burning, and the people were fleeing as we spoke. I relayed this bitter news to Sarajevo. We waited for the world's reaction and hoped that it would be condemnatory and that the Serbs would have to let us in to Cerska. A naive momentary thought.

I went to the barracks to find Pandorovic. I was told with arrogance that he was "at the front." I had no doubt that he was supervising the cleaning up of the place. I wanted to know about refugees.

– *Where has the population of Kamenica gone to?*

– *We do not know*—said the only young officer I could find.

– *For Christ's sake, let me forward so that I can at least see where they are going. These are women and children. They will need help. Now.*

– *No. I have orders that you are not to move.* I pressured Sarajevo. Sarajevo put pressure on Zagreb. I went back to the Serb headquarters.

– *Can I go forward without a convoy to see where the civilians are?*

– *No, but I can tell you that most of them have headed for Srebrenica.*

– *Srebrenica is starving and overcrowded now. The last thing it wants is more people.* But I got nowhere. The Serbs I was talking to were not going to let us go. The French escort commander asked his headquarters if we could try to advance without permission and without the convoy. The answer was a predictable "NO." I knew that if the Serbs had taken Kamenica, it would only be a matter of days before they continued their push onto Cerska.

Jeremy Bowen was equally desperate to get into Kamenica but was having no luck. He knew that the longer the Serbs kept him out, the more sanitised the place would be.

Then the Serbs sprang a surprise on us all. They had found a mass grave in Kamenica. Risto suggested that WHO should be present at the exhumation. Dakcic thought it would be a good idea but said that he would have to get approval. He then vanished and did not return.

The day ended with us getting nowhere. We were depressed, frustrated, and angry. Within a few kilometres of us, men, women, and children were trudging through the snow across the hills wearing little and carrying less. Their lives, like their homes, were destroyed. That night, I hid in my sleeping bag, I could not sleep. In the morgue in Gorazde, I had seen the bodies of those who had frozen to death on the walk from Srebrenica—black, contorted human blocks. How many innocents were shivering and shaking in the hills so close to where we lay? Too weak to move, too scared to stay. I could see fathers carrying bundles, mothers hugging babies to their bosoms as they slipped and slid in the deep damp snow, older children urged to keep up. I could hear the panic cries of the separated and the lost. We were so close and so far. That night, I hated Pandorovic.

The long night eventually ended, at least for me. Within minutes of waking, I contacted Sarajevo. Madame Ogata apparently had announced that if we failed to get into Cerska today, she would have to withdraw the convoy. General Morillon was encouraging us not to give up, and we did not intend to.

I went with Risto to see Dakcic. I was subdued but seething. As we were speaking to him, a busload of international journalists crossed the bridge. They had been invited to see the mass grave. Jeremy Bowen and his crew joined them. Risto was refused. Risto and I then heard that the majority of the bodies had already been removed and were in a warehouse in Zvornik. It was suggested to us that we could see them there. Risto runs a hospital in Finland and therefore does everything from medical consultations to major surgery, with a touch of forensic medicine thrown in. He was enthusiastic.

When I was about seven, an aunt of mine took me to the Claughton picture house in Birkenhead to see a version of Dracula. It frightened the life out of me. For months at night I could see faces in the grained wardrobe in my bedroom. I vaguely remember scenes from the film of stones creaking, graves opening, and bodies emerging. Now, many years later, I am being asked if I voluntarily want to see bodies exhumed. The true answer was—*No*. But Risto wants to go. The Serbs have half asked us, and I don't admit that I do not like the idea. If I say I do not wish to go, they will accuse me of wanting to see only massacres by Serbs.

Off we go. We chased around town.

We first went to the hospital morgue. There, we were told that the bodies had been taken to a warehouse in the town. We found the warehouse in a small street. There were houses on either side of it. A man appeared wearing rubber boots and heavy rubber gloves. Not the usual gear for a labourer in a warehouse.

— *We have approval to see the bodies from Kamenica.*

— *I have not got the key to the warehouse.* Ah! He did not deny they were here, just no key.

— *Where is the key?*

— *It is with the military.*

— *Risto, I think we could spend all day searching for the key. Let us wait until we can get a military escort.* Surprisingly, Risto rapidly agreed. Perhaps, as a child, he had had a wardrobe with faces in the wood. We returned to the convoy only to meet Jeremy Bowen, who began to give us a spade by spade account of the exhumations.

— *Jeremy, we have just come from the warehouse where the bodies have been transferred*—I said nonchalantly and truthfully.

— *Did you see the body without the head and the one with the wire around the neck? The Serbs were saying that it proved that the one had been strangled and the other had his throat cut*—continued Jeremy.

— *What is your view?*—I asked.

— *Well, the press consensus is that the one head had probably come off in the removal of the decomposing body from the mass grave and that the wire may not have been around the neck of the other but was in the grave and came out with the body caught up with the clothing*—replied Jeremy. I made a strong mental note not to find the man with the key. Headless, exhumed bodies were even worse than the Claughton picture house.

I kept in contact with Sarajevo and Dirk with Belgrade. There were all sorts of rumours. Madame Ogata was reported to be furious. She was on her way to Africa, but the plight of the convoys was uppermost in her mind. There were rumours that General Morillon was on his way to us. The Gorazde and the Tuzla convoys that had passed us yesterday were stuck. We were definitely stuck. At least with the other convoys, the escort and HCR vehicles were together. The press corps, fresh from the mass graves and en route to Belgrade, descended on us. I remember Dirk and myself giving an interview to both BBC and to Penny Marshall of ITN.

– *We are not turning back*—I said.

– *We are only going forward*—said Dirk.

At six in the evening we received the order from Sarajevo. Madame Ogata had ordered the recall of all convoys. The French escort commander Dirk and myself sat together. The escort was told by his headquarters to stay; Morillon had indicated that he would come personally to Zvornik. The transport battalion headquarters ordered Dirk back to Belgrade. Tony in Sarajevo sympathised with my wish to stay but reminded me that the decision was a UNHCR directive from Madame Ogata herself. Fortunately, it was too late to move, so we had the night to sleep on the situation and to see what developments dawn brought.

Another night at Milenko's. Sombre and sober.

Dawn brought more confusion. General Morillon was determined to intervene personally, New York wanted him to stay aloof. Tony brought me up to date on the UNHCR front. Madame Ogata was in Africa. She had made her decision to halt the convoys which was apparently causing chaos. No convoys could mean no aid. No aid meant no reason for UN troops to be in support of humanitarian aid. Therefore, her decision questioned the need for UN troops on the ground. He also told me the latest news from Sarajevo. Zlatko Lagumdzija was calling for the suspension of the airlift and for a halt to convoys entering the city. In effect, the city was going on a hunger strike in sympathy with Srebrenica!

– *Tony, you are pulling my leg.*

– *I am serious. They are not accepting our food. We have had to stop the delivery of aid in the city. We will keep the airlift going until we bulk out in the warehouses.*

This was one of those moments in the war when I wondered what the hell I was doing there. We were cold, tired, and hungry. And we were doing our best to reach those who were much more cold, tired, and hungry. The pilots were risking life, limb and aircraft with each sortie, the convoy drivers were hazarding their lives on dangerous roads and at violent checkpoints, and one of the sides was now saying—*You are not doing enough. Therefore, we are going on a HUNGER STRIKE.*

– *Tony, tell me this isn't true.*

It was. I went to see Pandorovic. I levelled with him.

– *Look Major, your action in stopping this convoy looks as if it might be the end of the humanitarian aid. You do not want that to happen. We are feeding tens of thousands of Serbs. Break the deadlock and let this convoy through.*

– *I do not have the power to do that.*

– *OK, what about a gesture, a humanitarian gesture. Let me go forward without the convoy to see what is happening to the refugees.*

– *No, it is not safe, also the Muslims may take you hostage.*

– *I will take my chance on that.*

– *You cannot go. That is final.*

– *OK then one gesture of goodwill. At least let the convoy cross the bridge.*

– *NO.*

By ten thirty Belgrade, Sarajevo, and Zagreb were all singing from the same song sheet. The attempt was over. The convoy was to return to Belgrade and the rest of us to Sarajevo. Final. No arguments, no discussions.

At ten forty-five I shook hands and hugged Dirk. He had been a tough, loyal companion and a great leader. He had kept the morale of his men high through five bitter cold days and nights. We said farewell to Milenko's family. God bless them, they had become so much a part of our team that they were as disappointed as we were. With heads low, we pulled away from the bridge. I did not dare call in on Dakcic or his men. If any of them had cheered or jeered, I am certain I would have knocked them to the floor. I took one last look down the Cerska road. I vowed to myself that I would be back.

Pandorovic, you may not have personally killed anyone, but you were in command when many innocents were mortared and shelled. You delayed my convoy whilst you captured Kamenica. You caused countless women and children to flee their homes and run in the snow to Konjevici where your troops pounded them again, forcing those that lived to slip and slide through the metre-high snow and the treacherous ice to join the already overcrowded, besieged, and starving Srebrenica where conditions rivalled the worst images of the middle ages.

As we passed through Podromanje, we were told that the Gorazde convoy was still at Rogatica. We arrived back at Sarajevo at five twenty in the evening. I went straight to the UNHCR office and was told that events were still moving. General Morillon had negotiated an agreement with the Serbs for the Gorazde convoy to be divided in two, half for Gorazde and half for Zepa. The convoys could move in the morning. The General wanted me to go to Rogatica as quickly as possible. I went and saw Pepe and Risto.

– *Do not unpack or unload—we are off.* But word came from the operations room that the escort was to change. The French would stay, and we would be accompanied by Ukrainians. They would not be ready until six thirty tomorrow morning. Secretly, I was delighted. I did not smell too good. I needed a shower, a change of clothes, and a change of company.

But first there was the matter of the hunger strike. I tried to track down Zlatko Lagumdzje but failed. I quickly contacted the Mayor of Sarajevo, Mr. Kreseljakovic, and he agreed to see me. I took Meliha with me. I told him how angry and disappointed we were. He supported the principle of the hunger strike but saw my point. He promised to see Zlatko and to do his best to get the policy changed. Back to the PTT.

I slept like a log. No recriminations. Normally, failure gave me days of depression and nights of sleeplessness, but this opportunity to follow up the failure with the immediate chance of another crack at either Gorazde or Zepa kept my adrenaline going.

We left at seven with four Ukrainian APCs and with some French engineering vehicles to clear the road. The trucks were so heavy, and the roads so icy that the convoy moved to Pale at about fifteen miles an hour. I spoke to the senior French soldier, and he was happy to go at his own pace without me. I therefore left him with the APC escort, and we motored on to Rogatica.

The Belgian convoy was lined up. It had been inspected and was ready to go. I introduced myself to the Belgian officer, a Lieutenant. He was in the cab of one of his trucks. I had had such a good experience with the two Dirks, I was looking forward to working with this one.

– *Hi, I'm Larry. I am here to go with one of the convoys into either Zepa or Gorazde. I have taken convoys into both places. What is the situation at the moment?* He did not smile, he did not shake my hand.

– *I am off to do reconnaissance*—he said.

– *Then I will come with you. I know both roads.*

– *When are you leaving?*

– *Now.*

– *OK.*

I returned to my vehicle. I told Pepe to move up to the front to join the Lieutenant. When we got to the front, the young officer had gone. I joined Francois, the French UNHCR convoy leader from Belgrade. He is an ex-French army officer. A small, bronzed, fit man who invariably wore a woollen ski hat. He is totally unflappable— nothing perturbs Francois, neither Serbs nor young Belgian officers. Francois briefed us.

– *The Serbs say we have approval to go to both Gorazde and Zepa. However, the Serbs are claiming that the Gorazde road is impassable because of shelling and mines, and the Zepa road is impassable because of barricades and fighting. So we can go, and we can't go. Simple.*

After about ninety minutes, the Belgian officer returned.

– *You did not wait for me*—I smiled.

– *I had to do the recce*—he replied curtly.

– *What did you find?*

– *here are barriers on the track in the woods.*

– *Before you left, I told you that I knew the road. Me, Risto the doc, our driver Pepe, and Francois took the first convoy into Zepa. We know the road.*

– *I am an officer. This is my convoy. I must do the recce.*

Uh-huh.

– *Look son, Risto is an ex-officer in the Finnish Army, Pepe is an ex-officer in the Yugoslav army, Francois is an ex-officer in the French army, and I am an ex-officer in the British army. We have been up the bloody*

hill, across the barricades and into Zepa. This is our convoy. OK?
Unfortunately, this officer proved to be a slow learner.

We went off to see Major Furtula. He was pleased to see us but was unable to guarantee our success. Once again, it was all the naughty Muslims' "fault." We thanked him for his concern and "reassured" him that we would succeed. Just before dark, the French engineering trucks arrived. I was ever so glad I had not stayed with them. At seven in the evening we heard several heavy explosions on the Gorazde road not far away from us. After five nights in beds in Serb houses and one night in our own in Sarajevo, we were again back to sleeping in the vehicle.

We were up and about at seven. You can't lie in when you are sleeping in a vehicle. But I knew that we were in for a late start, if we moved at all. The first unwelcome sight was the arrival of the Serb magpie Dr. Radomir Bojovic. Apparently, he had not had his customary root through the medicines. He lightened the load but not by much. A very stroppy soldier challenged him over every pill. The Belgian Captain decided that before his vehicles move, he must recce the complete route into Zepa.

– *Look my friend, you have been as far as the barriers. When you arrive with the convoy, the Bosnian government forces will move the barricades and you will proceed to Zepa. No problem. Take my word. If you turn up on your own and ask them to remove the barrier so that you can do a recce, they will not. You are a soldier, sorry, an officer, if you were commanding the defence of Zepa would you remove your barriers to permit a recce? You would not. For a convoy, yes. Not for a recce.*

– *But I am bringing them a convoy.*

– *Yes, but between the time you leave after your recce and the arrival of your return with the convoy, the Serbs could have raced in and taken Zepa.*

– *On my recce, I will take the APCs, and when I leave, they will stay to guard the Bosnian barricades.* I couldn't fault that. Good thinking. Our tactical discussions counted for nothing. The Serbs were not permitting movement along the Zepa road. So he decided to recce the Gorazde road. He liked recces.

The large explosions that we heard the previous night had resulted in huge craters in the road. *The result of Muslim shelling or mining*—the Serbs assured us. Why the Muslims would want to prevent a convoy reaching them was beyond me. The large French earth mover was sent down to repair the road.

There was an enormous bang.

The earth mover was pushing earth back into one of the craters when its blade hit an anti-tank mine. The majority of the shrapnel was contained by the blade. The blast was deflected around the curve of the blade, up the front of the vehicle and it shattered the windscreen. The French engineer, a true professional, was wearing his bulletproof helmet and jacket, protective goggles and gloves. The jet speed cloud of slivers of glass lacerated every surface in the cab. The curling pall of explosive smoke blackened every surface. The driver tumbled from his cab. The Ukrainians and the French standing near the crater were deafened and blackened by the noise and the smoke, but the few metal fragments not stopped by the great blade had missed them. They raced up to the driver. At first his face was black, but then drops of blood began to appear. Each fleck produced its own little stream. Within tens of seconds, his lower face was a smudge of red and black. Someone removed his helmet and his goggles. The contrast was startling. The top part of his face was clean, his eyes bright. Only his cheeks were cut.

What looked, at first, to be hideous, proved to be minor. A little war pitting and scarring even becomes a soldier. Risto and the French medics cleaned him up. He will always bless the discipline that made him wear his protective clothing. The mine in the crater further convinced me that the road had been damaged by the Serbs. It was too close to their front for even a very brave Bosnian to approach carrying mines and then to dig them in.

I casually mentioned this to Major Furtula. I could hear his gastric juices swirl.

The mine incident caused us to rethink on Gorazde. The craters blocked the road. Repairing the craters would now have to be done with more caution. The word came from Sarajevo that General Morillon wanted us to switch the whole convoy to Zepa. We went to see

Furtula and gave him the news.

— *The threat from the Muslims is very great. The road to Zepa is now heavily mined.*

— *By who?*

— *By us*—I heard the gastric juices again. We got back onto General Morillon. He was definitely in a gung-ho mood.

— *Take two APC's and the French engineers and clear the route.* We told Furtula of our intention. He was horrified. This was definitely out of his league. He stalled.

— *Please do it tomorrow. It is too late for today.* He was right—the light was failing. The General agreed.

Another night, Chez Land Cruiser discovered that today is Sunday. Furtula is on his way to see us. He arrived with a smile. *Last night we removed the mines on the Zepa road. You are free to go.* General Morillon must be putting the pressure on Mladic.

We moved off at eleven thirty. The road conditions were bad, but we found no signs of mines and no signs of mine clearing. The Bosnians met us in the woods. The Ukrainians helped to remove the barriers, and we were in Zepa by four thirty and unloaded by six. It was then dark and it began to snow. I suggested to the Belgian officer that we should stay overnight. But he was adamant that he should leave now. Some of his senior ranks and many of his drivers were not in agreement with him. A heavy discussion broke out. I had no intention of undermining the officer's authority with his own troops, so I moved away and returned to the hospital to see Benjamin. He predicted heavy snow and recommended that we stay as the road would be treacherous. I did not like being separated from the convoy, so at seven p.m. we left the hospital and went back to where the convoy had been parked. It was not there. We moved on, and after three kilometres, caught up with it. Many of the trucks were stuck in the snow. There was chaos, they were not going to go far this night. We decided to return to the home of Benjamin.

We had another enjoyable evening with the same team. This time, I did not try to eat the bread, but I did raise the subject of cannibalism. We were all seated around the table with a glass of slivovica. I

239

addressed Benjamin's father.

– Saban, last time I was here I wanted to ask you a difficult question.

– Go ahead—he said. Everyone fell silent.

– We had often heard that you were desperately short of food. We heard one report that in order to survive, some people had—here I paused—*well had, er, eaten human flesh. That there had been some cannibalism.* I then rapidly added—*Have you heard any such stories?* There was a silence. I blustered on—*Obviously the press were very interested in the reports and have asked me to comment when I return.* More silence. Then they began to laugh. And I laughed. *You know I wanted to ask you last time I was here. Especially when I saw all the dried meat in the room outside.* By "know," they were convulsed with laughter.

– You thought we were eating the patients? They now had tears in their eyes with laughter.

– Come on guys I cannot go back and say they just laughed. Has there been any talk or evidence of cannibalism? Saban stopped smiling and answered.

– We too had heard there were reports of cannibalism in Zepa. We were not shocked, we were not horrified. But genuinely we have seen no evidence, and we do not believe it possible.

I ate more heartily than on my first visit. We all slept in the one room, on the floor in sleeping bags.

We were up at six and we left at six fifteen. The road was densely thick with snow. The convoy was not where we had left it. We motored up the winding track. Even with the benefit of daylight, it was a treacherous journey. In the woods, we found the government soldiers. They were huddled together waiting for us to pass before they replaced the barriers.

Once out of the woods, we were in a blizzard, and visibility was zero. We moved on slowly until we literally bumped into the last vehicle of the convoy. It had been stuck in the most open area with the driven snow whiting out everything. They were freezing cold. The Serbs had stopped their convoy at twelve thirty. They were furious that a convoy had attempted to cross the front line at night in a blizzard. The convoy was very lucky they had not fired on it. When the Serbs realised that I was now at the back of the convoy, they braved the blizzard and came to our vehicle where they yelled and screamed at me for letting the convoy move at night and for not accompanying it myself. When the blizzard abated, they let us proceed to Borike and on to Rogatica.

Benjamin had given Risto a letter for Dr. Radomir Bojovic. He read it with no emotion, then derided its contents and passed it to the soldiers to scorn. He then passed to Risto a letter which he had written. It was addressed to The United Nations, and it stated that if we attempt to pass Rogatica without a drug delivery for Rogatica, a public demonstration of women would stop and detain the convoy.

We left the French engineering vehicles in Rogatica to continue to clear the route to Gorazde. I said a heartfelt farewell to the Lieutenant. We returned to Sarajevo. We still had not achieved Cerska but we had fulfilled our promise to Zepa to return.

Thirteen

Simon Says

The Bosnian Government and the media are pressuring New York and Geneva for something to be done about Srebrenica and Cerska. General Nambiar who was the boss of General Morillon and who ran UNPROFOR from Zagreb had completed one year of command. He is an Indian aristocrat. A man of honour and more especially a man of his word. After one year of Balkan deceit, deception, and double talk, he has had enough and wishes to return home. A Swiss, General Wahlgren, arrives to replace him. Whilst this is happening, General Morillon embarks on a course of action which has far reaching consequences. He informs General Mladic by telex that he will visit Cerska to assess the situation. The phone rings in the UNHCR office, and I answer it.

– *Larry, come and see me now.* I hotfooted to the residence where the General had his office and his bed.

– *I want you to accompany me to Cerska. No convoy, just an assessment. And bring a World Health Organisation doctor.*

– *Have we approval?* I asked somewhat incredulously.

– *I have told Mladic. He will find it hard to refuse me freedom of movement.* Back in the office, I rang Michelle O'Kelly, our protection officer in Tuzla. Eire born, Michelle is a lawyer who has practised in Dublin. A buxom woman with a gentle accent, she has a big smile and a warm personality, and excellent links with the Bosnian Government Military Corps Headquarters. More importantly, she recently has been invited to talk to the amateur radio stations in Srebrenica, Konjevici, Polje, and Cerska from the amateur station in Zivinice.

– *Michelle, what is the latest gen from Cerska?*

– *Grim. My last contact was yesterday when the Serbs were attacking. Some of the civilians have already left for Konjevici.*

– *Can the Bosnian government force prevent it falling?*

– *No way.*

We had a race on our hands. The arrangements made by General Morillon were swift and simple. The British Doctor Simon Mardell and myself were to make our way to the BiH Command headquarters at Kiseljak immediately. We arrived as self-contained as can be, with rucksacks, sleeping bags, some tinned food, and some high protein biscuits. Whereas Sarajevo has nothing, Kiseljak has a small duty-free shop, so Simon buys ten bars of chocolate and gives me five.

On a nearby football field, there are two helicopters. The General, his Military Assistant, the polyglot British Major Pyers Tucker, Mikhailov, the general's bodyguard, Victor Andreev, the Russian born Head of Civil Affairs, Simon, and myself all climb in and away we go the one hundred and fifty miles to Tuzla. There we are met by Major Alan Abraham who commands the resident squadron of the 9th/12th Royal Lancers. He puts us all into the back of his armoured vehicles and we are off to Zvornik. After ten miles, we reach the first Serb checkpoint at Kalesija and cross quite quickly. This could be a good sign. At Zvornik, however, we wait for hours. We sit in a conference room and are politely hosted. We are joined by Laurence Jolles, my UNHCR colleague from Belgrade. He is a bright lawyer, an outstanding linguist, and an excellent companion in a difficult spot. We are all given coffee and slivovica to drink and fed crumbs of information at infrequent intervals.

— *We are waiting for a Serb escort.*
— *The road is mined.*
— *There is fighting on the road.*

General Morillon keeps the pressure on. They can tell that he is not going to go away. Eventually we are told—*You will be escorted to the village of Drinjaca, the Serb front-line village. From there on, we give you no guarantees. We know that the Muslims have mined the road. We expect you to be back tonight.*

The first part of the journey is along a reasonable road. Then we turn off onto a narrow road which stays in the valley and runs alongside the Drinjaca river. This I know only from the map. There were five of us stuck in the back of the armoured vehicle, the usual crew and us passengers. We took turns to sit near the rear door from where you could at least see where we had been. The road was bordered by the sides of steep, snow covered mountains. The road was rarely used and was thickly carpeted with snow. It was ideal ambush territory. I hoped that the Bosnians knew we were coming. I would have felt a lot happier without the Serb escort.

At Drinjaca we stopped at a Y-junction just before the bridge leading to Konjevici. We all got out to stretch our legs. The Serbs moved freely and confidently. There were two routes into Cerska. One was via Kamenica, which I knew from my recent long stay at Zvornik was now in Serb hands, and the second via Konjevici Polje. By taking us to Drinjaca we were to enter via Konjevici which was only a couple of kilometres ahead of us but was shielded by a high col. Cerska lies about three kilometres to the west of Konjevici.

We had travelled south, so Konjevici was straight ahead around the mountain and Cerska was ahead and to the right. The Serbs did a quick head count in each vehicle and then the commander said— *Good luck. We will meet you here at eight p.m.*

He then left, not the way we had come, but by the road to the left.

Major Abraham placed one armoured car to the front, then his own with the General, ours was next, then an escort, and finally an armoured recovery vehicle. It was a slow move forward. In my opinion, when travelling over thick snow in a possible minefield, luck plays a bigger part than skill. I particularly hate being on a dangerous road, in the back of a vehicle I cannot see out of, especially when accompanied by people I do not know. If it is your own team you keep each other's spirits up. With a strange team, there is more silence, more time to think, more time to worry, more time to pass on or receive fear. Also, I hate not being in charge. My fate here was in the hands of Major Abraham. I trusted Alan implicitly. I just wished that I had been travelling with him; then at least, I could have had an input.

We stopped regularly, opening the rear door on each occasion, but we did not get out. It was tempting but would have been unprofessional. The valley was very quiet and still. The snow hung heavily on the branches of the trees.

After a couple of hours, we reached the beginning of the Bosnian barriers. The road was blocked by felled trees. By now it was dusk. Whilst we were working out how to tackle the problem, the Bosnians arrived. Unlike in other situations, these boys were not overjoyed to see us. They were not impressed that we wanted to tear away their barriers on the very road the Serbs could race along following our tracks. They were tired, tetchy, and nervous. *You cannot do anything until we have spoken to the commander*—they said. This made sense. Their commander is Naser Oric, a tough leader who rules with a rod of iron. General Morillon was impatient. *Take me to see Commander Oric*—he demanded. They told him that he and we were going nowhere and doing nothing until they had their instructions. The leader of the group was a tall, thin, lean and mean man.

– *Why are you here?*—he asked. *Have you brought a convoy?*
– *No*—we replied. *We want to go and assess the situation in Cerska.*
– *Cerska has fallen*—he said curtly.
– *When?*
– *Late yesterday.*

The bastard Mladic had played with us. He had delayed us in Zvornik whilst his troops were cleaning up Cerska. He had sent us via Konjevici when he could have sent us via Kamenica. He had made us take this route in order to clear the way for him. His troops would have observed our progress, they would now know there were no mines. We would have the barrier removed. These weary soldiers would never have the energy to replace it as it was. No wonder the Bosnians were not overjoyed to see us.

I had sat and listened to the death of Kamenica, I was now a guest at the wake of Cerska.

Naser Oric sent a vehicle to pick up the General. The rest of us struggled for hours, forcing a gap wide enough to let our vehicles pass. It was a bitter cold night. The Brits worked like Trojans pulling and pushing on the huge logs which were intertwined. They were designed to delay visitors. They were successful. I felt particularly sorry for Victor Andreev. He thought we were on a one-day visit. He had no kit with him, and being a good United Nations senior official, he is wearing a suit and shoes. He is very cold and very damp. Simon, the good soul that he is, dug out of his Bergen, some spare socks and a Gore Tex sleeping bag outer cover.

It was late when the main body entered Konjevici. None of us gave a thought to the Serb deadline of eight o'clock. The General was in the municipal building with Oric and the local authorities. Major Alan Abraham, Simon, the ICRC man, Laurence, and myself joined him.

– *You have heard about Cerska. The wounded from there are here. I have agreed with the commander and the authorities that we will try to evacuate those with the greatest injuries. We will stay the night. Tomorrow, Larry, will you organise an assessment of the situation here and the needs?*

– *No problem General. Simon can do the medical assessment.* The conversation then moved to medical matters. They discussed the situation in Konjevici and the terrible situation in Srebrenica. Simon then said—*I would really like to get to Srebrenica.* This was no surprise statement, we all wanted to go to Srebrenica. Konjevici was a halfway house. But the Bosnians said—*We can take you tonight.* I saw Simon's dark eyes light up.

– *No*—I said. *It is important that he assesses here first.*

– *No, Larry, no. It is good if he goes to Srebrenica*—said the General.

– *No, General, he has not got the equipment and the initial requirement is here.* Simon by this time has his Bergen on his back and is standing near the door. There is no doubt about his feelings.

– *I think he should go. He is fit, he has the boots, and he has some medicine.*

– *No*—I repeated.

– *Yes*—said Simon. True, he has his doctor's bag with him which is packed with emergency medicine including a lot of ketamine. Also, Simon is an excellent mountaineer and yachtsmen, so he will have no fitness problems. Besides, by now he was out the door with his guide. But I did not agree.

We are taken to a house. It is occupied by ladies. Three twenty-somethings and a couple of forty-somethings. We all throw in some food and a meal was prepared. It is then time for bed. The ladies all disappear. It is a sharp, bitter cold night. Somewhere close to us are the refugees and the wounded from Cerska. Somewhere out there, Simon is trekking through snow drifts. Victor is in the Gore Tex, suit, and socks. I thank God again for my sub-zero sleeping bag and am soon sound asleep.

I am up at dawn. I want to see Konjevici Polje. It is a bright, crisp, dry morning. The house we are in is at the end of a track on the top of a small hill. We are actually in the self-contained top half of the house. The ladies, whom I can now hear, are in the bottom half. From the doorway, I can see the whole of Konjevici. It seems to be just one long street with two or three rows of houses on either side of it. Everyone seems to be up.

I am soon joined by the ICRC man, Andreas Schiess, another old friend from my days with Somali refugees. We are to do a tour of the town, see all the wounded and identify those who need urgent evacuation. I hate doing this. I am a complete charlatan. At least Andreas is Swiss and is wearing a Red Cross badge. It matters little that I know that he is a lawyer. The sick will look imploringly at us. I do not know what I am looking at, and if it is too gruesome, I shall end up looking greyer and sicker than any of them.

We are joined by a medic from the Brits, a good start. Then the two locals, Huso Unvalic, a medical technician, and Almira Mombera, a nurse who has three children with her in Konjevici. In the absence of qualified people, these two have performed some major surgery. I have great confidence that they will guide us through the day. The first task is to find someone who speaks English. I am told that there is a young girl in one of the houses. I am taken towards the house by a young man. When we get near to it, I see a large group of fifteen to twenty-year-olds. They are playing on a slide they have made on the slippery slope near the house. Such simple fun, such happy laughter. The girl is delighted to work with me.

There are two main locations of the sick and a number of houses where one or two are billeted. Nasir Oric has told the general that there are seven hundred who need evacuating. We do not see many more than a couple of hundred in total. We reckon that seventy need urgent treatment. Some of these may not even survive being carried to the vehicle. I am particularly worried about a little boy with tubes and drains who has been hit by mortar shrapnel.

Whilst we are doing this job, General Morillon has left us and gone back to Zvornik. He has been told by Naser Oric that the conquering Serbs have committed a massacre in the village and that many homes have been burnt. The Serbs are initially angry with him because we stayed overnight in Konjevici. The General however goes on the attack and challenges them to disprove the stories about the massacre by letting him see for himself. They agree and take him to Cerska where he sees few burned houses, one wounded Muslim, one pregnant woman and no evidence of a massacre. He arranges for the two Cerskans to go to Zvornik hospital where he later visits them. On his return to Zvornik, he is told that we should have left the previous night and must leave now. For diplomatic reasons, he agrees and the message is passed by radio to Major Abraham that we are all to leave. We are to be at the bridge by two. This message is passed to us by Brit soldiers. I am confused and go to the vehicle of Major Abraham.

– *What about Simon?*

– *I know*—he says. *I think the General may have forgotten about Simon or it is part of a bigger plot. I will try to talk to him.*

We both agree that any such conversation will have to be guarded. We do not wish the Serbs to know that Simon has gone into Srebrenica. Soon we have an answer from the General. We are all to be out by two. He will meet us by the bridge. Major Abraham had already warned off the local authorities that we had to leave. They were displeased but understood that we would go out and then return with a convoy to collect the wounded. I went to see their leader—*Look, I need to speak urgently to Simon. How can I do it?* He arranged for Laurence and myself to go to the amateur radio station. The only transport available was a horse and cart. We were joined by Naser Oric himself, and we set off down the main street. It was an exhilarating ride. Everyone waved to Nasser. I had great difficulty staying in the cart. It slipped and slewed all over the road and there was nothing to hold on to. The soldiers were standing in the cart. I was also freezing cold. But not for long. At the far end of the town the horse and cart stopped and we got off at the foot of a very steep hill, on top of which there was a small house. *There is the radio station*—They said pointing to the house. It was a gruelling climb. My body soon thawed out and then sweated and then iced up. I slipped on the icy slopes. I panted and puffed and was passed by old ladies and young children.

It was a small house. The living room was comfortably furnished. Along one wall was a desk and on the desk was the "ham" radio. At it sat a young man in uniform.

– *I want to speak to Simon in Srebrenica. Is he there yet?*

– *Oh yes, he got there early this morning. He is in the hospital now.*

– *Can you get him for me?*

– *I will try. But do not forget the Serbs can listen in.*

After a lot of tweaking and crackling, we got through to Srebrenica and a message was left for "the visitor" to come to the radio. Within a few minutes I was told that the visitor was there. I passed a short and simple message—*We are off. Will be back. Get back here when we tell you.*

I felt very bad about this. Abandoning one of your team is not in the handbook. I felt pretty certain that Simon would feel low. I then went back down the hill quicker than I had come up. The cart was waiting for us, but we had no sooner got into it than a Brit armoured vehicle appeared to collect us. *The convoy is ready to go. The locals are upset. The General wants us out, at the bridge, as promised.* My kit was still in the house where we had slept, so we had to go back for it. I was still troubled about leaving Simon. He was alone. The place had no food and was regularly shelled.

– *Ask Morillon if I can stay*—I asked Major Abrams.

– *I have already asked and he said no.*

We left. We waited at the barrier whilst the logs were pulled back into position. We arrived at the bridge late. The General was not there. There was a small group of Serb military policemen. I was quite worried. If they counted us, they would find one missing. They asked for the vehicle door to be opened.

– *Are you the last out?*—I was asked. *Yes*—I replied truthfully but not accurately. The senior who was at the front of the vehicle asked his colleague who was with me.

– *Is the one with the beard there?*

– *Yes*—his colleague replied.

— Then let them move—was the reply.

Back in Zvornik we discovered that the General had returned to Sarajevo. We also heard that he had given his famous press conference.

— General, was there a massacre in Cerska?

— Non.

— How do you know?

— Je n'ai pas senti l'odeur de la mort—which my remedial level French tells me is—*I did not sniff the smell of death.* The journalists were not impressed. The mainly Muslim authorities in Tuzla were decidedly unimpressed. They declared him "Persona non grata."

We all agreed to keep quiet about Simon being in Srebrenica. We would get back into Konjevici as quickly as possible and pull him out then.

Not having a vehicle, I went to Loznica in Serbia with Laurence. We booked into a hotel. I lay on my bed and switched on my radio to hear the World Service News. *Simon Mardell, a British doctor, has walked into Srebrenica*—was the first item! The manure had hit the fan. I took my jacket off and discovered in the pockets five bars of chocolate. I knew someone who was going to need these more than me. The next few days were dominated by the Simon saga.

Simon left us in the municipal building. He was given an escort of three soldiers, who shared the task of carrying his rucksack, leaving Simon to carry his literally vital airline pilot type doctor's bag. The night was cold and dark, the track was narrow, there were Serb patrols to be avoided, huge snow drifts to be negotiated, there was indiscriminate poorly aimed fire, and there was shelling. It took them six and a half hours to reach Srebrenica.

He was taken straight to the hospital and introduced to the Army captain, Dr. Nedret Mujkanovic, who had been sent into Srebrenica by the Bosnian government. Nedret spoke English but was tired and weary. His first words to Simon were—*I am so glad you have come. There have been so many patients. I could not do any more than I have done.* An explanation to a fellow professional, an apology to his patients, living and dead, from a trained paediatrician who had carried out more than a thousand general operations without equipment, without drugs, without lighting, whilst being shelled. Nedret gave Simon a quick tour of the hospital and confirmed Simon's worst fears. There was no food, no medicine, and twenty deaths a day.

Simon was given a bed in the hospital and started work immediately. He shared his ketamine, an anaesthetic administered by needle, with the doctors. Besides Nedret there were five others. They were all trained with gas anaesthetics, none had used ketamine. Trauma surgeon Simon trained them as quickly as he could. Some were quicker than others. After working in the wards, he returned to the operating theatre. A mortar victim was being operated on.

– *Did you use the ketamine?*—asked Simon.

– *Yes*—said the doctor with pride.

– *Is the patient unconscious?*—asked Simon.

– *Not yet*—answered the patient. As Simon discovered, when you have had no drugs for so long, and then you receive some, the temptation is to use them sparingly—to make them last.

Simon rapidly realised that a priority was a translator. Srebrenica is not a university town. There was only one English speaker in the town, and he was there by accident.

Almir Ramic had left the suburb of Dobrinja in Sarajevo with his mother to attend the funeral of a relative in Visegrad. It was to be a one-day round trip by bus. Whilst in Visegrad, the Bosnian war erupted. The Bosnian Serbs drove the Bosnian non-Serbs out of Visegrad. Buses were burnt or stolen. The exodus headed towards Srebrenica. Sarajevo was cut off. Almir and his mother had less to carry than most of the other refugees. They had just the clothes they stood in. Almir was too young for university and was not a language student at school but had been an avid TV fan, especially watching English and American films. He became the resident translator and Simon's shadow.

When Simon received my call telling him we were off, I was right, he was not happy. He had come on an assessment mission. After a few hours, he had learned what he needed to know. Srebrenica needed all the aid it could get. It needed a medical evacuation programme. It did not need an international doctor with no medicine and no food.

He knew that his place was out of Srebrenica shouting for them, not inside screaming with them.

The question was: how do we get him out? General Morillon is racing around trying to get approval to go to Srebrenica. He has the support of General Wahlgren. He is also trying to arrange an evacuation of the wounded from Konjevici. I went to see Pandorovic.

— *I would like to go to Konjevici to bring out Simon Mardell.*

— *He is not in Konjevici.*

— *I know. He is in Srebrenica. You know he is in Srebrenica. It has been on CNN, Sky, and Serb tele.*

— *No. If I believe you, he is not in Konjevici nor is he in Srebrenica. You told my police that you had all left. If you had all left, then Mardell cannot be in Konjevici or Srebrenica.*

— *If you had not insisted on us all being out by two, he would have come out with us.*

— *But you only had approval to stay until eight o'clock. You stayed overnight. You had no approval to send anyone to Srebrenica.* I was the loser here.

— *OK. Can I collect him when he returns to Konjevici?*

— *Ask me when he is in Konjevici.*

I left furious. We were obviously expected to eat a large humble pie. Getting Simon back to Konjevici is the first task. Michelle becomes a key link in this. She can talk to Zivinice, they can arrange for a message to be passed to Simon. But there is a snag with this. The authorities, the doctors, and the patients in Srebrenica do not want him to go. They do not know about the alphabet of letters after his name, but they do know that he is a switched on, hands on, saver of lives. They also know that he is fresh, enthusiastic, and an international.

We ask for him to return to Konjevici by two p.m. the following day. Simon gets the message. He asks his translator to accompany him.

— *How much time will you need to get ready?*

— *I'm ready.*

— *But you will need to pack.*

— *I have nothing to pack. I have nothing.* He asked Oric to provide an escort. Simon and Almir are ready to leave at seven the following morning as instructed by Oric. No escort turns up. Over the next four days, Simon is ready to go on six occasions. Each time, the trip is delayed and an excuse produced. – *There is no escort available to take you to the front line.* – *There is heavy Serb patrolling.* – *The front line has moved.* – *There is increased shelling in Konjevici.*

Michelle regularly confirms to us that Simon is not in Konjevici.

The Mardell story is now a big media event. Back in the UK, his parents and his fiancée are reluctantly in the spotlight. I, myself, am also getting a fair bit of attention. *Why did you permit him to go to Srebrenica when he was on an assessment to Cerska?*—asked my own masters. I received a wonderfully polite letter from Sir Donald Acheson, the head of World Health Organisation in Former Yugoslavia, a man whom I admire and like enormously. The gist of the letter was—*You got him in. You get him out. And quick.*

From somewhere, comes a plan: when Simon reaches Konjevici, he is to be escorted by the Bosnian troops to their front line, then he is to walk along the no man's land valley road towards the Serb front line carrying a white flag!

I do not like it.

Then there is a Plan Mark Two: when Simon leaves the Bosnian front line carrying a white flag, L. Hollingworth Esquire is to leave the Serb front lines carrying a white flag. We are to meet in the middle! I like this plan even less.

Meanwhile back in Srebrenica.

Simon is worried. Almir has overheard conversations. *Simon, they are not going to let you go. They need you as a doctor, and as a focal point, a hostage.* We are blissfully unaware of this. Via the amateur radio, we inform him that he must, must, must be at Konjevici by two p.m. the following day. *Last bite of the cherry*—he is told. Simon is determined that this is going to be his last day in Srebrenica. He has already studied the map. He has learned all the village names, he has worked out all the routes. He has decided that tomorrow, with or without an escort, he leaves.

To be at Konjevici by two p.m., he must leave Srebrenica by eight a.m. He worked hard for the remainder of that day, seeing as many patients as he could. He then packed and went to bed early, not difficult in Srebrenica without light and with a temperature nearing minus twenty.

He was up early. By eight there was no escort, but he did have with him his faithful Almir. True to his plan, he set off without them. He headed north, the road was wide and good. He passed many refugees. He passed the football stadium—then the factory housing—where there were more refugees. After walking at a cracking pace for more than a mile, his progress was suddenly halted by shelling; direct hits on the road immediately ahead of him. He and Almir took cover in a building and waited for it to stop. Whilst they were waiting, the escort turned up, and strangely the shelling stopped. They set off together, still travelling north but looking for the track to the west which leaves the road close by the hill of Caus, which is in Serb hands. It was a clear winter's day. The Serbs could see the birds in the trees. Spotting Simon, his translator, and escort was too easy. They sent down a hail of machine gun bullets which zinged about their ears. Once again it was stop, take cover, wait, then move. Each delay was placing extra pressure and strain on Simon. His deadline was two p.m. They waited a few minutes, then moved quickly to the turning off to the left. Here they were a little safer. The escort began to saunter, they had no convoy to meet. Almir was cold, hungry, tired, and inadequately dressed. Simon decided to step out at his own pace. He gave his rucksack to Almir and strode off. He knew he was on the right track when he hit a wall of refugees, fleeing Konjevici. They helped his map reading but hindered his pace. He forced his way through family group after family group, all struggling in the deep snow carrying babies, holding onto toddlers, dragging bundles. Simon eventually reached the outskirts of Konjevici. He had fifteen minutes left. On foot, he was not going to make it. He saw a refugee with his possessions draped over the crossbar of an old bicycle.

– *How much?*—he asked.

– *Molim, please*—said the Bosnian uncomprehendingly.

Simon took a fifty dollar note from his pocket.

– *Me the bike, you the dollars. OK?*

The refugee could not believe his luck. His possessions plus the bike would not fetch ten dollars. Fifty may find his family accommodation in overcrowded Srebrenica.

Simon mounted the bike and pedalled with fury, forcing the ancient buckled wheels through the deep snow. And so passed into the brief remaining folklore of Srebrenica, the story of the sight of an international doctor, pedalling an old expensive bike, clutching, with one hand, a heavy bag against his chest and steering with the other, against the flow of traffic and TOWARDS a town being shelled. Near the centre of Konjevici he almost collided with Naser Oric.

– *Have you seen UNPROFOR?*—he asked him.

Oric knew everything that went on, but he pretended not to understand.

– *UNPROFOR?*

– *Yes, have they left?*

– *They left the day after you arrived*—Simon did not have time to waste amusing Oric. He pedalled on to the municipal buildings. It was after two. There was no UNPROFOR. He asked around. There had been no UNPROFOR. Simon sat at the side of the road exhausted, bitterly disappointed. He felt desperately thirsty. He had been running or pedalling for more than six hours. He asked for water, and a lady brought him a litre jug. Simon put it to his lips and drained it, and then a second and a third.

He left the bike and walked back two kilometres and up the hill to the amateur radio station. He asked for Tuzla and for Michelle.

Whilst he waited, Almir arrived with the rucksack. When Michelle came on the radio, the news she gave him he did not want to hear.

– *Simon, can you go back to Srebrenica? General Morillon and Larry with a small convoy are on their way there now. They will stay the night, pick you up and bring you out tomorrow.*

– *No*—said physically and mentally exhausted Simon. *I'm staying here in Konjevici.* Almir and Simon wearily made their way to the Medical Centre. With Almira and Uvalic, he did a ward round. He stitched and patched and cut and sewed. He found the young boy whom I had marked on my list. He drained his chest.

Whilst working, he considered his options: go back to Srebrenica,

256

stay, or walk out of Konjevici Polje the way he had come in through Serb lines. He decided that, for today, he would take the middle route.

Fourteen

Srebrenica

Alors, c'est ça l'enfer… L'enfer, c'est les autres.
"So that is what hell is. It's other people."
In Huis Clos by Jean-Paul Sartre

Michelle was almost right. We were on our way, but we were delayed for two days whilst the General finalised the approval to enter Srebrenica. We left when he had the full support of General Wahlgren, and when Milosevic and Karadzic had agreed.

We were a small convoy. The lot consisted of General Morillon; Major Pyers Tucker; Macedonian born Adjutant Chief Vangel Mihailov, his Legionnaire bodyguard; a Canadian tracked vehicle and crew; a team of UNMOs, a duet of American military communicators; a team of three from Medecins sans Frontieres; Eric, Muriel, and Branko; a jeep and two trucks from the Belgian transport company under the command of Dirk, who had spent so much time with me trying to get into Kamenica; and finally the UNHCR vehicle, with myself and Laurence. We had started out with a much larger convoy, but approval for the rest was not granted, and it was parked at the side of the road on the Serb side of Zvornik.

We apparently had permission to enter via Bratunac but only from Milosevic's Serbia. Our mini convoy was led from the front by our gallant leader. At a Serb town a few kilometres from the turning to Bratunac, we came upon a Serb checkpoint that was not aware of our permission to travel. We started off quietly discussing our position with the senior policeman, but he was adamant we would have to go back. So we produced our secret weapon, the general. This did surprise the policeman. He knew Morillon from TV. He did not expect to find him commanding a small convoy. But he stuck to his position. He was not aware of the convoy. He would refer the matter to his superiors. We waited patiently, and a more senior policeman arrived. He refused to let us pass.

The General is now steaming.

– *Pyers, this is ridiculous. Get Milosevic on the phone.* Pyers Tucker knows that the two Americans have a singing, swinging, dancing, military satellite radio with them. It is to be used for effecting more accurate air drops. The duet is commanded by an American major.

– *Rex, can you rig up the phone and get Milosevic?*

Rex looks a little worried, but this is day one of the attachment and this is the first request. He orders the other half of the team, Sgt. Chappel, to "get Milosevic." Sgt. Chappel has a great sense of fun and humour. *Get Milosevic*—he repeats. He and Rex then spend the next half hour setting up this compact but complicated radio set. The aerial dish is run out in different directions. But no Milosevic. The patience of the General, not his strongest feature, has run out. Pyers is sent to investigate.

– *What is the problem boys?*

– *We can't get through.*

– *But I thought this thing gets through to anywhere. Milosevic is about one hundred kilometres away.*

– *Yes, well, you see Sir*—says Chappel—*this radio goes only to our headquarters in America and occasionally to our headquarters in Germany. It takes normal speech, condenses it and sends a quick secure burst to the headquarters where it is decoded.*

– *Can it get (expletive) Milosevic now?*

– *No.*

We have halted near a post office. Mihailov is sent in with some small change, and after thirty second or so, reaches the office of Milosevic! We are allowed to proceed. But we have to wait a few minutes whilst the Americans re-stow their expensive, secure, technical white elephant, which, in truth, later did admirably the job it was designed to do.

We crossed the green River Drina at the Bratunac bridge and were waved straight through to the centre of the town. I catch a glimpse of my old friend the Mayor, Mr. Simic. He waves. He knows I am going to get further than last time. We meet a convoy of dignitaries, including the local military commander who tells us, surprise, surprise, that the direct route to Srebrenica is not possible as the Muslims have destroyed the bridge during the night. Why they should choose the day of the arrival of a desperately needed life-saving convoy to destroy the route in, confuses me. Why the Serbs should think for one moment that we believe them, I also do not know.

We are, therefore, to take the convoy in via a route through the woods which has not been used for months. A narrow, twisting, mountain route which is thick with virgin snow and which may be mined. In addition, thanks to the delays, we have about an hour of light left.

We move onto the track with caution. We agree that the Canadian armoured vehicle will lead the way. We also agree that it is the vehicle least at risk. Tracked armoured vehicles have an excellent weight distribution and can often go where heavy trucks cannot. The UNMOs follow the tracked vehicle, MSF is next then me and then the two Belgian vehicles. The going is tough. Beneath the snow, which is a metre deep, there is ice. The road twists and climbs. It is picturesque. The track is bordered by high, steep hills from which tall snow laden pine trees reach for the sky.

The General decides that our progress is too slow. He therefore zooms ahead in the tracked vehicle. The MSF vehicle fails to negotiate a bend. The convoy is stopped, and all the experts have a go at trying to extricate it. They succeed in digging it in, up to its door sills, in thick snow. The wheels spin as if they are sitting in butter. We decide to abandon the vehicle. MSF is to join the UNHCR vehicle. We set off again. Suddenly there is an almighty bang. The valley reverberates. I leap out of our vehicle. The Belgian truck behind me has hit a mine. The cab is shattered. The front wheels are blown away. The snow is stained black. A grey cloud is rising. There is a strong firework smell. My first thought is for the drivers. I yell for Eric the MSF doctor. We race towards the truck. I fully expect to find the bodies of the drivers. I do. But they are picking themselves up out of the deep snow. The vehicle is the only one in the whole convoy which has a Kevlar mine proof lining inside the cab.

The Belgian government had the foresight, the generosity, and the concern to ensure the safety of the drivers. As the cab disintegrated, the Kevlar cocoon protected the crew from the initial and deadly effects of the mine. They were thrown out into the white cushion of snow. Their ears are ringing. They have the odd bruise but they are alive. The Kevlar has absorbed the impact, the blast and the slivers of metal. The truck is dead. It is a write off. The cargo in the back seems to be alright. It contained sugar and medicine. The sugar protected the medicines.

The doc examined the drivers, they are suffering from shock but are otherwise fine. The damaged truck is blocking the road. The one behind it will have to go back. The two crew from the front one want to travel on but they have had enough excitement for today, they must also go back. As I walk past the damaged truck, I see the track of the left-hand wheels of my own vehicle. They have passed over the mine. My vehicle was not heavy enough to set it off. Just as well, as my vehicle has never heard of Kevlar.

All of this activity takes time. I expect any minute to see the tracked vehicle with the General return to see if we are alright. It does not happen. We proceed and eventually catch up with him. He has made contact with the front line of the Srebrenica troops.

– *General we have lost a truck.*
– *Is everybody OK?*
– *Yes General.*
– *Bon.*
– *Not bloody bon General. You didn't come back for us.*
– *Larry, I was negotiating here. It is their mine. They planted it. They never expected us to come this way. The Serbs lie. There is nothing wrong with the bridge. Let us go. We will soon be in Srebrenica.*

I remembered that "maintenance of the aim" is a principle of war.

We were still a long way out from the centre of Srebrenica. It was now very dark. The Bosnians put a guide in the armoured vehicle and away we went. The track is downhill and the incline is one in eight. We moved dangerously fast, but for all of us, there was the exhilaration of being almost there. At the foot of the descent, we were stopped at a checkpoint. A voice challenged us. I heard the reply which ended with "Morillon." I could feel the excitement of the soldiers as they repeated "Morillon." I could imagine how pleased the

General was feeling.

At the checkpoint, we turned right and moved along a fairly wide dirt road. It was very dark; if there was a town ahead of us, there was no indication of it. I could see no lights and hear no noise.

The road narrowed. Suddenly I saw the dark silhouette of a building on the left, then I could see shapes moving in the street. One, two, then many—huddles of people, bundles of people, little children. It was late, but visitors were rare. Mobile visitors rarer.

The armoured vehicle was stopped, we bunched behind it. On the left was a double storey building, on our right another but smaller. From the building on the right, a group of men appeared. Our guide leaped from the armoured vehicle. Again I heard the word "Morillon." It was uttered as if it were a greeting. It then became a mantra as it was repeated and passed on.

I could see him. He was out of the vehicle and shaking hands. He was wearing a parka with the hood down. He was half turned towards me. I could see his big smile. The smile of success. He had made it. He was in Srebrenica. On the faces of the reception committee, I could see awe. They too could hardly believe that they had in their midst in Srebrenica the Commander of UNPROFOR.

I was about to jump out to join him when soldiers appeared and pointed to the open patch in front of the building. They wanted us to leave the road and to park the vehicles. A large crowd was now gathering and they wished to cordon us off. The armoured vehicle revved, the driver locked a track and the metal hulk slewed around, scattering the startled crowd. It mounted the pavement and came to a halt close to the entrance of the building. There was deep, undisturbed snow outside the building, I was more cautious than the Canadian driver. His vehicle could flatten obstacles. I did not want to disappear in a hole and I did not want to puncture a tyre. The UNMO driver was quicker and bolder than me. He pulled forward then reversed up the pavement and parked alongside the Canadians. I was reluctant to pull forward, the crowd was now dense, so I mounted the curb and parked alongside the UNMO with my nose against the wall. We got out. I locked the vehicle and then double checked every door. Everything in the car we needed, but not as much as the crowds around us. We then joined the boss in the doorway.

The building was dark and cold. We went through the open double door. If it is mid-winter and a building has had no heating, there is nothing to gain by keeping the door closed. Just inside the doorway there is a staircase to the left. Our guide knew the way and moved quickly, we stumbled and bumped into each other. There is a small landing and then another flight of stairs. At the top, we turned left and were taken to the end room on the left. The door was opened and a warm fug wafted towards us. There was a small stove in the left-hand corner of the room. It had the most wonderful red glow. The blanket of warmth enveloped us. Each of us was drawn to it.

Our guide, a small, very friendly man, was in uniform and was introduced as the military commander of the town. That he may have been, but we knew that the real defender of the region was Naser Oric, whom we had met in Konjevici. We were then introduced to the Mayor of Srebrenica and other dignitaries. They were all overwhelmed by the presence of General Morillon who graciously introduced us, and his team, to them. Mihailov, the General's bodyguard, did the translating. We all sat down at a long, narrow table. The room was tiny, long, and thin. The table took up most of the room. The chairs were basic and sitting down behind the table was a tight squeeze. I scrambled around to the far end of the room and sat on the far side of the table. I noticed that behind me were windows. I looked out of them but Srebrenica was a wall of darkness.

The talks were short. General Morillon told them that we had come to look. UNHCR came to see the refugee situation, MSF, the hospital, the Americans, the air drop sites, and the UNMO's security situation. Almir was tired, the translation was poor. Basically, we were welcomed and told in brief outline of the terrible plight of the town. It was agreed that we would meet early in the morning and have detailed discussions.

The MSF team left for the hospital, which was the dark building on the opposite side of the road. Laurence and I decided on a walk-about. We left the building, checked that the vehicle was still there and was still locked, and then turned left, away from the hospital. The street was pockmarked, whether by shelling or disrepair I could not tell. Huddled on both sides of the street were family groups. Some sat around the dying embers of smoky fires and others just snuggled together for warmth. The temperature was minus twenty-two. These pavement plots were home to the latest refugee arrivals. Those who had arrived earlier in the day were in the better positions in the doorways of the buildings. We asked many groups—*When did you arrive? Where are you from?* The majority had arrived in the past twenty-four hours from Konjevici. Some recognised us from our visit there. They told us stories of heavy shelling, many deaths, and a mass exodus. We asked about Simon. Those who knew of him were full of praise for him. They told us that he had now left.

The pattern of conversation in each group was similar. All would answer our greeting. A man would be their spokesman for the initial questions, then the women would begin to answer, then the women would cry, always drying their tears on a scarf, which all the women wore around their necks. Few of the refugees wore coats, one or two had no footwear, the tiny children were bundled in the middle of the circle in whatever was available—blankets, rags, newspapers. The elder children, those over seven or eight, were treated like adults, they took their place on the outer circle.

We saw none with food. They were cold, hungry, tired, bewildered. Some were originally from Zvornik, the unluckiest had been "cleansed" from Zvornik to Kamenica, from Kamenica to Cerska, from Cerska to Konjevici, and finally from Konjevici to here. No wonder they had no winter clothes. Their misery had begun in April one year ago.

We walked back in silence. We had a little food we could give away, but to whom? To the largest group? To the one with the most children? To the one with the oldest couple? How could we give to one group without being mobbed by others? How could we favour one and ignore another? We returned to the building. The Canadians and the UNMOs with the general and his team were preparing for bed. They were all in one large room on the top floor of the building. I suggested to Laurence that we would be much warmer and more comfortable in the vehicle. We went to the car, opened it, and decided that we would give a bar of chocolate to the nearest group. This we did clumsily and guiltily.

Ideally, I would have liked to have gone to the loo. But I had failed to see one in the building. I knew that if I had found one, it would not have flushed. The front of the building was still a centre of curiosity. A group of twenty or so citizens were talking to our Srebrenica guards and to the group of two guards which Pyers Tucker had quite sensibly decided to deploy.

I took a walk to the back of the building without a torch and, with a little trepidation, almost fell over the rest of the team. All like-minded, all same-purposed. I was relieved that I got into the vehicle and into my sleeping bag, removing only my boots and jacket. We were in Srebrenica. I was metres away from families like my own in size, maybe like my own in background. I wondered how I would cope, snuggling my children to me, attempting to ward off the bitter cold. I know that I would have felt humiliated, impotent, so I came to the conclusion that I would have stayed and fought. I then realised that these people had been driven out not by an advancing army, that is not the Mladic way, but by shellfire. You cannot stay and fight shells. They land and kill and maim indiscriminately. You can run like a headless chicken, you can stay in the cellar like a mouse, or you can quietly and resignedly join the throng and leave. Perhaps that is what I would have done. I felt close to the refugees but not close enough to really understand. Even if I had sat on the pavement with them, it could not be the same. I can escape, they cannot. For me here is now, but for them here is now, tomorrow, and maybe forever.

Sleep came.

Dawn broke. Ice inside the windows of the vehicle. Unzip sleeping bag, put boots on. Open the door, and onto the snow. We have an audience already. I look down at the huddles. They are all awake. Too cold to sleep, they have started patrolling the streets. First task: clean my teeth. Use saliva and spit into the snow. I have a bottle of water, but it will be so cold it would crack my teeth. Brush my hair, brush my beard. Always brings a laugh. But what else do people expect me to do with it?

The Canadians are in good humour, but the big attraction is Sgt. Chappel. He has a circle of admirers around him. Perhaps big black men are rare in Bosnia.

Laurence and I enter the building and go up the stairs. In the big room everyone is up, some are shaving. The general has found a small annexe to the main room. He is there with his team. Laurence and I go to the little room we were in last night. The fire is out and the room is freezing. Next to the stove on the windowsill are bits of radios. Someone is trying to make one out of many.

MSF arrive. They have spent the night in the hospital.

– *How is it?*

– *Unbelievable. Not possible to describe*—says the doctor. Soon we will see it for ourselves. A man from Srebrenica arrives with a burning piece of wood. It is to get the stove going.

The general and the Srebrenica authorities arrive. With them are two journalists, Tony Birtley, the Englishman with ABC, and Philip Von Recklinghausen, a German photographer. Tony had been there a short while with a Hi8 video camera and had taken, and was to take, some fantastic exclusive film. He had arrived in Srebrenica on a Bosnian Government resupply helicopter which flew in at hedge-chopping height straight across Serb lines. The pilots were mad but had no option, the wounded they took out had no option. Tony felt he had no option; he is a dedicated journalist. He was to leave Srebrenica with no option, as a casualty in a helicopter. Philip is a strange loner. He had been in Srebrenica for a long time, longer than many of the refugees. He had walked in. By now, he had few rolls of film left but had captured on still film the history of the siege. He was as lean, as dirty, and as hungry as any Srebrenican. Not a man to stand too close to—he was wounded three times whilst I was in Srebrenica.

The Director of the town, Hajrudin Ardic, began the briefing. He is about forty, was once a stocky man, and has a greying beard. He has carried the responsibility of the problems of the town on his shoulders throughout the siege. He probably never was a talkative man, now he speaks wearily and almost disinterestedly.

– *The town had a population of six thousand five hundred. It was an undeveloped rural spa famous for its water and its rehabilitation centre. The population was seventy-four per cent Muslim and twenty-four per cent Serb. In the whole region, we had thirty-seven thousand. Now we have twenty thousand people in the town and eighty thousand in the region. All property is damaged. In the town, eighty houses have been burned, more than one hundred destroyed by shelling. The hospital has one hundred beds. It has one hundred and sixty patients. Twenty die every day. In the town, we have one thousand children under one year old; two thousand under seven, and four thousand five hundred under fourteen. Four thousand people are living on the streets. They have had no food for five days. We have an emergency stock of tinned food of about seven tonne. That is it.*

He ended abruptly.

General Morillon thanked him and then divided our tasks. UNMOs to check out if the bridge is down. UNHCR and MSF to assess the hospital, the school and the refugee centres. We would be back by twelve and leave at one.

We went straight to the hospital. It is directly over the street, but the entrance is at the back. We walked up the slight hill, which was icy. On the right is what used to be the clinic and lab building. Standing outside the main entrance to the hospital was a large crowd, outpatients and visitors waiting to be allowed in. A group of soldiers were controlling who entered and who didn't. Opposite the entrance was a long dismal building with an incongruously blue door. It was unmistakably the morgue.

We entered, turned left, and climbed the stairs. At the top of the first flight there were patients on beds in the corridor and on the landing. We were met by the surgeon, Dr. Nedret Mujkanovic, who was a captain in the army. He is a tall, heavy man in his late twenties. He has limited surgery training. He has done some pathology and some paediatrics. He is now an experienced war surgeon but a troubled man with deep dark rings around his eyes—a man who now moves in wild jerky bursts.

I am so glad you have come. There have been so many. I could do no more—were his opening remarks. He spoke rapidly as he took us through the wards.

— *I have carried out more than one thousand operations in seven months. Never less than five a day. We have no drugs, few instruments, no bandages, no electricity.* He was close to tears.

— *We must have another surgeon. Please get me another surgeon.* Eric from MSF promised he would.

The doctor then began to talk with great warmth and admiration about Simon Mardell concluding with—*...I have his assessment list here.* He gave me a list compiled by Simon.

— *There are one hundred and thirty-one patients who need urgent evacuation. Ninety-six are men of military age. The staff know who they are. There are a further three hundred and five elderly who should be taken out. There are more than two thousand in the town including many amputees who have infected wounds. The hospital is overworked, overstretched, and under equipped.* Nedret continued—*Ninety-nine per cent of our patients are war casualties. Most wounded are from shelling, then gunfire, then mines. Since the 12th of July, nine months ago, there have been more than fifteen hundred patients in the hospital.* Nedret was reeling off information as if it had been stored up waiting for the chance to tell someone.

In and out of the wards, packed with beds on which lay the wounded. Bandaged heads, bandaged legs, bandaged arms. Blood, puss, and the sickly, clawing smell. The bandages were a mouldy green. I later learned it was a wound infection bacterium called "Pseudomonas." It was not a blur of bandages and smell, each bandage wrapped a person. A soldier, a child, a woman, each reacting to our presence. Some smiled, some implored our help, some cried, some were bewildered, some dying. I tried to smile, to touch, to reassure. I tried not to swallow the smell. I wanted to spit it out.

In a doctors' rest room, which had the benefit of a stove and a huge old antique radio, we were introduced to the five other doctors including a young woman, Dr. Fatima Dautbasic, who had been a general practitioner before the war. One was a paediatrician. He told me that the birth rate in Srebrenica was up. Three hundred children had been born in the hospital and many more outside.

Nedret took us to the operating theatre. It was a war invention; there had been no operating theatre before the war. Ragged and stained bandages were drying around a stove. A pan of water, in which lay the surgical instruments, was bubbling away in an attempt to sterilize the overused and blunt surgical implements. The operating lights stood by the operating table; two lamps lashed to a frame which stood on wheels connected by a thin cable to a car battery.

– *I need blankets, mattresses, bandages, plastic sheeting.* Nedret was still firing away.

– *We have no food for the patients, no milk for the babies.* This desperate litany had been bottled up inside poor Nedret's head. It was unleashed with passion and desperation.

– *Yesterday we lost five children, four women, and eleven men. All casualties of the war.* Mercifully, we were now back out of the hospital. I took in a deep, deep gulp of ice-cold air.

– *Thank you Nedret.* He hugged me.

– *Please, Mr. Larry, come back soon.*

We walked to the school. I needed the wind and the snow to blow away the clinging film of death and disease.

The school is a short walk down the main street. There are small grey terraced houses on each side of the road, behind those on the left is the river. The road is full of people, some perambulating up and down, others, the new arrivals, distinguished by the bundles they carry or push or pull on wheelbarrows or sledges, looking for somewhere to stop and park and live. We passed the empty tail section of a huge aircraft bomb, evidence that the town was bombed from the air, probably from Serbia, but that has not been proved.

The school is on the left side. The entrance is set back from the road. The school playground is a large concrete square surrounded by a high wire mesh fencing. It has stands with basketball nets and football goalposts painted on the wall. The school is large but cold and dark and damp. The classrooms are full of refugees, huge dormitories. There are mattresses everywhere, pots and pans, blankets, old couples, young children. Noise, clatter but no laughter. The younger children are silent and soulful, the early teenagers are running about pushing and barging, the middle teens stand in groups. They are all males. The girls are somewhere with their mothers. No one is cooking anything. They all ask for food.

Women appear with babies, tightly wrapped like dolls, they have heard that there is a doctor "from outside." They want to show their babies to him, to discuss some problem, some illness. We patiently explain that our Doc has the knowledge but not the equipment.

– *But don't worry, we will be back soon with more doctors, medicine, food, and milk.* At least we are dispensing hope.

In the school playground, some of the children are kicking around a ball made from a bundle of rags.

Time is running out. We want to visit a small annexe to the hospital where the recent amputees recover. It is near to the Municipal building and is a couple of houses with the rooms converted to wards. We stay only a few minutes. There are many young men who have lost legs. Some above the knee, some below, some have lost only their foot. One man has lost his right leg and his right arm. He is lying on his bed. I wonder how he will be able to walk. He has a crutch so presumably he can. Their crutches are home made. They all ask only one question. *When can we leave Srebrenica?* They want rehabilitation, they want artificial limbs. They have heard that the earlier they are fitted, the better, the easier, the more comfortable. They all seem psychologically well adjusted to their loss. Presumably, this is because there are so many of them.

It is now time to return.

Murat Efendic was the mayor of Srebrenica before he moved to Sarajevo to represent the town's interests in the capital. He asked me to visit his sister and his brother in law and to have a peep at his house to see how it is. His brother in law had visited the PTT building last night and left his address asking me to call upon them. The house is close by, so we decide to call upon them to see if they have any messages for Murat. A neighbour in the street points out the building. It is a small, old block of greystone flats. On the ground floor is a shop which belongs to the brother in law. It has been destroyed by shelling. The neighbour shouts out the name of the brother in law. A lady appears at a window on the second floor. She is the image of Murat. There is no doubt she is his sister. She is thrilled to see us and calls us up the stairs to her flat. It is immaculate, with lace tablecloths and heavy furniture. She wants to offer us coffee. Here I can help, as I have brought a small jar as a gift. Mainly by smiles and sign language, we arrange that she will quickly write a letter for Murat and get it to the PTT before we leave.

We return to our vehicle, restow our kit, contact Jeff in Kiseljak and tell him we will soon be on our way.

The General wants a "wash up" conference before we leave. We assemble in the same small room. The stove is lit. The atmosphere is light and happy. General Morillon asks us all to give an outline of what we have done and what we intend to do. He promises we will all soon return; there will be land corridors for the convoys and air corridors for the evacuation of the sickest. He tells them that he is leaving with them the team of UNMOs and he promises them two more teams.

They tell us that they have recovered the load from the vehicle destroyed by the mine, they wish us a safe journey and a speedy return. We all hug, shake hands, and join our vehicles which are surrounded by a huge crowd of people, mainly women. Amongst them are Tony Birtley—camera whirring—and Phillip Von Recklinghausen—camera clicking. Murat's sister is there. She hugs me, hands me a letter, and begins to cry. The UNMO vehicle is in the lead, the Canadian armoured vehicle is next, and the General is on it waving enthusiastically to the crowd. My vehicle is at the rear of the mini convoy. I wave to Dr. Nedret, and he gives me a great warm smile. The Canadian starts the huge diesel engine. It belches out a black cloud of smoke, the tracks engage, and the great metal beast inches forward. – *Careful*—says the General to the women in the crowd who are dangerously close to the tracks. I shouted to Almir—*Make sure no one touches the exhaust pipe or they will burn their hands.*

It may have taken only seconds before we realised that the crowd were not waving us off. They were preventing us from going. They were blocking the path. The women were shouting to Morillon— *Zasto bi ti isao kad mi ne mozemo?*—*Why should you leave when we cannot?*

Our polite hosts, seconds ago, so diligently waving us away, were nowhere to be seen. Mihailov was next to the General translating—*It is vital that I go. I have to arrange the convoy and the air evacuation.* The women did not move. Hajrudin was sent for, and he joined the General on the armoured vehicle. He talked to the crowd but to no avail. The women were joined by others with children. They formed a human barrier across the road. Some even lay in the snow.

– *You are our only guarantee*—they told General Morillon.

– *Only you can break the siege.* The words were flattering and final. We were going nowhere. I motored back far enough for the armoured vehicle to return to its place outside the building. I parked in my usual spot. The crowd remained in the snow. We returned upstairs to the small heated room. The attitude of our hosts had changed. The General appealed for them to intervene; they refused, saying that they had no power.

We were then told that we were not to wander around. We were to stay in the building. They knew that I had slept in my vehicle, and they knew that our radio link was in my vehicle, so I was permitted to go to the vehicle but not to leave the car park. Pyers came with me. We briefed our respective headquarters. Jeff in Kiseljak was calm and very professional. *I will keep this channel clear and manned twenty-four hours a day. OK?*

– *Thanks Jeff.* BH command was also calm, given the circumstances.

– *Are you saying that you are prisoners? Are you telling us that the General is a hostage?* Pyers reassured them that he was not.

– *No, no, no. The road is blocked by women. We are just not allowed to leave.* A rope barrier was now across the car park. Keeping the crowd at its distance. And preventing us from talking to them to find out the real depth of feeling.

We returned upstairs. By now, the others had been told that we were all to stay in the one large room. It looked as if we had lost our liberty. I looked at the General. He was outwardly cool and calm. But I knew that his mind must be in a turmoil. There were many who had opposed his mission to Srebrenica, who had said that he was abandoning his whole command for a small corner of his patch. There were many detractors who, when they heard that he was a hostage, would say with perverse pleasure—*I told you so.* The Serb and the Bosnian Serb leadership would be saying not only—*I told you so*—but—*We told you not to trust the Muslims.*

To my mind, the worst event that could happen would be for him to become both a central bargaining chip and an impotent onlooker. Various scenarios flashed across my mind. Between the Bosnian Government and the UN—*You lift arms embargo, we release General.* Between Bosnian Serbs and the UN—*You obtain release of all our prisoners, or we bomb Srebrenica with your General inside.* Or between Bosnian Government and Bosnian Serbs with the UN in the middle—*You allow convoys in and our sick and wounded military out, and we release Morillon.*

For a brief moment, he looked troubled and vulnerable. But only for a moment. He was soon fast asleep stretched between two uncomfortable chairs. Pyers and I had our evening schedule. Our masters were not impressed with our predicament. Pressure was being applied at all levels from New York to Sarajevo.

Unknown to most of us, General Morillon had asked his team to wake him at two a.m. The man of action had a plan.

At two, he quietly left the building, wearing his parka jacket with the hood pulled over his face. He walked along the street to the far end of the town where he waited for Tucker and Mihailov to join him. They were to take one of the jeeps and to convince the women that they had to make an urgent radio schedule and that they needed to move the vehicle in order to get good reception. The general hoped that, without him in the vehicle, the ladies would agree. They did not. The vehicle did not move, and the General waited in the dark freezing cold until four in the morning when he returned. This was not the end of his plotting. When he returned, he placed his bed on the floor in a small room annexed to the large room where everyone was still sleeping. No one had seen him go. No one had seen him return. Perhaps, if they did not see him, they would think that he had gone. Whatever, he kept the initiative.

For most of the next morning we stayed in the room. The authorities of Srebrenica visited more frequently as the morning progressed. They were looking for a glimpse of the general. They were obviously worried when they could not see him. He sat in the big room with dignity. He still maintained his aura of leadership. He sat and thought. Then he emerged.

– *Larry, do you have a flag?*

– *Yes General.*

– *A UN flag?*

– *Yes General.*

– *Do you have a tannoy?*

– *No, but I am sure we can find one.* He sent for the Director of the town.

– *I want to speak to the people. Get them outside the window. Also, I want to use your amateur radio to send a message to the Serbs and to the Sarajevo Government.* Hajrudin agreed to arrange all of this. The General then explained to me his plot. *I am going to tell the Serbs that they must allow corridors for the wounded and for aid. It is a matter of honour for them to open them. I am going to speak to the people of Srebrenica. I need a translator and a tannoy, and I want you to have the flag ready on a pole. OK?* Hajrudin produced a large crowd outside the building. The General stood in the room on the top floor overlooking the entrance. He opened the window; the crowd fell silent.

– *I came here voluntarily to be with you. I have decided to stay. I am placing you under the protection of the United Nations.* This was my cue. I pushed the pole with the United Nations flag attached to it out of the window. The words matched the flag. The crowd clapped and cheered. The general beamed. At the beginning of the speech, he was a hostage—at the end a hero. All because he had decided to stay! We were now free.

– *Bang goes my Terry Waite book*—I said to myself.

We followed him down the stairs and out into the crowd. An astonished Tony Birtley, who had a world exclusive in his camera, asked him—*General, you have placed them under the protection of the United Nations. What happens if it does not work?*

– *Of course it will work*—he replied. The general went off on a walkabout.

One of the young Canadians asked me—*Larry does that mean we are free to walk around amongst them?*

– *No, my friend. It means that you are free to run around and protect them.*

Our next schedule with Kiseljak was interesting. The general sat in the vehicle himself. He spoke to the French colonel. I could hear the intake of breath as the colonel realised the implications.

Later that evening, by which time the Security Council in New York had sat and discussed the policy of safe havens vis-à-vis safe areas, the general was mapping out his plans and therefore had asked his deputy commander, the brilliant, irascible, British Brigadier Roddy Cordy Simpson, to be at the other end of the radio. The general sat in the vehicle in the seat behind me. I contacted Jeff, who handed it over to the Brigadier. General Morillon began—*Roddy, I want (tomorrow) helicopter flights into Srebrenica to evacuate the wounded.* There was a pause.

– *That is not considered to be a good idea Sir.*

– *By whom Roddy?*

The brigadier thought quickly—*BH command Sir.*

– *Roddy, I AM BH command.*

General Morillon had been able to leave Kiseljak to go to Konjevici and to Srebrenica only because he knew that in his absence his command was in the very safe hands of the British brigadier whose competence was respected by all sides and whose temper was feared by everyone. I could hear the sucking in of breath. The count to ten then.

 – *Of course you are Sir.*

There were no helicopters the next day. The General spent his time building up the confidence of the people. The towns' authorities moved him out of the big room and gave him the two balcony rooms. One as his bedroom and the other as office for Tucker and Mihailov.

Furthermore, they installed a wood burning stove. One of the women who had led the blockade was given the task of looking after him. She in turn employed two young girls who kept his suite neat and tidy. The ultimate accolade was the production of some fresh milk for his coffee. Not wishing to state the obvious, this did indicate that there was at least one cow hidden somewhere in the town.

Now that we had freedom of movement and were popular, we could start doing our jobs. I had no aid to distribute, but I met up with those responsible for the feeding of the town. I saw the empty warehouses, we discussed the distribution system but more importantly, in the company of Rex and Sgt. Chappel, we met the military authorities to discuss the air drops which were the lifeline of the region. The problem was the collection. The town authorities wished to collect the aid so that they could distribute it equably. But in a town of tens of thousands of starving people, local initiative, survival, greed, and other motives overtook common welfare. When the planes were heard in the sky, the streets filled with people rushing to the few likely dropping zones. We were told it was a free-for-all. That night we decided to see for ourselves.

It was much worse than we anticipated. We knew from our radio source, Michelle, where the airdrop would be. We travelled in my vehicle without lights, so as not to give the location away. We were on the outskirts of the town in a wooded area near to a clearing. We heard the drone of the aircraft coming closer. We also heard the sound of voices and the breaking of twigs and branches. Out of the dark, we saw hundreds of people rushing towards the woods—men, women, and older children. The aircraft passed overhead, all eyes looked skyward. As my eyes scanned the darkness, I began to see the pallets of aid slowly and eerily swinging under their umbrellas of silk. I was not ready for what happened next. As the chutes approach the earth there is a whooshing noise, like a train going through a tunnel, the chutes collapse and the one tonne pallets slam through the trees cracking off branches and landing with a shudder. There is no way you can avoid a pallet if you are standing in its path. They can demolish houses and squash people. As your eye is on one, another, unseen, is swinging menacingly towards you.

There were shouts of warning, screams of pain, whoops of joy as individuals and groups seized, dodged, pursued these cubes of life-saving aid.

Treat people like animals and they will act like animals. The strongest grabbed the biggest. Some hunted in packs, some as individuals. They growled, they barked, they fought. The cartons were ripped and torn, pulled and pushed. The innards spilled over the snow-covered, cold, earth. Unlike the beasts of the jungle, these were the starving in Srebrenica. Within minutes, all trace of the quarry was gone. The aid, to be eaten, the boxes, to be burnt, the parachutes, to be made into clothes.

There was nothing for the local authorities to collect. The fit and the brave had the aid; the weak and the vulnerable had nothing.

The following day we learned that during the airdrop, four people had been killed: three struck by pallets and one stabbed in a fight over the contents of a pallet.

The UNMOs and the Americans recced the area and studied the maps. They came up with more isolated and more distant sites. This would assist collection. The Americans used their swish radio pack to inform their masters of the new locations and timings.

More people streamed into the town throughout the day. Both from the West and the South. Some came to Srebrenica because they had heard that the UN was in town, others because General Morillon was in town. All had been forced from their homes. We went in search of accommodation for them.

At the far end of the town near to the mosque there is a small cross-roads. To the right, there is a high-rise apartment complex packed with refugees, to the left is a narrow road to the old spa hotel. Tucked away to the right, on the bank of the river, is the Rehabilitation hospital. We did a quick tour and were made welcome. It has excellent facilities, a few rooms are used to house wounded soldiers, mainly amputees. Further on up the road there is a hairpin bend, then another which leads to the spa hotel. It nestles against the side of the hill from where flows the pure clear spa water which gurgles from the taps to the rear of the hotel. The whole complex has been ransacked. All the public rooms are vandalised. The accommodation annexe is damaged, the doors have been stolen, all the windows are shattered and some of the frames have been looted, but it is repairable. The floor of the hotel is littered with small plastic bottles in which the spa water was sold. There are thousands of them lying in the snow.

We returned to the centre of the town, to the office of the man responsible for refugees. He fully supports our findings but warns us that there is opposition to the refugees being billeted in the Rehabilitation hospital. The hospital was a main source of revenue for the town before the war. Many of the townspeople do not want the building damaged or destroyed by housing thousands of refugees. They would prefer it to house the UN, who may pay rent and who may pay compensation for any damage or to use it as an annexe to the hospital.

He is keen on us taking over the spa hotel. He starts talking about the UN bringing in building materials, cement, and wood.

– *Wait, wait, wait*—I say. *We have brought in so far medicine and sugar from one truck which was blown up.*

– *But the material can come in on the empty helicopters which take the sick out.* They have faith in the General. To test his enthusiasm, I suggest that he gets a work party up to the hotel and cleans away all the debris. I make a mental bet with myself. *Morillon will bring in helicopters before this man cleans up the hotel.*

Some refugees have discovered a warehouse with a huge store of plastic crates probably designed to hold one litre soft drink bottles; they are bright red. My first thoughts are that they are to be used as seats. But as night falls, I see that they are multipurpose. Men and women are indeed sitting on them, but as the temperature drops, their occupants rise and set fire to the crates. They burn brightly and fiercely with an orange flame. They melt and drip, heat and light. They quickly burn to nothing, leaving a black stain on the floor, a temporary warmth to the body, a dazzle to the eyes and then a return to the cold and the dark. It reminds me of bonfire night. Watching to see who is setting off their fireworks. Children roam and run from

279

burning crate to burning crate. Each group has its moments of glory as its crate burns. The cautious wait until the night gets colder and darker.

Up and down the street, the burning crates illuminate the family groups. The flames reveal the drawn, gaunt faces accentuated by flickering shadows. They reveal mouths smiling during a brief moment of relief, mouths displaying broken teeth, black stumps, or dark gaps.

We wander from group to group, drawn like moths to the flames. Every group we talk to has someone in it who cries. It is usually the older women. Often the younger teenage children smile when the elders cry. Perhaps out of embarrassment, perhaps it is their bewildered reaction to seeing a respected elder display an emotion usually reserved for themselves. Younger children cling tightly to the legs of parents or to their arms. Only when asleep do they relax and shudder.

Some groups are eating, some have food to eat and are warming it over a burning crate. Towards the end of the town is a group of the most recent arrivals. They are on the right-hand side of the road. There are seven of them, three generations. They have no crate. The men are sitting on the icy floor, the women are sitting on the small bundles containing all that they possess. The children are on the knees of the two men, father and grandfather. They are eating, passing something between them, they are picking at it, sucking on it, probing it, in the dark I cannot see what it is. I move in and greet them, and then I can see what they are sharing. It is a horse's hoof. It is cold, and I think it is uncooked. They explain. They have arrived without food, someone has given it to them. There will not be enough for the adults.

I want to be sick. I want to cry. But I am so stunned I do neither. I know that people do eat pigs' trotters and frogs' legs. Maybe horse's hoof is a Balkan delicacy. I doubt it. All of these thoughts flash across my mind. I really want to scream. I want to drag the people who are responsible for this from their offices, from their trenches, to stand and share this scene with me. I cannot stay any longer with this family. I move on.

280

As I walk back, I try to identify where I fit in. We share some of this hardship. We are cold. Our building is cold. In truth I am hungry. But we are not them. We have good clothing, good boots. We have muscle, fat, and vitamins—in other words, hope. And a ticket home. This is how and why we cope. We are tourists in their hell.

Back in the PTT building, we huddle in our own groups and discuss what we have seen. We enter into our sleeping bags and pull the material as close to us as we can, leaving no channel through which the night chill can blow.

Sleep comes slowly, enveloping the images, blurring the scenes, dulling the sadness and calming the anger. But the mind has been scarred.

Whilst we sleep, New York is awake and in a flurry. The actions, the words, and the decisions of many a General have slung the cat into the birdcage. The feathers of BBG are ruffled, Shashi Tharoor is throatily singing his mellifluous words, ambassadors are telling their countries what they have signed up to do, the Sarajevo General is defining to the press the connotations of "Safe," as in havens or areas. Roddy Cordy Simpson is arranging helicopters for "BH Command" in absentia.

The girls tip toe in, light the stove and General Morillon breakfasts on milk. Oblivious, maybe, impervious, certainly, to the new direction he has sent the United Nations. We waken and wash the sleep from our eyes. There is to be another airdrop this evening. We have asked for one pallet for ourselves. We are running out of food and our Canadian Warrant Officer has decided to ration us to eating one meal every other day. Of equal importance, our glorious leader is out of Davidoff cigars. In our pallet, there will be a carton of cigars for him and a bottle of brandy. The remainder of the pallet will contain medicine for the hospital. The UNMOs have recced a dropping zone on the hill at the back of the building where we are living. The aircraft will drop the aid for Srebrenica on the first pass, then turn and drop ours. Rex and Sgt. Chappel travel out to the high ground to pass the coordinates to America on the singing, swinging, dancing non-Milosevic phone.

During the day, the UNMOs visit the southerly outer extremities of our newly designated "safe area" and receive a reminder of the presence of the Serbs. They are fired upon. I visited the hospital and the refugee centres. Laurence and I draw up a plan for the warehousing and the issue of food when convoys recommence.

Today, lunch for us is very special. Murat's sister and brother-in-law have invited us to their home. We feel very guilty and have got together, as a contribution, the few remaining goodies that we have left. They embarrass us with their hospitality. The table is set, we have the best china, the best glasses. There is soup and slivovica, and she has cooked a pie. God knows what effort she must have gone to finding the ingredients. It is delicious. They want us to have seconds. But they do not eat with us. We guess that they will have what we leave. We decline seconds. But she insists on wrapping the remainder of the pie for our colleagues.

If "our" pallet arrives, we know where some of our share must come. Night falls. We are all excited. The military are in charge of the recovery of "our" pallet. We hear the drone of the aircraft. They are on time. We can see the Srebrenicans moving off to where they believe the pallets will land. We have a little chuckle. We hear the aircraft on its return approach. The military is off.

Forty minutes later, they are back with all that they have retrieved. A few strips of cardboard. The pallet was a few hundred metres off course. They were beaten to it. Somewhere in this starving city, somewhere very close to us, someone has his feet up with a glass of brandy in one hand and a Davidoff cigar in the other!

The following day, the medicine arrives anonymously at the hospital. We offer a reward for the recovery of "our" goodies, but what use is money when there are no shops?

So far, I have been sleeping on the floor in one of the rooms on the ground floor of the PTT with the soldiers. It is in the area of the post office where the counter service used to be. We use the counter as the distribution point for our food. We have only Meals Ready to Eat, plastic packets containing a mess or pottage of some flavour or other. Some menus are more popular than others, so in order to be fair, the good Warrant Officer has devised a system whereby the packets are laid out on the counter face down so that you cannot read the menu. We each choose one, pick it up, he notes who gets what and throws the packet into the pan of boiling water. It is the individual's task to fish out his own packet which at least warms up the fingers. This ceremony takes place at about seven every other evening.

Four rooms have been taken over as sleeping areas. There is a wash basin and a toilet in one room, with, of course, no water. One room, which was the manager's office, has a stove in it. This has become our main meeting room. We do not have enough wood to keep the fire going all the time but when it is lit, there is a pan of water bubbling away. The MRE packets contain sachets of coffee, and I have tea bags.

The soldiers collect water and wood from the spa.

I have now found a small room at the side of the building, which I appropriate in the name of UNHCR. It is three metres by two metres and contains what I believe is the automatic telephone exchange. I have also found four chairs. Standing them side by side, I now have a bed. True, they are not all the same height, but at least I am off the floor. The room has one window which is shuttered. I therefore have no light, but the room is wind and weatherproof. The exchange machinery is in the centre of the room and extends from ceiling to floor. I place the chairs between the machinery and the inner wall to give me maximum protection in case of shelling. I do this without thinking. Later I wonder to myself if I will now go through life applying war instincts and rules.

The room is dirty and musty, but it is private. It becomes my little safe haven. Over the next few days, I learn that I do not need much to keep me happy. My torch is important but not absolutely necessary. I eat only with a spoon, but it is important that it is one that I brought with me. My little penknife keeps my nails clean and my pencil sharpened. My sleeping bag is vital. I am very pleased with my boots. I am fastidious about where my possessions are, each has its own place. I can find them in a hurry or in the dark.

The General has now built up such confidence in the population

283

that he can go anywhere. He is not happy with the tardy response to his requests for helicopters, so he decides to leave Srebrenica to pass through the Serb lines and to go back to Kiseljak. The Srebrenica authorities are happy with this. As long as the rest of us stay.

He is definitely a charismatic leader. When he leaves, we all feel vulnerable. To add to our vulnerability, the moment that he is in their territory, the Serbs shell the city for the first time since we have been in, they use multi-barrel rockets and kill one child and wound a few others. My first experience of the rockets was at the airport at Sarajevo. They are a frightening weapon. Six or twelve rockets are fired in rapid succession from the same launcher. They explode in the air with a puff of grey smoke and then throw out splinters of metal. The first burst takes you by surprise, the others follow so rapidly that you have no time to run or hide. If you are within its range, you have had it.

Just in case this shelling is a prelude to the Serbs taking the city, we have a meeting, a military "orders" group, and quietly we decide on a plan. We will abandon our kit and take to the hills. This is not O'Rourkes Drift, and we are not the South Wales Borderers. As the oldest, the least fit, a civilian, and having had a look at the terrain around us, I decide privately on a little plan of my own—to shave off my beard and to take my chance mingling amongst the locals.

We are hearing from the new arrivals that there is aerial bombardment on the front-line villages to the Southeast of Srebrenica. This is important. Are the aircraft Bosnian Serb from Banja Luka or are they Serb-Serb from Belgrade? The UNMOs feel it is their duty to investigate. The two journalists, Tony Birtley and Philipp von Recklinghausen, know it is their duty to investigate. They hire a truck which has fuel, a beast almost as rare as a unicorn. The driver agrees to take them to the village but warns them that there is one dangerous exposed spot where they may incur heavy Serb machine gun fire. Tony tells me that they are going and admits that he is worried.

An hour or so later they are back. Near to the predicted spot, the lorry driver parked his truck to listen and to observe prior to making a dash for it. He was too near to the spot. A burst of machine gun fire raked the rocks around the truck. One round ricochets into the cab, misses Tony but scores the hand of Philipp. The UNMOs had more luck. They reached the village and are shown fragments of aerial bombs. The frightened villagers believe that the plane came from Serbia. Both these reports are relayed via the radio to Kiseljak and high-level protests are made without apportioning blame. The following day, both Philipp and Tony are back on the trail of the story, Philipp with a bandaged hand, looking a sorrier sight than usual.

Every day I pass the school playground and watch the children playing football. The rag ball is getting smaller, so I contact Michelle by radio.

– Larry here. On the next airdrop, can you include some footballs?

– Some what?

– Some footballs.

– Sorry Larry, reception is bad. It sounds as if you are asking for footballs (here I hear her laugh). *Can you spell what it is you want air dropping?*

– I spell foxtrot oscar oscar tango bravo alpha lima lima sierra.

– Footballs. You want footballs.

– For the children to play with.

Michelle had fun with this one. Dieticians were agonising over the nutritional content of the food to be dropped. Doctors were debating the priority of medicines to be sent. Every milligram of airdrop space was argued over and prioritised. And the man on the ground wants footballs! She won. The next drop included a couple of footballs.

General Morillon was not having the success he wanted in arranging a helicopter evacuation. The Serbs were not happy. They suspected that "war criminals" would be included in the evacuation. Their definition of "war criminal" seemed to be any male between the age of sixteen and sixty. So, parallel to his air evacuation negotiations, the General was pushing with UNHCR for the entry of an aid convoy.

Peter Kessler was in Sarajevo as the UNHCR spokesman. He is a little ferret. He gleans UNHCR news and then bites journalists until they have presented it around the world. We were now in contact every evening. He gave me the great news—*Tomorrow you will receive a convoy.* I then received a call from Karen in Zagreb.

— *The convoy that comes in tomorrow will have Louis Gentile from UN-HCR Belgrade with it. The trucks will offload and then leave with the worst of the casualties. They must be women or children or men over sixty. Either you or Louis is to take the trucks with the casualties to Tuzla.*

I organised a meeting with the authorities and with Nedret from the hospital. Based on Simon Mardell's list, he chose ninety-seven patients. If we received ten trucks, that would be roughly ten patients per truck. The journey from Srebrenica to Tuzla will take up to eight hours. It will be a bumpy, miserable ride, but ten to a truck will give them room to breathe. I got onto the radio—*We need, with the convoy, at least one hundred mattresses and two hundred blankets.* Belgrade was quicker than I was. Each truck would have a co-driver with some medical training. They had blankets, mattresses, first aid kits, and water bottles all organised. I went around the hospital with Nedret and saw the patients he had approved. I made two or three substitutions.

— *Nedret, I do not want people who are going to die on the journey, putting it bluntly, it will be bad publicity for the evacuation. Both the media and the Serbs would be delighted with such a story.* With some reservation, he agreed and so some of the weakest and most urgent were earmarked to die in Srebrenica. I passed on to the General that we would evacuate ninety-seven. This number formed the basis of his negotiations with the Serbs. The atmosphere in the town was electric. I was starkly aware of the fact that we were to bring in, at most, one hundred tonnes of aid. Sufficient to keep the town going for a few days. But the new spirit in the town had nothing to do with food. It was the fact that the outside world was coming into Srebrenica. That they were not abandoned or forgotten.

If the convoy comes tomorrow, and if Louis stays, this will be my last night in Srebrenica. So I am determined that I will make the most of it. After my meal, I walk around the town. You can touch the excitement. Many approach me to confirm the news of tomorrow's convoy. They hold my hand as they talk to me. They hug me when I leave them. I then went across to the hospital.

– *Where is Nedret?*

– *In the operating theatre*—I walked along the corridor expecting to find him carrying out some chore in preparation for tomorrow. I walked in to find him operating on a patient.

– *Larry. Good. Please, have you a torch?*

– *Yes*—I say, offering it to him.

– *Can you shine it in here?*—he asks, pointing to the open stomach of the patient. He is assisted by another doctor. He has rigged up the operating light to the car battery, but the light is weak. Fortunately, the operation is almost over. I spend the next half hour with my eyes mainly closed. The patient was to have been one of our evacuees but complications set in. I returned to the PTT. The boys are chatting around the stove. Pat Hoorebecke, the Belgian UNMO is, as ever, keeping morale high. He is an excellent officer. I realise that he has been a quiet but very positive influence here. I feel I know him well. I know about his wife and his dog. They are both very fond of England. I know quite a bit about the personal lives of the whole team. We have all become very close. I wonder how much they know about me. I make some tea and take it to my room. This may be my last night here. It has only been home for a week, but I am quite attached to it. I awake early and get up right away.

Tonight I may be in Tuzla. If I am, I can get a bath. So I decide not to wash, just to clean my teeth. I get onto the radio.

Peter, what news?

The convoy is at the other side of the bridge near Zvornik. It is all ready to go, but we are awaiting approval. I spent almost a week at Zvornik trying to get in here, but there is a big difference this time. New York is now aware of Srebrenica thanks to the action of mon general, and the man himself has gone out to meet the convoy to bring it in. Dirk, who spent so much time at Zvornik with me, has gone with him.

Throughout the day, I keep in touch with Kiseljak and Sarajevo. The convoy moves very slowly. By late afternoon, I make the decision that if the convoy arrives, it will stay overnight, and we will carry out the medevac tomorrow at dawn. There is great disappointment amongst the patients but relief amongst the hospital staff that we are not attempting to outload in the dark and the bitter cold. I spend most of my time in my vehicle on the radio. Peter Kessler is in the radio room in Sarajevo. He has half of the Sarajevo press corps with him. They are hungry for news.

Darkness falls. The UNMOs tell me the convoy has passed Serb lines. The tension and emotion is overpowering. The majority of the population are out on the streets waiting. The Srebrenica authorities are trying to keep the road clear. There are huge crowds outside the PTT building. I first hear the noise from the people as they hear the lead vehicles of the convoy. They are cheering and clapping. Then I hear the roar and the rumble of the lead APC. The chant of the crowd changes to "Morillon, Morillon." The APC trundles to a halt outside the PTT. In the cupola is the unmistakable figure of General Morillon. The crowd is wild with joy. I am shouting into the radio for Peter Kessler and the world to hear—*We have a convoy. We have a convoy.* My cheeks are warm with tears.

I leave the vehicle and find Louis Gentile, the UNHCR man. He is a tough young Canadian diplomat on loan to UNHCR. I am thrilled to see him. Together, we lead the convoy down to the warehouse where it is unloaded in the usual siege town slow style. When the trucks are empty, we lead them back to outside the PTT. The drivers are given the big room on the second floor where we began what Morillon calls in his book "La legende de Srebrenica." Louis and some more UNMOs have brought biscuits, sweets, fruit, and booze. Someone has donated a bottle of wine. It is a strange feeling to share the "stove room" with new people and with such food. Von Recklinghausen is like Ben Gunn. He has found some cheese. Louis is not sure what his future will be. He has received the same message as me. One of us stays and the other takes out the sick.

– Louis, what do you want to do?

– Stay—he says without hesitation. In truth, so do I.

– *OK, I will take out the sick.* Louis beams from ear to ear. His time in Srebrenica was more traumatic than mine. I showed him where "our" office was. I suggested that he move in right away, and I would move back into the main room. He would not hear of it. I then took him around the hospital, introduced him to Nedret, and discussed the evacuation plan. After a drink or two, I left for bed. I knew that the following day would be eventful, but I underestimated how much. I was up very early. I packed, said farewell to my room, and joined the drivers. It was still dark, and the slope leading to the hospital was icy and treacherous. Removing stretcher borne patients was not going to be easy. Inside the hospital, the staff had moved those who were to travel into the corridors. There was one big problem—there was a crowd of thousands outside the hospital, including whole families. Many had their possessions. I went to see the mayor and the military commander. He was saying farewell to General Morillon who was leaving to the Serb front line to ensure that the convoy had no hassle there.

— *Please move the crowd back. They are blocking the entrance to the hospital. It will be very difficult to load the sick onto the trucks.*

— *We will try*—was the best answer I got. We sent all the blankets into the hospital to wrap the patients. The drivers laid the mattresses on the floor of their vehicles. The co-drivers stood in the back to assist the loading. We reversed the first truck up the slope as close as possible to the hospital entrance. The first casualties were carried out and placed in the truck. Some were children. It had been agreed that wounded children would be accompanied by their mothers and that if their mothers had other dependent children, they would also travel with their mother so that we could keep the family together. Whether it was the sight of fit women and children climbing onto the trucks or whether it was planned, I do not know, but suddenly, the crowd surged forward and within seconds, the trucks were full of people—desperate people pushing, shoving, fighting, kicking, all of them determined to escape from Srebrenica. The trucks were full. Worse, they were surrounded. We could not get the stretcher borne patients anywhere near the trucks. They were shivering with cold. We sent them back into the hospital. I climbed onto the first vehicle and began to throw people off, physically. I was grabbing them by their limbs, their hair, and throwing them off. I was punched and kicked and bitten. As fast as I was throwing them off, others were

289

climbing up.

Everything was out of control. There were thousands of people on the trucks. Women had thrown on babies and young children to give them the chance of escaping. The babies were howling, the young children were screaming, the women crying.

I jumped off the vehicle. There was no one from authority in sight. I ran into the PTT and bounded up the stairs. The mayor was hiding in the room with the stove. I dragged him out and down the stairs. *What the hell are you going to do about this?*—I yelled. In his customary lethargic way, he went back into the building and returned with a policeman who began firing into the air with a Kalashnikov automatic rifle. For maybe thirty seconds, there was silence and peace. Then the mayhem broke out again as family fought family for a place on the trucks. The police tried another burst of fire. It was totally ignored.

I pleaded with the mayor to let us at least get the wounded on first and then we would fill up the vehicles. But it was a waste of time. He was powerless. We were all powerless. Mob rule had taken over. I stopped running around and told the drivers to move forward two hundred metres to at least escape from the thronging crowd. This they did. The police at least tried to form a cordon behind the trucks but this was soon breached. I got onto the radio and talked to Kiseljak and Zagreb.

– *Look it is chaos here. I have hundreds on the trucks, maybe even a thousand. Few are the sick I intended evacuating. I can call off the whole evacuation and try again or go ahead with what I have.*

– *You are on the spot. What do you think you should do?* I had already worked this one out. If I called off the evacuation, eventually the people would leave the trucks. Would we then send the trucks out empty after all the negotiations that had been conducted to get this far? If we emptied the trucks and waited, would the crowd go away? Highly unlikely. They had nothing else to do. Could the local authorities prevent the people from boarding the trucks? I felt that Nasir Oruc and his troops could, but that the rest could not. Would Oruc? Why should he alienate his own people? A few less in the town would not detract from its defence.

– *I think I should try to get as many sick on as is possible and then fill the trucks.*

– *OK*—said my masters. *But be careful we are not accused of cleansing the place.* I did not even deign to comment on this one. I then spoke to General Morillon down at the Serb checkpoint. I explained what was happening.

– *General you have approval for ninety-seven. I can cancel it or turn up with almost a thousand.*

– *Larry, you come. We are waiting.*

– *General, that does not answer the question.*

– *Larry, you leave now.*

– *OK General. Leaving now.*

– *Larry. No men under sixty, OK?* So that was his answer. Get moving. Bring what you have. Make sure there are no men under sixty. I explained to Louis what I was about to do, shook him by the hand, and wished him well. I was just leaving the building when Tony Birtley approached me—*Larry, will you do me a favour? Will you take my films out and give them to ABC in Tuzla?* I took them from him and stuffed them in my various pockets. I climbed into the lead vehicle and left. In the rear mirror, I could see women running alongside the vehicles holding their children aloft and arms on the trucks pulling them aboard.

I got the convoy moving at quite a speed, because at every corner there were crowds waiting for the chance to go to Tuzla. We motored for about fifteen minutes. We were then out of town, exposed to Serb fire but not to crazed crowds. I then stopped the convoy and attempted to do a head count. I also made it clear that any males under sixty would be arrested by the Serbs at the checkpoint and that I would do nothing to help them. There were a couple on board.

– *What can we do?*—they asked.

– *Get off and walk back*—was my reply. By now I hated Srebrenica. I was so angry. These people had betrayed their own wounded. I reckoned that I had on board forty of the ninety-seven sick and about eight hundred sanctuary seekers. The sick were squashed and trampled under the fit. I tried to rearrange the trucks, but this just caused more panic. We stopped the convoy just before the Serb front line. I got out and walked forward and saw the General with Pyers. I explained what happened.

– *Will the extra numbers cause chaos here?*

– *Larry, the Serbs would be happy if you brought everybody out.* He was so right. I walked back to the convoy. There was a Serb officer standing by it.

– *Mr. Larry, I have some old people here from Bratunac. They are Muslims. Please take them to Tuzla.* I looked at them. They were old and bent and certainly more infirm than the majority of my convoy of so-called sick.

– *Do you want to go to Tuzla?*—I asked each of them.

– *Yes*—they answered enthusiastically. I put them on board. Despite the fact that we may have been doing the Serbs a favour, they took their time at each checkpoint. They counted and recounted and leered and threatened and provoked and humiliated my lot.

It was early evening before I arrived with them at Tuzla. We were escorted by the police and a fleet of ambulances to the football stadium which had been converted into a huge reception centre. There were hundreds of media people watching as the convoy unloaded its human cargo. They were carried down and escorted up the steps to the line of doctors waiting to grade them. I realised that in truth, they were all ill. The citizens of Tuzla had been affected by war, but they were fit and healthy by comparison to those whom I had brought. "My lot" were thin and emaciated; physically and mentally battle-scarred and weary. I felt better for this.

ABC News soon found me and took from me the Tony Birtley tapes—the first films out of Srebrenica. He was filming as the trucks were loaded. I hoped that there were no reels of me throwing people off the trucks. I was taken to the main Tuzla hotel. I was desperate for a bath. There were no rooms, and the place was full of journalists.

I was at my lowest ebb. Then I heard a voice I knew so well. *Larry I have been looking everywhere for you.* It was Michelle.

– *Did you get the footballs?* We both laughed. *UNHCR has a party in its office. We are waiting for you.* At the party, I met Rod Kay of UNHCR, a fellow Merseysider, who had a room in the hotel. He had twin beds and offered me one of them. The party was full of attractive women, but Rod's was the only offer I received. The following day, the Serb radio vilified me for negotiating the removal of ninety-seven wounded and then evacuating "almost a thousand." They congratulated themselves on their compassion. The Bosnian Government television vilified me for aiding and abetting the cleansing of Bosnians from Srebrenica.

I made my way back to Sarajevo and went straight to Simon's room to find out what had happened to him. Simon told me that whilst we were on our way to Srebrenica, he had assumed the role of resident doctor in Konjevici Polje, where there was the constant rumble of shelling in the distance. The day after he arrived, he awoke early and worked hard. At one o'clock he stopped for a break. He went down to the river and decided to take off his boots and to wash his feet in the icy cold water. It was a peaceful spot, especially in contrast to the urgency and the smoke and the smells of the houses containing the patients. The peace was shattered with whistles, the whine, and the deafening bang of an artillery shell. Huge howitzer shells from a single gun began to punctuate life in the village.

Simon again had three choices: to abandon his boots and socks and to run for cover, to put his boots and socks on and run for cover, or to pick up his boots and socks and run for cover. He went again for the middle course. He raced to the house where he was staying. Not to the nearest house, but to the house that was "home," even though he had only been there one night. Home is where your kit is. Home is where you want to be in a time of crisis.

The shells pounded the village every few minutes. At about two o'clock Simon heard another loud rumbling noise, but this one was friendly. Like in a B movie, the cavalry had arrived. Alan Abraham was back. At first, Simon cheered and waved and shouted. Then he realised that they were driving past. He had seen them, but they had not seen him.

Simon eventually caught their attention. They had come in to evacuate the seventy wounded and to take out Simon. They had two armoured vehicles, of which one was unserviceable and being towed by a recovery vehicle. With them was a UNMO vehicle and a vehicle from ICRC with Andreas Schiess. They had been forced to leave some trucks at the last Serb checkpoint. The Serbs had insisted that the whole convoy be out before nightfall. The aim was to find the patients and shuttle them from Konjevici to the Serb checkpoint where they would be put into the trucks and taken to the hospital. The Serbs had added the usual proviso. The wounded could not include men between the age of sixteen to sixty. This caused problem number one. Naser Oric, the Bosnian commander, was insisting that the most ill were taken out. Not surprisingly, the most ill included his wounded soldiers. More than this, Oric was insisting that if there were no soldiers, there would be no evacuation.

A huge crowd surrounded the UN convoy. The wounded were brought by cart to them. The shelling of the town was still ongoing. More casualties were occurring by the minute. Captain Nick Costello, the ever-brave British Army translator who was in the thick of so many incidents through a long and dangerous tour in Bosnia, attempted to quieten and reason with the crowd.

John McNair, the British Royal Army Medical Corps medic, brought to Simon a young woman whose shoulder had been blown away. She hardly had a pulse; she had lost an enormous amount of blood. John put up a drip. John, Simon, and Andries, the ICRC rep, quickly checked the houses to assemble the medical evacuees. They were looking for children, old men, and women.

Whilst they were working, the senior UNMO, a Russian Sasha Vasiliev, came running up to them. *We must go now. The Brits are surrounded by a frantic crowd.* Simon ignored the order.

– *I felt I was going to be OK. The convoy had come in to do a job and to fulfil a promise. We had to deliver.* Sasha, who is a small, tough, happy-go-lucky man, stayed with Simon, but soon they could hear the noise from around the convoy. Hundreds and hundreds of angry women were around the trucks. They were demanding that they be evacuated. They made it clear that if they were not, then no one was going anywhere. Rebel rousing them was a toothless old crone. Alan Abraham was attempting to reason with Naser Oric who was taking the usual line in these circumstances—*I would love to help, but I cannot. I cannot shoot on our own women.* Alan Abraham quite wisely gave the order that everyone was to stay with the vehicles. If he saw a chance to move then he would go for it.

Simon was, as ever, independent. *We are not able to move. I have patients to look after.* He went and found the woman with the damaged shoulder. He gave her a local anaesthetic, and for the next ninety minutes operated on her. His translator assisted. He returned to the vehicle. Alan Abraham was still controlling the situation. His vehicles were still in his hands. The crowd was not a mob.

Simon went to one of the houses where there was a group of young children crying and sobbing. They had just witnessed the death of their parents who were killed by a shell. By now it was late. Alan gave the order to stay overnight. Simon did his rounds. The following morning, Simon was up early and performing minor operations. His lady with the damaged shoulder was still alive. At one o'clock very heavy shelling began causing many casualties. A woman came running up to John McNair. She was hysterical. In her arms, she carried a baby in a bloodstained sheet. *Do something for my baby!* —she screamed. John pulled back the sheet. The baby had no head. It had been decapitated by shrapnel. Simon treated a little girl with a leg shattered by a shell. He took a scarf from the neck of an old lady and applied it as a tourniquet. Simon watched a nurse and mother of three, Almira Mombera, perform minor surgery on a young child. He was impressed with her skills—all learned during the war—and mainly without supervision.

The British soldiers helped to staunch blood, to bandage, and to console.

– *Simon, Simon, we must go. The UN has been hit.* They all ran to where the vehicles were parked. The UNMO vehicle had been hit. Sasha had been inches from it. He and his colleagues were OK. Alan Abraham made the decision—*I am sorry we must go. We are not stopping the shelling. We are not protecting the people. Our vehicles are being hit. Soon we will lose men.*

He was right and everyone knew it. The next few moments were ones of great sadness. The soldiers said farewell. There were hugs, kisses, and many tears. *Please let me come with you?*—asked Almira the nurse. Simon quietly explained that she could not and that far more importantly, she was needed with the people and by the people. She understood, but it did not make leaving her any easier. The convoy left. By nightfall, Konjevici was on the move. The following day it fell to the Serbs, but by then, most of its inhabitants had walked to Srebrenica. Some carried the patients whom I had seen in Srebrenica and tried to evacuate.

Fifteen

Of Papers and Prime Ministers

Deputy Prime Minister Zlatko Lagumdzija kindly hosted a dinner to welcome me back to Sarajevo. Murat Effendic, in the presence of several displaced Srebrenicans, presented me with a superb bronze picture and a thank you letter from Srebrenica. I was very touched.

Later, I learned that the order to detain us in Srebrenica had come from Murat Effendic. I bear him no ill will. In his shoes, I would have done the same thing. Morillon's bold move to force Srebrenica onto the world scene needed an extra tweak. Murat provided that twist. His action kept the enclave alive for another two years but sadly with disastrous results.

Much later, I had the chance to clear up another mystery. In a quiet moment, I visited Zlatko Lagumdzija in his office. He was relaxed and in a frank and open mood. I seized the chance and asked him about the "Sarajevo Hungerstrike."

– Zlatko, Sir, what were you thinking of when you ordered it? His mood changed immediately.

– Larry, you are running humanitarian aid. We are running a country. You think your job is difficult! I will tell you exactly what happened. Then you can see how difficult ours is. The story he told me made me like him even more.

– I was told that a small delegation from Srebrenica had come to Sarajevo. They had taken a great risk, as they were all well-known and would have been easily recognised if they had been caught as they crossed the Serb lines. They came to see me. I sat them down around my table. They told me that the situation in Srebrenica was so desperate that it needed desperate action. They were angry that the only city mentioned in the world news was Sarajevo. They believed that no one knew about Srebrenica. They had a plan of action. For each citizen of Srebrenica who was killed, they would kill a Serb in Sarajevo. Zlatko paused whilst I took this in, then he continued. *I said to them, 'OK. In the block where I live, there are Serbs living above me. I will give you the addresses of their apartments.'* Zlatko paused again—*They leaned forward in their*

chairs. They looked at each other. I then said to them, 'I will also give you the address of my apartment.'

Zlatko now had me in the palm of his hand. He paused and then continued—*I said to them, 'Before you get to the Serbs, you have to pass my apartment. Before you get to the Serbs, you will have to kill me. These Serbs are my neighbours. They are from Sarajevo. They are Bosnians. When I have no food, they have no food, when I have no water, they have no water. When I am shelled, they are shelled.'*

He told me that his reply stunned them. He asked them if they really wanted innocents to be killed. He weaned them off violence, but he promised a tougher stance on Srebrenica. Hence the imposition of the "Sarajevo Hungerstrike." Little picture Larry left the office a humbler, wiser man. Big Picture Deputy Prime Minister Zlatko returned to his deep in tray and his outer office full of supplicants.

Only after I returned to Sarajevo did I begin to hear criticism of the actions of General Morillon. By placing Srebrenica "under the protection of the United Nations," he had "put the place on the map" and forced New York to do something about it. What Morillon wanted was a detachment of Canadians to be sent in, an increase in the numbers of the United Nations Military Observers, and an air evacuation of the wounded. What he got was a ceasefire, the demilitarization of Srebrenica, the entrance of the Canadians, an increase in the numbers of UNMOs, and, amazingly, a UN Security Council Resolution declaring Srebrenica a "safe area."

He also got an air evacuation. It included some of the victims of a vicious, barbaric, obscene shelling, which took place on the twelfth of April, which killed fifty-six, including many children who were playing football in the school playground with the ball which had arrived by airdrop. Louis Gentile, brave, calm Louis, informed UNHCR that—*...fourteen dead bodies were found in the schoolyard. Limbs and human flesh clung to the schoolyard fence. The ground was soaked with blood. One child had been decapitated.* He concluded his gruesome, disturbing message—*I will never be able to convey the sheer horror of the atrocity I witnessed. I do not look forward to closing my eyes at night for fear that I will relive the images of a nightmare that was not a dream.*

298

Simon Mardell and I attended the press conference in Sarajevo the following morning. I made the following statement—*Simon and I wish to speak, as we have shared some of the anguish of the people of Srebrenica. When, yesterday, I heard the news about the shelling, my first thought was of the Army Commander who had ordered the shelling. I hope that he burns in the hottest part of hell.*

I then thought of the soldiers who had loaded the guns and fired them. I hope that they suffer from nightmares. I hope that their sleep is broken by the screams of the children and the cries of their mothers.

I then thought about Doctor of Medicine Karadzic, Professor of Literature Koljevic, Biologist Mrs. Plavsic, and Geologist Dr. Lukic. I wondered if today they will condemn this atrocity and punish the perpetrators, or, will they deny their education and condone it?

I then thought about my Serb friends whom I had met on my travels. Do they wish to read in future history books that their army has chased innocent women and children from village to village until, finally, they are cornered in Srebrenica, a place from which there is no escape and where their fate is to be transported like cattle or slaughtered like lambs?

Later that day at the airport, there was a conference attended by the generals and the top negotiators from Zagreb. The evacuation of Srebrenica was the subject. The senior person present was Cedric Thornberry, the distinguished Irish civil rights lawyer who was now UNPROFOR's most senior civil servant. He approached me and smiled a smile that must have devastated many a prosecuting counsel.

– *Larry, heard your spontaneous speech to the press. It was outstanding. Must have taken you all night to write it.* The first air evacuation of the wounded involved a very brave "hot extraction." The designated and agreed helicopter pad came under mortar fire, and some of my Canadian friends were wounded.

The helicopters—French crewed Pumas and Royal Navy Sea Kings of 845 Squadron piloted by crews led by Lt. Commander George Wallace—took off from Tuzla and flew to Zvornik football stadium where they were inspected by Serbs who checked who was on board and ensured that nothing was taken into Srebrenica. Everything was stripped from the helicopters on each and every trip, to test the patience of the crews.

In the football stadium at Srebrenica, Louisa Chan, a doctor from the World Health Organisation, ran what is known in the medical profession as a triage—a new word for me—a place where patients are categorised. Some she rejected, others she prioritised.

I was supposed to travel in on the first helicopter, but the Serbs were still smarting over my "Hottest corner of Hell" speech, which had received a slice of media coverage. But in fairness to them, they let me travel on the first flight on the second day. We took in a Muslim doctor from Tuzla and a Serb doctor from Zvornik. They were to examine the patients and to ensure that only seriously wounded would leave. The Serbs were still insisting that there would be no "war criminals" amongst the wounded, which was supposed to eliminate all men between sixteen and sixty. Fortunately, the Serb doctor who we took in was kind, considerate, and genuine. He was a doctor first and a Srpska Republika Serb second. He was also very kind to his Muslim colleague. They were slightly wary of each other at first but soon swapped stories of colleagues and friends. The Serb gave some money to the Muslim to give to a relative who was living in Tuzla. The Muslim stood close to the Serb when the helicopter first landed in Srebrenica, when he was at his most nervous and his most vulnerable.

The negotiations with the Serbs had been for the evacuation of five hundred wounded. It was easy to categorise the first two hundred. They were stretcher borne and painfully and visibly very sick. The remainder was a lottery. The amputees with suppurating stumps were an obvious category. Many had been identified by Simon Mardell, who was not allowed by WHO to go to Srebrenica for fear of reprisal for his previous behaviour. He met the helicopters at Tuzla. He saw many of his patients from Konjevici Polje as well as from Srebrenica. He saw the nurse Almira and the lady whose shoulder he had patched under shellfire.

In Srebrenica, when the word got around that amputees were included in the evacuation, every amputee in the valley moved to the football stadium. They came on crutches, in the arms, on the backs of friends, or in wheelbarrows. Some hopped, some ran, some shuffled. It was as if a Pied Piper had played a magic tune that attracted only limbless people. There were hundreds and hundreds of them.

So many that we had to block off the road with barbed wire. Myself and a few soldiers were the keepers of the gate. For the first hour, we were sympathetic as stump upon stump was unwrapped and raised for our inspection. But as we realised that we had few helicopters and jumbo jet-loads of applicants, we became more ruthless. Fresh wounds, young children, women, and Oscar-winning actors passed the first hurdle and were handed on to the doctors. There was good humour on both sides. So essential in so bizarre and tragic a setting. We knew that not only were we giving the chance of treatment but also escape from the risk of further shelling. We did not then know that many whom we left behind would brutally lose their lives two years later.

When Louis left Srebrenica, he also brought out a convoy of wounded. He brought out more than I did. He had the same mad chaotic scenes. So crowded were his trucks that some died of a lack of oxygen as they fell to the floor of the trucks. He also had the truck from which a little child fell. The picture of the child crying as he watched his frantic mother waving as the truck she was on sped away was in many newspapers. The child was eventually reunited with his mother.

Back in Tuzla, this time, I had a hotel room of my own. I found it very difficult to put the experience in context. It was as if I had been in a Fellini film or in a circus. My mind was full of images of bandages flying and crutches waving. I could not put a face to anyone, just a huge anonymous canvas of deformities. In and out weaved cameras and tripods and notebooks and questions. More compartments to close down.

I was glad to return to the measured insanity of Sarajevo where the talk is of extending the "safe area" concept to Tuzla, Bihac, Zepa, Gorazde, and Sarajevo itself. Apparently, tens of thousands of troops will be requested for the task. We have had fun trying to get one hundred and fifty Canadians into Srebrenica!

My next aim is to get back into Zepa.

The six areas are now "safe" according to the UN definition. Boutrus Boutrus-Ghalli has asked for thirty-five thousand troops to make them safe. So far, he has a handful. "Safe" Zepa is taking a beating from Serb artillery. There are rumours that the inhabitants have abandoned the town and are now living in the hills, in caves. Simon Mardell and I are part of a small group led by a very tough Dutch Military Police Colonel who are to go in and see what is happening to our new "safe area."

We hang around in Pale for a few days awaiting approval. Our base is in the UNMO house. But Simon, Zlatan, and I are staying with the hunter and his lovely wife. Today is the day. We have approval. We are to go in with an escort of Ukrainians. All is well until we get to Rogatica. The Serbs insist that we stay the night and go in tomorrow. They do not seem to be too keen on me. They make oblique references to a certain corner of hell, but they make it absolutely clear that they are not allowing any Muslims into Zepa. This is a real nuisance. It eliminates the UNMO translator and Zlatan, my doctor's driver. They will have to go back to Sarajevo tomorrow. The Dutch colonel, who is world-famous for a television clip in which he physically sorts out an angry Serb who is recklessly toting a Kalashnikov, argues for them to stay—normally my job. But I am very happy to hand over the task of Duty Rottweiler to him. He does not succeed. We decide that one UNMO vehicle will go back with Zlatan and the translator. The UNMO is a Norwegian and is new to the Serb scene, which is a pity, as between Rogatica and Sarajevo there is a three-hour drive and many a checkpoint. The result is that he is not forceful enough, and at one checkpoint the Serbs haul out of his vehicle Zlatan and the translator—both of whom are arrested and thrown into prison. We, of course, know nothing of this.

The day gets worse. The Serbs decide that I cannot go. We argue. I argue. We fail. So, I say farewell to the colonel and to Simon as they prepare to leave. Then one sharp-eyed Serb spots "walk into Srebrenica" Simon and he joins the lengthening list of no go's.

The Ukrainians and the Colonel leave for Zepa, which is the cue for Simon and me, each in his own vehicle, to leave, but we decide to be difficult and to stay and complain. At first, we are ignored. Then we are verbally abused. We still stay. A young captain then arrives. He is not at all pleased with us, and as the day wears on, he becomes aggressive. He demands we leave Rogatica. He threatens to arrest us, then to shoot us. We are not going to be allowed into Zepa today, that is obvious. So, together, Simon and I agree that we will go but with dignity. This means slowly turning our vehicles away from the direction of Zepa and even more slowly leaving Rogatica checkpoint. The captain is now frothing at the mouth. He is waving his weapon and urging us to leave more quickly.

We proceed with a little more dignity than is necessary, moving away at very few miles an hour. The captain stops us and threatens us once again. He then moves away, and we set off only slightly faster. We are acutely aware of the fact that during all of this escapade neither of us has been able to contact Sarajevo by radio. We are in a valley, a communication black spot, and maybe a black situation.

The crest of the hill, a source of good communications, is six or seven kilometres out of Rogatica. Up the winding hill, past the first Serb checkpoint, is a caravan manned always by a delightful old soak who cheerfully waves everyone through.

At the crest, we try to make contact but fail. The next good spot is a couple of kilometres further on. Here we try again, with no success, but we meet a boy playing with a ball in a field. Soon he has introduced us to his friends. One of whom would like a lift into the next town, another would like a letter taken to Sarajevo. We do not notice the arrival of the irate captain. He gives us an ultimatum, shoos away our new friends, and tears up their letter. The one who wants a lift climbs into Simon's vehicle. This is a real provocation to the captain. He insists the young man get out and walk.

We proceed to the next checkpoint at Podromanija. They are expecting us. We are stopped and told we have to await approval before we can move. They delay us until it gets dark, then let us go. At the next checkpoint, we are again delayed. We arrive late in Pale. Late, tired, and exhausted. The following morning we motor to Lukavica. There, I am told that I can have approval to go to Zepa. Simon cannot. They give me a piece of paper which says that General Mladic permits me to enter Zepa. I race back. At Podromanija I am delayed for hours and hassled by a drunken Serb soldier. Fortunately, my radio is working and, even better, Simon is listening in on the other end. I begin to think that being on my own is not the best of ideas. Eventually, they let me go to Rogatica. My arrival at the checkpoint causes quite a stir. I wave my paper and demand to be allowed to motor on to Zepa. A soldier with a Kalashnikov is placed in front of my vehicle, and I am told not to move. I still have communication with Sarajevo and Simon. My favourite captain then arrives.

– *Why are you here?*
– *I am going to Zepa.*
– *I tell you yesterday you are not going Zepa.*
– *But*—I said waving my piece of paper—*I have the approval of General Mladic.*
– *Let me see.* Now the golden rule is never to let anyone take hold of your identity card, which is why we have them on a chain around our necks. And never give anyone your approval to travel.
– *Here it is*—I say holding it up against the windscreen.
– *Give me.*
– *Terribly sorry, cannot do that.*
– *Then sit*—says the captain. Ah! This is not in the rule book. I start the engine and try to move forward, but the Kalashnikov stands firm.
– *I demand to see your commander*—I shouted. The soldiers laugh. The damn captain just drives away. In the next hour, Kalashnikov only moves once, to urinate on my front tyre. More menacingly, he is joined by a Serb soldier who is very much the worse for a drink. He has a bottle with him, which he shares with Kalashnikov. Even worse for me, I lose radio contact.

After a while, I begin to shout and wave my paper, they laugh. I am in truth worried. The longer I stay at this checkpoint the later I will be leaving for Zepa, a long and lonely road, especially when you are on your own. Also, I do not fancy staying the night on my own at this checkpoint. *Get me the captain immediately*—I waved my paper—*Get me the major. Tell him that I have a piece of paper signed by General Mladic.* This time at least the soldier does something. He uses a phone.

I am a little happier. I think that I have got through to Sarajevo. Not a two-way conversation, but I think they have heard me. The captain returns.

– *Give me paper from Mladic. I want to show it to Major. If you do not, you stay there all night.* Foolishly, I gave him the paper. He grinned and the soldiers laughed. He got back into his car and drove away. About an hour later, he returned. *Get out of the car*—he ordered, pulling open the door which was not locked. But only because I was talking through the open door, as the window does not wind down. I am aware that I am breaking all the rules. Never leave the safety of a car—another golden rule. But here I had no option. I was "assisted" out of the car.

– *I go to Zepa now*—I said, half as a statement half as a question with as much confidence as I could muster.

– *Where?*

– *Zepa.*

– *Zepa, I told you yesterday, you not go.*

– *But today I have approval from General Mladic?*

– *Where?*—He laughs. All the soldiers laugh. Oh God. I knew then that I could be in trouble.

– *You took my paper from me.*

– *No I didn't. What paper?* The soldiers are crowding around laughing, I can smell the alcohol fumes. They are enjoying this. I can either be frightened or strong.

– *Get out of my way, I am going to your headquarters to see the commander.* I went to walk past him and to move towards my vehicle. The captain drew his pistol from its holster. I looked at him. His face was white. He looked nervous and very angry. The soldiers were suddenly silent. A bad sign.

– *I have approval from General Mladic. I have every right to go to Zepa.*

The captain aimed his pistol at my head.

– *Sarajevo*—he said. *Go.* He got hold of me by the shoulder and was still aiming the pistol at me. He pushed me into the seat of the car. I remember that I needed to step back in order to get into the car, but he was pushing me forward. I therefore struggled into the car and then slammed the door and locked it. He still had his pistol in his hand. He pointed up the road with his pistol. I turned the key, and thank God, the engine started. I knew that I must show no fear. This man was dangerous. Slowly I moved forward. Kalashnikov moved out of the way. I turned slowly in order to make sure I could do the U-turn in one movement. I then moved away slowly hoping that he would not fire. I had none of the bravado that I had the previous day when Simon was with me. I was acutely aware that on my own I could easily disappear.

I looked in my mirror. I thought if he follows, shall I speed ahead or slow down? I decided that I would stay ahead, but he did not follow. At the crest, I decide against stopping to attempt comms. As I approached Podromanija, I was stopped. But not for long. I am able to talk to Simon who has been great. Knowing that I was in trouble, he has monitored the channel all day. I arrived safely back in Pale and had a number of drinks with the hunter. I vowed never to travel on my own again. A rule I broke many times.

Back in Sarajevo, I am delighted to see and thank Simon. But I am not happy to hear what has happened to Zlatan. Tony is working hard on getting him released, which he does, but not before my poor driver has had a real fright. I promise myself never to let my staff out of my sight. Another rule I later break. The Dutch colonel reached Zepa. There was no one there. He sent the Ukrainians into the hills. When the Bosnians saw that the UN was in the town, they began to return. First a trickle and then a flood. I have a message from Zagreb. They want me to fly there and to see Neill Wright.

Neill is very professional. He takes me to the bar in the Intercontinental, buys me a glass of wine, and suggests that, as I have been in Sarajevo for a year, I should have change. He recommends Banja Luka, where, at the moment, we have no international staff member.

It is a critical spot. The minorities, the Croats and the Muslims are the most vulnerable groups in the whole of Former Yugoslavia. The UNHCR staff are constantly hassled by the authorities. We do not have freedom of movement, no aid is moving into the region, and the international staff were withdrawn for their own safety. The local staff are magnificent. They are keeping the office open. UNHCR wants to re-establish its presence. Would I like to be the man to do it? I told Neill that I would very much prefer to stay in Sarajevo, but if I cannot, then I like the challenge of Banja Luka. I suggest to Neill that I should have a word with so-called Prime Minister Lukic to see how grata my persona is in Serb held territory. Neill thinks it is a good idea.

Brane fixes me up with an appointment with Prime Minister Lukic who says that, for a change, he very much would like me to work on the Serb side. I am not too sure what he means by this! I am running around tying up loose ends and saying farewells, not helped by the fact that the shelling in the city is very bad, when I hear that Deputy Prime Minister Zlatko Lagumdzija has been hit by mortar shrapnel. I go immediately to the hospital to see him. The legendary head of surgery, Dr. Abdullah Nakas, meets me at the door. A mountain of a man, in stature, strength, and power. He was a surgeon before the war, God knows how many operations he has now carried out. He is a man who exudes confidence. He is worshipped by his staff. May God preserve him and keep him. Sarajevo needs him more than any other citizen.

The intensive care ward is up flights of stairs. There is of course no light. The windows are sandbagged. Getting casualties to the wards is a big problem. I was here once with Dr. Edin Jagjanic when patients from a shelling incident were brought in. He bounded up the stairs in the dark like a white-coated bat, leaving me to bump into walls and banisters and to trip over the stairs. I was overtaken by nurses and orderlies carrying patients. Suddenly they had all gone. I was alone and lost. Many minutes later, I emerged into the hustle and bustle of candlelit activity.

Today I followed the surgeon. At the door of the intensive care ward

307

stood Zlatko's bodyguard, whom I knew so well. He had been with him but was uninjured. His clothes are bloodstained. He took me in to see Zlatko. In the dim light, I could see the overcrowded ward. It has been a heavy day and many were wounded. The Deputy Prime Minister was getting no better service than anyone else. The beds were very close together. Zlatko was unconscious, tubes and drips protruded from his face and arms. His face was grey. His injuries were in his stomach. His bodyguard stood with me—strong and faithful. I stayed a few minutes then gently touched his hand and left the ward. I gave a big hug to the bodyguard and left.

On the way down I talked to Dr. Nakas.

– *How is he?*

– *He may live. He will have a better chance if we can get him out of the city, but he is not fit to move yet.* I briefed Tony Land. When Zlatko was stronger, Tony got him out to Sweden. He is now fit and well. No longer Deputy Prime Minister. Now a professor, at Sarajevo University, of course.

Sixteen

Banja Luka and Its Characters

So the die was cast. It was decided that I was to leave my beloved Sarajevo and go to Banja Luka. Jerrie Hulme, who at that time was in the chair in Sarajevo, expressed a wish to travel with me "for the ride." I was delighted, as up until then, no one had motored from Sarajevo to Banja Luka via Brcko, which is a Serb held town of strategic importance with Croat forces to the north of it and Bosnian Government forces to the south. It is a hotly contested strip of land and a very active front line.

Jerrie and I went to Pale to see if we could get Serb approval for our trip. I particularly wanted to motor, as I liked my vehicle, 333, and it was coming with me one way or another. Going by car also meant that I could load it with all my gear, and, as I am an inveterate "this will come in handy" man, there was lots of it. Furthermore, it prevented me from having to struggle with suitcase upon suitcase as I swapped from aeroplane to aeroplane.

At Pale, we met with the Deputy Commissioner of Refugees Mr. Milan Simic, an interesting character who is making the best of a bad war. He is a small, neat, dapper man, who likes and is liked by the ladies. Before the war, he was in senior administration on the board of the University of Sarajevo. He was born in the Serb stronghold of Ozren and was an unashamed xenophobe. It is very difficult not to like Mr. Simic, and it is very easy to be carried along by his plans and sucked into his schemes.

Mr. Simic thought there would be no difficulty in our motoring to Banja Luka. He arranged a meeting with the Commissioner of Refugees, Mr. Ljubisha Vladusic. They were delighted that UNHCR was reopening the office and even more pleased that the hand on the tiller was to be old, mature, and gnarled. Mr. Simic confirmed that the route was dangerous and difficult. He therefore very kindly volunteered to accompany us. This was great news, as we were aware that the value of any piece of paper signed in Pale would diminish the further away from Pale it was presented. We agreed to set off the following day, with Mr. Simic, en route Pale-Brcko-Doboj-Banja Luka. We left Sarajevo early, with 333 stacked to the roof with my kit and a bag or two of Jerrie's. I had to leave behind some paintings and some brass plaques. The plaques were gifts from the Bosnian army and the paintings, gifts from the senior citizens of Srebrenica and Gorazde living in Sarajevo, bore inscriptions thanking me for my endeavours in breaking the "aggressor" siege of those towns. Items which I felt would not win over the friendship of Serb fighters at the numerous checkpoints we would have to pass. It would be a year before I would see them again. My colleagues in Sarajevo looked after them despite shellings, moves, and covetous glances.

As befits two ex-military men, we arrived at Pale five minutes before time, entirely thanks to the discipline of ex-Major General Hulme; a long beard is not the only unmilitary aspect of ex-Lt. Col. Hollingworth. Mr. Simic was a little late, and when he arrived, he had one or two tasks to do before we left a couple of hours late. We motored for two or three hours towards Zvornik on a beautiful picturesque road with high wooded hills on our right and the river Drinjaca on our left. Real tourist country, if it were not for the war and the constant reminders of it, the checkpoints, the burned houses, and the men with guns.

Quite out of the blue, Mr. Simic asked me to take a left turn down a narrow country lane—*where we could have a cool drink and if we wished a meal.* Mr. Simic was our guide, mentor, and guarantee for safety—we were in his hands. If this is the way we go, then this is the way we go. We followed his instructions, came off the main road, down towards the riverbank along a winding, twisting road which became narrower as we progressed. We eventually came to a beautiful, idyllic country cottage at the side of the river. Simic indicated that this was it, this was the location. We were met at the gate and made very welcome by a family consisting of a Mum, a Dad, a young boy aged about fourteen, and a young girl about eighteen. We were offered juice and coffee, but we were not actually offered any food. We wandered down by the garden. It was a pretty spot. Then Mr. Simic announced it was time to go and, surprise, surprise, Mr.

310

Simic and the young lady get into the vehicle. We had been, for the first time, "Simiced," a new verb but one we were to get to know very well. The young lady was to travel with us to Banja Luka. She was to assist with translation duties. As "yes" and "no" and an all-encompassing smile seemed to be her limit, Jerri and I did not use her services. From my occasional glances in the rear-view mirror, she was better at saying "yes" than "no."

The four of us proceeded in the direction of Zvornik and then on to Brcko. This was the dodgy bit; it is a narrow strip, heavily fought over. It was pretty obvious to me before we had gone very far that it was not a road which Mr. Simic knew well. Mr. Simic was reading the rare road signs probably a fraction of a second before I was. If the road led us into cul de sacs, then it led us into cul de sacs. I could have done as well myself. We had a few false starts, but eventually, we got through the bad bits and arrived at a large crossroads checkpoint close to Doboj. We handed over our paperwork and we waited quite a long time. Mr. Simic left the vehicle and joined us. The paper from Pale was impressing no one. But with smiles, a little cajoling, and the fact that Mr. Simic was from the Ozren, which is close to Doboj, we were allowed to proceed.

Eventually, we reached Serb dominated Doboj, "Cowboy Town." Doboj is the Crewe of Bosnia. It is an enormous railway town. Like Brcko, it is a town of strategic importance, with a Bosnian government stronghold on one side and a Croat force opposing it on another. It is a town which is heavily fought over. He who has Doboj has the gateway to the South. It is the gateway to Zenica and to Tuzla. He who has Doboj also has the main entrance to a dense, difficult pocket of land—the Ozren with its Serb majority. If the Bosnian government forces could take Doboj, then they could encircle the Ozren. If they could besiege the Ozren, they themselves would then have a large Serb enclave which they could use as a barter factor against the Muslim enclaves of Gorazde, Srebrenica, and Zepa.

All of this we knew but had not seen. Mr. Simic first took us to the office of Mr. Gogic, the Regional Commissioner for Refugees, a man whom I was to learn to admire as the bravest of Serbs in the so-called

Srpska Republika. A genuine humanitarian aid worker and a man of immense courage. Mr. Gogic had organised a translator, Lidija, a woman from Radio Doboj. She has a young son and an aged mum. Her mum was born and bred in Doboj and does not want to leave. Her daughter has such loyalty to her that she is sacrificing her own future to stay with her. Mr. Gogic took us to see the Mayor of Doboj. He was in uniform but had been the administrator in peacetime. I liked him. He made us very welcome. Our whole group then moved to the main hotel in town, the "Bosna."

Not only is Doboj a front-line town, but it is also where the Serb soldiers come out of the trenches and go to for a little "R and R," rest and recuperation. They are allowed to drink, and they are allowed to drink heavily. As we approached the hotel, we could see on the left side of the road a small gathering of very, very drunken soldiers, shouting, jeering, heavily armed with weapons and bandoliers and heavily loaded with slivovica. We parked our vehicle outside the hotel and Mr. Gogic warned us to take inside anything of any value. I valued first my flak jacket, then my helmet, and then my sleeping bag. The rest I could live without. I was very pleased that I had not brought the Bosnian army plaques. They would have been a crimson cloak to a raging bull. We went into the hotel where we found that we were the only occupants. We were booked into two, quite small but adequate, rooms. We met again down in the dining room where we were joined by two or three men in uniform. There was a strange atmosphere. The noise of the revelling soldiers outside contrasted with the contrived peace within. We were probably the first humanitarian aid people in Doboj for some while, and we were not too sure how we would be received. We had promised Sarajevo that we would keep in touch, and we had arranged a radio sked for six p.m. We were a little late. It was now six ten, so we excuse ourselves, explaining very clearly to all what we were going to do. We went outside, got into the vehicle, switched on the radio, and tried to make contact. As usual, whenever you want to get through, you never can. Mercury is the most overrated of the gods, and he has a twisted sense of humour. He allows trivia to pass with crystal clarity and then squelches or garbles words of import. Perhaps if we called him by his Greek name Hermes, he might be more amenable.

We could not get through, so Jerri suggested that I motor back or forth a few yards to see if it is local interference. So, for about ten minutes, I moved the vehicle back ten metres, forward twenty, back five and in this manner, we progressed up and down the street. Jerri has the handheld microphone to his mouth saying—*Hello Sarajevo, hello Sarajevo? Hello Zagreb, hello Zagreb? Hello Metkovic? Hello Mum?* All to no avail. We parked back on the same spot and returned to the dining room where we were brought some wine—delicious wine. Mr. Gogic proved to be not only a splendid companion but also an excellent host.

We were drinking our wine, and my attention was attracted by some commotion on the steps by the main entrance. The soldier who had been making the most noise on the corner of the road—a young, ugly man with hardly any teeth, wearing a red beret and fatigues, bandoliered and pistoled—was making some sort of protest. Mr. Gogic was called out, he returned and looked serious. *Which one of you was out filming?*—he asked.

– *Filming?*—we asked.

– *The soldier, who I admit is drunk*—said Mr. Gogic—*is claiming that you were moving up and down the street filming the soldiers.* We carefully explained that we had been out in the street, moving up and down trying to contact Sarajevo. Mr. Gogic went out and explained to the soldier, but from the noise, it was pretty obvious that the soldier was not going to accept this. Mr. Gogic returned. *The soldier wants the movie camera. He has both military and civilian police with him. They want to see the movie camera so that they can remove and view the film.* Now here we were lucky, we were able to say to Mr. Gogic—*Dear Mr. Gogic, if the civilian police, if the military police, if the drunken soldier, wants to see the movie camera and wishes to remove the movie film they are welcome to do so, but first of all, they will have to find the movie camera. We do not have a movie camera. We were out in the car on the radio.* Mr. Gogic could tell that we were telling the truth so he went out and brought in the military police.

313

We explained to them—*This is our kit, if you wish to go through it, you are welcome. If you wish to examine the contents of the vehicle, you can look with pleasure. There is no camera and there has been no filming.*

The police were quite happy with our explanation, but it was obvious that they were frightened of the drunken soldier. They left, but I knew that we had not heard the last of this issue. We continued to drink our wine. I was casually looking out of the window when I saw a sight which I could not believe. I turned to Jerri and said—*Jerri, I think we are about to lose our vehicle.* Jerri looked at me and then looked out through the window. Our drunken soldier, red beret, no teeth and all, had returned. On his shoulder was an anti-tank weapon. AN ANTI TANK WEAPON! He was pointing it at our vehicle. I quietly motioned to Mr. Gogic and asked—*Do you think that man intends to destroy our vehicle?*

Poor Mr. Gogic looked through the window, and his face dropped. He hurried out to the steps. This was a lot of fun. We could not fail to see the funny side of it. This swaying, drunken soldier had this heavy anti-tank weapon on his shoulder which was disturbing his ability to maintain the balance.

It was easy to see that the military, the police, and Mr. Gogic were wary of him. The police would go nowhere near him. Mr. Gogic approached him and told him that we were friends here to bring in humanitarian aid. But the boy was having none of this, none of this at all. Mr. Gogic did however appear to persuade him to put down the weapon. I felt a little relieved. I watched him through the window. He dragged a box across the pavement, opened it, and took out an anti-tank round. He placed it on the ground near the anti-tank weapon. He then went away. Mr. Gogic returned. We returned to drinking our wine. The incident seemed to pass. We were relaxing and musing on the event when, all of a sudden, the doors to the dining room where we sat crashed open, and through the doors came our drunken soldier with the loaded anti-tank weapon on his shoulder. He came across to me, and he pointed this lethal tube about six inches from my nose. Now, if he had pressed the trigger, not only would I have disappeared, but probably half of the street ahead of us as well. The back blast would have destroyed the hotel. Jerri looked at me, I looked at Jerri and no matter how frightening the situation was, we could not help but smile. This drunken individual accused me of having done the filming. If there had been a camera and there had been a film, I was the one doing the driving, so Jerri would have been the one doing the filming. So this menace was wrong on all counts, and without being disloyal to Jerri, I tried to tell him. He was not for placating, and his finger was dangerously, perilously close to the trigger of the anti-tank weapon with all its potential devastation. The army officers around the table froze and did nothing. The only man who got up was Mr. Gogic, who said to the soldier—*You have got to leave here. We will talk about this outside.* I do not know what else Mr. Gogic said but he was firm, straight, direct, incredibly courageous and, most important, successful, for he managed to quietly and gently take the man away to outside the hotel, where, through the window, we watched him put the anti-tank weapon down, remove the round from the tail, undo the wires, and place the round back in the box. We then had the fun of watching him, guided by Mr. Gogic, load into the car the anti-tank weapon, the round in the box, and finally his drunken self. All bundled into one lonely little VW Golf. Mr. Gogic returned, and we congratulated him on his courage. After that, we ate. Later on that night, Mr. Gogic's car was stolen. That was his reward by the locals for interfering. His car plus his possessions were never seen again.

Jerri and I then went to our rooms. Before we went to sleep, we drained a bottle of whisky and recounted the story of "the anti-tank weapon in Cowboy Town." A story and images which will stay with us forevermore.

We awoke early the following day and went down for breakfast where we met Mr. Simic and the two-word translator. We were told that there was a change of plan. We were to motor to Banja Luka and then return to Doboj for a visit to the Ozren. What we did not know is that we were about to be "Simiced" again. We set off on the road to Banja Luka. Mr. Gogic led the way in another Golf he had borrowed for the day. It is a very pleasant drive. It was obvious as we approached every checkpoint that Mr. Gogic was well known and well respected by the soldiers.

I was thrilled when I arrived at the UNHCR office in Banja Luka. All the staff were at the window, and as I got out of my vehicle, they gave me a great round of applause. They came down to the car and helped us to unload. They were delighted to have a boss once again, to have a new head of the family. They gave me a lovely welcome. I saw my new office, and I knew that I was going to be happy in Banja Luka. We had only time to unpack and say hello, before we were off to meet the hierarchy of Banja Luka. We called first on the office of the Mayor Predrag Radic. A man I was to get to know very well. We met him with Mr. Simic in the mayoral parlour, a large open office in an old building that looked the part. We were about to commence our meeting when for some strange reason, never subsequently explained, the building was buzzed by a lone single-engine aeroplane. The first fifteen minutes of our meeting were drowned by the penetrating growl of this little plane as it lined up, approached, dove, and turned away. The Mayor made us very welcome and told us he was pleased that we were back. He had great aims for us and great targets for us to achieve. He was very unhappy that HCR had fled, very impressed with ICRC who had stayed. We had a reputation to recover. He hoped that I was the man able to do it. After the meeting, I went to the little house where I was to live and then returned to the office to leave for Doboj and our trip to the Ozren. We were told that the Ozren was an important Serb stronghold, never conquered by the Germans, never conquered by the Turks, isolated, and had had no aid at all and desperately needed a visit.

So, back to Doboj, back into the same hotel. We met the same interpreter and were told that at the evening meal we would be met by the Commissioner of Refugees from Pale, Ljubisa Vladusic, who would come with us on our trip around the Ozren. The evening at the hotel was fun. Ljubisa said—*I am going to drink you under the table.*

Not a wise statement to make to two ex-army officers with, between them, seventy years of service. Especially when one of them was Jerri Hulme. If drinking ever becomes an Olympic sport, Jerri Hulme would be the national coach to a gold medal side. I suppose it took two hours before Ljubisa quietly and slowly slid to the floor. Jerri and I were then able to finish off a couple of bottles of wine and off to bed. The following day, we were up at dawn, out and into the Ozren. It is an interesting trip, there is no doubt about it. We visited the Ozren radio station "Radio Ozren" where the station manager is Mr. Ozren! A big bearded giant of a man. He gave us first-class hospitality and an excellent lunch.

We motored down the Ozren from north to south on the western side. We almost covered the whole area, but we were stopped at a distant checkpoint because of a battle close by between the Ozren Serbs and the Bosnian force from Zavidovici. We turned back and took the eastern route. Our guide was Mr. Simic. He took us to, surprise, surprise, the home of Mr. Simic. He had wanted to see his home to make sure it was safe and sound and that all was well with his brothers, sisters, and his relatives.

He had decided that in these days of fuel shortage, we would be his means of transport. We had been well and truly "Simiced" again. After visiting his house, we wearily returned to the Doboj hotel and passed a night with few incidents. The following day we moved to Banja Luka to start the Banja Luka bit.

The market in Banja Luka is near the heart of the town. It has been a centre of trade since 1494. The stalls are bordered on one side by the river Vrbas. Today there are many stalls selling fresh vegetables. Farmers and smallholders have brought in their produce. Entrepreneurs have stalls full of knick-knacks—lighters, combs, toilet paper. The local genuine gypsy community has cornered the market in tobacco, which is sold by the kilo, and in cheap gaudy watches, some bearing famous names. New arrivals on the market are the women from Muslim families. Some manage to find a corner of a stall, others place their wares on the ground. They are selling their possessions: lace tablecloths that have taken weeks of winter nights to make, pieces of crystal, vases, dishes, glasses, all beautifully cut. They were wedding presents, birthday presents, anniversary presents bought with thought and love, cared for with pride. They are truly heirlooms,

317

pieces that were destined to be handed on and coveted by daughters, daughters-in-law, and grandchildren. Pieces that now are to be sold for a fraction of their worth to buy bread, pay for medicines, buy exit visas, pay for coach tickets, or for the escape of a loved one. The market traders have licenses obtainable from the local authorities, they cost next to nothing. Muslims are not allowed to buy them.

Amira is sixty. She has found a space on the grass and laid out on a blanket her goods for sale: a mirror, some pots and pans, a tray, some glasses, cups, and saucers. She lays out a pair of curtains that fitted the windows of the little house where she had lived for more than forty years. There is no window in the flat into which she has been forcibly moved. This flat she shares with a family who previously she did not know.

The pride of place on the blanket is given to a small crystal vase. It was the first present her husband bought her after they were married. At the time, she would have preferred a pretty scarf or some make-up. Thankfully, she never showed her disappointment and time had proved him right. The vase had given her so much pleasure. She had cut many flowers from their garden in Vrbanja and placed them with care in the vase. Even washing it gave her pleasure. The blue streaks, which her husband told her was the lead in the glass, sparkled. The rim of the vase was crenelated and the peaks were sharp. She loved rubbing her fingers over them. Her daughter had told her to ask twenty marks for the vase but a neighbour, who had sold many items on the market, said she would be lucky to get ten.

She heard the shouting and saw the group of men in uniform. Some were police, some army. She saw the women around her gathering their items. Some women ran. Amira had time only to stand before the man in uniform who asked her for her licence. She was so stunned and frightened she could not speak. The soldier was joined by others. One asked for her identity card. Before she could get it out of her bag, one of them snatched the bag, pulled out the small square card, and read her name.

The events that then took place happened at such speed that she was unable to comprehend what was happening. Now at night, she can recount it, frame by frame. She was slapped and pushed away from her possessions. She saw one soldier pick up and pocket the mirror. Another grabbed the four corners of the blanket, picked up the bundle, and thrust it into her hands. Uncomprehending, she took it. She was then pushed and dragged to the edge of the river by two of them. She remembered thinking that both were younger than her grandsons. At the river's edge, she was told to throw her bundle into the river. It was at this point, she remembers she cried. Her sobs angered the soldiers who grabbed the bundle and slung it into the flowing water. In the slow-motion replay which now haunts her nights, she remembers the vase flying through the air before she was pushed away.

Samir is a Montenegrin by birth. He has a Muslim surname. He is now sixty-five. He was a very handsome man. In his wedding photograph, he looks like Clark Gable. He first visited Banja Luka when he was fourteen. There was no work in his home village. He was the eldest of seven children. He arrived, found a job, sent for his parents and his brothers and his sisters, and never left. He worked for one company his whole working life, rising to senior management. His skill is in negotiating. He believes passionately in communism and old Yugoslavia. He lives with his Banja Luka born wife in a large flat, which he bought twenty years ago. He has three sons, and, in the Montenegrin manner, when they married, they brought their wives to live with Samir and his wife. In a flat one floor below lives Samir's mother, now in her late eighties. Samir's youngest brother used to live with his family on the ground floor. He was the family miser. He never wasted a penny and banked all of his money. He worked regularly in Germany and returned with cheap souvenir presents. He never gave parties and contributed little to the upkeep of his parents. When the war broke out and the government confiscated all hard currency, he lost everything. His moaning could be heard blocks away. At least his contacts in Germany enabled him to get refugee status for himself and his family. For permission to leave, he relied on a local senior Serb army officer, who in return for this favour, accepted his flat and contents, down to the last knife and fork.

Samir's sons did not want to fight. Many neighbours, with less contacts than Samir, managed to help their children avoid the draft. True, they did not have Muslim surnames. Samir had no success. All three were to be drafted, and as has become the custom, boys with Muslim names invariably get sent to the front line to prove their loyalty. The boys therefore decided to leave. Leaving costs money. Samir has spent more than three thousand marks on getting his next generation out. One family to Libya, one to Sweden, and the youngest boy, so far, only to Belgrade. This boy is married to a Serb girl who was previously married and has one child with her former husband's surname. Getting the family to Belgrade was easy. Getting out the young boy with the Serb surname proved almost impossible. Whilst they moved from Embassy to Ministry and days passed, their money dwindled and more of Samir's possessions appeared on the market.

The colonel in the flat below has friends who like Samir's flat. It has been suggested that it is too large for one man and his wife. Especially for one man whose sons have left. Samir is prepared to leave if they find a smaller flat for him. This will prove no difficulty. Soon he will move. The new flat will not be large enough for his furniture, but the new occupants of his flat will help him out there.

Samir is an obliging man. He will go along with most suggestions, But he is a Montenegrin, and despite having had two heart attacks, he is still a tough, wiry man. When a group of soldiers stopped him in the street and started beating him calling him "Muslim shit," he fought back. He lost, of course, but not before he had bruised a few of them and they had learned that by nationality he was a Yugoslav, by religion a communist, and a Muslim by name only.

Soon after I arrive in Banja Luka, the market is full of apples. There are many orchards. The crop is vital to the economy. The young men who would normally gather the apples are in the trenches and barracks miles from home. Someone has to harvest. The Muslim men understand this, they accept that they cannot sit in overcrowded apartments, with no job to go to, and watch the crop rot. They fully understand that the Banja Luka authorities must call upon their services, that they must "do their bit" for the war effort.

Mustafa is a leading consultant bone specialist. He was at the Banja Luka hospital. He was not included in the first purge of Muslim professionals. With so many war wounded, it looked as if he would survive the duration of the war. He lives in a lovely house, with a pretty garden. At the bottom of the garden, there is a small shed containing a pool table. Behind the shed, on the other side of the fence, there is a mosque.

In the second wave of purges he was dismissed. He went home and spent his days in the garden, playing pool with his friends. He had no shortage of partners—psychiatrists, lawyers, architects, all debarred from practice because they were Muslims. Amazingly, Mustafa was reinstated. Some of his patients, wounded Serb soldiers, demanded his recall. But when they moved out, Mustafa was out again. He is a man who has enjoyed the fruits of his labour. A big man, who has relished good food and who serves delicious slivovica. When he was bussed out to the apple orchards along with many of his friends, he must have felt that his soft, tender, caring hands could be better used in the hospital than in collecting apples. On arrival at the fields, his work group was allocated "a norm." The Serb soldiers, young, heavily armed men "supervising" their work, made it clear that the norm would be multiplied by the number present and that they would not leave until it had been achieved and that tomorrow was another day and another norm. The farmers and the labourers amongst them found the norm achievable; the doctors, dentists, lawyers, teachers, found it almost impossible. The soldiers encouraged them by shouting, pushing, and occasionally beating. The soldiers were insistent that the apples were removed from the trees carefully. One university professor with an aching back and blistered hands constantly dropped apples, bruising them. He was singled out by a soldier as young as any of his undergraduates, told that he was clumsy and careless and ordered to extend his hand. He was whacked on the hand with a stick till his hands stung and his cheeks ran with tears.

321

The soldiers laughed. His colleagues turned away in shame. At the end of the long day, norm achieved, they were bussed back to Banja Luka for a short sleep before another day and another norm dawned.

How can I reconcile each of these stories with my task of providing aid in the Serb dominated territories of Bosnia? This was my dilemma whilst in Banja Luka. The office had closed down. I had been sent to reopen it. I was welcomed with open arms by the Serb authorities who wanted whatever aid I could bring in. I was welcomed by the minority populations and their leaders for whatever protection I could offer them. Could I give aid only to the oppressed? No. Without the approval of the Serb authorities, I would never get aid in. They controlled the entry checkpoints. Without bringing in aid, could I minister to the minorities? No. The Serbs would only grant approval for us to move if we were carrying aid.

Did that mean, as the press regularly stated, that we were buying or bribing our way in? Not quite. In the Serb held territories, there were about 300,000 displaced or vulnerable people. At least a third of them were Serbs—Serbs who genuinely needed aid, Serbs who had fled from towns and villages now in Croat or more usually Bosnian government hands. We were in the business of providing to all three sides. Provide we must.

My first days in Banja Luka were spent assessing the problem and the players. The problem seemed simple. There were at least twenty-six towns with warehouses to where we could easily deliver aid. If from these warehouses the aid could be fairly distributed to all three communities, depending on their needs, then all would be well. I was assured by the Banja Luka representative of the Commissioner of Refugees, COR, that all I needed to do was to hand the aid over to him and he would issue it fairly and squarely. The Regional Representative for the Red Cross assured me that his organisation had the best distribution network. He further confided in me that to give aid to the Commissioner of Refugees, would inevitably mean a large percentage going to the fighting forces. The Catholic agency Caritas and the Muslim agency Merhamet both guaranteed me that unless

322

they were given their share direct, they would never see a kilo of aid. To further complicate issues, two local Serb charities, Dobrotvor and KSS, demanded "their share" to be delivered directly to them.

I had come from Sarajevo where people were genuinely starving. From Sarajevo where we were bringing in only a fraction of needs. I had travelled to Banja Luka through kilometre after kilometre of fields sown with crops. I had visited the market in Banja Luka, where there were items for sale which had almost been forgotten in Sarajevo.

When you come from a place where there is nothing to a place where there is plenty, what hits you is colours, the yellow of the bananas, the greens and the reds of peppers and tomatoes, the orange of the citrus fruits. Banja Luka market was ablaze with colour. In Gorazde and Srebrenica, people would fight for a cigarette. In Banja Luka you could buy packs of 200. There were restaurants open where you could buy steak, and for me, joy of joys, a bottle of wine.

I was here to deliver aid. Valuable life-saving aid. Was it really needed here? Here, where the agencies are all in conflict and the odds on the minorities receiving their share, long. In my first week, I visited and was visited incessantly. The office had been closed and many people wanted to express their delight that we were back in business or their anger that we had left.

Mr. Tutnjevic, the Regional Commissioner for Refugees, annoyed me from the start by asking for a breakdown of all the aid brought in from the beginning of the year, and its distribution. The import of the latter was, I am sure, to make a case that, proportionately, we were giving too much aid to minorities. He made a strong plea for all aid to be given to him for a "fair" distribution. He also complained about the quality of the aid we were bringing in. I reminded him that I had just come from Sarajevo where there was no opportunity to supplement what we brought in. I then learned that he is a Sarajevo man and has relatives there.

Father Tomislav Matanovic, the representative from the Catholic charity Caritas, interested me. He told me that he was bringing in some aid on a weekly basis. I presumed that he was paying off the

Serbs both at the checkpoint and in Banja Luka, but I did not ask him outright. It was too early in our relationship to ask such leading questions.

The main supplier of aid to the Muslim community was the charity Merhamet. I asked to see their rep only to find out that there were two Merhamets and that they were in dispute. I could not believe it. Senad Sirbegovic was the deputy leader of Merhamet One. He was a professor of electronics at Banja Luka University. He was one of the few professional Muslims to still have a job. I liked him. He spoke very good English, but preferred to go through a translator, which gave him time to think. He explained the rift between Merhamet One and Merhamet Two. The powers in Two had been expelled from One. There were hints of misappropriation and mismanagement. I was exasperated and told him that I could not believe that in the most dangerous environment in the whole of ex-Yugoslavia the Muslim community was fighting within itself. The ever-reasonable professor agreed and hoped that I could solve the problem by closing down Merhamet Two. He then amazed me, by telling me that until recently, Merhamet had been able to bring in truckloads of food from Zagreb. They had struck a deal with Tutnjevic to give twenty per cent to his government organisation. What they had brought in was only enough for schools, public kitchens, social institutions, and retired people. This deal had recently been stopped, for reasons he could not understand, by the army. So he wanted me to get it going again and provide the balance to feed the majority of the Muslim community who were unemployed and dispossessed—a total according to him of 90,000.

A further small task, which he gave to me with a charming smile, was to recover seventy-two tonnes of food which had been stolen from the Merhamet warehouse by the army and taken to the Red Cross warehouse from where it was being distributed to the army.

My next visitor was the senior Croat politician, Mr. Nikola Gabelic. He began by telling me that one third of the Croat population had left the area and the other two thirds wanted to leave. Fifteen Croats had recently been murdered in the Banja Luka region. *All Croats go to bed in fear of their safety, none sleep peacefully. Croats are beaten up, many have lost their houses, all have lost their jobs*—he explained.

He also identified the biggest nightmare for each household, the draft. All males between the ages of eighteen to fifty-five were eligible for mobilization. No Croat wished to be forced to fight against fellow Croat. If they refused the draft, they were evicted from their homes. If they accepted the draft, they would be sent to the front lines. He told me that for 200 DM per person a family could get to Croatia, for 450 they could go to Sweden. *Sadly*—he said—*all the rich have gone, only the poor remain.*

He concluded our first conversation with a warning that the remaining Croats were ready to fight to the last man if they were pushed much further. He was doing his best to keep the lid on, but only because he feared massive reprisals.

– *I want a Croat community in Bosnia. I want human rights, and I expect you to help. What can you do?*—I did not tell him, but the answer to his question was very little except to listen, like a father confessor. And listen I did. And report certainly to whomsoever would listen. But was that why I was there? Why was the UN there?

The next visit was from a group of four men led by Mr. Muharem Krzic who was the leader of the Muslim political party SDA. To the Serbs, he was like a Black man at a Ku Klux Klan convention. A sincere but difficult and demanding man, he began abruptly by stating that he wanted a Bosnian state, not a Muslim state. He then asked, no, he demanded regular meetings with me, "as the situation for Muslims is so tense."

Events proved him right. Of the four men present on that day, I was later to spend a lot of time getting two out of jail. Mr. Krzic told me that of the 700,000 Muslims who had lived in the Banja Luka region, only 70,000 were now left. He told me the same story as Mr. Gabelic, his Croat counterpart, only on a grander scale. The majority of Muslims were unemployed, many had lost their homes, many were beaten. He told me in detail of robberies, looting, and beatings that had taken place the previous evening in Gornji Seher, a suburb of Banja Luka City. He retold the story of the mobilization rules. He

325

outlined the plight of most of his people.

– *Firstly, Mr. Larry, the man is sacked. If he has no work, he is deemed to be unable to pay his rent, so he and his family are moved to cramped shared accommodation. No job means no social security. No social security means no medical treatment.* Mr. Krzic was full of praise for the Swiss ICRC chief Michel Minnig, who had responded, after midnight, to a call from Mr. Krzic and had prevented Serb violence on Muslims who had been herded into a local mosque.

He asked for my home number so that I could help when the next crisis happened! As he was leaving, he asked me to support Merhamet Two—*especially their soup kitchens.*

It was now time to talk to the "home teams." Mr. Spahic of the Red Cross was the first to bat. His main message was that the Red Cross had successfully distributed aid to the poor and the needy for many years. They had warehouses, transport, and well-informed compassionate staff. They pleaded with me not to hand the aid over to the government agencies. They guaranteed me that they would ensure that the minorities were fed. They seemed honest and sincere. My question was—*Fine, but can you guarantee delivery to Croats and Muslims? Can your man on the ground feed the minorities when faced by an angry Serb soldier with a gun?*

I liked the Red Cross reply—*No, but nor can you, or any other agency.* The representative for the Serb charity Dobrotvor was a large, domineering woman, a doctor of medicine, who was a refugee from Zenica. Outsized, outspoken, and outrageously Serb—the sort of woman who could cure malingerers with a stare at a hundred paces. Slobodanka Hrvacanin wanted aid to be given directly to Dobrotvor. She was not happy with the distribution system of either the commissioner or Red Cross. Whilst not agreeing with her policy and her extremism, I could easily see that any aid given to Slobodanka would go to wherever she said. In our conversation I discovered that she was a great friend of Mrs. Plavsic, the Vice President of the so-called Srpska Republika. The lady whom, of course, I knew well from my Gorazde convoy. She informed me that Mrs. Plavsic was in town and was with Prince Tomislav. She further promised to get me an invitation to dine that evening with all three of them. Which she did. I was frequently to battle with Slobodanka, she was a formidable adversary, but always consistent. She is a member of the Srpska Republika Parliament, the Assembly, and a hard-line Greater Serbia Monarchist.

My next session was with the rep from the Banja Luka Association for the Deaf, Mr. Nicola Djukic. In a war it is easy to forget the needs of the disabled. When you are trying to provide basics for the starving majority, the blind, the deaf, the immobile, those with mental illness, are almost ignored until their problems come screaming at you. The deaf in Banja Luka just wanted food. Mr. Djukic, his two colleagues, and myself shouted and gesticulated our way through a half hour meeting.

Finally, I met with Merhamet Two. Mr. Amir Novalija, a tall handsome man, came with two ladies. He was charming. He runs ten kitchens in the town, he feeds about 750 people every day, twenty per cent of them Croats and the remainder Muslims. We apparently have only helped him twice, and he needs food or he is out of business. One of the women with him, Vesna, is a doctor of medicine. Vesna is an unusual name for a Muslim. I presume that she is the product of a mixed marriage. She used to work within the government system, but now is out of work, so she runs a clinic, which they call an ambulanta. She also does house visits to the old and the infirm. Right now, all she can dispense is knowledge and sympathy. She really impresses me. I promise to help to get some drugs for her. I will have to tap up WHO or MSF in Zagreb. I talk at great length to Novalija. I explain to him that by running a splinter group, he is doing the Serbs' work for them. Divided they will fall. United they will probably fall. I ask him if he would amalgamate with Merhamet One. Surprisingly, he says he would but that his management would want some positions of authority in Merhamet One.

I ask myself, can this petty squabbling be true? It took me a long time to realise that when murder and mayhem are your companions, you need something else to occupy your mind. A good simple dispute or argument with your neighbour can be therapeutic.

My next call was on Michel Minnig, the International Committee of

Red Cross (ICRC) chief delegate, so highly praised by the Muslim leaders. He offered me tea or coffee—I opted for tea. When it came it was herbal tea, bright red and horrible. Mental note, next time I ask for coffee.

I had been warned by my own office in Zagreb that Michel was not pro UNHCR, so I went in a little warily. I need not have worried. I found him to be open, frank, and helpful. The UNHCR staff in Banja Luka were one international and five local staff. He had seventeen international and seventy-three local! He warned me of the security situation against his staff. His staff were frequently threatened by armed men, homes were burgled, cars broken, some stolen. I asked him about freedom of movement for his staff. He said that all of his staff had a freedom of movement certificate, but its validity depended on the check point commanders—*All movement is difficult, unpredictable, and dangerous.* We talked about the essential difference between his convoys and mine. ICRC worldwide refuses to be escorted by local uniformed or armed escorts. UNHCR had agreed with the Serbs that we would be escorted by a Serb military or a Serb police escort. Therefore, theoretically, we should have an easier passage than ICRC. Michel was sceptical.

He emphasised that whilst convoys were vital, protection for the minorities was the number one task. For the most vulnerable, even protection was not enough, evacuation was the only solution. Evacuation needed greater ICRC/HCR cooperation. He could organise the mechanics of movement, but they had to have somewhere to go. Resettlement was a UNHCR problem, and in his opinion, we were not providing enough overseas places for those that had to go.

He warned me that my number one task in Banja Luka would be protesting to the authorities. How right he was. We discussed aid; ICRC was bringing in almost 2000 tonnes per month and was not happy. The authorities wanted more and more, and he was convinced the aid was not going to the most needy. However, he was of the opinion that we had no option. If we wanted to feed any of the minority we had to cooperate with the Serbs. In my naivety I told him that I disagreed. I remember my words—*When we have so little food, I cannot see why we should feed people who are living in villages surrounded by lush green fields.* I was, of course, still conditioned by my Sarajevo experience.

– *You will*—replied Minnig. He pointed out to me that to feed vulnerable minorities, and not to feed the majority, made the minorities even more vulnerable.

Minnig had taken a bold, controversial stance on the feeding of the prisoners in the infamous Manjaca prison. He refused, because the Serbs would not allow him free access to the prisoners. My first thought was that this was wrong, but on reflection, if you cannot visit the prisoners, how do you know if the food you deliver gets to them. Finally we discussed who I should see. We agreed that the big five were the Corps Commander General Talic, the Chief of Police Zupljanin, and the Mayor Predrag Radic on the Serb side, and the Catholic Bishop and the Mufti on the minority side.

I decided to begin with the General. I asked Davorka, the Croatia born office interpreter, to fix me an appointment. She told me that he had always refused to see my predecessor. I was luckier. I got into his small, neat office the next day.

General Talic is a large, benevolent looking man with a round, red, open face, gentle eyes, and a relaxing smile—Pickwickian. If his reputation is anything to go by, then his looks are very deceptive. I was told that he is a tough commander with a blood lust who likes to be in at the kill. He welcomed me and praised the work of UNHCR. He said that he was very unhappy that we had left, that he knew of me by reputation and looked forward to working with me. I told him that in order to work at all, we would need freedom of movement. This he immediately granted "within the constraints of the security situation." Another document for my "Neville Chamberlain" file. He then went on with words so significant, I have never forgotten them—*HCR has saved certain areas from certain death. Thanks from me is not enough. Your thanks will come from God. But you can do more. Not only are there refugees but also the destitute. Serbs, Croats, and Muslims.*

Then came his best line—*You are here to help all. I want all to stay.*

This land will be much richer if it has a multi-ethnic base. My interview with him lasted ninety minutes. I came away believing him. Time and events would strain that belief.

I next went to see the Regional Chief of Police Stoyan Zuplyanin. He met me in his scruffy office in his scruffy building. He is an extrovert. He had with him his Banja Luka Chief and, for some reason, the commander of the Air Force base. He offered us drinks and said many things about UNHCR, all complimentary. He regretted the incidents against the minorities and promised to do everything in his power to protect them. He blamed "uncontrollable elements" for the aggression. He brought to my notice the fact that the main Muslim suburb of Banja Luka was on the outskirts of the town.

– *As our soldiers return from the front, they pass through it. To some, who had just lost comrades, brothers, and cousins in the trenches, killed by Muslims, the sight of the Muslim men lolling against their gates, idling their time, Muslims who refused to defend the territory where they were born, is too much.*

The Chief of Police said that he did not agree with their actions but that he could understand them. During my interview with him, there was much humour, much slivovica, many promises, and very little sincerity.

There has been a Catholic Bishop in Banja Luka since the twelfth century. The present incumbent is the right man at the right time. Franjo Komarica is a fighter. He is a Banja Luka boy, born and bred. He knows all the locals, the goodies and the baddies. He lives in the religious house next to the church. The church is a monster. The architect who designed it achieved neither warmth nor beauty. The bishop's residence is neat, clean, and has character. The quarters of Bishop Komarica give a great insight to the man. They are opulent. The room where he meets you has Persian carpets on the floor. Excellent paintings, mainly of people, cover the walls. There are shelves full of porcelain. The table at which you sit is covered with a beautiful cloth. The slivovica is in a decanter, the glasses are cut and of the finest lead crystal. The Bishop wears a well-made dark suit, his pectoral cross is small but good. He is neat and immaculately groomed. His wavy hair is greying slightly. After a few words of welcome and some comments on my "prophet's" beard, we are straight into business. He is delighted we are back, we are needed, if only as an observer. But he hopes for more, much more. The war has hardly touched this area, therefore the cleansing, the beatings, the burnings, were out of character with the people and the situation. He was devastatingly critical of the international community. *You watched them pen us like sheep and kill us like wolves.* He continued—*You are content to feed us to die. You should protect us to live.* He ended with two statements—*The minorities here have not provoked the Serb, they do not deserve the treatment they are getting*—and—*The situation here is desperate. Do not be fooled by the calm outlook.*

He took me to an adjoining room where he had a large map on the wall. It was the map of his diocese. All his parish churches were marked on it. Some had XXX's covering the church, others a circle around the church. The XXX's were churches burned down by the Serbs, the encircled were churches that had been damaged. The Bishop had tears in his eyes as he gave me the numbers of parishioners who had fled. Komarica could be the last in a long line of Banja Luka bishops.

As I was leaving, he was called aside to see a parish priest who had just arrived. The priest had come from the village of Ljubija, where a Serb gang was, as we spoke, driving the Croats out of their homes and burning their houses. *Your first test*—said the Bishop as he bid me farewell at the door.

I went back to the General. He saw me immediately. He sent an aide to investigate. The aide returned. He and the General chatted and the General explained to me that Serb extremists had indeed gone to the village to taunt or rob. Croat villagers had opened fire on them thus inviting an attack. The General said he abhorred the burning of houses, but he was convinced that the provocation had not come from his soldiers. He had another good line—*I want peace more than you. This war has taken our young, our economy, and our land.*

To go back to the Bishop and explain that his naughty Croats had fired on advancing, robbing Serb extremists thus provoking military intervention seemed a little hollow.

I went back to the office to think and found a large group of Muslims waiting for me. They were committee members from the suburb of Gornji Seher. Some of the men were crying. Last night in their suburb there had been an attack by armed men. During the attack, one of their men had been killed and two were injured and were now in hospital, seriously wounded.

Apparently, for weeks small bands of men had arrived in the village after curfew to loot the homes of the Muslims who had fled. The empty homes were now stripped so the bands are robbing from occupied homes. Any resistance is met with violence. The committee's request was simple. They wanted me to evacuate the whole population of seven hundred. NOW!

I tried to explain that to evacuate you have to have somewhere to go. Nations prepared to take seven hundred could not be found. A sad fact of life. After a terrible emotional half hour listening to their sobbing and their terrible stories, I persuaded them to return with the reassurance that I would seek the intervention of the Military and Civil powers.

I contacted the General again. I told him that I intended to stay the night in the village and requested him to give me an escort. He was weary, and I am sure genuinely concerned. He told me that it was a police matter, that my staying there could be considered provocative and more importantly that having reported the matter, I should give the powers the chance to sort it out. He promised that protection would be provided.

I went back to the committee, explained what had happened and hoped for the best. I then went to my house, where at that stage, I lived alone. I got into bed feeling really guilty. I felt that I should have gone and stayed in the village. I questioned why I had not. Was I scared? Did I believe the General? As darkness fell, I heard shooting in the distance. I hoped it was not in Gornji Seher. If it was, and I had been there, what could I have done? The next day I contacted the committee. They were very frightened. No government protection had turned up. At dusk a van load of looters had arrived. They attacked an occupied house and the son of the owner was murdered. The Muslim community retaliated, and in the ensuing gun battle one of the Serb criminals was killed.

The General was not available. He was "in the field." The Regional Chief of Police Stoyan Zupljanin was "away." The city police Chief told me that the Criminal Investigation Department was handling the case and that the police were fearful of reprisals and were attempting to ease the tension. I was told not to visit the area. He recommended that later I take a food parcel to the family of the dead Muslim!

I tried to get to the village but was turned back at the police checkpoint. *Too much tension*—I was told. I went back to the office, contacted Neill Wright and asked him to urgently send me a protection officer and an international lawyer. He told me that an outstanding Sri Lankan lawyer, who had previously been in Banja Luka, was on his way back and that he was looking for another.

Mr. Krzic and his gang of three turned up at the office to complain about the night's events. I was less than polite, but I did feel that I had let them down.

My next visitor was Mrs. Malbasic, the Director of the Central Pharmacy. She is responsible for the supply of drugs to the hospitals and clinics. She gave me a list of needs. She had received some drugs from ICRC. She had received a lot from Serbs living overseas, but this source was drying up with the embargo. There was a thriving drug production potential in Belgrade, but they could not get the raw material because of the blockade. I promised to get Medecins Sans Frontieres and the World Health Organisation involved. I remembered Dr. Vesna and her Muslim ambulanta and asked Mrs. Malbasic if she could provide some drugs for her until I could get some. With a smile and great charm, she assured me that she could. But she had a much better counter proposal. She wanted to open a humanitarian clinic for all who could not afford medicine. Could I find for her a charity agency to run it and to provide the drugs? Meanwhile, she was certain that if Dr. Vesna's patients turned up at the hospital clinic, they would not be turned away! If I had been unable to get into Gornji Seher the chances of a sick Muslim getting out to collect some drugs from the hospital seemed remote.

It was beginning to look as if getting aid into besieged towns was far easier than achieving anything in Banja Luka. I prayed to God and to Neill Wright to send me reinforcements.

Seventeen

Banja Luka

Neill heard my prayer. The arrival of Indrika Ratwatte was great news. I needed another international, for credibility, for the sake of the minorities, and to have someone to discuss events with. He is from Sri Lanka. He is a clever lawyer, with a background spanning the quiet corridors of the World Bank and the violent world of the banks of the Jordan. He spent a few years in the UNRWA Palestinian refugee camps. He is a Buddhist. A very gentle man, he is outstanding at listening to the problems of vulnerable people, at assessing what he can do, and then doing it with speed, courage, and efficiency. Women tell me that he is devastatingly handsome!

He was part of the old team who had moved from Banja Luka when our activities were temporarily suspended. He did not agree with the decision. The staff loved him and the authorities respected him. I wanted more protection officers and was promised another "soon."

Out of the blue, a Frenchman arrived. He had no experience in UN-HCR. He was a doctor of philosophy, right hand man to the Secretary General of the OECD, and had volunteered his annual leave for humanitarian aid work in ex-Yugoslavia. Philippe Montigny had a Clouseau-like English accent, tremendous energy and enthusiasm. He rapidly became a vital part of the team. I made him a protection officer, and under the guidance of Indy, he was excellent.

The key player I still had to see was the Mufti—the leader of the religious in the whole of the Banja Luka region. Mufti Ibrahim Halilovic had his office in a building in the grounds of the Ferhadija Mosque. The mosque was built in 1574. In this century it had survived two world wars and an earthquake. It did not survive the night of 27 May, 1993. This ancient, revered and UNESCO protected building was dynamited. In the days that followed bulldozers attempted to level the site. The window in the office of the Mufti overlooked the flattened mosque. A daily reminder to the leader of the Islamic community of the trials his people were undergoing.

Muftis and their subordinates, Imams, can be rigid, dour, humourless people, and I was not too sure what to expect on my visit. I found, instead, a saintly man—a man whom I grew to admire enormously. He has none of the fire and none of the urbanity of the Bishop. He is more the cloistered academic, the scholar cleric. He is medium height, fit, with an open, smiling, slightly tanned face. His voice has been trained by many packets of rough cigarettes. It is mellow, quiet, and considered. His deep blue eyes twinkled in laughter and moistened in sadness. He carefully explained that he was the spiritual leader of those Bosnians who considered themselves to be Muslims. He made it clear to me that he was neither their political leader nor their cultural guide.

Humanitarian aid was the task of Merhamet. Politics was the domain of SDA. He recognised that he, his clergy, and his religious buildings were the symbols of Islamisation so hated by the extremists on both the Croat and the Serb sides. He wanted a return to the multi-ethnic state that had been for most of his life Yugoslavia and was now the still-born Bosnia. We drank coffee. All the time I was to know him, he never offered alcohol. He asked me if I thought that he should advise his people to leave. I told him that I did not, that I believed that it was vital that they stayed. I reiterated the words of President Karadzic, Prime Minister Lukic, and at the local level General Talic that they wanted a multi-ethnic state. The Mufti was pleased with my words. It was what he wanted to hear. He would tell his flock that the new HCR man, the new UN man, thought it was safe to stay. At that time, I believed what I told him, because I believed those who had told me. I later had to revise my advice, my opinions, and my judgement. We parted, and I knew that I had met a good, honest, brave man. I hope he survives.

Now that we were back in the protection business, we had a constant stream of visitors, mainly Bosnians classified as Muslims by the local Serbs and under great pressure. They all wanted "out." Sadly more and more nations were closing their doors to refugees. The international community cannot have it all ways. The choices seemed simple. Either come in strong and sort the situation out or let the oppressed escape and give them somewhere to live. These poor people were stuck. They could not stay. They could not go.

Meanwhile their nightmares were our breakfasts.

I arrived at the office as usual at about a quarter after seven. There were a couple of men waiting for me. One was very distressed. The previous evening at dusk, a car had arrived in his neighbourhood, four men in uniform got out. They came straight to his house, kicked open the door, came in and took away his seventeen-year-old daughter. It all happened so fast. He, his wife, and his younger daughter watched her go. He heard her screams and her cries. He did not do anything. He said that he knew that had he moved they would have killed him. They probably would have killed his wife as well and still taken his daughter. His daughter had not returned. Could I help to find her? And a second question. He wanted to know how he could explain to his daughter that he had let her go. He heard her screams, her pleas, and let her go without a fight. I was able to help find his daughter. My advice as to what he should tell her was irrelevant. She was pulled out of the river, naked and dead.

On the aid front, we had success from the start. I issued the contents of the warehouse to Banja Luka, Doboj, and to Petrovac. This meant that UNHCR convoys became high profile. I appeared on local TV, on the radio, and in the press. Wherever the convoys went, an international staff member went. Whilst the trucks were being unloaded it gave us the chance to talk to the local distributing agent, to assess his honesty and his integrity. We also tried to see the local community leaders. This was never too easy. If we announced our intention in advance we could get fobbed off with "tame" minority leaders. When we returned we discussed our findings with Sirbegovic of Merhamet, with Krzic of the SDA, and with any of the priests from Caritas. We were soon delivering aid to all the towns in the region.

On the 8th of July, the Special Envoy Nicholas Morris visited. He is a tall, thin, quiet, self-effacing man, an intellectual with a complete grasp of the situation. He was excellent to take around. The Bishop was at his most aggressive. Nicholas quietly explained the reality of the limitations of both UNHCR and UN.

The Mufti, who was banned from wearing his Mufti clothes, was so pleased by the visit of Nicholas that he wore them. He greeted Nicholas with fez, turban, and flowing robes. He had prepared a speech, which he read. The concluding words brought tears to my eyes.

– *We are asking only for the right to live. A piece of land under us. A piece of sky above us. May Almighty God replace the evil of today with the goodness of tomorrow.*

In the middle of July, I was invited to return to London for the launch of "Bosnia, Bloody Bosnia" week. This turned out to be a superb series of programmes made by Channel Four. I was flown back to the UK, where the UNHCR public information officer Nanda na Champassak had organised a really heavy schedule—meetings, lectures, appearances. I thoroughly enjoyed it. Nanda was a dynamo. She kept my adrenaline going and shepherded me from venue to venue from dawn till way after dusk.

After four hectic days, I returned to Banja Luka. I thought it had gone really well. What I did not know was that on the back page in "The Guardian," next to a huge photograph of Ian Botham, was a half inch column, in tiny print, on Bosnia. It credited me with stating: "the UN's programme in Bosnia is ineffective." I am quite capable of hanging myself with the statements that I do make. I did not need any help from inaccurate reports in "The Guardian." Some cricket fan must have spotted the article and run to Mr. Stoltenberg with it. He called Madame Ogata. For a day or two, it was a crisis. It was defused by the professionalism of Nanda who pursued the issue and the honesty of the Guardian reporter Ed Pilkington who explained that the article was severely compressed and distorted and that the offending statement was his, not mine.

My next contribution to a newspaper was refused. On the night of the 14th of July, two mosques in Banja Luka were blown up. This brought the total to eighteen destroyed in the previous year which included five that had been built in the sixteenth century. When lives are being destroyed, it may seem a little strange to get worked up about the destruction of buildings, but these acts indicated to the minorities that they were to be driven out and that all traces of their culture were to be removed. I knew that I could not get these people out. I was trying to persuade them to stay, quoting the words of the Serb leaders. How I could expect them to believe in a multi-ethnic state when gangs could turn up with explosives and blow up mosques!

I went to the site of the two mosques. They were not far away. From the stories told to me by the local residents the modus operandi was the same. At dusk a van arrived, and out went some soldiers carrying boxes. They entered the area of the mosque, placed the charges, withdrew, and up went the mosque. These two mosques were surrounded by houses. The first three homes were damaged. One was severely hit, it lost a third of its roof. There were only minor casualties. At the second location, one house was abutting the mosque and was no longer habitable. Two others had been shaken to their foundations and would need a lot of repair. I went to the destroyed house. The owner was swathed in bandages. When the van had arrived, the villagers knew what was about to happen. So the men ordered their families into the fields where they had slept the night. The men had stayed in their homes to prevent looting. They had telephoned the police in Banja Luka. The police said they would investigate tomorrow!

When the explosion had gone off, all the men were lucky. They had suffered only cuts from flying glass. As I walked around the shattered house, the wife of the owner was in what remained of the kitchen. She was washing the dishes. Her way of coping with the loss of her family home, her possessions, and life as she had known it.

I went to see the police chief. How could a van with explosives pass at least three police checkpoints? Why had the police not responded to the telephone call? What did he intend doing about the incidents? His reply was truly Balkan—*How do you know that the Muslims did not do it themselves?* He then went on to tell me that the Muslims had, themselves, destroyed the ancient Ferhadija Mosque in the centre of Banja Luka. The evidence was a masterpiece of detection. *After the blast, we were very soon on the scene. We found no priceless carpets amongst the debris. The Muslims had removed the carpets before they blew it up and blamed the Serbs.*

The article refused by the newspapers in Banja Luka was my open letter to the editor.

Dear Editor,

UNHCR deplores the destruction of another two mosques in Banja Luka. The Civil, Military, and Police authorities continually state that it is the intention to encourage a multi-ethnic state. The destruction of religious buildings is aggression. It is intimidation. It is not in accord with a policy of integration. It is difficult to understand how explosives can be taken to religious sites after the curfew hour, placed around the building and detonated without, at least, the tacit connivance of certain official organisations. The activity around the mosques was reported to the police before the explosions. No action was taken to prevent the destruction. There are now only four mosques left in Banja Luka. They are an important part of the history and culture of this region. UNHCR implores the authorities to publicly condemn this outrage and to preserve and protect the mosques which remain.

I hand delivered a copy of the above to a wide list of people. The best comment it elicited was from Bedrudin Gusic, the leader of the Islamic Community and confidant of the Mufti—*Thank God you did not publish the addresses of the four remaining mosques. We do not want to make it too easy for them.*
Sadly "they" needed no help from me.
Life goes on in other parts of Bosnia. And death. On the 30th of July I received a message from Sarajevo.
– *Message for Larry. Mrs. Kira Sparavalo wants Larry to know that her husband Veljko, whom Larry knew well, was killed by a mortar about an hour and a half ago. The children in England do not yet know.*
I remembered the last time I saw him. Every inch the successful actor. Immaculate. What will Kira and Denis, their son, do without him? Who will tell Aris and Enesa?

On the first of August, as we arrived at the office, the phone rang and we had a strange message. A Serb woman in a place called Liskovac said that her Muslim neighbours had asked her to pass on a message. During the night, there had been a massacre in the village. Could we get there urgently? We took two cars and raced to the village. There were few people about. One man who looked very scared told us to proceed to the top end of the village. Unfortunately, as we arrived there a large group of police were walking towards us. They stopped our car and told us that they were the crime scene team and that we could go no further. We argued and pushed. One man came forward. He was wearing blood stained rubber gloves. He identified himself as a doctor and the local coroner. He quietly pointed out to me that if there was a murder inquiry in the UK, aid workers would not be allowed on the scene. I reminded him of my human rights responsibility. He promised that if I went to the police station in Gradiska, he would ensure that I received all the information. Behind him stood a gorilla of a policeman whom Indy had clashed with before. We were not going forward. We moved slowly away. Some of the Muslim villagers approached us, they wanted us to stay. They were frightened. They told me that there were five dead, two were women. They were about to tell me more when the gorilla arrived, and they all melted away. At the police station we met the Chief and his deputy. He convened a meeting with detectives, doctors, and police. He promised thorough investigations, prosecutions for the guilty, security for the minorities. He was so plausible, I almost believed him.

We were in a difficult position with this man, as he controlled the one and only entrance and exit from Zagreb to Banja Luka. All our aid convoys passed over the Gradiska bridge, metres from his office. Every refugee who left went out over the Gradiska bridge. This man and his associates inspected the baggage of every refugee leaving. Few, if any, refugees got over the bridge without losing something. On his whim depended the food of many and the freedom of some. He promised to keep me up to date with progress. I called a meeting in the village for that evening.

I got the full story. At dusk a car had arrived. Out got the soldiers.

341

They went to the first house where an old lady lived with her son and his daughter. They burst in and grabbed the girl. The old lady was brave. She fought with them. One of them picked her up and threw her outside into the yard. She continued screaming so he shot her dead. Her son then tried to protect his daughter. He was shot dead. The girl was repeatedly raped. Some of the gang moved next door. They killed an old man and his son and repeatedly raped the wife of the son. They did not leave till dawn. Throughout the night, other villagers had telephoned the police, but they refused to come. I met the neighbour who had called the office. She described a night of screams and terror. The whole village asked for police protection for the night. The police chief promised to attend the meeting but did not. When it ended, I went back to see him. He said that he would happily provide police patrols in the evening but that he had no fuel for the police vehicles. I knew that this was another scam. Another cheap, nasty way of getting something for nothing out of us. I also knew that no fuel meant no patrols. I further knew that if I gave fuel once, I would have to give it forever. Fuel I just did not have. I went back to the village and explained. For the rest of the summer, as dusk approached, they moved out of their homes and slept in the fields.

On the fifth of August, another one of our parked vehicles was damaged—a sure sign that we were doing our job well.

On Saturday, 14th of August, one of our drivers in Zenica was shot dead. Boris Zeravcic was driving a UNHCR armoured vehicle in Stari Vitez, a Muslim besieged village. A high velocity round went through the vehicle, through the shoulder of Boris and lodged in the windscreen. In the vehicle with him was the young Dorothy Finnemore, a UNHCR Canadian lawyer, and a veteran of the UN-WRA Palestinian camps. Boris was a big happy basketball star, recently married. Dorothy watched his life blood drain away. She is a girl of great courage. She served on in Bosnia's trouble spots for at least another year.

In August, I received a real boost. Two more protection officers. One, big tough Greek Georgios Karamatzogolou, and a great surprise for me, Louis Gentile, who had worked so well out of Belgrade and who took over from me in Srebrenica. Louis was one of the best, and if I could have chosen one person to join the team, it would have been him. Sadly, Philippe went back to the Ivory Towers where he has written an excellent book on Banja Luka. With the arrival of Louis, I was able to reorganise the office. Louis ran protection, giving me time for everything else. My only problem with Louis was reigning him in. He is a stocky, cocky, uncompromising fighter.

His first suggestion was that he and his team should patrol at night the Muslim areas. I had been down that path and saw the flaws. I vetoed his suggestion but never his boundless enthusiasm. Whilst Louis and his duet were daily overwhelmed in their attempt to offer protection to increasing numbers in an ever worsening internal and external environment, I concentrated on pushing aid through. Only one Serb helped me unreservedly. This was Milko Gogic, the Commissioner for Refugees for the Doboj region, who was so brave on my first trip to Doboj. He is a humanitarian worker par excellence. He always wanted more aid than anyone else. If I sent a convoy to his area, he was always there to meet it. He knew where every kilogram had gone to. He had accounts to prove it. More importantly, he fought for his beneficiaries. He is a Serb in a volatile front-line area. He had enormous pressures put upon him. The minorities in his area did not get all that they should have, but they got as much as Gogic dared give them. Gogic gave me total support and encouragement to attempt to reach besieged minorities. At the end of the war there will be rogues who must be punished and there will also be heroes who must be honoured. Milko Gogic is my nomination for selfless, honourable, brave humanitarian worker in a vicious and dangerous environment. May God grant that his health does not fail and his enemies do not succeed.

On the 19th of August, as I arrived at the office, I received a call from Colonel Vujinovic. The Commander wished to have breakfast with me. I took Louis with me, and we went to the Corps headquarters to look for General Talic. However, the Commander they had in mind was the Commander in Chief of the Army, my old friend General Mladic.

Seated at a large table in the dining room were many of the top brass of the army of the so-called Srpska Republika. General Mladic was on top form. As I entered, he got up and gave me a big bear hug. Then with a great flourish, he introduced me to his top table.

– *Gentlemen, my friend Mr. Larry, the Muslim Ambassador to Banja Luka.* The joke was enjoyed by everyone.

As our activities expanded, we needed more local staff, but the recruitment of them was a problem. In Sarajevo, the government complained that we had too many Croats or too many Serbs. In Banja Luka, there were many hints that we had too many Croats. We had, of course, no Muslims. The locals seemed to be telepathic. The moment that I thought about extra staff, before I spoke to anyone, my staff were sidling up to me offering the services of their brother, mother, sister, cousin. This was not surprising, as we were paying about six hundred dollars a month in an environment where brain surgeons were on two a month. I decided to rock the boat. I needed three extra staff. I informed the local authorities that I was about to recruit three people, one Serb, one Muslim, one Croat.

The authorities came back to me very quickly with a statistical argument. The Muslim and the Croat population of the region represented less than ten per cent, my staff total was about to increase to nine, therefore I should employ less than 0.9 from the minorities. As I already had one Croat, they wished me to take on three Serbs, and they would provide their names in due course. OK!

– *Wrong*—I replied.

I had a novel plan of my own for the recruitment of my three. I went to Merhamet, Caritas, and Dobrotvor and asked for a person from each. The qualifications were that the candidate spoke English and was prepared to work for one sixth of the salary. The remainder was to be distributed by the charity to the poor. I would hand over the salary to a rep from the charity who would provide me with a breakdown, complete with signatures, of all those who received money. After a few false starts caused by nepotism, I ended up with Igor, Aida, and Sanja. Only Merhamet kept to its bargain and produced monthly accounts, but all three new recruits assured me that they only received one hundred dollars per month. Merhamet paid seven dollars each to forty-two families.

Therefore, Aida kept forty-two families alive. I hope she felt as good about it as I did. The local authorities' response was interesting. You win one, you must lose one. They decided that I must pay for their services.

Each convoy that entered their territory was escorted by one police car, in that car, they said, were five policemen. They demanded twenty Deutsche mark per person per day plus 210 litres of fuel per convoy for inspection teams. There was a cunning caveat to these charges. They were only applicable to those convoys which were transiting through the Serb territory. The implication being—*Why should we Serbs finance, in any way, aid going to the enemy?*

I went to see Colonel Vujnovic. I explained that the bulk of the aid we brought to the so-called Srpska Republika remained there and kept his people alive. This aid came in through Croatia. The Croats did not insist on us having an escort, and consequently, there was no payment to them. I reminded him of the many promises, declarations, and statements "guaranteeing the free and unhindered passage of humanitarian aid" made by Dr. Karadzic, his Vice Presidents, and his Ministers. Vujnovic refused to drop the issue. I refused to pay. The ever-increasing bill became an agenda item at our weekly meetings, but we never paid.

They did, however, sting us for fuel for the escort vehicle, twenty litres per trip, and for a food packet if the escort was out late. On the 26th of August, I was called to the house of the Mufti. Some "extremists" had fired seven shots from an automatic rifle into his living room. Amazingly there were no casualties. It was the first time that I had been to his home. It was about one hundred metres from his office, adjacent to the destroyed mosque. He lived in a first floor flat in an old building on a narrow street.

I went with Vesna and was met at the bottom of the stairs by a small group of Muslims who had come to congratulate the Mufti on his good fortune, or his narrow escape or on God's great mercy or whatever excuse they used to visit and to show their solidarity with him.

As we entered, his wife was praying. We walked round her and went into the living room to await the Mufti. We could see the bullet entry holes in the large window, and the spray of pock marks across the ceiling. The rounds had been fired from the street at a fairly tight angle and had entered too high to hit anyone seated. Allah had indeed been merciful. The Mufti entered the room. He had his usual happy and serene smile. We greeted him, he ordered coffee for us, and we sat and talked. We both agreed that the attack must have been to frighten him and his community. If anyone wanted to shoot and kill the Mufti, there were so many occasions when he presented a better target.

During our conversation, he introduced me to a house guest, Vadhet Alemic, a young Imam who had walked from Srebrenica to Gorazde and then to Banja Luka. He was about twenty-five or six—and a lot of fun! He had a problem and, as I was there, took the opportunity to share it. He had no papers, no identity card, no nothing. Could I get him out to Zagreb and then to Germany?

Could I fly him to the moon? I asked myself.

The Mufti explained that without papers, the Imam was at great risk in Banja Luka. He had confined him to his house. Could I employ the Imam, give him a UNHCR card, and send him to Zagreb never to return? I slowly, patiently, and I hope kindly, explained the pitfalls. If I employed him, the authorities would know within a day. At least one of my office staff was in direct contact with the police and the military. But, as I knew it, I did not mind. I could understand it. He was storing favours for the future. Other staff members were married to loyal Serbs. Could I expect them not to discuss office matters with their husbands?

If I employed the Imam, and we sent him towards Zagreb, he would probably be stopped at the border crossing. If he made it to Zagreb and never came back, then the freedom of movement of the rest of my staff could be compromised. My advice was to use local influence to get the Imam papers and then for us to get him out. Later, I was to wish I had been more helpful. After her prayers, Mrs. Mufti joined us. She was as noisy and outspoken as he was serene and reasonable.

As UN and a Brit, I came in for a verbal beating. Lord Carrington had persuaded the Germans to recognise Slovenia and Croatia too early. Lord Owen's map was appeasing the Serbs and rewarding aggression. The UN, by not lifting the arms embargo, was making the Muslims fight with their hands tied behind their backs. The Mufti and the Imam enjoyed my discomfort. Vesna enjoyed the challenge to her vocabulary, and I enjoyed the coffee. Before leaving, the Mufti loaned to me a pretty Koran in English and Arabic. I still have it and will return it when the war is over and I know that the Mufti and his possessions are safe.

The 10th of September started out a normal day. I left the house at a quarter after seven. The office was very close, left turn, right turn, left turn, right turn and you are there. Not this day. As I took the second left, there was a tank blocking the road. A second was manoeuvring into position. Troops were on the streets. Not the usual, jaded, aimless, scruffy local soldiers but smart, fit, tough and surprisingly polite soldiers. I could see that they had ringed the military headquarters of General Talic. I could also see that they had blocked off the entrance to the municipal headquarters where I normally went to see the mayor. I found an alternate route to the office, radioed back to my breakfasting staff, giving them the new route, and waited for the local staff to come in to see what they knew. When they arrived at eight, they were as excited and as amazed as I was. They told me that Radio Banja Luka was not broadcasting its usual programme, and that the street rumour was that the town had been taken over by soldiers from the crack 16th Brigade. I knew the commander of this unit, Colonel Topic, a pre-war JNA regular officer. His troops had been in the front line since the very beginning of the war. He had fought against Croatian Army forces before taking on the Bosnian Army. He and his troops were considered to be the best. We were in for an interesting time.

We rang General Talic. He was "at a conference." I'll bet he was. It can't be much fun for a Corps Commander to wake up and discover his headquarters surrounded by mutinous troops. How had the tanks rumbled along miles of road at night, through many check-

347

points, without at least one officer checking with the headquarters? We were unable to raise anybody. All our contacts were unavailable. The radio then announced that the town was under the control of a "Crisis Committee." The plot unfolded. The "Crisis Committee" was commanded by a captain. They had come from the front line and were refusing to go back until demands were met. Basically, they were fed up with fighting on the front line and were returning home to find that their families had received little, but seeing that some people were profiting very nicely from the war. One of their first actions was to close the restaurants and the bars. The office girls used their contacts and found out what they could. There were two cordons, one blocking off the city centre and another on the outskirts of the town. We were scheduled to deliver aid, to receive aid, and we had a convoy coming back from Zenica, which had told us by radio that it was stopped outside Banja Luka at a "new" checkpoint.

The general was not answering his phone; neither was the mayor nor the chief of police. I decided to visit the "Crisis Committee." I walked from the office with my bold and brave Vesna. We got through two checkpoints, and we were close to the civic building opposite the municipal headquarters. It was in this building facing the old seat of power that the "Crisis Committee" had brazenly made its HQ. Here we were stopped. I explained that I wished to present my compliments to the commander. We were ushered into the building and told to report to his deputy.

We met him on the second floor. He was small, toothless, and ruthless. We later learned that he had more notches on his gun belt than anyone else in the battalion. He told Vesna that he was pleased the UN was recognising their presence. I was not too happy with this interpretation, but I needed them. Without their cooperation, I was temporarily out of business. He took us in to see the captain, who looked worried, tired, and not in command. I was amused to discover that his name is Zec, rabbit in Serbo Croat, as he looked like a frightened rabbit. I explained to him that if one of his aims was to stamp out corruption, then he had my one hundred per cent support. I outlined the aid which we brought in and expressed my doubts about the integrity of some of the distributing agencies. I then told him that I wanted the usual freedom of movement that HCR enjoyed. He told me that he would authorise the "release" of the convoy returning from Zenica, and that he would allow the freedom of movement of my convoys as long as they did not come into Banja Luka.

I asked about the freedom of movement of my staff, local and international. He told me that I had to submit an application for each vehicle and each staff member to him for his approval. I was quite happy with this. I returned to the office. My staff were not so happy; they were reluctant for their names to be given to the "Crisis Committee." Whilst I was discussing this point with them, the phone rang. Colonel Vujinovic wished to speak to me. I went to see him but got no further than the "rebel" troops.

Back in the office, we spoke by phone. He had heard that I had been to see the "Crisis Committee." He wished me to have nothing further to do with the "rebels." He told me that—*The Corps Commander is still in charge.* I gently pointed out that he was not even in charge of the access to his own headquarters. I explained all that I had done and said. He asked me not to give legitimacy to the new committee by submitting requests to them. I promised to do my best.

The next week was fun. The "Crisis Committee" strong man proved to be a warrant officer. He upped his demands on a daily basis. Eventually, he overstepped himself and demanded the resignation of the whole government. General Mladic came from Pale to sort out the situation. The rebels would not at first let him into the city. They demanded to see Dr. Karadzic. General Mladic said that no way would he allow the president to suffer the indignity to have to pass checkpoints manned by dissenting troops. He invited the rebel commander to the airport outside Banja Luka to meet the president. The crafty warrant officer was not that stupid. He knew where his power base was. Eventually, General Mladic came in and spoke to the troops. They were not as respectful as he expected. From this moment on, they were doomed. The question was: would they be outmanoeuvred physically or mentally? Mladic decided on the mental approach. I think he chose this course because he was not too sure just how widespread this dissent was throughout the army. We had a good source of information from within the rebels; the boyfriend of one of our girls had served with them throughout the war and was manning one of their checkpoints. He believed that there were other battalions as equally prepared to rebel as his. The sadness to me was that their cause for complaint was not the futility of the war but their disappointment at the behaviour of those who were not fighting alongside them in the trenches.

In the midst of all this excitement, the deputy leader of the SDA party came to see me. Their leader Mr. Krzic had disappeared. I immediately spoke to Michel Minnig of ICRC. He had also heard the news. We both tried all of our contacts. The facts seemed to be that Krzic had left his house in the morning of the 11th of September, was seen heading towards the centre of town by some friends, and then was seen in a police car by one man standing on a street corner near the military police barracks. We asked the legitimate authorities, but this proved difficult. We could not contact the mayor; apparently the "Crisis Committee" had placed him under house arrest. The General was too busy to worry about the safety of one Muslim activist.

The Chief of Police seemed to have lost some of his power to the Military Police, who looked as if they were leaning towards the "Crisis Committee." I sent a polite letter to the "Crisis Committee" asking for their cooperation in establishing the whereabouts of Krzic. I never received an answer to this or to any other letter which I wrote to them. Meanwhile, my happy band of protection officers, led, once again, from the front by Louis, proved to be extra zealous in their investigations and were themselves arrested by the Military Police and were carted off to the MP barracks. They were not to know it at the time, but they ended up only a cell or two away from Mr. Krzic. When I arrived at the MP headquarters, I was told the arrest of my staff was a misunderstanding. They were released immediately.

A few days later, on the 16th at one thirty p.m., we answered the phone to hear the terrible news that the Mufti had been arrested.

This made me feel sick. He is such a gentle man that I knew he would suffer mentally more than physically. I made the wisest decision that I have made for a long time. I rang Geneva and told Sylvana Foa, the head of UNHCR's Public Information Department, what had happened. This was one of those days when the phone worked when we really needed it. I then went to the old mosque to see Bedrudin Gusic, the head of the Islamic Community. He was very frightened. The Mufti had been at home, a carload of troops had arrived and arrested him and the young Imam from Srebrenica.

I left Georgios Karamatzoglou with Bedrudin; if the soldiers returned to arrest any more from the Muslim community, they would have a hard time with Georgios. He is a two meter plus, very stocky Greek with a bad temper, a short fuse, and an over inflated opinion on the value of a UNHCR card.

I went back to the office, wrote a protest note to the "Crisis Committee," and contacted Predrag Radic, the Mayor who despite having problems of his own, promised to help. By three o'clock, Sylvana had the news of the arrest of the Mufti on CNN, Sky, and BBC World Service. I spoke to Mr. Gogic and to my contacts in Pale. By five o'clock, the Mufti was free. He had been threatened but was unharmed.

It took a further five days to get the Imam out. Five days of constant aggravation and irritation. When he was released, it was done in a bad, bad way. Louis and his team went to the Mufti's house to see him and realised that he needed urgent medical attention. They got him into the Banja Luka hospital. No easy achievement. Serb doctors are reluctant to treat Imams beaten up by Serb Military Police. It took seven days before the Imam could be moved. During this time, the UNHCR protection team got him papers and a place on a convoy to Zagreb. Because he was then an ex-detainee, he was able to find a third country to take him. Most countries, whilst not accepting refugees, will take, as asylum seekers, refugees who have been in prison. It is a cruel way to qualify. *Every violent thunderstorm has a silver lining*—as I told each released prisoner, hoping that it translated into Serbo-Croat.

Getting the Imam out meant that we could concentrate on Mr. Krzic. On the 17th, the "rebel" troops disappeared as quickly as they had arrived. Assurances were given that their leaders would be safe. I would not take a bet on the lives of the instigators at any odds. The Sarajevo-published pro-Bosnian government newspaper, Oslobodjenje, had an interesting theory. It suggested that the whole episode was organised by Mladic to prove that the troublesome independent Banja Luka corps commander Talic was not in control, and therefore could be removed. Very Balkan. As Talic is still there, this theory is either incorrect or failed. Another mystery to be cleared up at the end of the war. Throughout this interesting week we had a fistful of fame from CNN, and the "Bob and Bobby Show" from Time and The Independent.

CNN was not allowed to film a frame, despite the presence of Dave Rush as cameraman and the ace Christian Annanpour. The Indie and Time filed many a good column.

With the rebel troops out, the Mayor was back in his office. We went to see him to discuss Krzic. He amazed me; he told me that Dr. Karadzic was taking an interest in the case of Mr. Krzic. He assured me that he did not know where he was, but that he would do all in his power to help. Both UNHCR and ICRC spent hours every day chasing up leads on Krzic or pleading his case with the authorities. I have to confess that I thought he was dead. But on the 22nd, he was released.

The first week of October brought tragedy into the office itself. Our administrative officer Irena Benda, tall, with long dark hair, an excellent pianist with a degree in music, a most sensitive woman, lost her large, loving father. He was pedalling home at dusk on a bicycle with no lights and was hit by a passing lorry. His death was a great loss to a close family. At his funeral, I watched his son lose his hard-fought battle against tears. In pre-war fuel-available days, Mr. Benda would have driven home, in pre-war pre-sanctions days, his bicycle would have batteries for its lights. He was indeed an indirect victim of the war. Irena stayed at home for a week to comfort her mum. During that week, I realised what an influence she had on the office. She is a very understanding, calming, soul. I remember one day we had a highly emotionally disturbed girl in the office—a girl who had suffered too much and could take no more. There was the usual queue, but she pushed her way to the front. The crowd sensed her tension and did not hold her back. In the office we tried to deal quietly with her, but she suddenly flared from sobbing wreck to screaming siren. She was threatening the staff, I came out of my office with the intention of organising her removal. As I approached her, so did Irena. The girl was spitting and swearing, Irena talked softly to her, then put her arm around her and quietly led her away for counselling.

Sadly, Irena was not the only staff member to lose a loved one. The boyfriend of Ljiljana Stojakovic, who was the 16th Brigade soldier who had kept us in the picture during the Banja Luka mutiny, was to lose his life as the result of a traffic accident. He had fought in the front-line trenches in every hot spot since the war began and then was knocked down by a car. My mind's image of him is sparkling eyes, big smile, and damaged teeth. Typical of the fighter that he was, he initially survived the accident and lived on in intensive care for months before he eventually died. I remember Ljiljana telling me— *I have lost my man.* So submissive, so possessive.

On the 28th of October, Indy went to Sipovo to follow up on reports of severe harassment against the Muslims. We last had trouble in Sipovo on the 30th of June, when three Serb soldiers from the village had been killed at the front line. When their bodies were brought back for burial, some of the Serbs went on the rampage. Three Muslims were murdered, and fifty houses were burned down and the Muslim occupants driven out. Indy found only three hundred of the original three thousand Muslims still living in the village. The majority of these would leave today if we could find somewhere for them to go. Those that remain are those with no money, no contacts, and not a lot of hope.

Eighteen

Tesanj and Maglaj, A Delayed Entry

There should not be rivalry between aid agencies. We all share the same aims and the same goals. I am the most open aid worker that I know. I share all my info with any agency, I assist all fellow aid workers. But I like to be first. I put a lot of effort into trying to get into Tesanj and Maglaj. I had had that breakfast with General Mladic, where he promised me that I would get in.

So, when I heard that ICRC had approval to enter Tesanj, I was rocked. Inwardly, I was fuming. Only the girls in the office knew how much it affected me. I rang Michel Minnig.

– *Michel, I have just heard that you have approval for Tesanj.*

– *Yes. Have you also?* It seemed a genuine question.

– *No, I have not.*

– *Pity, we could have gone together.* Could he be as sincere as he sounded?

– *Are you going or just Patrick?*

– *Non, we are all going.* I rang Colonel Vujinovic. The phone was answered by Major King.

– *Is the Colonel there?*

– *No. He is out. May I help?*

– *You, help!* I said to myself. King I never trusted an inch. I could be wrong about him, but I doubt it. Perhaps Major, we can have a drink when the war is over, and I can find out where you really stood.

– *Please ask the Colonel to ring me on his return.*

– *OK. By the way, Mr. Larry, have you heard that ICRC have approval to enter Tesanj?*

– *Yes*—I replied. *My approval is on its way from Pale*—I lied. King had the arrogance to laugh. I hated him. I got into our office in Pale. We had two staff there. One, with the Scrabble defying name of Esko Kentrschynskyj, a Swede with a flat in Paris and a house in Chieng Mai, was far too much of a bureaucrat and a diplomat for my liking. He wanted everything done by the book. His deputy, Jacoba Van Der Vall, a Dutch woman, was much more my style. Her voice alone was enough to calm me down. But Sod's law being what it is, if ever I was in a fury, it was always poor Esko who answered the phone.

– ICRC have approval to go to Tesanj.

– I know.

– Where the hell is my approval?

– They tell me it will come soon.

– When the hell is soon?

– Don't you shout at me!

– I am not shouting at you! A little tug on my arm from one of the girls.

– You are.

– Look man, for weeks the reason they have given for us not going is security. If it is now secure for ICRC, it is secure for us. Please, please ask them for approval for us. We, at least, must go in with ICRC.

– What difference does it make who goes in first as long as someone gets in?—my colleague asked, sensibly. The girls in the office braced themselves for my reply.

– To you, who sit on your backside all day, not one jot. But to me, my friend, it matters enormously. Get up the bloody hill and get my approval. Not for the first time did I hear him saying, quite rightly—*Don't you talk to me like that.* For the next forty-eight hours I sat and simmered. I rang everybody who could help. They all agreed that it was cruel that ICRC should get the approval to go and that I, who had kept the name of Tesanj and Maglaj in the news for months, should be denied the joy of entering. They all also agreed with my patient colleague in Pale that all that really mattered was that someone entered with a convoy. I knew this, and Vesna and I went to the ICRC offices to see if we could assist in any way. Michel and Patrick were pleased to see us, and I am sure were genuinely not gloating.

Colonel Vujinovic and my faithful friend Mr. Gogic both knew how I felt. They tried every avenue to get approval for me to go with ICRC. I suggested that we try for approval for just one vehicle from UNHCR. They tried and they failed.

– Mr. Gogic, why ICRC and not me?

– Mr. Minnig never told the Serbs to burn in the hottest corner of Hell—

replied the frank, honest, and amused Mr. Gogic.

The day arrived for ICRC to leave. I sat in the office. I rang them, wished them luck, and watched them go.

Early in the afternoon, I received a call from ICRC, from Patrick's wife. Their lead vehicle had hit a mine. The vehicle was totally destroyed. No one was too sure about casualties.

My first reaction was one of anger. ICRC in Banja Luka had limited experience of crossing active front lines. Of all the ICRC delegates that I have dealt with, I liked Michel best. I hoped he was alright. Furthermore we were very good friends of Patrick and his wife. News came back slowly. There were no deaths. Then we heard there were no casualties. Finally, we heard that the convoy was returning.

Now I could smile. Sorry, but smile I did. The way was open for UNHCR. The Serbs had shown that they wanted a convoy to reach Tesanj. They were obviously claiming that the mine which blew up the vehicle was a Muslim one. ICRC as an organisation was not going to race back in. I pressed hard.

– *We have a convoy ready. We have experience. Give us approval.* The following day I went to see Michel and Patrick. They were OK. They had had a fright but were in good spirits. More importantly, Michel was determined that I should succeed. He and Patrick drew maps and briefed me as thoroughly as possible. Thanks, guys, for your magnanimity.

Approval followed for me to go to Tesanj, followed rapidly with approval for me to go to Maglaj. Zagreb reacted rapidly. A Scandinavian convoy for Tesanj and a Brit one for Maglaj. I was to take the Tesanj one in, return to Teslic and then pick up the Brit one and head for Maglaj.

I rang Tony Land in Sarajevo. I was very excited. *Tony I am so happy. To quote from the good book, 'My cup runneth over.'* Tony, as quick and as realistic as ever—*As long as your vehicle does not turneth over.*

The convoy from Zagreb arrived in Banja Luka. The drivers were as hungry for success as I was. Hauling humanitarian aid from warehouse to warehouse along rough terrain and crossing checkpoints is exciting, but the chance of delivering the aid directly to a besieged town is why they all joined. MSF Holland were to join us as well. They had a vehicle full of vital medicine. Their team was a bright, happy, handsome and charming Dutch doctor, Bert Schilte, and a real character of a Brit, Peter Milne, whom I had first met when he was a driver, part of the very first successful convoy into Sarajevo. He had motored from Split in Croatia with two of his trademarks; wearing a kilt and smoking a pipe. Peter is one of those men that every small team should have, perennially happy and a fixer.

Stowed away in their already overcrowded vehicle was Brien Mc-Closkey, a World Health Organisation doctor, originally from traumatic Northern Ireland, where, I think, he was a neurosurgeon. He was now a public health specialist in soporific Worcester, loaned to WHO. Brien, who is very much a "hands on" doctor, had "escaped" from the WHO office in comfortable Zagreb. He had visited part of our Banja Luka region patch and had, a few days earlier, been rebuked by his WHO security masters in Zagreb for stepping beyond his areas of responsibility and putting himself at risk. If they thought he was a naughty boy last week, then volunteering for Tesanj was going to make them apoplectic.

At the last minute, I was called to the Army Corps headquarters. I went with trepidation. I knew that Colonel Vujinovic was away. Major King met me at the door with a sinister smile. The route was changed. No explanation. As I was expecting the bastard to cancel the convoy, my smile was much broader than his. New routes I could cope with. In fact the route was awful. It would take us along a track with a very poor surface and some pretty wicked bends. The aim presumably was, at best, to slow us down, at worst, to prevent us getting through. One day I will find out whether this excursion through the woods was the work of the authorities at Pale or the little joke of Major King.

After hours of driving, the Scandahooligans got us to the Serb front line at Vukovici. The track passed through a clearing in the woods. On both sides there were Serb soldiers in trenches. All were soldiers of the renowned 16th Brigade. They were quite friendly, but the convoy was halted. We had to wait for Colonel Topic, the commander, to arrive. Topic I had met before in Pale. He is one of the Serb battalion commanders with an almost legendary reputation. He is tough and independent. It was his merry men who had barricaded Banja Luka and his captain who was still incarcerated in some Serb military "kalaboos."

Whilst we waited for Topic to arrive, Vesna and I got some friendly banter going with the soldiers. They teased us about the ICRC convoy. Topic arrived. He is about five feet nine, solid, intelligent, and quite a handsome man. He was obviously in charge. He greeted me courteously, remembered our previous encounter, and asked me how things were in Sarajevo. I introduced him to Serb Vesna, they chatted, and the ice was broken. We discussed General Mladic, Banja Luka, and the war.

Meanwhile, the convoy stayed in line with engines running to keep the cabs warm. Colonel Topic asked me if I had been debriefed by ICRC. I told him that I had. *OK. I know I have orders to let the convoy through, so let's do it quickly and as professionals. You go forward about fifty metres, then you turn left. On the left you will see my front-line trench, in front of it is the remains of the ICRC vehicle. Immediately ahead of you is the road. That is no man's land. To the right is Croat and Muslim territory. Once around that corner they can see you. Do not be surprised if they fire on you. Once you pass my front-line trench, I cannot guarantee your safety. I said the same to Minnig of ICRC. He ignored me, he lost his vehicle, he could have lost his life.*

– *Will you accompany me to your front-line trench?* His face broke into a big smile.

– *Are you scared?* He asked me.

– *No. Cautious. Are you coming?* I replied.

– *No.* Big smile from me.

– *Are you scared?* I asked him.

– *No. Cautious.* He replied and smiled. I liked Topic.

I went forward, wearing a bullet proof jacket and helmet.

Vesna stayed with Topic. I noticed that they moved forward, keeping a safe distance but ensuring that Vesna was within earshot. As I turned left, I saw the Serb trench. There were two soldiers in it. They

were relaxed and smiling. One of them pointed over to my right where, about fifty metres away, I could see movement on the hillside.
– *Muslims*—the Serb said.

In front of the trench were the remains of the ICRC vehicle. It was badly damaged. How they all got out safely I do not know. Immediately in front of me, there was a large mound of earth half the width of the road. The remainder of the road was blocked by boulders.

– *Mines*—said the Serb, pointing to the mound of earth. It was obviously the route that Michel's vehicle had taken. There may be more mines, there may not. Just off the right-hand side of the road, there was an unexploded hand grenade. A further twenty metres ahead, there was a small makeshift bridge spanning a gap caused initially by subsidence and then enhanced by the Minnig mine. The left-hand side of it looked fairly solid, but on the right-hand side, the track and bridge disappeared in a heap of rubble, stone and twisted metal. I was hoping to send twenty-tonne trucks over this.

From the right side of the tracks, I could hear voices from the Bosnian held hills. I shouted that I was UNHCR and raised my arms to show I was unarmed. Normally at this stage, the Serbs would fire a single round. They would claim it had come from the "Muslim" side. They would hope that the shot would frighten me off and that I would go back. They would also hope that the Bosnian forces would reply thus allowing them to say—*You bring a convoy here and they fire on you.*

Topic is a thorough professional. He knew that one stray round would not frighten me away. He also knew that one stray round could start a fire fight, putting his soldiers at risk. When Topic decided to fight or to be difficult then he was vicious. War was no game to Topic.

I could see almost the whole length of the road between the Serb foremost trench and the first Bosnian post. The no man's stretch was about one hundred metres long. I turned to walk back and found Topic and Vesna standing by the Serb trench.

– *Colonel, I want to walk forward and make contact with the other side.*
– *Fine.*

I walked back to the MSF truck, briefed Peter and the two docs, then called forward the convoy leader. I explained what I had seen, the destroyed vehicle, the mound of earth, the unexploded grenade, the damaged track, and the proximity of the Bosnians. I told them of my intention to go forward.

Vesna walked with me to the mound of earth. She was wearing her bulletproof jacket and her helmet. She looked worried and very vulnerable. I asked her to wait at the mound, to watch, to observe, and to try to hear any words shouted to me from the Bosnian side.

I approached the mound of earth. I could see the track taken by the ICRC vehicle. Where the thing had blown up there would have been a fair bit of reckless movement, so I could safely presume that there were no anti-personnel mines in the mound. There may be more anti-tank, but my twelve-stone was not going to set these off. It was possible that the Serbs would place some anti-personnel mines there at nightfall, but I felt that I trusted Topic.

Slowly, I walked onto the mound. Step by step I advanced, carefully choosing a place to put my foot that looked "clean" and firm. Once over the mound, I walked to the point where the track was at its worst. I could see that this was going to test the driver's skills.

Once over this obstacle and round the corner, I was on a stretch of tarmac. Excellent. It is much easier to see mines in or on tarmac. At a glance, I could see shrapnel and tails from mortars which had hit the road. I walked very slowly, hands up in the air, shouting that I was —*UNHCR Mr. Larry*. It is a strange feeling. You feel like a ham actor in a "B" film. You feel conspicuous. You feel slightly ridiculous. And you feel really, really high.

One nervous soldier, one psychopath, from either side, and you are dead. I could hear words shouted back at me from the opposite hill. I looked back. Vesna was at the end of the road. Too close for her safety but close enough for my morale. *It's OK*—she said.

Whatever was being shouted was not detrimental to my health. I passed the halfway point and began to see soldiers at the Bosnian end. They were smiling. Any thoughts of quickening my pace were kept in check by the sight of anti-tank mines. The mines were wired together in threes on long thin wooden boards, which had been laid on the road to form a deadly zig zag chicane. I stepped over them. When I reached the Bosnian location, I first saw a Croat flag flying from a house to the right down a lane. This was the Croat checkpoint. But the first man to approach me extended his hand and said, "Mustafa." He was in uniform and on his sleeve was the Bosnian shield. He was a very tall, gangling, garrulous man with an almost overpowering friendliness. My first thought was that he was drunk, but I could smell no alcohol and he was steady on his feet.

– *Bring convoy?* Mustafa continued.

– *Yes*—I said with pride.

– *Serbs OK?*

– *Yes. I have a message from Topic for your commander. Where is your commander?*

– *Comes.* By now, I was surrounded by Bosnian soldiers all wanting to talk to me.

– *Wait, I go get translator*—I said, accompanying my words with my best "charades" hand movements.

– *OK.* I walked back. No, I remember, I strolled back, I felt good. Vesna was waiting with Topic.

– *Come on I need you*—I said to Vesna, then to Topic—*Colonel, if the Bosnian agrees, will you meet him in the middle?* Topic smiled.

– *No weapons. No bodyguards.*

– *I'll try.*

Vesna and I walked to the Bosnian lines. I introduced Bosnian Vesna to Bosnian Mustafa. She was then bombarded with questions from every direction, especially when they heard that she is from Sarajevo. It appears that everybody has somebody living in Sarajevo. Apparently, we were in the village of Kriz, a combined Croat and Muslim post.

Soon the Bosnian commander arrived. A very tall, handsome, intelligent looking man. Younger looking than Topic, but I sensed that they were equal adversaries. He was very pleased to see me. He knew that we were coming. He had hoped that we would not be put off by the ICRC incident. I asked him if the mine had been laid by him.

– Five metres from a Serb trench? I wish it had.
– Have you planted any mines in the no man's land?
– No.
– Have the Serbs?
– I do not know, but I doubt it. We dominate the road. But on a dark night...

I put to him my suggestion that he and Topic should meet in the middle of the no man's land. The Bosnian commander was agreeable. I left Vesna with them. I walked down to Topic.

– OK. Let's go—I said. He called over his number two and handed to him his belt, holster, and pistol. It was an understated, very professional and very brave gesture. We walked to the centre together. He stood in full view on the empty road. The Bosnian commander followed his lead and came with Vesna to the centre. He tried to come alone but Mustafa would not stay behind. They were both unarmed.

– Shall I send Mustafa back? I asked Topic.

– No, he is harmless. I know him well. They all greeted each other, their first "face to face" contact for almost one year. I watched Mustafa. I was worried that he could be dangerous.

They began to talk. I left them. Vesna and I walked back. I collected a bottle of whisky from my vehicle and gave it to Topic's number two.

– Take this out to them. He readily agreed. I was happier because then it was two and two.

Vesna and I discussed Mustafa. Her observation was much more accurate than mine. *He's shell shocked*—A diagnosis from a Sarajevo woman that I would never dispute.

After ten minutes, and half the bottle, I returned. *Do you mind if I get my show on the road?* Topic spoke to his deputy. He came back to the Serb lines with me. The first problem was the "blind" grenade. To my surprise it was no longer there. How it had been removed, who removed it, I do not know, but there it was (or rather, was not)—gone! Next problem was the earth mound, forward of the last Serb trench. Did it contain any mines? A few of us had now walked over it, but that was not a sufficient test. I asked for volunteers amongst the convoy drivers to dig a path through the mound. I was swamped with volunteers, but we had only two shovels. I asked the Serb deputy if I could borrow some shovels. His men were living in trenches, there could be no shortage of shovels. To my great surprise, not only did he provide shovels but men as well. This was a really good sign. If the Serbs had recently laid any mines in the mound, then they were unlikely to stand over us as we picked our way through.

The ICRC mine was either laid by the Bosnians and their commander had denied it, or by the Serbs who had then forgotten it was there, or by the Serbs who knew it was there and had let Michel motor over it. The fact that they watched us dig led me to believe that they were pretty sure there were no anti-personnel mines in the area.

Digging the tracks was slow, hard work, and in truth the shovels soon all found themselves in the hands of the Danes. They cut through the mound of rocks, rubble, and clay, two tracks the width of the wheels of their trucks.

We now had a path for the trucks, but we still could not guarantee that under our newly made tracks there would be no mines.

I went to see both commanders and explained the next part of my plan.

– *I am going to bring up one of the heaviest trucks, reverse it and motor it backwards over the tracks through the mound. Ten tons of flour will set off any anti-tank mine. With a bit of luck, the driver will be sufficiently far away from the blast to be OK. Please warn your men so that if there is a bang, we do not start a war.*

Both commanders thought it was a good idea. In truth, I had hoped that they would both agree that it was an unnecessary precaution, which would imply that they both knew that there were no more mines.

Mines are evil. Especially in the hands of irresponsible troops who lay them indiscriminately. As a Sandhurst cadet I can remember drawing minefield maps. In Hong Kong in 1968, I saw a brave young sergeant earn a George medal carrying two injured Hong Kong policemen out of a minefield. The minefield was marked, but the wind and erosion had caused the mines to slip down the hill. In Bosnia they are sewn like seeds, strewn about the countryside. Seeds which reaped their own evil harvest.

Neither of these commanders knew what their predecessors had left. I went to see the convoy leader. We chose the heaviest, longest truck. I suggested that I should drive it. *You?*—said the Danish driver. *Not bloody likely. You may scratch it.* Wearing his bullet proof jacket and his helmet, he reversed his truck up to the mound. We moved away. He backed his rear wheels over the tracks we had made.

Silence.

Back and forth went his rear wheels, defining a safe path for the trucks. He re-joined the convoy. We lined up. I shook the hands of Topic, agreed a time of return, nine the next morning, and away we went. The tracks of my vehicle and that of MSF were not as wide as the truck's, but my trip into Srebrenica had taught me that my vehicle was not heavy enough to set off a landmine. The ICRC vehicle was armoured and therefore two tons heavier than mine. Peter Milne knew this, I knew this, though the docs were not as convinced.

We paused at Kriz. A Bosnian soldier with a TV camera asked if he could travel on the bonnet of my vehicle and film the convoy. I thought he meant for the initial few yards, but he perched on the bonnet for the whole ten or so kilometres! It was pouring with rain, and he got soaked, but so did we in the vehicle. I could not use the windscreen wiper, for fear of knocking him off. So we had to wind the windows down and see through the side windows. As we passed through tiny villages, the population lined the route and waved and cheered. Their waves were returned by our ecstatic, acrobatic camera-man. I was really worried that he might fall off and end up under the wheels. We had two doctors in the following vehicle, but we had come to save lives, not to hazard them. The Bosnian commander in a battered police vehicle led our way into Tesanj. By now it was late. They had chosen a warehouse on the outskirts of the town, where we would unload. We motored the convoy in. This was a little disappointing as we were unable to see Tesanj itself or to meet many of the people. The drivers were undeterred, they knew that they had brought in the first aid for five months. They unloaded rapidly and prepared themselves for the night. There was the rumble of distant shelling, but we felt safe.

On our arrival at the warehouse, I reminded the commander that we had the MSF truck full of medicines for the hospital.

A short while later, after darkness had fallen, a civilian came to collect us to take us to the hospital. This was a short distance away, but in the city itself. We were therefore able to see, by silhouette, the extent of the destruction. It was bad, but not as bad as I had anticipated.

At the hospital, we were met by the Mayor of Tesanj, Muhamed Clanjak, who is a doctor himself, and his charming wife who is a dentist. We were taken to the office of the hospital director Dr. Ekrem Ajanovic who was formerly a professor at Tuzla University. He briefed us on the medical situation. They had wired up a bulb to a car battery to illuminate the office. They had had no visitors for more than four months. No supplies for ten months. They were desperate to talk. Brian McClusky and Bert listened patiently to their many tales. We met the two surgeons who had carried out two thousand operations in ten months. Their eyes were red, their faces drawn and lined, but as they recounted their successes and saw the wonderment and admiration in the faces of the visiting doctors their eyes sparkled with pride. Ninety-five per cent of the two thousand cases were caused by war trauma. An average day brought three deaths. Surprisingly there had been six hundred births in the past ten months. Two hundred down on the previous year's figure. There were one hundred and thirty TB patients whose treatment had stopped for lack of medicines.

We then toured the hospital by candlelight. Nurses held makeshift lamps containing homemade rag wicks and burning oil. The hospital had been designed to have one hundred patients. It now had one hundred and fifty, the majority of whom lay in beds in the corridors of the hospital. The wards had windows, the windows faced the Serb positions. Many Serb shells and Serb sniper rounds had landed in the wards. The beds in the corridors, the burning oil lamps, the smell, the stained bandages, the blood, the gore, the shadows. It was how I had imagined hospitals in the Crimea. These latter-day Florence Nightingales took us from bed to bed. Accompanying and assisting them was a tall, slim young man aged, maybe, sixteen. Gentle and innocent, his face untouched by a razor, his voice still not broken, he had volunteered for work in the hospital at the beginning of the war, almost two years ago, and never left.

We had been told that some of the patients were victims of mushroom poisoning. This was particularly poignant as these people are really rural dwellers. They knew the risks but preferred the risk to starvation. In one bed, lay a very pretty ten-year-old girl. She had been brought in with mushroom poisoning. Her sister had already died. Her mother was at her bedside. As she lay sleeping with her shallow breathing and her dainty looks, I was convinced that she would live. She was surrounded by amputees and open wounds, but in the flickering candlelight she looked like Sleeping Beauty.

Sadly, it was the Prince of Death who visited her in the night.

As we stumbled out of the hospital in the pitch dark, the doctors reminded us of their most urgent needs, fuel to run the generator, so that they can perform operations at night, run dialysis machines and incubators, anaesthetics, blood plasma, vaccines.

We returned to the warehouse. The drivers were surrounded by people from Tesanj, sharing their cigarettes, their food, and their stories. We, who had visited the hospital, were quite depressed. But not for long. The irrepressible Peter Milne had found out before leaving Banja Luka that today was Brien McClusky's birthday—his fortieth. Peter produced a four-course meal which included salmon and was concluded by whisky. All that then remained was to find a place for Vesna to have her nightly ablution and a discreet wee. Then sleeping bags out and the enveloping sleep of the emotionally drained.

The following morning we left at seven. There were quite a few people to see us off and to wish us a speedy return. Despite the fact that it was a misty and wet morning, we made the front line much quicker than I had anticipated. I had said that we would cross at nine. We were at the Croat/Bosnian checkpoint at eight. Visibility was about thirty metres. I had no intention of emerging unannounced, out of the mist, at the Serb front line.

The Bosnian commander had occasional radio contact with the Serb front line. The radio operators at each end were both local boys, had been to school together and were in the same class. The callsign of the Bosnian Serb was "Geneva" and the Bosnian Muslim "Paris." Paris alias Hakija tried to raise Geneva alias Mirko, but the batteries were too weak.

In the meanwhile, Vesna went off to explore Kriz and found a three-year-old boy called Mario. He lived in Kriz, in a house on the very front line. His parents, a young Croat couple, refused to leave their home. The detritus of war were the playthings of Mario. Vesna gave him cuddles and chocolate. By eight thirty, the mist had cleared sufficiently for me to feel safe in walking down no man's land. Vesna insisted on accompanying me.

At the halfway point, we were met by a happy and smiling Topic and his deputy. He had a Serb TV camera crew with him. The interviewer was Lidija, my lovely friend from Doboj. It was really good to see her. Topic invited the Bosnian commander for slivovica. I brought the convoy forward. There was much self-congratulation on all sides. For at least thirty minutes Serb side soldiers mingled with those from the Bosnian side. I shook hands with all, thanked them all, especially Topic. I watched as the Bosnian commander returned to his lines. We drove back to Banja Luka, arriving at ten thirty.

By then the Serbs had shelled Tesanj. Back in Banja Luka, we had time only to write a quick report, make a number of phone calls, go to the loo, eat, wash, and change. I said a fond farewell to the Danes and awaited the arrival of the Brit convoy, whose leader, big "Ginger" Dawes, I knew well. "Ginge" is an ex warrant officer in the Parachute Regiment. Paras are either lean and mean like greyhounds or big and square like bull mastiffs. Ginge is more than six feet tall, very heavy looking, with a bright, cheerful, open face, topped by a good head of ginger hair. He has a ginger moustache, a Northern accent, and a "let's get it done lads" attitude. He has a great sense of humour and a gentleness which belies his size and former training. I often watched him and found it difficult to see him as a bawling, beasting para senior rank. Also, with his size, it is not easy to imagine him dangling on the end of a parachute. Perhaps he has mellowed and spread with retirement.

The convoy drivers always fascinated me. The Scandinavians were young, smart, bright, and arrogant. The German team was slightly older and were a mixed but disciplined bunch. The Brit teams were special. They looked as if they had been recruited by a press gang touring motorway transport cafes. They were, in the main, ex-soldiers, tattooed, crude, rude, and vulgar. They wore T-shirts bearing convoy logos or obscene graffiti. T-shirts which they pulled on over their eleven-month pregnant stomachs. T-shirts which never quite managed to stay in their trousers and which therefore constantly revealed the first month or two of their brewery bellies. T-shirts which revealed in grotesque detail their belly buttons forced and stretched to protrusion by breakfasts at "greasy spoon" cafes and the foaming brown contents of pint glasses.

The mere hint of a ray of the sun is a magnet to all lorry drivers. As it peeks through the sky, they divest themselves. The Scandinavians do so to turn their ski toned muscles a subtle brown, and the Brits to blur their tattoos a lobster pink.

– *Are we going to get through, Larry?* asked big Ginge.

– *No question, my friend. If the Scandies could get me into Tesanj, we can get into Maglaj.*

– *My lads won't let you down. Just show us the way.* We set out in the early afternoon with a Serb police escort of one battered Golf and two men. The police had been briefed by Major King and surprise, surprise, we were going the scenic route, not the direct route. A route full of bends and potholes that would add on at least twenty-five kilometres.

We had moved only a few kilometres when Ginge told me on the radio that it was time to stop and tighten the canopies over the trucks. This was a routine, especially British. The trucks were filled to capacity, and with the shaking of the load on the tracks and roads, the contents of the trucks "settled." It was therefore necessary to tighten covers. It was a practice which, although necessary, irritated me. No sooner was it "Wagons Roll" than it was time to stop.

During this first break, I spoke with the police escort. The driver was nervous and tired, his escort much more laid back.

— Why are we going this route? I asked.

— I do not know—he genuinely answered. Then he surprised me.

— Are we returning tonight?—he asked.

— My friend, the convoy is going to Maglaj. This floored him.

— Maglaj is Muslim. We can't go there.

— You take me to the front line and wait for me.

— But the front line is in Croat hands.

— Correct. You are taking us to the Serb/Croat front line. There you wait for us.

— But we have no food. We have only enough fuel for Teslic. We have no money. Where will we stay? The questions tumbled out of him as if he were a child. Vesna translated and was irritated by him. I needed him on my side but was annoyed at the route he was leading us along. It was not his fault, but he was part of the system which would probably now prevent us from entering Maglaj until the following day.

I promised him food and fuel and insisted that he got us to Teslic quickly. We set off and approached Teslic, where we were stopped by a checkpoint. The escort driver was useless. He knew we had approval. He would not have been leading the way if we had not, but the checkpoint commander told him we were "unannounced." The police driver came to tell Vesna. He looked relieved. Unannounced equals no approval, equals back to Banja Luka, equals tonight with his wife. *Tell the commander to wave us through. Tell him that you got your orders from King, who got his from General Talic, who got his from General Mladic.*

It worked. We moved on through the town and out onto the road leading to Maglaj via Zepce. I was pleased. Vesna was not. *Too easy*— she said. She was right. On the outskirts of Teslic we were stopped at the entrance to the military headquarters which was in a large house on the right-hand side of the road. A group of heavily armed and aggressive soldiers told our police escort that we had no approval to proceed and that we must return to Banja Luka. Their spokesman was a huge Serb with a shaven skull. He wore a uniform but with no hat. An aggressive brute with a smirk on his lips and the smell of alcohol on his breath. Our police escort was frightened. They did not want to be associated with us.

With Vesna, I got out of the car and we walked to the group of soldiers. They were all noisy and some were not sober. The sneering giant barracked Vesna.

– *Why are you, a Serb, helping them to feed the enemy?* Whenever this happened, we had a pattern for defence.

– *She is here to speak my words. Not to answer your questions. Get me your commander immediately.* Even translating someone else's words is not easy when the atmosphere is hostile and electric. She got back a stream of abuse. I waded in with very heavy words demanding in the name of military discipline that I see the commander. The harsh words, the tone, and the noisy response eventually produced from the house a young officer, a captain, who was the adjutant to the commander.

– *The commander is out. He will return late. Please go back to Banja Luka. By tomorrow the whole thing will have been sorted out.*

– *Yes*—I said—*but not to my satisfaction.*

– *Vesna*—I continued—*tell him that I will stay here until I see the commander.* The young captain was reasonable but made one telling point.

– *I am sorry, Mr. Larry, but I cannot guarantee your safety here, especially when it gets dark. Please return.*

– *My dear friend, we stay.* I walked away with Vesna and briefed Ginger and the MSF crew, Bert and Peter. Brian, the WHO adventurer, was returning to Zagreb with the jubilant Danes to inform the world on the conditions in Tesanj.

I returned to my vehicle. The large bald Serb hurled an obscenity our way which brought laughter and jeers from his companions. Vesna and I got back into the vehicle and locked the doors. Vesna was white.

– *Are you scared of him?*—I asked her, nodding in the direction of the large, vulgar Serb. Her answer was simple.

– *Horribly*—she replied.

As we waited, the aggro built up outside the headquarters. More soldiers gathered. More crowded around the vehicle and some banged on the bonnet and kicked on the tyres. I contacted the Banja Luka office and asked them to get hold of Mr. Gogic in Doboj and to ask him to intervene if possible, also to ask them to see General Talic.

Rod Kay was holding the fort, a dour, doleful but witty Liverpudlian who is an excellent logistician but not one of life's natural diplomats. Ginger, Rod, and myself: the "A" team, if the "A" stood for aggression.

Eventually, the commander and a number of his officers arrived in a convoy of three cars. He was briefed by the soldiery. Vesna listened to what was going on through our car window. She firmly warned me that the situation was explosive. I left our car and we approached. I offered the usual courtesies but received a torrent of insults which needed no translation.

The commander was about fifty. He looked to be a petty but educated man. His message to me was simple—*Go back. You have no approval. We do not want you here. Get out of here before it gets dark.* I hate rudeness when I am trying to be nice.

– *Commander, I have approval from Dr. Karadzic, Mr. Koljevic, General Mladic and General Talic to go forward. I have in my possession a piece of paper signed in Pale approving this convoy and this route. I respectfully ask for your cooperation in permitting the convoy to move forward.* Now, I have to tell you that at this stage I am bluffing not only him but myself. I know that, if I get his approval, it is now too late to move off towards the Croat front line. It is too easy at night to lob a lone shell onto a slow moving, un-armed, unescorted convoy, in a war zone at the front line.

If he is really clever, he will wave me forward. That will test the Hollingworth hot planning facility! However, I judge that the battle is one between being forced back to Banja Luka or staying where we are till dawn. Back to Banja Luka will mean the end of this convoy's chances.

The commander taxes Vesna's vocabulary with a range of Serbo-Croat invective. She, poor girl, knows that English has twice as many words as German and four times as many words as French, but has a paucity of swear words. She conveys the mood if not the mode.

It transpires that this particular war-lord, like so many others, has little respect for his seniors or his superiors. Time for me to huff and puff—white beard, white hair reflecting red cheeks, puce lips, and green eyes.

– *I am amazed by your disloyalty. What hope is there for you. You claim to be fighting for a sovereign state, Srpska Republika. You, you are a rebel commanding a rabble. This convoy is for women and children. Where is your Serb humanity? Where is your Serb chivalry? Where is your Serb loyalty? I have come here with approval, where is your famed Serb hospitality?* Vesna translates all this, word for word. I know that she is frightened. Her face is white. She, of course, can hear the soldiers' comments, hear the taunts aimed at her Serbness or more specifically, what they perceive to be her lack of it. She began by saying— *He says.* This is good, as it at least slightly distances her from me. If she had begun to translate in the first person—*I am amazed by your disloyalty*—she may have gotten no further.

Somewhat unfairly, I prefer a female translator. They can say far more than a male can. The recipient is not likely to knock them down or arrest them. Also, very few males have the courage to translate harsh words to men of violence in a dangerous environment.

The commander is shocked by the vehemence of my attack. It provokes much discussion amongst his colleagues. I pester Vesna to tell me what is going on. She asks me to be patient.

After a long minute or two, the commander tells me to wait, and he enters the headquarters. Vesna advises that we get back into our vehicle away from the soldiers.

Back in the comparative safety of our vehicle, she briefs me on all she has heard.

– *They do not want the convoy to proceed, but they know that it has approval. The commander is being pressed by the toughs to send you back. The young officer is advising that we are parked here for the night. They have gone inside to discuss to avoid pressure from the drunken soldiers.*

With the leadership inside, the soldiers moved around our vehicles. Using the radio, I advised all drivers to stay in their locked cabs but discovered that Ginge had already ordered this.

Every fifteen or so minutes, Vesna and I got out of the vehicle and walked to the gate to see if the commander wished to see us. It was important to show that we were not frightened and that we would not go away. After about an hour, the crowd of soldiers had thinned out. It was cold and dark.

On our next visit to the gate of the headquarters, we were invited in. The atmosphere was entirely different, the young officer took us into a room with armchairs, at which were seated the commander and some of his officers. We were invited to sit down and offered slivovica.

– *You cannot go forward tonight. You cannot stay where you are. You will have to park your convoy in the hotel car park a few kilometres back at Banja Vrucica*—said the commander. They all waited for my reaction.

– *Very wise decision, commander.* They were all delighted, not half as much as I was. *But*—I continued—*I have been guaranteed safety whilst on the Serb territory. I demand a guard, preferably police, to guard the convoy during the night.* The commander told me that a police guard was beyond his ability but that he would produce soldiers. Reluctantly, I accepted, knowing full well that they would be the same gang that had given us so much hassle already. *Furthermore, I wish to leave for Maglaj at seven in the morning.*

The commander said—*OK.*

The next problem was to turn the convoy round. The road we were parked on was far too narrow for the trucks to turn in. Ginge and I went ahead and found an entrance to a field where each vehicle could drive past and then reverse. This we would have to do ten times. It was going to be a long tedious night.

Whilst one of Ginge's crew sorted this out, we went off to the hotel escorted by our police car which had reappeared. The hotel was a famous spa centre before the war and had some excellent buildings. I had been there on a number of occasions with Mr. Gogic for conferences.

The car park was large, tarmacked, and excellent. However, we were directed by the police and the soldiers to park on the farthest side of

374

the empty car park, farthest away from the hotel entrance and next to a line of trees. I made it clear to the police that they would return to escort us to Maglaj at seven the following morning.

Slowly, the trucks arrived and were parked up. Noisily, the guards arrived, all tanked up and with a "ghetto blaster" radio. They looked far more like the local street gang that they were, than the soldiers they pretended to be. The drivers began to cook and brew, the soldiers to cadge and barrack.

The local Teslic Red Cross supervisor, whom I knew, came to visit us. She confirmed that our office had contacted Mr. Gogic and that he had contacted her. Furthermore, Mr. Gogic was a very good friend of the manager of the Spa Hotel, and he was expecting a visit from us.

I briefed Ginger and Peter Milne, left the convoy in their capable hands, and went to the hotel. The manager met us, bought us a drink, and offered us rooms in the hotel—all of us. His offer was genuine, but I knew that if we left the vehicles unattended and to the mercy of the so-called guard, we would have nothing left for Maglaj by morning.

He was determined to be hospitable, so he invited the Red Cross lady, Vesna, and myself to his house, which was about one hundred metres on the other side of the line of trees where the convoy was parked. We went for one drink, but whilst there, discovered that his hobby was collecting mushrooms and that he had a fridge full of frozen dried mushrooms. He was insistent that we try them, and his wife cooked an enormous pan of them. I still had the vision of the Sleeping Beauty in my mind and was not much in the mood for them. Also, I was not absolutely certain that all those he had collected were safe to eat. Some were enormous, some of strange shapes and colours. But once the smell wafted from the kitchen, I threw caution to the wind. They were delicious. The manager then offered Vesna and myself a bed for the night at his home. I was already feeling guilty at having left the convoy for so long, so we declined but used the facilities. He kindly completed his hospitality by walking us back to the convoy.

The guards by now were dangerous. They had no officer with them, they were taunting the drivers and attempting to steal anything. Bert Schilte, the MSF doctor, had pitched his camp bed on top of his Land Cruiser. One of our drivers in the vehicle next to Bert's found one of the guards attempting to steal one of his jerrycans and pushed him away. The soldier replied by letting off a burst from his Kalashnikov. The hail of bullets whistled through the sky, the initial trajectory missing the reclining Bert by millimetres.

Ginge, Peter, and myself reviewed the situation. The drivers were tough and were determined to protect their load and their possessions, but we were all unarmed. The burst of fire had brought no visitors from the headquarters. We were on our own with a lawless, drunken bunch. I had the added complication of Vesna. Would they respect her? Should I take her to the house of the manager? Would we get there safely? What would we do if there was a serious incident and no translator? I had a lot of faith in her ability to charm and to tame.

I made a decision. All the drivers into their cabs. If they heard noises around their vehicles, they could shout and bang on the cab, but no one was to leave the cabs. There was a quick flurry to the bushes, a return to the cabs, and a clicking and locking of doors. The night air was frequently penetrated by shouts and bangs. Sleep came to few. By morning, we had lost a hundred or so litres of fuel and four or five bags of flour. It could have been a lot worse. I cannot remember the time when I was happier to see dawn break. We were ready to roll by seven but there was no escort. The police eventually turned up an hour late and went directly to the hotel for breakfast! I was livid. I went in and bawled them out. But even the meek driver had been emboldened by the behaviour of the soldiers. He kept us waiting a further twenty minutes. I marked his card and had my revenge later. We set off for Zepce. The route was a killer. It was a track, barely the width of the vehicles, with some very tight bends. The first, a hairpin, was after only a few minutes of driving. The track was muddy and each of the vehicles had to run at it. The drivers, who had had so little sleep and so much hassle, were marvellous.

We eventually reached the Serb/Croat front line on the top of a hill

376

at a place called Tadici. Why it was called anything I do not know—there was nothing there but a barrier.

Going into Tesanj two days previously, we had passed through the Serb lines to the joint Muslim/Croat post. The northern end of the pocket was defended by Muslims and Croats against the besieging Serbs. Here at the southern end of the same besieged pocket, the combined might of the Serbs and the Croats were encircling the Bosnians! How very Balkan.

Our police escort stopped on the Serb side and said he would await our return. He asked for some food, I refused, but this was not my revenge. That was still to come.

The Croats were not surprised to see us. The commander told me that we had to wait as the route into Zepce was blocked, and he wished to send down a crane to clear the road for our benefit. From the top of the hill where we were parked, we could see the whole road. It was not blocked, and traffic was moving up and down. At intervals, I got out to talk to the commander about the progress of the road clearance. He kept a straight face as I became more irritated. We had heard two sides of the tape when permission to move came through.

Whatever plot they had in mind was now in place. We were free to find out and face it. The Croat army, the HVO, provided an escort. It sped away ahead of us. We followed at what was obviously too slow a pace, for after a short while the escort car stopped and told me to speed up the convoy. I replied that for the last hour we had proceeded at his pace, we would now proceed at mine.

The road to Zepce passed through Ozimica, which had taken a lot of damage. The track was full of craters and bordered by shells of houses. In Ozimica itself, there is a small field hospital which Vesna and I had visited when we had taken the first convoy into Zepce some weeks previously. On that occasion, we had come in from another direction on a much better road.

We turned left at Ozimica and headed towards Maglaj. The military escort vehicle was still pushing the pace. We passed the Catholic church on our right and turned the bend to approach the last Croat village before the run into Maglaj.

As we came out of the bend, my heart sank. The escort car slowed. Blocking the road were a large group of women and children. The convoy came to a halt and the soldiers in the escort car disappeared into the crowd. I got out of my vehicle and approached the crowd. Through Vesna, they told me that they were the wives, mothers, and children of thirty-four Croats who had fought for Maglaj against the Serbs but had been imprisoned when the Croats changed overnight to the Serb side. They believed that the Muslim action was treacherous. They had with them two soldiers who had been part of the group but who had escaped. They told me stories of being used as forced labour, digging trenches on the front line and of collecting air dropped aid which had landed in the minefields. The atmosphere was not tense. The women were emotional but rational. They would not let the convoy go through until their loved ones were released.

My first task was to make sure that they understood that I had no intention of driving the convoy with force through them. I therefore turned my vehicle around, so that it faced away from Maglaj. The convoy, of course, remained facing Maglaj. I then went and explained to Peter and Ginge what was happening. I asked them to keep their drivers near to the cabs but no forward movement. Friendly fraternisation was to be encouraged.

My next task was to try to find the decision makers. There was a Catholic priest amongst the crowd. I approached him and asked him if he could find the leaders of the ladies so that I could meet privately with them. He agreed and quickly arranged a meeting. We met in the garden of a large house on the left-hand side of the road at the corner of the women's roadblock. We sat at a wooden bench and table. However, too many people gathered around, and the proceedings were becoming orchestrated. The priest seemed to have a lot of influence. He was aged about forty-five, was the local parish priest, and looked forceful and fit. He had a stentorian voice. I suggested that we find somewhere quieter. He had a word with one of the crowd, and a group of about six of us was taken off to a building to the left of the garden. We went up a flight of stairs, entered a small room, and sat at a table. Coffee was produced for everyone and, for me, slivivoca accompanied it.

I sat at the head of the small table, Vesna to my left and the women on my right. The priest, who was quiet, sat in between the women and slightly behind them. One woman opened the talks, she was about thirty-five and was very sincere.

– *My husband is a prisoner in Maglaj. My children are downstairs. You can see them. They want their father. I want my husband. If he can come out, you can go in.*

A second woman interrupted—*You can go, on your own, bring our men out and then take in the convoy.*

– *I can't*—I replied. *I cannot link aid to prisoners. I cannot buy my way in and buy my way out. I just want to take food in. You know that they are starving in there. Women and children, mothers, like yourselves. They too are victims of the war. Please let the convoy go in, let me feed them. Whilst I am in, I will try to see your men. At least I can bring you news from them.*

The priest spoke to them. *Can you negotiate their release whilst you are there?*—one of the ladies asked me.

– *I can try. I cannot guarantee that I can bring anyone out. But I can try. But, to be able to try, I need to go in, and I can't go in without the convoy.*

They talked amongst themselves. The priest occasionally interjected. Vesna listened. I observed her. It seemed to be going well. Some of the women had tears in their eyes as they spoke. The priest seemed to steer the conversation but not to lead.

The priest then asked—*Will you take in with you Father Stipo, who is the parish priest of Maglaj? We would like him to see the prisoners.* I knew that this could be a big problem. Implicit in the request was that I guarantee his safety. I could not guarantee my own. It had oc- curred to me and to my masters that the Maglaj authorities may take us hostage. To the Bosnian Muslim authorities in Maglaj, a Catholic priest could be an incentive or an added bonus. Furthermore, would Maglaj think that I was bringing a spy in their midst? Nevertheless, with the sniff of Maglaj air in my nostrils, I replied—*Of course.* I then rose from the table, determined to keep the initiative with me.

– *I will do all I can for you*—I told the ladies. *I can guarantee nothing. At least I will make sure that your priest sees your men.* We left the room, and I strode positively towards the vehicles to brief Ginger and MSF.

– *I think we are on our way.* MSF were looking very pleased with themselves. Peter had visited a house close by in order to fill up his water bottle and had found the lady of the house in bed. Her daughter was with her, and she told Peter that her mother was dying of cancer. Peter went back and brought Bert. The old lady had had a breast removed and was in great pain. Somehow she also had a broken arm. She had been prescribed the drug "Fortral," but none was available. Bert had some in his truck and had given it to her. *She'll die soon, but her last days will now be more peaceful.*

Taking in the priest worried me, so I contacted Zagreb. I asked them to contact Tuzla to contact Maglaj to tell them a priest was on his way with us. The word spread amongst the crowd that we were on our way. Some seemed pleased, others, mainly men, continued to look surly and to be obstructive. We waited for the priest to arrive, for the barrier to be removed. Whilst we awaited, a family came across to us, led by a woman, aged about forty-eight.

– *Are you Vesna?*—she asked of my translator.

– *Yes.*

– *Vesna Stancic?*

– *Yes.*

– *I am your Aunt Lucija. Here is your cousin.* Vesna had found a long-lost branch of the family. The aunt had last seen her more than ten years ago but had recognised her features and knew that we had come from Sarajevo. There was much hugging and kissing and swapping of stories, which helped to pass the time whilst we allowed the locals to prepare for our departure at their own pace. I felt it was important that we left with dignity and accord. We still had to return, and I was pretty certain that we would return empty handed.

Interestingly, Vesna's relatives were hard line and against the convoy. Perhaps with good reason. They were refugees from nearby Zavidovici—until recently, a happily integrated multi-ethnic town.

When fighting broke out between Croats and Muslims, the Muslim son of a near neighbour was murdered. His family sought revenge and had attacked the house of Vesna's aunt, killing her eldest son and seriously wounding her second son. Her husband had taken the wounded boy to Zagreb leaving her and their youngest son to survive in Zepce. There were no bystanders in this war. Some were guilty, some were innocent, but all were victims.

With the arrival of the priest, the convoy was ready and the barrier removed. A police car pulled out and we were off. Vesna and I leading, MSF behind with the priest, then Ginge and the boys. We approached the first Serb checkpoint. There were four Serbs in the middle of the road. To the left of the road there was a house about fifty metres away. From the shattered downstairs window frame, a machine gun barrel glinted. To the right was another house. In it I could see both Serb and Croat soldiers. To our front was a barrier blocking the road to Maglaj. Lying on the road, clearly visible and menacing, were anti-tank mines. The leader of the group on the road was a middle-aged man. There was no bravado, no smell of alcohol. He knew we were coming. We smiled, shook hands. He raised the barrier. His soldiers removed the mines blocking the road.

– *Are there any more mines ahead?*

– *Yes. These here were laid by me. We are from Teslic. Further ahead there is the Doboj brigade. They have also laid mines. Then, after that, you are in no man's land, there may be Serb mines, there may be Muslim mines.*

– *Do the Doboj Serbs know I am coming?*

– *I have no contact with them.* I waved to the Croat escort, shook hands with the Serb.

– *I will return at eight tomorrow morning.*

– *Sretan put*—he said. *Good luck.* Luck we were going to need.

Slowly, I moved the convoy forward. I watched its progress in my rear view mirror. I heard the voice of Ginger—*Last vehicle clear of the barrier.* I smiled and stopped the convoy. Ten metres ahead of me, I could see the first of the mines of the Doboj brigade. I got out of my vehicle and looked back. The Serbs at the first barrier were nonchalantly replacing their mines.

Our little unescorted thirteen vehicle humanitarian aid convoy was now mined back and front. The road was silent and still. It was fenced on both sides. I raised my hands in the best "B" movie style.
– *Humanitarna Pomoc. UN. Komesarijat*—I shouted. No reply. I tried again. I heard voices to the right but in the distance.
– *I think there are Croats over there in the hills*—said Vesna. I looked but could see nothing. To our left there was a small gap in the fence. It led to a path which crossed a stream by a makeshift footpath. The path was well worn and ended at a small house.

I yelled my plaintive message in the direction of the house, breaking the stillness and the silence. The reply was deafening. From the woods behind the house a machine gun opened fire. This brought a response from the right-hand side of the road, a more distant, more muffled rattle from another machine gun.

I stood still. I looked towards the vehicle at Vesna. I had left the door open. The bullet proof helmets are heavy and large; Vesna looked so tiny beneath hers. The helmet was white, her face even whiter. God knows what colour mine was. I repeated my message to both sides of the road. Vesna called me to the vehicle. *Someone is coming across the field from the right.* Three soldiers in a single file were approaching us. I went by the side of the road to greet them. They were Serbs, they were from Doboj. They were friendly but firm. They told me to wait whilst they contacted an officer in the house to the left.

After a short while, a young, scruffy, tired but polite officer came to the road. He was almost apologetic—*I do not know anything about your convoy. You will have to go back.*
– *No chance, my friend. Speak with your colleagues at the first checkpoint. They know we have approval. Otherwise they would not have let us through.* He told Vesna and myself to accompany him to the house. I briefed Ginge and we followed the officer down the track over the rickety bridge to the house. At the house he told us to wait outside, he went in and after a few minutes returned.
– *OK, you can go.* He came with us to the road, and as his three colleagues picked up just enough mines to permit the width of a truck

to pass, he said—*When your last vehicle passes this point, you must stop the convoy and let us put back our mines before you go on, OK?*
– *OK. Are there any more mines ahead?*—I asked.
– *I do not know. I'd be surprised if there wasn't.*
– *Thanks. We will return tomorrow at eight in the morning.* The Serbs left. I moved down the road to tell Ginge to halt the convoy when the last vehicle passed through the gap in the minefield. *Then my friend*—I said with all the false bonhomie I could muster—*we will have two minefields behind us and the unknown ahead of us.*

We were not given time to dwell on this situation. Suddenly all hell broke loose. We heard the heavy crump of mortar fire from both sides of the road and heard in the near distance the shells exploding in Maglaj as the Serbs detracted from the excitement of the inhabitants, especially those who were brave and foolish enough to be in the streets awaiting us.

I walked back to my vehicle. Ahead of us there were approximately two hours of daylight and about a thousand metres of tarmacked road. I had not come this far to risk a vehicle on a mine.

I had brought with me a six-foot-long thin twig. My aim was to patiently and painstakingly search every centimetre of the road. With the twig lightly held between two fingers at the end of my outstretched left hand, I slowly paced forward. I was looking for wires, anti-personnel mines, anti-tank mines.

One, two, three, four, five paces. Eyes slowly scanning from left edge of the road to right edge. If the twig brushed against anything, or showed any resistance, I stopped. If there was a hole in the road, I stopped, lay beside it, and examined it. Mounds of earth, clods of grass, piles of stones, especially the edge of the road, all received the same concentrated attention. If at the end of my five paces, all was clear, then I lay the twig across the road. I stood and looked at the next five paces. I walked to both sides of the road, looked along the fence on both sides, visual only, all the time ensuring that I did not advance forward of my marker twig.

Visually prepared, I physically advanced the next five paces, twig at arm's length. Forward, down, examine, up, forward. Vesna later described it as a—*bizarre, primitive, sinister ballet.*

My actions may have been elaborate, they may have been melodramatic, but I had been mined coming out of Gorazde, and had lost a truck going into Srebrenica. Every twenty paces, I called the convoy forward, ensuring that the lead vehicle travelled over the safest path. This way the trucks avoided the unexploded mortar bombs and the mounds of ammunition which my search uncovered.

Regularly during our movement forward, there was heavy machine gun fire from both sides of the road. At first, I was worried, but I soon realised that the fire from both sides was parallel to the convoy. The Serbs were playing with us.

They were not playing with poor Maglaj; throughout the afternoon, they continually shelled it. At one stage, as I lay at the side of a large hole, I had the feeling I was being closely watched. God was not with me, but one of his representatives was. Father Stipo had decided to give me moral support. It was a genuine, sincere gesture, but it was reckless, and in truth, it made me feel quite foolish. Me in my helmet, bullet proof jacket, complete with twig, ritual and gravitas. He in his shirt sleeves, angelic smile, and peaceful air. I sent him to my vehicle to be with Vesna. For the rest of the trip he looked after her. Ex para Ginge visited me at several of my five pace break times.

It was important that he always knew what I was doing just in case anything went wrong. To better observe my actions, he left his vehicle and drove mine, always briefing his patient, fascinated, determined drivers who later irreverently referred to my actions as "Larry's Papal impersonation."

As we neared the Bosnian Muslim front lines, there was a derelict, destroyed cafe outside of which there was a large milk crate with bottles in it. I took some time over this. My fear was that they may be filled with petrol. A crate of Molotov cocktails we could do without. They turned out to be innocent.

Eventually I reached within ten metres of the Maglaj front line. I could see the Bosnian soldiers in their trenches. I shouted to them. They shouted back. Vesna left the vehicle and came to tell me:

– *They are telling you that there are no mines here.*

The temptation to run forward to greet them was overpowering, but I had not spent the last ninety minutes inching myself forward to throw it all away in the closing metres.

My last pirouettes were within their enchanted gaze. As I reached their location, I shouted a greeting. I was relieved and elated. They looked so young. They were down in a deep ditch at the side of the road.

I wanted to share this first contact. I waved forward Ginge. He came up to join me. The leader of the defenders, a boy who turned out to be eighteen but already an established front-line veteran, shouted something from the trench.

– *Come up and join us*—I said. Vesna translated and he replied.

– *We can't. They can then see us.*

– *No*—I said. *The firing is parallel to the convoy. We are OK.* He and his number two climbed up onto the road. A hail of bullets came whacking in from the woods on our right. These were not parallel to us. They were aimed directly at us. They smacked into the tarmac and ricocheted around us, some hitting the canopies of the trucks. The two Bosnians leapt back into the trenches. Ginge and I did a little dance, a sort of retired military two step. Poor Serb Vesna dodged the Serb bullets by taking refuge in the UNHCR vehicle, her own little safe haven! I clearly remember screaming into the woods—*Stop that firing!* I have no doubt that my words had no effect on whoever had fired. He had achieved his aim by scuttling the Bosnians. But shouting made me feel better and the firing did stop. I turned and spoke to my big companion—*Ginge. What ARE we doing here?*

– *I was just thinking that myself*—he replied grimly.

We called the convoy forward, and Ginge parked it along the road by the side of the Bosnian trenches. Thus protected, the defenders emerged once again. The Bosnians told us that we had to wait for an escort from Maglaj. They had had all day to get an escort there, but they waited until we arrived at the front line to call him forward. I was a little put out. We were parked in the middle of a very active front line. But it was easy for us to forget that being parked in a very active front line was everyday fare for these boys. Whilst we waited, the whole front line emerged from their various hidey holes. They were desperate for cigarettes. The drivers looked after them. I had brought in many jars of coffee and I handed some out.

Eventually, one man walked in from Maglaj to escort us in, fuel and vehicles were for the seriously wounded, not to be spent on meeting convoys. He climbed into my vehicle and we set off for Maglaj.

No traveller ever approached Samarkand, no explorer ever entered Timbuctoo with any less excitement than I entered Maglaj. We passed the bridge where my colleagues, the Danes, had died, mortared in a railway tunnel. They were the last convoy in. As we approached the outskirts of the town, the people came out to greet us. Tears, flowers, cheering, and no shells. The Serbs had given their word that they would not shell Maglaj whilst we were inside. It looked as if they intended on keeping their promise, the shelling had stopped as we left the Bosnian front line.

It was dark by the time we parked up, but light enough to see the massive damage. Almost every building was hit. The people looked dirty, hungry, tired, and confused. Ginge took charge of the unloading. Vesna and I went off with Bert and Peter of MSF to meet the mayor and her team.

The first person we met was the Maglaj interpreter, Violetta. She was from Sarajevo and, amazingly, had been a student of languages at the university there in the same year as Vesna. Violetta is a Croat married to a Muslim. Sadly, she was closely watched the whole time we were there.

The meeting was held in a secure building. There was no power and it was dark, but they had rigged up a small light from a car battery. The meeting room was crowded with dignitaries, some in uniform, some in civilian clothes, all active defenders of Maglaj. The table configuration was two very long tables placed at the edges of a smaller top table, making a large U.

We awaited the arrival of Aida Smailovic. There was a flurry of excitement once she came. She is a tall, large boned lady in her middle thirties. She has a beautiful head of dark hair. She has the presence and the bearing of a Margaret Thatcher. When she is in a room, no one is in any doubt who is in charge. She took her place at the centre of the top table. I greeted her. She shook my hand and welcomed us. I immediately introduced my team and included Father Stipo. I explained that he was there to visit the prisoners and that I trusted that he would be made welcome and given protection. I could see that some were not happy with his presence. Aida promptly guaranteed him both cooperation and safety. I placed some cigarettes on the table and a bottle of whisky. I was not too sure how the bottle would be received. I saw some of the men looking at Aida for guidance. She took one of the cigarettes but did not take any whisky.

She was straight into business. She gave to me a many paged letter which outlined, in English, the plight of the town. It gave details of the destruction of the buildings, of the shelling and the sniping and of a new hazard introduced since the commencement of the air drops over Maglaj: the Serbs were shooting at the townspeople, the starving townspeople, as they attempted to recover the lifesaving packages. Ten people had been murdered in the past week. This crime I found particularly horrendous. The Serb snipers were in the hills no further than three hundred metres from the dropping zones. The snipers could hear the aircraft overhead, see the packages land, could hear the men, women, and children racing out to recover them, could hear their excited conversations, and yet could raise their weapons, focus their eyes through the sights, fire, and cut down innocent, desperate, starving people. I find it hard to put a face to any man who could do this. Who, at three hundred metres, could listen to the screams, the cries, the panic, the despair and the agony inflicted by his squeezing of the trigger? Can these men ever be at peace with themselves?

Aida concluded by giving to me a list of the most urgent needs of the town, mainly medicines and fuel. It was explained to us that the wounded from Maglaj were taken to the hospital in Tesanj by night along a narrow but serviceable road. The road conditions were poor and many wounded died en route. Bert and Peter were able, with justifiable pride, to tell the assembled crowd what medicines they had taken to Tesanj two days ago.

Throughout her long diatribe, there was no praise for the UN, no thanks for our coming. There was criticism, there were questions, and there was regret, but no thanks. Later we were thanked profusely by the town administrator, but Aida wanted to make it clear that Maglaj had come close to total destruction and that the world had stood by and listened to its plight and watched and waited. During her speech, I heard the sound of shelling. It sounded to me very much like outgoing shells. I interrupted Aida and asked her military commander Esad Hidic if I was right. I told him that the Serbs had promised there would be no shelling on the centre of Maglaj whilst we were in. No incoming shells meant no outgoing shells. I felt bad for demanding this, as I had seen and heard the pasting Maglaj had received whilst we were attempting to get in. The commander assured me that it was incoming shelling but sent a man to investigate. Within minutes, the shelling stopped.

The meeting was not easy. Aida and her closest associates could not understand why the UN did not blast its way in and lift the siege. She was scathing about any linkage between future convoys and Croat prisoners. At one point, I somewhat foolishly mentioned that recently Croats in villages close to Maglaj had been murdered by armed groups from Maglaj. My point was that defensive action by Maglaj was understood and accepted by all but that offensive action, especially against civilians in neighbouring villages, placed them in the same category as the Croat and the Serb. This caused great anger, only a little ameliorated by the production of a second bottle of whisky. The conversation mellowed. We agreed to adjourn until seven the following morning.

When we left the building, it was very dark, there was no moon.

I was asked if I wished to go to the warehouse to supervise the unloading. I didn't. Ginge was far more efficient at this than me. I was therefore escorted around the town to where we were to park for the night. It was in one of the main streets with high rise blocks of flats on either side, thus giving us some protection from shelling. We moved without lights. The warehouse, which was quite close, could only accept one vehicle at a time, so the whole convoy was in the street. The loaded ones were at the front. Those unloaded were already parked up for the night. There was a heavy police presence surrounding our location, preventing the people of Maglaj from getting too close to us. I objected to this, but we were told it was for our safety and protection. We would have welcomed a little fraternisation and an exchange of news.

I parked my vehicle at the head of the convoy, and Peter and Bert parked theirs behind mine. They had Father Stipo with them. Now he was the most vulnerable. We could hear shells landing in the distance, so my first concern was to establish what we would do if they came any closer.

— *Vesna, ask one of these many policemen if there is a basement we can use as a shelter.* She returned with the head of police, a middle-aged man who looked very fit and who wore a leather jacket and carried a pistol. He took me to the entrance of the nearest building and unlocked a metal grill leading to the basement.

— *Will this be ok?* I entered, went down the steps and shone my torch. It was a huge cellar. We could all get in and it was close to the vehicles.

— *Tell him it is perfect.* I then took those drivers who had returned and made them walk from their vehicles to the cellar.

As each driver returned, they carried out the same recce. Bert and Stipo decided to sleep in the back of one of the empty trucks where they could stretch out. Peter opted for staying with the still full MSF vehicle. They would not be able to unload their vehicle until the following morning. It was too dangerous and too dark to unload this late at night. I should have gone to visit Ginge, but I felt very tired. I sent a message to him by the next truck to go forward.

— *Ginge, do you need me?* Vesna and I then got ready for the night. She moved into the driver's side. I moved into her seat. She is much smaller than me, so she could cope with the steering wheel and the pedals. I could stretch out more comfortably in the passenger seat. Vesna unrolled her sleeping bag and snuggled down into it. I waited for a truck to come back with a message from Ginge.

Vesna began to talk to me about Violetta. *She has a small child. Her husband is not trusted because he is a Croat. He is sent to the front line and is used to collect the airdrops if they are near the Serb lines. She is very frightened. I would like to give her any food we have left.*

We had brought in quite a bit of our own food to be given away. *She can have whatever you like.*

As we were talking, there was a tapping on the vehicle window on Vesna's side. I lowered it. It was Violetta. She looked scared. She began to talk to Vesna, and I noticed the man in the leather jacket moving towards her. With a great flourish, I got out of the vehicle and asked her to sit in the passenger seat. I could see that this did not please the policeman. I joined Bert, Peter, and Father Stipo who were rigging up beds in the back of a truck. They were also taking a surreptitious bite of food hidden from view. In a besieged town with starving citizens, you feel so guilty if you eat.

Out of the dark, a man approached me and asked if I had any spare torch batteries.

– *No I haven't, my friend, and I will need my torch tonight, but tomorrow you can have the batteries out of it.* He beamed brighter than my torch could.

The next truck back had a message from Ginge—*Unloading will take another couple of hours, but you are not needed. Go to sleep, you old bugger.*

Whilst I was talking to the driver, the dark street was briefly illuminated by a red glow. It happened again and again. I suddenly realised it was the brake lights on my vehicle. I just got to the door before the leather jacket. I could hear laughter from within the vehicle. As Vesna laughed she was stretching out in the sleeping bag and hitting the brake pedal with her feet!

– *Signalling, signalling*—said leather jacket.

– *Rubbish*—I replied, opening the door. I explained to Vesna what had happened. She was blissfully unaware, but then saw the face of the chief of police. He spoke to her and accused her of signalling with the lights.

– *To whom?*—I asked him.

– *To the Serbs*—he answered.

– *Why?*
– *So that they know where to shell*—he replied.
– *Shell you, shell me, shell herself, come on?*—I asked in exasperation. I looked at Violetta. She was trembling with fear.
– *I must go now*—she said, getting out of the vehicle.
– *Just wait a minute, I will walk you home.* I realised that I may have insulted the policeman in front of Violetta which would not help her when we had gone. I therefore apologised to the policeman, explaining what had happened. I gently rebuked Vesna. The policeman seemed happier. He agreed that I could walk with Violetta. *But only to the corner of the street, for your own safety.*
He left. Vesna hurriedly got together a large bag of food, which I stuffed under my jacket. I walked with Violetta a couple of blocks, and in the dark gave her the bag. I turned to walk towards my vehicle and fell into a very large shell crater scraping the skin off my knees. God loveth a cheerful giver!
I hobbled back to the vehicle, unfurled my sleeping bag, and turned to Vesna.
– *Goodnight. God bless and no signalling to Serbs.* It was a long night. I heard every vehicle return. Whenever I closed my eyes, images of the day filled them.
At one stage, I heard a mini commotion around the vehicles. Someone was looking for Father Stipo. They were not after his blessing. They were kept away by the police and an ancient, primitive, highland curse.
As dawn broke, the drivers awoke. Vesna and I were up quickly. The vehicle was freezing. As we clambered out, we met the man to whom I had promised my batteries.
– *Come with me, I can show you where you can wash.*
– *Great*—I said. *Vesna, you go first.*
After a few minutes she was back. It was my turn. For some reason I thought he was taking us to his house, but he took me to a water pump in the square between the flats. There was already a large line of people. The morning chilly mist had risen only a few feet. I was taken to the front of the queue. A man pumped on the handle, and

391

a thin silver stream of water trickled out of the pipe. I cupped my hands, and the water hit them. It was ice cold. I splashed my face and was instantly awake. I stuck my toothbrush under the tap and wet it. I put a helping of toothpaste on it and realised that I was being watched by every pair of eyes. Toothpaste, for them, was a long-forgotten luxury. I gave the tube to the woman at the front of the queue whose husband was pumping the water. As I left, I gave away my soap. I saw many sets of covetous eyes. I went back to the vehicle, where I had a carton full of soap. Vesna returned to the queue and handed it out.

The convoy remained in the street. Peter, Bert, and Stipo left to visit the hospital and then to see the prisoners. I went back to the office of Aida. She was waiting for me. She took me around the town. On foot. She pointed out the Serb gun positions. You could see the barrels glinting in the rising sun.

She showed me the Catholic church. There was very little damage to it. She showed me the Orthodox church, it was badly damaged. – *Damaged by Serb shells*—she told me with a big smile. She did not tell me that it was in response to a mortar attack fired by her troops from the rear of the church. The Serbs told me that later. She walked over the bridge, defying the Serb snipers to show me the damage to the ancient mosque.

She pointed out aid pallets in the river. We went to see the hospital. There were few patients; during the night there had been an evacuation to Tesanj of the wounded. The hospital staff were unpacking the medicine brought in by Bert and Peter. They were smiling from ear to ear. I met the hospital director, surprisingly not a doctor but a dentist. She thanked me profusely.

I saw the blocks of flats, all damaged. Children were emerging from the cellars. They were raggedly dressed and ingrained with dirt. They looked tired. Old faces on young heads. They smiled and waved.

We visited the collective centre, which had initially been a school and then became a centre for the elderly and the mentally sick who now mingled with the refugees. Each group looked bewildered—the patients whose lives were temporarily disrupted and the refugees whose lives had been shattered.

The centre was also a soup kitchen, and families were collecting their meal of the day. They carried all manner of containers from pans to jars. I watched the distribution. It was some form of greyish soup. It smelt terrible, but those collecting it walked with care so as not to spill a drop.

Time was running out. We had told the Serbs we would be there at eight. I said farewell to the mayoress and promised that I would return in one week. I re-joined the convoy. Peter and Bert had been with Stipo to see the prisoners. They had seen twenty-eight of them. They were told that two had escaped and two were in Tesanj. The visit had not been without incident. The parcels had been examined by the guards and some items confiscated. But far more annoyingly, Stipo wanted to hear the confessions of the prisoners, prisoners who may die from shelling, gunfire, or be executed. The guards had refused. It was too late for me to do anything.

We had promised that we would take out mail—the first to leave the town for four months. Peter kindly accepted responsibility for it. There were sacks of it, mostly urgently written messages to all corners of Bosnia, assuring the recipient that the sender was still alive. In Zagreb, Peter posted them all, presumably at considerable personal expense.

We left. We were escorted by a police car as far as the bridge. Then we were on our own again. We sped along the road, slowing at the Bosnian front line, where one young hoodlum threatened Father Stipo, drawing his hand across his throat. Then a sedate slow drive down no man's land, visually checking for mines. We met only those we had seen the previous day. We paused as they were removed by the Serbs who were waiting for us. First the Doboj lot, then the Teslic lot.

We returned to Brancovici. There was a group waiting at the barrier. It was clear they were at least hoping that we would bring some prisoners out. I could both sense and hear their disappointment. We took Stipo to the house of Father Simic. He was very friendly and gave us coffee, food, and slivovica. He seemed happy with the outcome of our convoy.

393

I then went to the office of Lozantic and briefed him. I was convinced that I could get at least some of the prisoners out in the next few days and get convoys in on a regular basis. We then headed back for Banja Luka. At the Croat checkpoint at the top of the hill, we met up again with our Serb police escort. They led the way back into Serb-held territory. As we passed through Teslic, they sped ahead to the junction to warn them of our arrival. I quickly spoke on the radio to Ginge. The convoy bunched together. As we approached the Y-junction, I could see our escort. Their vehicle was parked on the right fork, the road we had used to come in, the long diversion. They were out of their vehicle talking to their colleagues.

We approached the Y-junction sedately, and then I turned the convoy to the left along the direct and shortest route. I saw the police run to their car. I accelerated, the convoy accelerated, and we sped along the narrow road. By the time the escort had started their car and turned it around, it was too late. We were on our way. For the next few miles, I could hear the police car hooting its horn as it attempted to overtake each vehicle. It received no assistance from any of our vehicles. Perhaps one or two of the drivers even used up a little more of the road than was necessary! We were well on our way before the police car overtook mine, thus blocking the road.

– *You are on the wrong road. You have to go back.*

– *No, we are on the right road.*

– *You have no approval for this road.*

– *No approval, I have a police escort*—I said pointing to his car parked at the head of the convoy.

– *We only have approval to use the other road. Major King will be furious. You must go back to Teslic and go the other way.*

– *I am sorry, but the road is too narrow for us to be able to turn the trucks.* This was untrue, as the Brit drivers can turn their vehicles on a sixpence.

– *You must go back. We will be in trouble with Major King.*

– *You are wrong. WE are not going back, and YOU will be in trouble with Major King.* There began a discussion between the two of them which I cut short with a suggestion.

– If we get along this road quickly, Major King may never know. So let's move now. I walked a pace or two and then stopped and turned.

– Next time, when I say we move at seven, we move at seven. OK? I got back into my vehicle, started the engine, and watched with satisfaction as they slunk into their car. Revenge is sweet.

A few kilometres outside Banja Luka, we were stopped at a checkpoint. They were surprised to see us. Our escort came back to see me.

– We are not announced. I knew we would be in trouble. I got out of my vehicle with Vesna and spoke brusquely to the checkpoint commander.

– Get on to Major King immediately. We have full approval. We have a police escort. Our escort went white, but the checkpoint commander saved their day. He waved us through.

We returned to Banja Luka to a great reception from the women. They were as thrilled as if they had been with us. They had shared every moment listening to our radio contacts. Vesna was their hero. Ginge and the boys stayed the night in Banja Luka and carried out a little quality control exercise on the local beer. They left for Zagreb the following day.

Neill Wright rang and asked me to go and see him in Zagreb. *Larry, let's meet in the Intercontinental Hotel for a glass of wine.*

Ugh ugh. Last time I met him there, I was moved from Sarajevo to Banja Luka. What is the plot this time?

– Larry, how is Louis doing?

– He's great.

– Is he 'Head of Office' material? Could he run an office on his own?

– No problems. He is a good leader—tough and a better administrator than I am. Where are you thinking of sending him?

– Well we are looking for a head of office for Central Bosnia, which of course is the largest office, and, at the moment, is the busiest and maybe the most dangerous. We need an old hand. We think you could do the job well and Louis could hold the fort in Banja Luka. Another drink?

I drove myself back to Banja Luka. The drive through the Croat bit is along the old Zagreb Belgrade highway. Once one of the busiest motorway stretches in Europe, it is now deserted.

– Do I really want to leave Banja Luka?—I asked myself. I knew the answer—*NO*. There was so much to do. I will feel as if I am abandoning the Bishop and the Mufti. I don't think I have achieved as much as I could have. It is only now that I feel I know my way around. And in truth, Louis is very gung-ho. Great with me there to hold onto his shirt tail. Louis has that wonderful arrogance of youth. He knows that he is not yet senior enough to be able to save the world, but he is convinced that he can save his corner of it.

I will miss the whole team. Indie is tremendous. Georgios—strong and stubborn. The women are all outstanding. The best I have had. The little house we all lived in was also special. As I cross over the bridge into so-called Srpska Republika, I feel none of the trepidation I did on my first trip. I have enjoyed the challenge. I will be sad to go.

When I arrive back in the office, Louis is waiting for me. Before I left for Zagreb, I offered a job as assistant logistician to Rade Kosic whose duties are as an interpreter for the Military Corps Headquarters. Before the war, he was in senior management in the electrical factory in Banja Luka, a company which made electrical motors under licence for many of the leading car manufacturers. Rade has an excellent command of English. He is a tall, lean, slightly grey man with angular features mellowed by business lunches. A precise, meticulous man with an annoying and arrogant manner of speech. He is loyal to his masters. So he must be. They can transfer him to the trenches if they wish. He was receiving little or no money from them and asked me if we had a vacancy. I had met him socially. I knew his family and some of his friends. He knew who was who and what was going on. He knew the police in the headquarters, and he knew the soldiers on the checkpoints. In conversation, he was opposed to the ethnic cleansing of the town.

I weighed up the possibility of him being a potential government plant. All of our local staff were open to persuasion. His background would make him more suspect than most.

I decided to offer him a one-month post. I would make sure that he got nowhere near our protection files. I would give him the task of getting aid to our most vulnerable villages—all Croat or Muslim—

and see how effective he was.

Louis wanted me to attend a staff meeting with him and the other Internationals—*No problem.*

– Larry—said Louis—*we do not agree with Rade Kosic working for us. We think he is a spy. The least he will do is put lives in danger. His presence here may prevent people coming to us with their accusations.* Heavy handed, Georgios the Greek, wanted to twist the knife.

– And we think you should have discussed his recruitment with us. I like meetings to be short.

– Thank you, gentlemen. I did not discuss his recruitment with you because I knew that you would disagree. If it is your consensus of opinion that he should not work here, then I respect that. I will fire him immediately. Thank you. Before you go, Louis, please give me a minute. The others left.

– Louis, I think you are all wrong. We have to put up with Rade as the military interface whether we like him or not. If he worked for us, we would have more pressure to put on him. Namely, the pressure of a monthly salary. However, as I am going to be the new Head of Zenica and you are going to be the new Head of Banja Luka, I bow to your advice. In this manner was Louis informed of his elevation.

The following morning, Rade arrived as usual—early, bright eyed, and bushy tailed. I told him that Geneva had blocked the further recruitment of local staff but that they had approved the payment of one month's salary in lieu of notice. Rade was delighted. I think Rade the spy would have been disappointed. Rade, when the war is over, you must tell me were you or were you not (a spy)!

I agreed to leave in three days' time. I requested travel permission from the military headquarters. I had a few farewell meals, deliberately avoiding offering hospitality to Major King but making a big fuss of Colonel Vujinovic. I sat with the Mufti and Bedrudin. I really felt low when I left them. I took a last lingering look at his office standing in the rubble of the Ferid Pasha Mosque. I had lunch with the Bishop and then we sat for quiet drinks. I promised that I would not give up on Banja Luka. But fighting for a cause from a distance is never the same as fighting in the front-line trenches. The office staff gave me a super farewell evening. Lots of food and wine, kind words and an excellent farewell present—a little work of art, a clay mask. Very much my style. On the morning of my departure, I packed 333, the vehicle I brought with me to Banja Luka, and hugged and kissed a tearful staff. I then set off on my own. At the first checkpoint, less than a kilometre from the office, I was stopped.

– *Hello, Mr. Larry. Where are you going?*

– *To Zenica.*

– *Sorry Mr. Larry, but you are not announced.* I got on the radio to the office. They spoke to the Military Headquarters, the checkpoint commander was contacted, and I was waved on. At the next checkpoint the same procedure. This happened at every checkpoint. Halfway along my journey, at Jajce, I was stopped.

– *Papers?*

– *It is me, Mr. Larry. I am on my way to Zenica from Banja Luka.*

– *You have no approval.*

– *Please contact your Headquarters.* They did and they came back.

– *You have no approval.* I got onto my "old" office. They contacted the Military Headquarters. The Military Headquarters spoke with the checkpoint.

– *You have no approval. You must go back.*

– *Look my friend, I have passed through many checkpoints today. I have approval.*

– *I have just spoken. You have no approval. You are to return.* I had a sudden thought.

– *Who did you speak to?*

–*Major King.* Back I went.

Two days later. More hugs, more kisses. Away again. This time with a piece of paper signed by Colonel Vujinovic, King's boss. At the crossing point at Turbe, I met my old friend Salko Beba. A Bosnian army officer, a pre-war businessman, and an ace fixer. By late afternoon, I arrived at the Zenica office. All the staff were waiting. Sanja, my new Secretary, took me to my new office and then to my new home, the upper floor of a nearby house.

Nineteen

Zenica

Zenica is the main city in Central Bosnia. It has a huge iron and steel works and is surrounded by coal mining towns. It had a pre-war population of one hundred thousand. It is now mainly Bosnian Muslim. It used to be an hour drive from Sarajevo. Now you can hardly drive an hour in any direction without hitting either a Croat or a Serb front line.

Once again, I took over a "cold" desk. The previous Head of Office, Jorge de la Motta, had left before I arrived. He left everything in good shape. There were three internationals in the office: the brilliant, witty, and laconic Canadian lawyer Steven Wolfson, who was Protection Officer and acting Head; Mark de Guilio, an American Field Officer with a very high reputation for getting aid through; and Amir Saaed, a Pakistani who was in charge of administration. He is a fine example of the Raj legacy, a meticulous bureaucrat. Amir had a form for everything and could quote UN regulations, including the punctuation marks. I may mock such men, but every office seems to need one.

With Amir producing and controlling the paper mountain, I would have time to get on the road and to get aid moving. I looked forward to working with Mark, but on the day that I arrived, he was in the Croat military headquarters in Kiseljak and read a few palms. He told a local commander, Ivica Rajic, exactly what he thought of his aid blocking tactics. A source of information told the Brits that the Croat commander had left the meeting threatening the life of Mark. The Brits recommended that Mark be moved for his own safety. Mark was happy to stay and brave it out, but field work involves a lot of travel. A single car is vulnerable. Also, if anyone is going to take out Mark, they may include those travelling with him. Furthermore, I knew that Mark was engaged to an Irish girl and was soon to be married, his life is just beginning.

I decided to move Mark on... to Banja Luka. Where I knew he would fit in. Neill agreed. Mark moved the next day.

Steven briefed me on the events of the past six months. He showed me the reports he had sent to Zagreb. They were like legal briefs, beautifully written, concise, and accurate; all they lacked was a red ribbon. I discovered that Steven had an M.Phil. from Oxbridge, had worked as "bright young assistant" to the most senior judge in Canada, and was extremely good company. I installed him as Deputy Head of Office and put him in the second largest office in the building. He would keep the reports flowing and make Zagreb and Geneva very happy. The office would run itself. I could now concentrate on aid.

– *Excuse me, Larry, may I have a word with you?* It is Amir.
– *Of course you may, my friend.*
– *In UNHCR regulations, there is no appointment 'Deputy Head of Office'.*
– *Amir, there is now.* As I sat at my new desk, I sent a radio message to all the other UNHCR offices: "Greetings from the Master of Zen." The best reply I had was from Jerrie Hulme:

"Welcome to your new appointment."

(To be sung to the tune of *The man from Monte Carlo*)
Larry's song.
as he steps down off the antropov
with his kit bag on his back
you can hear his colleagues crack
he's been through a lot of flak
when the bullets fly, he won't be shy
he's certainly not afraid to die
he's just the chap we want for old Zenica.

There are no convoys coming in. They were suspended after an incident at Novi Travnik when convoys were moving across a front line which became active. One Danish Driver, Bjarne Nielson, was killed and eleven Dutch soldiers injured. Despite no convoys, the UNHCR warehouse had some food in it which surprised me.

400

I sent for the Acting Logistic Officer Billy Bilic. A very interesting man, a pre-war senior policeman. He is a Croat, but his parents were clever. Instead of giving him an "ethnic" name they had called him Yugoslav Bilic. Very clever until Tito died. Everybody called him Billy. I was tempted to call him "Former Yugoslav" or "Ex Jugoslav," but he is a very big man with an uncertain temper.

– *Billy, if we have had no convoys in, how come we have food in the warehouse?*

– *It's emergency stock.*

– *When did we last issue any food?*

– *Two weeks ago.*

– *So some people have had no food for two weeks?*

– *Yes.*

– *How many weeks do they have to have no food before you call it an emergency Billy?* We emptied the warehouse. House in order. Time to look outside and meet some of the principal players.

The British who are based at Vitez, a thirty-minute drive away, are changing over battalions and commanders. I see the tail end of "The Prince of Wales" with Alastair Duncan and the arrival of Peter Williams and the Coldstream Guards.

Peter impressed me greatly. He is not a military martinet. He is not a gung-ho cowboy. He is just a thoroughly professional, caring, Commanding Officer. He told his men that he had three aims for the battalion. First, he wanted them to do the job they had been sent to do, to operate "in support of humanitarian aid." Second, he wanted for everyone to return home safely, and third, for everyone to enjoy the tour. In my opinion, he achieved all three. He was a good father of his battalion.

He allocated to me a Liaison Officer, Captain Harry Bucknall. A tall, handsome, blonde, archetypal young Guards Officer—an Old Harrovian who hides a good brain and a fit frame behind a bluff personality. Harry spent at least four months shadowing me, overtaking me, and standing on my toes. He kept me in the picture as to what the military were doing. And, by diligence and guesswork, kept the military in the picture as to what I thought I was doing. He called this the Hazza/Lazza show.

I needed to know and to know well the two warring faction commanders. So an early visit was vital. In the centre of Zenica, next to the iron and steel works, is the Bosnian Army Corps Headquarters whose commander Alagic was also new. Not an easy man to get to know; he is a man who thinks in parables, speaks in riddles, and acts stubbornly.

The Croat military commander Tihomir Blaskic was an old friend. A sharp military man with a disarming ingenuousness and frankness bordering on naivete. His office was in Vitez.

Even more important to me were the civilian leaders. The Mayor of Zenica Besim Spahic is a cunning politician. The Mayor of Croat Vitez, Mr. Santic, is a saintly looking man with guile and charm. The link between Zenica authorities and aid was Mr. Dzeferovic, a tall, elegant local factory manager, who oozes the salesman charm and street credibility of a successful car dealer.

The UNHCR office was freezing cold. The house where I lived was even colder. Thank God I am happiest in the field.

President Alia Izzetbegovic visited Zenica today. He looked worn out, but at least he travelled in style and with ease... in a vehicle stolen by his army from an international humanitarian aid agency!

The Croats have in their territory an ammunition factory. Colonel Blaskic informs me that if the Muslims invade, he will blow it up. He seems to be unaware that this may be a spectacular piece of self-immolation. I'm not too sure what Peter Williams thinks of this Croat agenda item. His barracks is about three seconds away from the ammunition factory flash to bang.

When I question him about it on his next visit to me, Peter assures me he has an evacuation plan should the ammo factory blow up. If it blows up, I shouldn't think he needs one.

In the middle of the Croat dominated territory, which is surrounded by Muslim territory, there is a little besieged Muslim enclave, an island within an island, called Stari Vitez with a population of twelve hundred. It, too, is very close to the ammunition factory, which is unfortunate, as the Croats are short of shells but not short of gunpowder. Therefore, they shell innocent Stari Vitez with any heavy chunk of metal they can stuff into a piece of tubing. The heaviest calibre is a fridge freezer. An engine block is common. This would be funny if it were not true.

Kakanj is a coal mining town near to Zenica. I have been invited by the mayor to visit him. He is disappointed by the lack of food he is receiving. We still do not have convoys. I agree to see him soon. Perhaps not soon enough, for today my senior driver Emir Kratina, who, before the war, ran a very successful veterinary surgeons practice in Zenica, was visiting Kakanj in a very clearly marked UNHCR vehicle and was set upon by soldiers who told him they were starving. They had been to the municipality buildings begging for food and had been told that there was none because UNHCR had failed to deliver any. As he motored away, they fired into his vehicle. He is very lucky he has only one bullet in his shoulder. The rest miraculously missed him.

There is a strong rumour that soon we will be able to start convoys again. I am being harassed by all the mayors, dignitaries, and men of influence. They all want the first convoy to come into their fiefdom. They all hint darkly that if aid travels through their area without stopping and delivering, then the trucks will be hijacked. We in UNHCR therefore work out a master plan. The first convoys will drop off aid as a rolling barrage. They will move forward delivering aid so that the first villages on the route get fed first and the most distant get fed last. This way we effectively "buy" our way in. I visit all the local warlords. They all sign up to this.

Brigadier John Reith, late Parachute Regiment, who tells me that he has run ten thousand trucks in the Gulf, knows better than my carefully laid and agreed plan. He bombasts his way into Central Bosnia with twenty-eight trucks. He is successful but buggers up my arrangements and confuses the locals. We at UNHCR bring a ten-truck convoy into Travnik from my old stomping ground of Banja Luka.

Now that we have some food, we can start delivering it. With Peter Williams and an American civilian affairs officer, J. Carter (who is

403

late forties, very fit, speaks fluent Vietnamese, and may just conceivably have had a military background), we agree that an early convoy must be sent into Stari Vitez. We persuade Blaskic that we should link deliveries, one mini convoy into Croat dominated Vitez Colonia, one into Muslim Stari Vitez, and another into Muslim Kruscica. The split is a little unfair. The Croats get seven vehicles, Stari one, and Kruscica two, but at least they get something and we get in. We have a great day. The commander Sevkija Dzidic is a character. His enclave is so small he can hear the Croats breathing heavily as they load their weapons. He shows me the scrapyard of metal which the Croats have aerially delivered. It really is a dark comedy.

The highlight of the day for me is a visit to the home of the lady who is responsible for the delivery of the aid within Stari Vitez. This involves a run through a garden exposed to active sniper fire. Her old mother has insisted that we visit her for coffee. The roof of the house has a shell hole in it, the walls are bullet scarred, but the house is immaculately clean and tidy. At the doorway, the daughter shouts to her mother:

– *Mother, it is Mr. Larry!* Mother comes to the door, welcomes me, and invites me in. I step forward into this little war damaged gem and receive a tug on my sleeve. *Take your muddy shoes off*—demands the old lady. I did as I was told. Here was a lady who did not compromise, war or no war, siege or no siege.

Stari Vitez was such a plucky place. A microcosm of the war. It had, in miniature, all its share of the tragedy of a besieged enclave, and therefore was so much more personal and tangible and emotional. Because I had "been in" and been able to put faces to many of its incredibly brave ordinary people, I felt part of the place, which made it harder when we could not achieve results.

For instance, the time when the British battalion were informed that a wounded child was desperately ill and needed surgery. They tried every Croat avenue to get approval to take the child out to hospital in Zeniza. They failed. The child died. It must be so hard to lose a child—to lose one when you know that treatment is available but that you can't get the child to it because someone is blocking you for political reasons, that your child is a pawn in petty power politics. Dario Kordic is the political master of Croat affairs in the Lasva Valley. A tall, thin man with bright eyes. He looks like a Jesuit missionary. An image he encourages by wearing an oversized set of rosary beads, which he wears around his neck like a Bishop's pectoral cross. After the death of the boy, we went to see him. He explained in an infuriating, condescending way that—*the policy on medical evacuations from Stari Vitez is that those who are critically ill can be evacuated to the Croat hospital in Nova Bila. They can only be taken to the major facility in Zenica if critical patients in Nova Bila can be transferred to the Croat town of Kiseljak.*

– Mr. Kordic, can we not isolate dying children from political point scoring? The UN is prepared to collect and transport the wounded. Could you just allow the UN to use its discretion as to where patients go?

– Mr. Larry you do not understand. Mr. Kordic you are so right. You will need more than a set of rosary beads around your neck to get into heaven.

The Bosnian Muslims were not much better. They were insisting that Stari Vitez patients should be taken to Zenica. The mother of the little boy who died would have accepted treatment from an itinerant quack. This squabbling, linkage, bartering, and bargaining went on throughout the hostilities. Water from the Muslim side for access to the road on the Croat side. Live prisoners for dead bodies. The civil affairs officers and the military liaison officers spent their whole tours negotiating.

An armoured vehicle from the Canadian Battalion slipped off the bridge on the outskirts of Zenica and fell into the river. Two of the three crewmen were killed. Bizarrely, a Golf car was following carrying Mujahideen. They were so involved in watching that they went over the side as well. They all survived. I wrote a letter of condolence to the Canadian Battalion Commander. The regiment has been here only a few weeks. It is a real blow to morale to lose men so early and in such a manner.

November has ended. We managed to issue nine per cent of needs this month. Nine per cent of the minimum food needed to keep

people alive. I heard from a translator a wonderful true Guards officer story. Peter Williams, the C.O. of the Coldstream, was asked to attend the office of the Croat HVO Commander Colonel Siljeg.
– *We do not agree to you or to the United Nations employing Muslim interpreters. You must not employ them on Croatian territory.* Peter's reply was pure P.G. Wodehouse. Drawing himself up to his full, shoulders back, guardsmen-on-parade height—*Colonel, a gentleman does not comment on another gentleman's servants.*

It is approaching Christmas, there is talk of a cease fire. But the omens are not good. This time, the Bosnian Government forces seem to be to blame. They attacked a place called Krizancevo Selo and killed perhaps sixty or seventy Croat soldiers. Rasim Delic, the Bosnian Government Commander in Chief, is reported as saying there will be no ceasefire, as—*there is too much unfinished business in Central Bosnia.*

Christmas Eve. I have today received in one envelope three messages from Tihomir Blaskic. The first letter states:

Respected Gentleman,
.... A special Muslim unit has broken into the villages of Dubravica and Krizancevo Selo where they set on fire several houses, murdered ten civilians, and captured or killed thirty-three.
We request you to visit the Muslim prisons in Zenica and Travnik so that you can register the imprisoned.

The second:

Respected Gentlemen,
HVO Officer Fabijan (Ivo) Tadic has been murdered in the recent attacks. Muslim soldiers have cut his head off...
Since the above mentioned officer is to be buried very soon, we request you demand III Corps of the Bosnian Army to do their best so that the head of the officer is urgently brought back to us.

406

The third is a Christmas card:

Merry Christmas, Mr. Larry.

There is of course no Christmas ceasefire. The Bosnian Army Corps headquarters blames Mujahideen for the beheading. I have to confess, I progressed it no further. I was fearful that, if successful, I may have to go and collect it. That I could not do.

Another year begins, the war still continues. For December, we achieved twenty-one per cent of needs. It is not good enough. I have received a letter from the refugee groups that they will demonstrate outside my office in one week's time.

The demo takes place—peaceably. I bring the leaders in to see the empty warehouse. The Bosnian police, however, keep the remainder out of my compound with a whiff of CS gas.

We are definitely not bringing in enough food. We now have civil unrest and more significantly, civil unrest on our convoy routes. At a place called Lisac, there is a sharp bend at the bottom of a hill. The trucks must slow down especially if the roads are icy or wet. Traditionally, the local kids have gathered at Lisac corner and begged. Traditionally, the generous convoy drivers have thrown sweets to them. Lisac corner therefore became known as "BonBon Corner." Convoys at "BonBon Corner" are now surrounded not by children but by adults who are hijacking the contents of the trucks. This self-distribution is not helping me. If we lose the food before it arrives, we will have even more trouble in the cities.

Trouble in the cities and trouble on the routes is serious but not as serious as the reports coming out of Maglaj, which I have not forgotten.

Twenty

Well Done, Hard Luck

Will no one rid me of this troublesome priest?
—Henry the Second.

As so often happened, the relieving of a besieged town was a momentary joy. The minute the convoy left, the siege was reimposed, the shelling began, and life for the inhabitants returned to its previous perilous tempo. Getting into Maglaj in October had achieved nothing more than a quick feed. We took in three days' worth of food. In November, all convoys were stopped because of the death of the Dane at the crossing point near Travnik. In December, we tried to make amends, but the cooperation of the Croats was minimal. Maglaj was relegated to a low priority, and I only managed to bring into Central Bosnia nine per cent of needs, a mere 1.7 kilograms per person for the month, when the temperature fell to as low as -22 C!

Maglaj began to look possible again in January. We were on target for twenty-two per cent of needs—not good but better than nine—and the plight of the people of Maglaj had deteriorated because of a combination of shelling and starvation. As ever, my first aim was to get the media interested. Media pressure was always more successful than my words in the wilderness. Louis Gentile, tough "pull no punches" Louis, was a great ally. He was as equally determined as me to get into both Maglaj and its neighbouring besieged town of Tesanj. Together we bombarded the Bosnian Serb and the Bosnian Croat authorities to give us approval. The Serbs in Pale gave Louis approval to mount convoys from Banja Luka but refused permission to me. Louis had a few attempts but failed because of the usual Serb disjoint between approval and intent.

Eventually, we agreed to try to do a combined "go" at Maglaj. Louis would bring the Maglaj convoy from Banja Luka, from where it would have Serb approval. I would come from Zenica with a matched convoy for Zepce, to be delivered if the Maglaj convoy went through. The Croats would not like this distrust but that is war. I would also bring an agreement from the Bosnian government forces that they would cease firing as the convoy approached and, more importantly, that they would not antagonise the Serbs in the run up to the convoy arriving.

Louis achieved his bit and arrived with the convoy at Croat held Zepce. The convoy was of Danish drivers; the leader was Ole, a short, heavy, red bearded man whom I at first misjudged and then learned to like. I had done my homework. Firstly, I had contacted Lt. Colonel Hap Stutt, the Canadian ECMM, who had a very good working relationship with the Croat hierarchy in Zepce. He agreed to warn Zepce of my intentions. Then I went to see Colonel Tihomir Blaskic. He was very friendly, he said that he would issue the order that the convoy could pass but could not guarantee its success, as he was sure the women of Zepce, whose husbands were prisoners in Maglaj, would again try to prevent the convoy. Over a jar or two of whisky, which I brought him, I reminded him that the Croat army had in November signed the latest agreement permitting the unhindered access of convoys.

I showed him the document signed by his boss, General Ante Roso. He was, as ever, courteous and friendly, but he warned me that neither he nor the local Zepce commander would use force to remove Croat civilians who might block our way. The two Brits with me at this meeting were pessimistic. But I left the room, as ever, the eternal optimist.

I then went to Zepce to deal with the duet—Mayor Ivo Lozancic and Commander Niko Jazinovic. Our group was larger than I would have liked. Hap was accompanied by two other ECMM monitors. The British Liaison team, a trio from Hereford, also came in with us, and we had the local UNMO team. All in addition to me and my interpreter, the beautiful Emilija, and my Britbatt LO Harry Bucknall. To make matters worse my driver Kenan, a Muslim, was not happy to sit in the vehicle in Croat held territory, so he stuck to me like a limpet. Lozancic saw us all in his office, a spartan room like all Croat headquarters, except that Mostar was dirty and untidy. He sat at the head of a long table. I explained my aim to take the convoy, which was about to arrive from Banja Luka, into Maglaj. I told him that his convoy containing an identical load to the Maglaj convoy was on its way from Zenica and that it would park up in Bosnian Government territory, close to his front line, and cross into his territory when the convoy entered Maglaj. Lozancic smiled at my caution but was most co-operative and friendly. *No problem*—he said. *Maximum coopera-tion*—he continued.

Hap and the SAS man were amazed. Only hours before, Lozancic was telling them that there was no chance the convoy would get in. Lozancic concluded—*As long as you have approval from the Serbs, you will have no problem.* Serb approval we had. He concluded by asking me to liaise with his military commander.

We left his office, and I said to Emilija—*I do not like this. It is too easy.*
– *You are right.*
– *But I am certain we will succeed. We will get into Maglaj.*
– *Would you like to bet on it?*
– *Definitely.* She set the stakes as a dinner in Zenica.

We then went off to the military headquarters, another unglamorous Croat location. Jazinovic always met me in the same place—a grotty conference room dominated by a round table with tatty chairs which were too large for the room. At one end of the room there was a small cigarette-stained table on which stood a telephone. There was always a soldier sitting at the table manning the phone, always a different soldier, but all had the same habit of chain smoking. This phone was what passed for the "hotline." Jazinovic sat with his back to the wall. On the wall was "the map" on which was plotted the Bosnian and the Croat dispositions as known to Jazinovic. It was never the most accurate of maps. We all trooped in and Jazinovic immediately began to berate me. He accused me of breaking my word with the people of Zepce, referring to the fact that on my successful visit to Maglaj in October, I had "promised" that I would bring out the thirty-four Croat prisoners. He went on to accuse me of having smuggled in weapons on my last visit. *How else can you account for the fact that im-mediately after your convoy, the Muslims were able to attack our villages?* He concluded, as ever, by calling me a Muslim sympathiser who had

411

starved the population of Zepce. I heard this from him every time I saw him. I reacted in my usual manner. A slow start, thanking him for seeing me, asking about his son and his family, then gently refuting each accusation, building up to a climax where I questioned his intelligence for making such ridiculous statements, then slowly defusing all by explaining away his accusations as the understandable actions of a tired military commander carrying such huge responsibilities. Jazinovic was always accompanied by Zoran, a tall, dark, pleasant looking man who spoke excellent English. His task was to listen to conversations and to pick up our asides. He also interrupted if he felt that his Commander's words were being misinterpreted. I never knew if I trusted him or not. He would frequently whisper and smirk during these exchanges.

After the usual opening session, we got down to business. Jazinovic had heard on one of the infrequent calls on the table telephone that Louis had arrived with his convoy and that it was now parked up at the back of the hospital in the village of Ozimica a few kilometres away. Jazinovic informed me that the convoy would have to be inspected to ensure that it contained no contraband (i.e. no weapons). The convoy had already been inspected minutely twice by the Serbs but another would not harm. I agreed. Jazinovic mentioned that I may meet some opposition from the women of the village. I reminded him of his obligation to assist the convoy in accordance with the agreement signed by General Roso and told him of the support that I had received from Colonel Blaskic. This annoyed him, and he reminded me that he was the commander on the ground. On this happy note, I left to meet up with Louis and the convoy. I briefed them. They were in good spirits. Louis was determined that this was the convoy to get in. I must confess that I thought so myself. Louis and I were quite a team. Neither of us would take no for an answer. The inspection went well. Big Ole sat on the tempers of his boys as their loads were once more subjected to the hassle of an inspection designed to humiliate and to inconvenience. Canopies off, boxes off, packages opened. We had the usual try on, they wanted to inspect the cabs and the personal possessions of the drivers. We always tried

412

to draw the line at this.

The inspection of the drivers was done at a pace to ensure that we would not leave for Maglaj that day. Soon it was too dark to risk going forward. The HVO had therefore achieved their aim for one day. I contacted the "Zepce" convoy which was parked near the front line. This convoy was military. It was accompanied by my logistician, the Dane Steen Fredricson. He was disappointed. He made the wise decision to return the one hour to Zenica, sleep the night in the warehouse, and come out again the following day.

There was a small restaurant near where we were parked. The journalists told us that it served wine, a then forbidden substance in Zenica and my favourite libation. Louis, Hap, Harry, myself, and the interpreters hotfooted there to discover that the journalists had drunk the place dry. Fortunately, the resourceful Louis had a bottle of whisky with him. We ordered a meal and were tucking in happily, when Zoran, the English speaking HVO, entered, called me to one side and said that he had been sent to invite our group to a meal that evening in the same restaurant but in a private room. I needed all the cooperation I could get, so I quickly accepted.

Two meals in one day was never a problem in a place where tomorrow may bring no meal. We met the HVO crowd at about seven. They produced "stock" brandy, a local sweet, not too strong, version of the French variety, and the inevitable slivovica. The meal was large gobbets of lamb. The anti-freezing effect of the pure alcohol loosened up our hosts, and I was able to gauge who was for me and who was against. The boss Lozancic seemed sincere. He was worried that we may have problems with women demonstrators but felt that we would get through. The military commander was still difficult with me. He was forever cursing Muslims and constantly referring to a Muslim massacre in one of his villages. The military police chief, Dragan, I watched with interest. He said little to us but spoke in whispers to Zoran who behaved like a giggling schoolgirl. I got the impression that we were being set up. I did my best to keep the small talk going and ignored the provocations of Jazinovic. I was impatient to get out and talk to my interpreter Emilija who, thank

God, I could trust entirely. I wanted to know from her the gist of the Dragan/Zoran conversations. We left at about nine and returned to the carpark. It was a bitter cold night. The drivers had a fire going. We parked our Land Rover and prepared for the night. Emilija was to sleep across the two front seats, Kenan the driver and I would sleep in the back, one down each side. We unrolled our excellent sleeping bags, arctic variety, provided by UNHCR via the US Army, and tried to make our bed spaces comfortable.

Two tasks remained, the vital pre-sleep wee, easy for Kenan and I, not so easy for Emilija. The temptation is not to go. *I'll be OK. I'll last till morning.* You never are and you never will. Furthermore, it's a damn sight more difficult to get out of the sleeping bag and a damn sight more cold at three in the morning! The second task was for me to apologise to Kenan. Earlier in the day, he had reversed the vehicle and slightly altered its shape. I had been furious. I never treat a vehicle as a "company" vehicle, I always look after them as if they were my own. Furthermore, the vehicle is absolutely vital to the task. If, whilst out on a convoy, the vehicle becomes unserviceable you are left without wheels, equipment and a home. When he banged the vehicle, Kenan had said something like—*It is OK. It doesn't matter.* Well it did to me, and I let him know. As the day proceeded, I realised that the vigour of my venom was actually fuelled by my own tension; I so desperately wanted to get into Maglaj. I further realised that Kenan was also very uptight. He was a Muslim in the Croat territory. He had heard all the threats by Jazinovic. It was no surprise that, as I led him into the lion's den, he had other things on his mind. We ended up apologising to each other.

Whilst we awaited the return of Emilija, I spoke to Louis whose translator Nidal was also obeying the last call of nature. We agreed that the convoy should be ready to move at seven the next morning. I then saw Harry, parked at the far edge of the car park. He took on the task of briefing Ole and checking whether or not the guard the Croat commander insisted on giving us was likely to be more of a help than a hindrance. They were neither; they never turned up.

Back in the vehicle we wriggled into our sleeping bags, tossed and turned to establish where the bumps, the ridges, and the edges were. Emilija thanked her petiteness as she negotiated the steering wheel and gear lever, while Kenan had the driver's side of the back. He had the task of switching the engine on whenever he awakened during the night, just a few minutes of heater to chase away the sharp cold of night. On convoys, we normally slept in our clothes. You never knew what the night might bring. I always took off my shirt and pullover but left on my trousers and socks. The last drill for me was to mentally check where my helmet, flak jacket, and boots were. Then, glasses off, I find somewhere safe for them and close my eyes. The first round of sleep came easily. The night is always coldest at about three; the fog, the smoke, the fumes which built up in the vehicle during the day have gone, the warmth of the vehicle is stolen by the dark night, and breath turns to moisture as it hits the cold walls of the vehicle. Three o'clock never fails to wake me up. This is the time for original thoughts, for clear assessments, for inspiration. Maybe. Personally, I praise the quality of the sleeping bag and snuggle down deeper into it—cocooned by it, enwombed and warm.

Dawn breaks and wakes. Find glasses, shirt on, pullover on, out of sleeping bag, boots on, out of vehicle, morning wee, clean teeth, roll sleeping bag. Ready for the day. The only other vehicle awake is Harry's. The Brits have a fire crackling and they are drinking tea. Harry gives me a sip from the cup of his flask. Kenan is a slow starter. Ole is up and he is doing the rounds of his trucks banging on cabs. The Brits and the Danes are into making some form of breakfast. We in "Refugees" don't run to breakfasts. At a quarter to seven the boys from Hereford arrive, bright eyed and bushy tailed. They have a house in Zepce. Louis and Nidal awaken last. By seven, we are ready but with nowhere to go. I contact Zenica. Steen and his "Zepce" convoy are on the way. They will, as yesterday, halt near the front line.

By seven thirty, we are joined by Dragan the military policeman. We can go.

Now the adrenaline runs, the stomach twitches. This is why I joined. We move out, slowly, sedately, I lead. So much can go wrong, but we are on our way, we are moving towards Maglaj. Towards besieged, hungry Maglaj. Out of the car park, left turn, round the sharp bend, up to the junction, left onto the Zepce-Maglaj-Doboj road. Past the church of Father Simic who assisted me last time in a strange way. On to Brankovici. I look in the mirror, the convoy is spread out behind me. We turn the bend into tiny Brankovici. My heart sinks. The road is blocked again. On it there is a line of women and elderly men. They stand behind logs laid on the tarmac. It is so cold that they have lit a fire at the side of the road. I slowly take the convoy right up to the barrier. They stand firm. I tell Kenan to halt; he does and the convoy stops. My experience is to sit in the vehicle, not to get out. Just sit and watch. Observe the mood. See who talks, see who moves, who sneers, who laughs. I can see the village idiot, the drunk, the shrew. I will avoid these. I see some of the women from my last attempt. I look for the woman who, last time, was the most compassionate. She is there. I am prepared to sit a little longer, but glancing in my mirror, I see that the Hereford boys are out of their vehicle and advancing with Harry towards the barrier. They are accompanied by at least two TV camera crews. It is very important that this civilian barricade sees this convoy as a United Nations humanitarian aid convoy, not as an UNPROFOR siege breaker. I open my door, walk to the back of the vehicle, collect Emilija, and walk towards the barrier heading for the compassionate woman. There is a barracking from the crowd, but it is good natured.

I hear my name mentioned. I wear my broadest front-line smile.

– *Dobar dan*—I greet them. My arm is outstretched and I step over the logs. I tell Emilija to tell them that we are headed for Maglaj and that I have approval from both the Croat and the Serb authorities. She gets no further than the word "Maglaj," and I do not need to be a linguist to know that they are not happy. At this stage, we are surrounded, and many people are tugging or pulling, attracting my attention to give me their version. I ask Emilija if she can arrange for them to elect a few spokespeople to meet me. There is a hum of discontent, and Emilija says that they do not wish to discuss with me. I decide that the best course is to return to my vehicle and sit and see what happens. I quickly brief Harry and Louis, everyone to stay in their vehicles. Back in mine, I am able to watch the reactions to my proposal. I see the key player, Father Simic, arrive. A car arrives. Dragan the military policeman and Zoran the English speaking Croat get out and pass easily through the crowd. I decide that it is time for me to get out again. I approach Father Simic and ask if he can organise a meeting with the leaders of the barricade. He agrees to have them together in fifteen minutes. I watch from my vehicle who he contacts. Certainly some of the women seem powerful, some just vociferous. What I do not like is that there are two or three mouthy men in civilian clothes. One is armed.

The two military take no part in the organization, but Zoran is into a lot of whispering and smirking.

I attend the meeting with Louis, Harry, and some of the media. We sat on one side of a wooden garden table on wooden benches. The home team is in two groups; two of the women who led the barricade during my successful October attempt and Father Simic are seated, and a group of women plus the two male agitators are standing. Hovering close by are Dragan and Zoran.

I outlined what I wanted, a convoy into Maglaj, to feed starving civilians. Significantly, Father Simic began the reply; he accused me of having betrayed the women of Brankovici on my last visit. He told me that I had promised that, if the convoy went in, I would bring out the prisoners. They had allowed me in, the prisoners were still there. The women, who had tears in their eyes, stated that they wanted their men out. The male agitators were muttering that no convoy to Maglaj would pass. I explained that I had the full approval of the Serb and the Croat authorities to go to Maglaj, and that I objected very strongly to any accusation that I had betrayed the women. I outlined the chain of events following my successful October attempt; the death of the Dane near Travnik, resulting in the complete stoppage for more than a month of all convoys in Bosnia-Herzegovina; and the subsequent refusal of the Serbs to permit a convoy to cross their front line into Maglaj.

I reminded them that the only hard knowledge they had of their loved ones was from my October visit, and that I had taken in with me Father Stipo and arranged with the Maglaj authorities the deal "Convoys in, some prisoners out." It was not my fault that I had been unable to get back into Maglaj, that I was here now in good faith ready to take a convoy in to see what I could do for their men. The women, through tears and emotion, stated their position: they wanted their men out. The male agitators insisted that I listen once again to the history as to how their men had become prisoners through Muslim treachery. I agreed with them that their men had gone from being defenders of Maglaj to prisoners in Maglaj and that it was very unfair on them.

But it was at times like this that I felt cheap. For the real reason why the Maglaj Croats suddenly became prisoners was simply because the Herceg-Bosna Croats changed sides and stabbed the Muslims in the back at their hour of weakness and need. However, explaining this truth was not going to advance the convoy. I appealed to the women to permit the convoy for the sake of the women and children in Maglaj—women and children whom many of them had known as neighbours. This brought more tears and the women replied by saying that they understood the plight of the residents of Maglaj but that I must see their side. They had children who needed their fathers. They were not preventing the convoy, they just wanted their men out. I agreed. I told them that it was expressly forbidden for me to link convoys with prisoner exchange and that I had written agreements from all sides for the unhindered access of the convoy but that, as I felt an obligation to them for their kindness in the success of my previous convoy, I was prepared to discuss with the authorities in Maglaj the release of their men. I was prepared once again to take in Father Stipo and together, we would see their men.

I seemed to be getting somewhere with the women, but the priest cut me short with—*Prisoners out, Convoy in.* I said—*Sorry, no can do.* I explained in words of one syllable that I was not permitted to accept "linkage." "Prisoners out, convoy in" is direct linkage and is unacceptable but that, "Convoy in. Discussion on prisoners leading to prisoners out," was not direct linkage. Slowly but surely, I was becoming Balkanised! We had reached impasse number one, so I called a halt to the meeting, told them I would refer the matter to Sarajevo and Mostar, but that the convoy would remain on the road where it was—facing Maglaj. I returned to the convoy, briefed the convoy and the press, and sat in my vehicle and observed the crowd. They were good humoured. It was a cold day, they had lit fires. They had no television. This was the nearest event to a village fete since the war began, and they were settling in to enjoy it. After a few minutes, Military Police Officer Dragan came to my vehicle to inform me that he wanted the convoy to return to the hospital car park, as he could not guarantee my safety where we were. In my gravest voice, I reminded him that, in accordance with the agreements signed in Mostar and Sarajevo, he was responsible for our safety. I further reminded him that I had the full approval of his military and civilian leaders for this convoy and that it was going only one way and that was forward. He did not seem best pleased. We were then into the inevitable waiting game. Bluff and bravado would decide the outcome.

I contacted Zagreb and spoke to Karen Landgren. As ever, she was fully supportive and quick to act. She got Jerrie Hulme, late British Army retired Major General and UNHCR incumbent in Mostar, to speak to General Roso, late French Foreign legion, retired Colonel, and incumbent Herceg-Bosna military commander. Jerrie's feedback was not good. Roso was supporting the local line. Time for a bluff. I left my vehicle and headed off to meet with Lozancic. I informed him that General Roso had assured UNHCR that he agreed with the principle of unhindered access for humanitarian convoys and respected the agreement to which he was a co-signatory. I told him that I presumed that his communication link with Mostar would confirm this and that he would assist us to move forward. The pear shaped ex-military leader, now mayor, wore his most sincere look and explained to me that the influence of Mostar diminished in proportion to the distance from Mostar. *Ah*—I said—*thus giving you, the senior man on the ground, greater power.*

No. No—said Lozanjic. This apparently was not what he meant. I have to confess that he was reasonableness itself. He agreed to come with me and help me to plead my case with the committee. I returned to the convoy to await him, briefed everybody and started on the next chapter of my book. The convoy drivers were in good spirits. By now, those civilians not actually manning the barrier were chatting, smoking, and drinking with the drivers. The local children were being well provided with sweets. The press were happy. They were carried along by my enthusiasm and thought we were going to get in and that they would be able to file a good story. They were a little worried about whether the Serbs would allow them to proceed once we passed this Croat barrier. I reminded them of the words of my favourite hymn. *Lord for tomorrow and its needs I do not pray, keep me Oh Lord just for today.* On the side of the road, near where we were parked, there is the small farmhouse where the old lady with cancer had been treated by MSF on my last visit. Outside the house is a large Doberman dog chained to a kennel. This Doberman hasn't read the dog books; he is as soft as a pantomime horse. Along with the man from The Independent, I visited the house. The old lady sadly has gone. Her husband was there. He produced some coffee and some slivovica. I gave his daughter a jar of Nescafé, and we were allowed to use his loo. A vital negotiation, especially for the female translators and the ladies of the press. The old man thought we would get through to Maglaj but insisted that I would have to do something about the prisoners.

In the afternoon, Lozancic duly appeared. He told me that he had not yet received any orders to cooperate. We met with the ladies and the priest. Lozancic was excellent. The priest was becoming more obviously the leader of the opposition. I also began to suspect that two of the women could cry to order. At this meeting it was suggested that I go to Maglaj on my own to see if the Maglaj authorities would agree to releasing the prisoners. My first thought was that this would be a great idea. With luck, I would get the Croats to agree to the medicine that was on the convoy going in with me. But I was very wary of the linkage problem. I said that I would have to refer this to Zagreb.

Lozancic left. Jazinovic arrived. He demanded that the convoy return to the car park immediately. Tempers were high, he could not guarantee our safety. I told him I had no intention of moving, but I thanked him for his concern!

In my vehicle, I mulled over the prospect of a trip to Maglaj on my own. I could see one big danger. Here I was, going in saying—*Prisoners out. Convoy in.* What would happen if the Maglaj authorities said—*Convoy in. Mr. Larry out?* I could be there for a long time. The rest of the day passed with radio calls to Zagreb, Sarajevo, and Banja Luka. A new little complication set in. The leaders of the Danish convoy back in Zagreb told Ole that they did not intend leaving the convoy tied up in Zepce. If it failed to advance, they wished it to return to Banja Luka and thence to Zagreb where it could be used for more productive convoys. This attitude I continually had to face. Logisticians saw the trucks as tonnage deliverers. Tonnage delivered was the yardstick by which they measured their success. I measured success by where we delivered as well as by how much.

I discussed this development with Louis. We decided on a little subterfuge. I informed Ole that the Croats had made it clear to me that whilst the convoy could not go forward, it could not go back either. The inference being that the Croats would demand the convoy for themselves if it did not go to Maglaj. Ole did not believe me, but he was as equally determined to get to Maglaj as we were, so he happily reported this problem back to Zagreb. This kept them off our backs. We had enough enemies without, we needed none within. By four o'clock, light was beginning to fail. Even if the barrier were removed, it was too late to cross the Serb front line with the likelihood of mines. I saw Lozancic and Jazinovic. They invited a group of us to dine with them in their headquarters.

They asked me to move the convoy back to the car park, as they could not guarantee that we were not in range of the Muslim artillery fire from Maglaj. I was more concerned about the safety of the convoy from looting by locals. Furthermore, I wanted to appear to the locals to be the good guys, so I proposed that we would guarantee not to move forward so that the locals could go home to bed. But the locals were in carnival mood and made it clear that they would man and woman the barriers throughout the night.

To the annoyance of Jazinovic, and to the amusement of Lozancic, I insisted that the convoy stay where it was. The boys from Hereford organised a guard for the convoy from amongst the Brits and the ECMM. I decided that I would go to Maglaj but that I would take two vehicles. Then, if I was taken hostage, we might get one vehicle back with the latest news and the conditions. We might also lose two vehicles and provide two sets of hostages! The joy of command. A real plus about going in was that we would be a recce for the convoy. We would establish the attitude of the Serbs and the condition of the road in no man's land, we would also get the medicine in. The Croats were delighted with my decision.

I got on to poor Steen. He and his convoy had sat the whole cold, bitter day waiting for us to move forward so that they could enter. We agreed. *Same time, same place, tomorrow.* In order to go into Maglaj without a convoy, we needed to do some liaising with Maglaj itself.

The Croats had a radio in the Ozimica post office. They monitored Amateur Radio Maglaj and knew the time skeds and the frequencies. Dragan and I went together with Emilija. With very little difficulty, we were through to Maglaj. I briefly explained the position and asked their approval to come to Maglaj without a convoy. They were not happy. There were silences, and the request eventually was put before the Mayoress Aida Smailovic. She came to the radio and spoke with me. She could see no reason why I could not bring in the convoy and discuss other subjects whilst there. Eventually, she agreed that I could come and that she would warn off her front-line troops. We agreed I would enter her territory at eight o'clock. Dragan promised that he would go and see the Serbs.

The convoy hierarchy dined with Lozancic and his senior staff, who produced brandy and whisky as the drinks. Jazinovic was at his anti-Muslim worst. He was going to eliminate thousands that night on a raid into Maglaj. He would lead us into Maglaj at the head of a conquering Croat invasion. The poor man was obviously cracking under the strain. Dragan goaded him into making more ridiculous statements, and the other Croats present teased him without him realising. I was glad to leave the table and go to bed. I appreciated their hospitality and their generosity; they gave freely from the little that they had, but the bigotry was too much at the end of a tiring and frustrating day. I particularly felt sorry for Emilija. She had to listen to all this rubbish and then translate both that and my reply.

We returned to the convoy. The local villagers were settling into their self-imposed watch, with lots of noise and lots of drink. Fortunately, in the military HQ there had been a loo and washbasin, so we had all at some time during the evening performed our nightly chore. The convoy drivers were all in their cabs, most had the engines running. I took particular care to ensure that Kenan did not park opposite a vehicle exhaust pipe. The air was already thick enough with diesel fumes to make your eyes water. Within minutes of unrolling our sleeping bags, we were all asleep. The noise from the barricade could be heard all night. Occasionally a villager strolled across and banged on the side of one or other of our vehicles. Innocuous enough in a war zone.

I was one of the first up and about. Our military guard had done well. We were all safe and sound. There were a few bleary-eyed civilians still at the fire next to the barrier. The moment we stirred, children appeared, hoping for the odd goodie. It is a little disconcerting to be cleaning your teeth and spitting when surrounded by kids. Teeth cleaning is important in the field, washing isn't. Not that I have much face to wash.

Teeth cleaned, hair combed, beard brushed, I was ready for action. A quick call to Zenica, Steen is on his way. A quick touch base with Sarajevo and Kiseljak.

The Maglaj group comprised two vehicles, with the senior SAS man, Harry, Hap, Louis, myself, Kenan, Emilija and Nidal, the medicine, and, as agreed, Father Stipo. Dragan was always a good timekeeper. We set off at seven thirty. The barricade was removed sufficiently for us to weave our vehicles around. There were hugs and smiles from those already up and about.

As we pulled away, following Dragan in his red Golf, I got that exciting feeling again. I also knew how the others would feel, for them it was new ground. Emilija was also excited. Maglaj had been her patch before the place became besieged. At the Serb front line, they were expecting us. I got out, greeted them and handed out a couple of jars of coffee, whilst Dragan spoke. I could see the mines on the road. There was some negotiation and a phone call before a path was cleared for us.

Once through the first barrier, I knew from previous experience that we had cleared only the Serb Teslic command barrier. We still had to go through the Serb Doboj one. There is a mere hundred metres between them, but on a bad day, they can be on different planets. At this stage, my vehicle took the lead. Dragan sensibly became number three. We proceeded very slowly. Stopping regularly, me getting out, looking for trip wires.

The Doboj Serbs gave us no trouble, and we were then on our way through no man's land to the Bosnian Government front line. This was where Ginger Dawes and I had danced during my October outing.

When we got to the front line, I stopped and got out of the vehicle. Our second vehicle stayed opposite the white building. I was surprised to see that Dragan had motored up with us. Once I had identified the Bosnian soldiers and they were happy who I was, they came up to the road. Dragan, with a lot of courage, left his vehicle and came up to join us. Dragan is about six foot two, thin, dark, and wearing a Croat HVO uniform. The Bosnian defenders were a motley bunch in a variety of clothes. They carried a selection of weapons from hunting rifles to Kalashnikovs. Their leader was still the bright young nineteen-year-old. The Bosnians stayed in their roadside trench whilst we conversed from the road. Perhaps they remembered my last visit. With or without a Croat present, they were not going to trust the Serbs whose positions were no more than a hundred metres away and in higher ground.

Dragan had the gall to ask the Bosnians why they did not surrender instead of living like rats. The young man (whom I liked more and more) asked Dragan why the Croats did not return to Bosnia. Dragan was put down by these remarks. From his lofty height and his besieger's position, he thought that the Bosnians would be at least apologetic if not afraid. This young man was neither. We were told that we were expected but that we had to wait for an escort from Maglaj. This took about fifteen minutes. I handed over with pleasure some coffee to the young man. I agreed with Dragan that we would be back at one. He was to meet us at the Serb checkpoint and make sure they did not fire on us as we returned.

A man from Maglaj squeezed into the vehicle and we headed for Maglaj town. The road is straight, then a turn to the left, where the Serbs have you in their sights at a distance of no more than 200 metres, then under the bridge, past the tunnels where the Danes and the UNHCR interpreter died, along the river bank, one left turn, and the destruction is before your eyes on both sides of the road. Every house, every building—damaged. No glass anywhere. We went to the municipal building where the majority of the leaders were waiting for us. The building was boarded up. There was no electricity, but in honour of our arrival they had, as last time, rigged up a small source of light using car batteries. There was lots of backslapping, handshaking, and tears. Even Father Stipo was greeted warmly. It was good to see them again. I handed over some jars of coffee, put a bottle of whisky on the table, a single malt provided by Louis, and some cigarettes—the first they will have seen for three months.

We sat down and awaited the arrival of the Lady Mayor, who liked a grand entrance. Aida Smailovic was, as ever, immaculate with the works—lipstick, powder, eye shadow—even in besieged Maglaj. I greeted her with a kiss. She sat and presided. She welcomed us and reminded me that last time we met, I promised I would return one week later. She outlined the present troubles, told me of their needs, their hopes, and their fears. She then invited me to explain my absence, presence, and lack of convoy. I suggested to her that the Military with me should be given the chance of seeing the town, that Louis should see the hospital and deliver the medicines, that Father Stipo see the prisoners, and that she and I should discuss the convoy. She agreed.

My companions went leaving Aida, Emilija, and myself. I explained

425

to her everything that had happened. I made a great point of explaining that it was not my habit to link convoys with prisoner exchanges. If she wished, I would say no more about prisoners but that I felt I was not going to get a convoy through Zepce unless there was some cooperation from her. She started to give me the rhetoric. Where is the strength of the United Nations? Why must the Bosnians be the victims of aggression? I cut her short—*Aida, do you want a convoy in this week? If you do, then compromise someway, somehow, on the prisoner issue, and I will guarantee a convoy. If there is no give from you, I do not believe that I will get a single truck up the road.*

– *What is the best deal I can hope for?*—she asked me. I had pondered over this long and hard.

I suggested to her—*What about three prisoners per convoy. You have thirty-two prisoners. If I can get in eleven convoys, then you can feed your population with the World Food Programme suggested minimum every day for the next two months.* By even suggesting this, I was breaking every rule in the aid delivery handbook. I was leading with my chin and risking a knockout blow on it. The flaws with my proposal were numerous. Was I setting a precedent? Gorazde for instance has Serb prisoners. Our convoy was of nine vehicles. Was I establishing a rate of three trucks per prisoner? Was the rate two trucks of flour and one of tinned meat or two of tins and one of flour? If the exchange went well and we stockpiled eleven convoys worth of food in Maglaj was that an extra incentive for the attacking Serb? Would the Serb let eleven convoys in to release thirty-four Croats? If I did not make a proposal and no convoy came in, had I done my best? If there were no convoys and many people, innocent women and children, dying of starvation, was that better than compromising our rules?

Why, oh why, could I not just deliver aid without all this hassle? Every bloody time there was a catch, a compromise, a condition.

Aida listened, she told me that she would have to discuss the issue with her military commander. She is a tough girl. *I want to negotiate from strength. The message you take back is: 'Convoy in. Discussion on prisoners. No convoy, no discussion.' Understood?*

This was fine by me. It meant that I bring the convoy in without any

obvious previous precedent setting deal. I was also optimistic enough
to think that the women in Brankovici might see a glimmer of hope
for successful negotiations. I agreed with Aida that I would return
the next day, early, with or without a convoy, to bring back the reply
of the Croats.

Aida then took me on a walkabout around the town to show me the
damage that had occurred since my last visit. Maglaj had a Lowry
look about it. Matchstick men and women against a backdrop of
snow and grey and cold. Aida is a born leader. She wore an expensive
fur coat, black high heeled shoes and walked like a retired ballroom
dancer. The Serb positions were visible. She advised that we did
not stop as we crossed the bridge into the old part of the town, but
she did not quicken her sprightly step either. The Serbs appreciate
strength; they must admire Aida. Few seemed to live in the old town,
it was too exposed and too vulnerable. The mosque had received
a few more hits since my last visit but it still stood. Back over the
bridge and a quick visit to the hospital. The dentist remains in charge
and still sends the badly wounded by night to Tesanj for treatment.

They were overjoyed with the medicine we brought, mainly anaesthetics and antibiotics. So pleased with so little. I know that if I can
get the convoy in tomorrow, I will bring in ten tonnes more! I discuss
this with the hospital director. She assures me that she will send the
majority of it on to Tesanj. I tell her that Louis, with his terrier-like
tenacity, will try to get into Tesanj from Banja Luka. It is now time
to meet back at the municipal building to return on schedule at the
Serb checkpoint.

Everyone is happy, the SAS man has done a good recce; Louis has
visited homes, centres, and the hospital.

Father Stipo has seen twenty-eight of the thirty-two prisoners and
can account for the others. ECMM have had a good look around,
and I have shuttled the Croat proposal and am about to bat back
the Bosnian reply. The most important fact is that we are in Maglaj.
We can see on the faces of the locals that they are delighted we are
there. Today, all we have brought is hope. They all enquire about the
convoy. We are saying—*Tomorrow.* Emilija is still convinced she is

going to win a dinner. I hope she is wrong. I have lots of cigarettes in the car; I wonder whether I should give them all out now or wait until tomorrow. With or without a convoy, I decide I will be back, so I take the cigarettes with me. Our return is easy. Dragan meets us at the Serb checkpoint. He is disappointed that I have brought no prisoners out with me. I can sense the anticipation as we approach the barricade. People are looking in our vehicle to see if we have any released prisoners. We stop at the convoy, quickly brief the convoy and press, and then proceed to the office of Lozancic to give the Maglaj reply. On route, we stop at the house of Father Simic and drop off Father Stipo.

Lozancic is glad to see me. I try to be my most enthusiastic. I explain to him the conditions in Maglaj, the scale of the suffering, the responsibility which he bears, his chance to demonstrate to the world, via the media with us, the humanity of the Croats. I am carried along by my own enthusiasm, I tell him that I am certain that a convoy going in will return with some gesture from the Maglaj authorities. Lozancic listens politely. He then tells me that he has been told by his headquarters that he is not to use force on the local population. I ask him if he has any objection if I organise another meeting with the leaders of the Brankovici barricade. He seems relieved. I think he feared I might ask him to address them.

On returning to the convoy, I contact Zagreb and Sarajevo. Karen Landgren promises to talk again to Jerrie Hulme to see what the latest is from Roso. She gives me every encouragement to succeed. She tells me that Nicholas Morris, the Special Envoy, has spoken to the office of the Croat leaders in Croatia and in the so-called Herceg-Bosna. She outlines the considerable media interest. Tony in Sarajevo is fuelling it. His public information king is briefing the pack twice a day. Jerrie comes back from the HVO side in Mostar with the distinct feeling that it will be "no go" without the prisoners being released.

Time to put words in the General's mouth again. Back at the barrier, the committee is waiting for my brief. Father Simic has orchestrated the meeting. He is to conduct, sitting opposite me at the end of the wooden table; next to him are the women with the best tear ducts. I describe the town of Maglaj, the condition of the people, and the vital need for a convoy. I tell them that I have full approval from General Roso to take in the convoy. I point out the presence of the world's media hovering by, the opportunity for the women of Brankovici to show to the world their compassion, their humanity. As I talk, I can sense the meeting dividing into two camps. I can see the disapproving glances of the priest as the women warm to my words. The priest has a hard face, his dark eyes are neutral, his power is in his voice. It is deep but flat, clear, and loud. For the first time, I realise that those around the table fear him. He demands the return of the prisoners before a truck enters. He accuses me of betrayal, of being a "Muslim sympathiser." The mood changes for the worse. The women cry, the priest rants, the other men jeer. I call an end to the meeting and return to the convoy. I brief the press and convoy. We stay close to our vehicles.

Father Stipo visits me and tells me that we are unwelcome. He advises me to be careful. This he does as a friend. Suddenly, there is trouble near my vehicle where a crowd has gathered. I push my way through it to find my driver Kenan very frightened. I can hear in the crowd the word "Muslim." Kenan tells me that he has been identified as a Muslim and that men in the crowd are threatening to kill him. Emilija hears the name Nidal also mentioned. She is the Banja Luka interpreter with Louis. She too is Muslim. The crowd jostles us, and the men shake their fists. One draws his hand across his throat and points to Kenan. I get everyone into their vehicles. We sit tight, we stay still. I have made up my mind that we will move back to the hospital car park, but I will let some time pass first. I do not want the crowd to feel that it has routed the United Nations. My dilemma is solved for me with the arrival of Jazinovic. He tells me that it is not safe to stay where we are and this time insists that we return to the car park. I make a pretence of weighing up his words and then tell him that as a mark of respect for him I will agree. He is amazed. The SAS boys turn the convoy round in a dignified and unhurried manner. We return to Ozimica.

That night, we refuse the invitation of the HVO for a meal, but we are pressured into accepting an invitation for a drink. I do not want to offend at this crucial stage. Lozancic tells me he thinks we will not get through, but he supports us staying and trying. I suggest that I go into Maglaj the following morning on my own to have a final discussion with Aida. They are all very keen on this. Dragan agrees to do the liaising with the Serbs and Maglaj. Lozancic asks me to tell Aida that he can send at least eight hundred Maglaj people living in Zepce to Maglaj, all of whom want to return. *Eight hundred Muslims for thirty-four Croats.* The Croats seem to be pleased with this ratio. I am irritated by the conversation. Firstly, very few Maglajans in Zepce want to go back now knowing full well that the place is starving and constantly shelled. Secondly, I know that Lozancic has recently forced thirty-six old people to return to Maglaj on foot against their will and without negotiation—a heartless and reckless act. Surprisingly, Lozancic did it believing it to be a conciliatory gesture to Maglaj. Thirdly, these numbers are people. People like me and you.

We are in our sleeping bags early. I miss Jack Frost's three o'clock call and sleep on till six. The strain is getting to me!

Leaving Louis in charge, I left Ozimica at seven thirty. Just myself and Emilija. No sense in taking Kenan and exposing him to unnecessary danger. Dragan is not around so we go alone. At Brankovici there are few people, but it is obvious that they did man the barrier even though we had returned to Ozimica. The fire burns and the late duty stag is standing hunched yawning and scratching. We approached the barrier slowly. I stopped the car, opened the door and said, to no one in particular—*Going to Maglaj?* No one moved. I drove over the barrier and on to the Serb front line. There was no one there. I parked the car, Emilija and I got out. I shouted—*Visoki Komesarijat.* To the left of the road, about fifty metres away, there was the shell damaged house. A soldier waved. I wave back. We then waited for about five minutes before two soldiers came. One of them I recognised. I had given him coffee. This time I gave him a packet of cigarettes. They were very friendly and happy, they knew that we were coming, and they knew that I was going up to discuss "prisoner

exchange." Not strictly true. They were not interested in verbal nice-
ties. They had a neat little request of their own. There was a Serb in
Maglaj. He was confined to a wheelchair. Could I bring him out
today?

Aida was going to like this one! I promised nothing more than that
I would contact the Serb and alert the Maglaj authorities of the request. They removed their mines, and we motored cautiously to the
Doboj Serb front line; there were no mines there. We drove slowly,
slowly through no man's land, towards the Maglaj front line. My
marker was always the white building. As we reached it, I stopped,
got out, and walked forward. The Maglaj troops in the trenches
waved. I continued on foot, greeted them, handed out cigarettes,
went back to the car, and motored on to Maglaj. I went straight to
the office of Aida, but it was closed. Not a good sign. We went to an
alternate location. She was not there, but our presence in town had
been noted and the military were soon on our tail. We were escorted
back to the building where we normally saw her. This was now open.
We sat inside and waited for her. The translator Barbara was present.
I like her, she is full of life but in an invidious position. She is only
one of two qualified English interpreters in Maglaj. The one we met
on our first visit was a Croat. I notice that she is not around this time.
Questions about her are ignored. Barbara is also a Croat. She must
be vulnerable too. I asked Barbara if she could get any information
for me on the Serb in the wheelchair. She promised to do her best.

Aida arrived with her deputy. I summarize events in Zepce. I am
frank, without prisoners out, there will be no convoy in. Before her
tongue gets into condemnatory autopilot, I tell her that I have a
short time only and that I want to see the prisoners and compile a
list of their names. I mention the offer of Lozancic. She gives a quick
burst on the elderly thirty-six he "expelled" from Zepce earlier in the
week. But she seems interested in getting some people from Zepce.
This is the first bite on the hook. She knew that I wanted to see the
prisoners. They are ready and waiting. Dragan had done well. She
promises that she will have a list of people she wants out of Zepce on
my return from seeing the prisoners. A soldier took me to the place

where the prisoners were detained. It is close to the Catholic church which, ironically, is the least damaged building in Maglaj. Emilija and I entered the prison through a small door which led into a large open courtyard. All the prisoners were there, lined up, waiting for us. They were all clean shaven, wearing clean clothes, and amongst them there was a great air of anticipation. I quickly addressed them as I did not want them to think that I was there to release them. I told them that I was about to bring a convoy in, that I hoped they would be released soon. Emilija compiled a list of their names. In an attempt to verify who each was, I asked them to give me their name and their next of kin in Zepce. There were twenty-nine of them. One was a German. Two were mentally disturbed. The remainder seemed as fit and as alert as any other occupant of Maglaj. We handed out cigarettes and smiles. Hope and heartache. We left and raced back to Aida. The prisoners looked to me as if they were ready for handing over. Why else make them look so presentable?

Aida took us into her little office, the first time I had been in there. We went straight to lists. I asked her—*Are you prepared to release any prisoners?*

She replied—*Yes.* Such a sweeter word I have never heard. Her military commander then joined us. He had a list of those Maglaj men whom he wanted out of Zepce. It was twenty strong. Aida agreed to five Croat prisoners out. She and her commander were not happy that the Croats could choose them from the list of twenty-nine. Here I began to shout.

– *You want to choose your twenty, but they cannot choose their five! Why don't you take any twenty and they take any five?*

Aida was amused by my temper. The military man was not. He started to accuse me of being more interested in prisoners than aid. I hit the roof. I told them to stick their prisoners. I got up as if to go. Poor Emilija was halfway through trying to find a Serbo-Croat equivalent of "Stick your prisoners," and I was on my way.

Aida called me back. She agreed that the Croats could choose their five as long as they got their twenty plus a convoy. I was so elated I could not get out quickly enough. If we really moved, we could still do convoy and exchange today. As we were leaving, one of the military handed me a letter from the Serb in the wheelchair to his relatives in Zepce.

I still had a large quantity of cigarettes left. I was so convinced that I was coming back I did not give them out. At the Serb checkpoint, they were pleased with the letter from their man in Maglaj until they opened it. It was one long plea to come out!

I did not stop at the barrier. I headed straight for the office of Lozancic. He was pleased to receive the list of Croat prisoners. He was not happy with the list of twenty Muslims wanted by Maglaj. They were —*all war criminals*. He promised to talk to his military leaders and to the authorities in Grude.

I was deflated. I tried to push him. It was "convoy in, five prisoners out, then twenty in." Surely this is what he wanted. Whilst the convoy went in, he would have time to discuss and arrange the twenty. *Just get the women off the streets, remove the barrier, get the convoy moving*—I pleaded. *Euphoria will do the rest*. No. I had to wait. He promised he would come to the car park. I returned to Ozimica, briefed everyone, and waited and waited. On a reporter's phone I spoke to Karen in Zagreb. She was still prepared to support the convoy. We both hoped that if it succeeded, the press would ease off on the prisoner exchange angle. I was convinced that if we could get them in, they would have a big enough story. We both agreed that, morally, our job was to get aid to the desperate and that there was no community more desperate than Maglaj.

Lozancic turned up with all of his henchmen. He said that he had orders that the convoy was not to move until the prisoners were released. I was furious with him. I tore into him. He seemed genuinely shocked by the force of my invective. I accused him of deceiving me all week. I summarised our efforts. We had risked our safety by going into Maglaj without a convoy. We had gone against our principles and discussed prisoner exchanges. I concluded that we had a right to deliver aid, a right accepted in written agreements, signed by his so-called President and his military commander. Lozancic looked guilty, and he left meekly.

We sat in our vehicles and waited. I knew that this could not be the end of it. Lozancic returned. The convoy could go. Furthermore, the convoy waiting in Bosnian territory to deliver aid to Zepce could also go to Maglaj. The prisoner exchange was off. There was no obligation to bring back Croat prisoners. He was not offering the release of the twenty but—*all those Muslims who want to return to Maglaj are free to do so.*

This reversal was too quick; the concession too dramatic. But it was not an opportunity to be missed. I informed Zagreb. I spoke to Steen, still sitting on the front line with his convoy. He later told me that when he told his drivers they were going into Maglaj there was cheering, clapping, and even some tears. We lined up, revved up, and set off. The excitement amongst us was touchable. Our smiles could have melted ice. I kept the pace slow and dignified. We had no police escort. At the crossroads we turned left, and I watched in my mirror as each vehicle turned the corner.

We drove past the church of Father Simic and on to Brankovici. As I turned the corner, I could see that the barrier was no longer there. My heart raced. In its place there was the detritus of the picket. Ashes where the fires had burned. Broken chairs where they had sat.

I looked up from the scene of so much hassle at the road ahead to Maglaj. One hundred metres ahead, a large blue truck was reversing into the road. A small car overtook the convoy at great speed. I recognised its occupant as Father Simic. The driver of the truck jumped out of the cab and abandoned the vehicle in the middle of the road.

I slowly brought the convoy to a halt and sat and watched. The priest, Father Mathias Simic, Man of God, was barking orders to a small group of men. Father Simic, Catholic priest, directed the placing of oil drums on the road to complete the barrier. Simic, spiritual leader of the parish, approached my vehicle and banged on the door. *What do you think you are doing?* he shouted in his most dramatic pulpit manner. *Where do you think you are going?* I got out of the vehicle. Simic looked violent. The small crowd that had gathered were very noisy, angry and aggressive. I tried to explain that I had approval from Lozancic. His name brought jeering and spitting. I was pushed and jostled, there was lots of arm waving and shouting. The message was clear. *Go back.* I returned to my vehicle, and by radio, I told the drivers to stay in their vehicles.

Jazinovic, the military commander, was next on the scene. His attitude was, as ever, that he could not and would not remove his own civilians by force. He warned me that the mood was the worst it had been. I asked for Lozancic. He eventually came. He was wearing a fawn raincoat, which for some reason has always seemed to be significant. Perhaps it made him look ordinary and vulnerable.

I may never know if I was conned from the start on this particular convoy. I may never know if Lozancic and Jazinovic played me like a fish on a hook. I do know that when Lozancic arrived he was worried. His actions over the next half hour were, I am certain, genuine and brave.

Lozancic moved into the crowd which by now was larger than it had ever been and contained far more men than women. We opened the door of our vehicle so that Emilija could hear what was said and translate.

Lozancic told the crowd that the convoy had approval to go to Maglaj and that it was the duty of everyone to obey that decision. He told the crowd I was a good man, I had a duty to deliver to Maglaj, the press were present, and the world should see how honourable Croats are. He was shouted down. He raised his voice. The crowd began to push him, to assault him.

Throughout this, the priest Simic was rabble rousing. He was muttering to some, prompting others. I watched him malevolently pace back and forth on the periphery of the crowd. I saw him push people towards where Lozancic was speaking. I have no doubt that the leader of this blockade, the force behind the stoppage of this convoy, was Catholic priest Father Mathias Simic.

The final words of Lozancic were—*If you do not accept the orders to permit this convoy to go to Maglaj, I resign.* This provoked a howl which drowned any further attempts at translation. Lozancic turned towards his car and climbed in. I got out of mine and thanked him. He left. We were now the sole attention of the crowd. There were

435

many threats, much drawing of fingers across throats, a lot of banging on the vehicle.

I thought that we should sit it out. Harry Bucknall and the SAS man approached my vehicle. The SAS man told me that he was responsible for the security of my convoy, which was news to me. He told me that he was ordering it to turn around and to head back to the car park. I was not happy with this. I will never believe that the UN should be seen to run. I preferred to sit it out a little longer. I knew that we would have to move, but we should move at our pace in our time. This was neither the time nor the place for there to be division in our ranks. I therefore reluctantly agreed.

I insisted that the convoy be turned around in a slow and orderly manner. During this manoeuvre, I went across to talk to the senior man from Hereford. He was rude and vulgar. He is off my Christmas card list.

I had a conversation with Louis. He was all for staying in the car park for another attempt the next day but was prepared to look at alternative solutions. Next to Maglaj, the place that most needed aid at that time was Central Bosnia. So, the choice seemed to be: another day with two convoys trying to get into Maglaj or to release both convoys to Zenica and Central Bosnia.

We decided to cut our losses and to deliver both to Central Bosnia. Our suspicion was that the Croats would not let our convoy back into Bosnian Government territory but would insist that we give it to them. We therefore decided on a quick run straight across the front line. No asking permission, just go.

Go we did. The Croats at the checkpoint were a little confused and let us pass. We sped to Zenica where we met up with an equally disappointed Steen.

Back in the office there was lots of—*Well done but hard luck*—which I hate. As we unpacked my vehicle, I saw that I still had the cigarettes with me. I remembered my promises to Aida, to the doctor in the hospital, to the people in the streets of Maglaj. I left the office, went to my house, and quietly wept.

Twenty One

The Darkest of Dark Days

The convoys and the drivers become part of my life. Without their courageous tenacity, there would be no aid to distribute. The Danes, the Swedes, the Germans, and above all, the British Government ODA funded teams kept the aid coming. The convoy leaders that reported into my office swapped gossip, told me of the hazards on the road, the latest developments, and the changes of personnel. Sometime during the unload, I would try to visit the drivers and chat with them. I knew them all by sight and many by name.

All of the convoy leaders were aggressive, some recklessly, others cautiously. They had to strike a balance between achieving the aim of the convoy and ensuring the safety of their drivers. Big Ginge, who got me into Maglaj, was most in accord with me. "Mack" Court, another ex-military man, a marine, was more serious. I had a couple of differences of opinion with him over the crossing of convoys from Banja Luka to Zenica. These were professional disagreements and never interfered with my respect for him.

In late January, he travelled down from Tuzla, where his convoy "The Nomads" was based. He came down with three trucks and his own Land Rover Discovery. The convoy arrived in Zenica in the early evening. The vehicles were parked in the compound of the European Community Task Force (ECTF) close to UNHCR where labourers were to load them. The team then left to book into the Mettalurg Hotel. This was not the usual hotel for the drivers but was used when the two better hotels were full. The meals in the Mettalurg were not to the liking of the team, so they moved to the best hotel for the evening meal. Shortly after seven, they received a call that two of the vehicles were loaded. Mack took two of his drivers, Paul Goodall and Simon King, to the ECTF compound to place the loaded trucks into the parking bays.

An hour later, they left the ECTF compound and set off back to the hotel. They slowed down at a notoriously bad patch of road where the road surface had been washed away. As they slowly bumped over the corrugated road surface, they were overtaken by a green Volkswagen Golf car. The car cut in front of the Land Rover. It stopped and four men leapt out of it, three from the rear and one from the front passenger seat. They were carrying Kalashnikov rifles. *Get out!*—shouted one of them. The ODA team got out of their vehicle. Mack Court immediately offered the keys of the vehicle to them as is the training and practice in such a circumstance. We can always buy a new Land Rover. He noted that all of them were wearing some sort of uniform, were dark haired, and that three of them were bearded. There was some confusion amongst the men with the guns as to what was to happen.

They then ordered them back into their own vehicle. Simon first, Paul in the middle, and Mack behind the driver. One of the gang sat in the rear of the vehicle behind the team and another two sat in the front. The team were told to put their heads into their laps and their hands behind their backs. The man in the passenger seat then said—*You are to be taken hostage to exchange for one of our people who is being held prisoner.* What thoughts went through the minds of the team I do not know. But they now knew that this was not a robbery. The gang spoke amongst themselves. Mack believed it was in Arabic.

The vehicle travelled about three kilometres. The Land Rover was parked off the road. They were told not to look up. The one that spoke English told them not to worry as they were to be exchanged. The driver however was more agitated and shouted at the one who was interpreting. They sat looking at the floor. A second car arrived. There was some conversation and they then followed it a further two or three kilometres. The team were ordered out of the vehicle. They were taken forward to the side of a small hill. They were near the bank of the river. Here they were told to kneel, searched, and lost their wallets and valuables. They were then moved down to the bank of the river and again told to kneel. They could see that the river was a few metres below them, was fast flowing from left to right and was thirty or so metres wide and looked deep.

Paul Goodall was on the right, Mack Court was in the middle, and Simon King was on the left. One assailant fired two rounds into the back of the head of Paul. As the first of these rounds was fired Mack leapt forward and threw himself into the river. His action was followed by Simon. The attackers fired their weapons at the two escapees. Mack was hit in the back and Simon in the arm and the leg.

They both attempted to swim across the river but the current was too strong. They were carried downstream away from their captors. They swam under the icy water to avoid being seen. Mack was the first out of the water. He was alarmed to hear footsteps behind him but discovered that it was Simon. They were both wet and exhausted, but the icy water had staunched their wounds. They walked towards Zenica fearing pursuit. They arrived at a small group of houses. They knocked on a few doors before finding one that answered. It is not surprising in a war zone that people in houses without electricity (who after peering out through their windows late at night seeing two men wet and wounded) do not answer. Eventually, one house did show courage and let them in. They sent a member of the family to the telephone to call the police.

The police arrived and took them to hospital. Amazingly, Simon was bandaged, discharged, and sent to the Mettalurg hotel! Mack was admitted to the surgery ward. At the hospital, the police rang me. They told me that two British drivers were in the hospital and one was dead. I contacted John Adlam, the head of the ECTF and de facto head of the Brits. Together we went to Zenica hospital where we saw Mack. He was only concerned about Paul. In his usual gruff manner, he told me to leave him and to go and find Paul. To make sure that Paul was OK. I did not tell him that Paul was dead.

The British battalion in Vitez were informed and they were excellent. It was after eleven, but they sent an armoured ambulance which had to cross a heavily mined Croat checkpoint.

They collected Mack from the hospital and Simon from the hotel and took them back through the minefield to Vitez where they were treated by the outstanding Royal Army Medical Corps Lt. Col. David Jackson. The Brits sent a Warrior armoured vehicle to pick up the body of Paul. He too was taken to the Brit battalion to be with his own.

John Adlam and I had one more task to do. We phoned England and told Jack Jones of ODA what had happened. ODA sent a man to the home of Paul to inform his family. He was the father of four beautiful girls.

The next day, Tony Winton, the extremely caring and sensitive boss of the ODA in Zagreb, whom I had served with in the army, arrived with the equally caring, equally sad, Karen Abu Zayed, the UNHCR Chief of Mission. Tony went to see his boys, all three of them. Mack looked weak and tired. Simon was alert and talkative.

Karen and Tony with John and myself attended a meeting with the authorities in Zenica. They were shocked by the murder and ex-pressed genuine and deeply felt condolences. They were extremely worried that the murder would cause the aid programme to stop. They assured Karen and Tony that every effort would be made to find the "terrorists" as they called them. The chief of police made it clear that the aim of the crime had been to murder, not to rob. He believed it was a political crime. The one slightly annoying note was that a man calling himself the Head of the Military Court was critical saying that, we, UNHCR had hindered the investigation by removing the three victims to the British battalion.

Within a few days, the police had found the Golf and detained some suspects for questioning. The ODA Land Rover was discovered, after being involved in a strange incident. It was spotted trying to cross into Sarajevo. The police chased it. There was a shootout and all the occupants were killed.

Many letters of condolence were received by the office from various Bosnian authorities and from Bosnian members of the public. I got together with all the aid agencies in Zenica and told them everything I knew. Most were stunned by the fact that murder was the motive. All of us knew that the hijacking of a vehicle was a likelihood. It had happened to many agencies. But to be stopped with murder in mind was new. Regardless of this all, the agencies agreed to stay on. All ap-preciated that there are few safety and security precautions that we could take.

The greatest tribute to Paul was that the Nomads, his team, took a convoy from Zenica to Tuzla within hours of his death. They stopped at the site of his murder and laid a wreath. It was not the first. Many citizens of Zenica had left small posies of flowers.

The suspects arrested in the Golf were released except for one who was positively identified by Mack and Simon the morning that they were evacuated to Britain. Bizarrely and ominously, he was being transported to Sarajevo in police custody to be a witness in another case when he escaped. He was a Saudi member of the Mujahideen. The case was closed.

Two other incidents arose from the case. We received a phone call in the office purporting to come from the Turkish Mujahideen threatening "to kill a member of UNHCR by 1100 hours." This I gave maximum publicity. As a result, the local Mujahideen commander requested for me to visit him at his headquarters in an isolated part of Zenica. I sought advice. The Zenica chief of police thought it would be extremely dangerous to go. His relationship with the Mujahideen was not cordial. Karen in Zagreb was clever. *Invite him to our office*—she suggested. Surprisingly, he agreed to come.

I had to clear the compound. I sent the staff home early and we awaited his arrival. He arrived with a small but well armed bodyguard. He was a Turk, but he spoke Arabic. No problem, our ace convoy controller Nijaz has a degree in Arabic. He translated.

The Mujahideen commander was thin and tough. His message was heart-warming—*We, the Turkish Mujahideen have never issued any death threats against you or your staff.* Then the bit I really liked—*You and we are here for the same job. You are supporting Bosnians, so are we.* Then the real beauty—*And we are having the same success. No matter what we do, it is not enough. If anything goes wrong, we get the blame. Neither of us gets any praise or thanks, only criticism and blame.* I liked him.

Zagreb has decided that it is time for Steven Wolfson to move. He is replaced by Mark Cutts. I really am lucky with staff. Mark has a degree from Durham University in Theology and is the son of the former Anglican Archbishop of the Argentine. Tall and dark haired with looks that make women stop in the street. He is a fluent Spanish speaker. He has a studied, measured hesitancy in his speech delivery. A man who weighs his words but brings them from his soul. He is a passionate humanitarian aid worker as well. He too writes excellent reports. He also enjoys chairing meetings. Mark will rise to the top. With him as Deputy Head of Office, I am still free to roam.

The piracy of our convoys is increasing. At Lisac, at Opara, at any place where there is a sharp bend which slows the convoy, the trucks are swarmed and emptied on the move. We give an ultimatum to the Bosnian authorities. You stop it happening or we stop the convoys. They say they have no fuel. *Give us fuel and we will do our best to patrol the danger spots.* We give them fuel, some of which will be spent on the problem!

The UK charity Feed the Children are doing a great job. They are delivering their aid to the children on the hijacking route and trying to persuade them to leave the convoys alone. Much appreciated.

The British Government Overseas Development Administration has stopped its convoys running and withdrawn some of its advisers to safer Split. When the bigggies do this, it has a knock on effect. The smaller agencies will feel obliged to follow. I called an interagency meeting. It was well attended. I explained that we at UNHCR are here "for the ride," we will not be pulling out. ICRC is equally as determined to stay. Unfortunately, most agencies are thinning out. The stopping of the convoys is a real blow.

Commander Alagic tells me he has arrested twenty-one people for bushwhacking our convoys. Now we have no convoys to bushwhack. You take one step forward and two backwards here. I am fed up today. Harry Bucknall pleases me—he offers to ride shotgun on any convoy which is brave enough to set out.

I have sent a radio message to Enda Savage in Metkovic. *Convoys to Zenica, Please be assured there is no extra danger to convoys entering or operating in Central Bosnia. There are more than fifty internationals who live and work here. This includes twenty females under thirty-five. No one has expressed a wish to leave. We desperately need the convoys. Please continue to send them.*

It is true that no one has asked to leave, but many are ordered to leave by their masters who are out of the theatre and do not understand the play. By the end of the week, we are no more than a handful.

Received radio message from Zagreb:

We have been informed by Bosnian Embassy that three persons working for 'Benevolence International' have been wounded and need UN assistance to be evacuated. Biodata is: Sulaiman abu Maluh. Year of birth: 1967. Nationality: Jordanian.

Abdul abu Alghol. 1963. Nationality unknown.

Majid abu Nasser. 1970. Jordanian.

Thank you for your assistance. Best regards.

I replied:

There is just the slightest chance that either the Croats or the Serbs may have a teeny weeny suspicion that these three wounded Arab aid workers may be, dare I say it, Mujahideen. If this outrageous thought were to cross their minds, they just might object to granting free passage. Please advise. Best regards.

If they really are aid workers, someone will continue to put pressure for their evacuation. I never heard any more.

I then had a long conversation with Jerrie Hulme. He had a bad incident in Mostar, which he is not yet able to compartmentalise. He was about to enter Mostar, where he is Head of Office, to arrange for the medical evacuation of a little girl, and to escort in an aid convoy, when he was approached by an Italian TV crew who also wanted to enter the city. They were accredited journalists and had the right papers and stamps from all sides. Kind old Jerrie agreed to take them in with him.

Before crossing the front line, he checked on the security situation and learned that a UNHCR convoy in Mostar on the East bank was hampered by shelling. Jerrie advised the convoy he was escorting to go back. They agreed, but before they left, he explained the situation to his passengers and gave them the offer of returning with the convoy. They opted to go on with him. They arrived at the Presidency building in the city centre at one thirty p.m. The journalists were briefed by Jerrie on the hazards of sniping and the risk of random shelling. They were then taken over by the local authorities who provided them with an escort and an interpreter. Jerrie agreed to meet them back at the Presidency at three thirty. The city was quiet as they left.

At a quarter to three, heavy shelling began. At a quarter after three, Jerrie was told that the journalists had been in an incident. He went to the area, no more than a few hundred metres away, and found the three journalists dead. They had been filming in a cellar, the light was bad, they decided to continue outside. They were interviewing a six-year-old boy who stood in front of them with the interpreter at his side. A rocket came whooshing in and exploded behind them. The three journalists took the blast, the boy survived uninjured, the interpreter had minor cuts. Jerrie used the radio to bring in the UN Spanish Battalion. The bodies were recovered. But nothing is easy. The Bosnian Government wanted to carry out a post-mortem on the bodies. The Italian Government asked Jerrie to prevent this. The Croats amazingly admitted responsibility for the incident. This allowed Jerrie to plead for the release of the bodies. He got them out by two o'clock the next day. Only twenty-four hours after they had entered, in his vehicle. The journalists were part of the day's toll of nine dead, fifteen wounded.

We chatted around the incident. I knew what bothered him. First, if you, an old hand, take someone into a dangerous area, you know that they say to themselves—*If he feels it is safe enough for himself to go in, then it must be safe enough for us.* But we go in because we have a job to do. We cannot sit around and wait until it is absolutely safe to go in. And we do not take unnecessary risks. Standing outside in heavy shelling is not something that Jerrie would have done. Second, three young excited professional individuals, with whom you have shared the confines of your car, suddenly become three dead journalists. Swift and final. You are at one end of their bridge from life to death.

— Jerrie, what happened to the little girl you went in to evacuate?

— I got her out of course, she's fine. Big, bluff, blue-eyed bear of a man with a heart of gold.

Today we are visited by Paddy Ashdown. I cannot offer him the excitement of a night in the bunker a la Sarajevo, but as usual, he gets his nose into the offices of all who count. He asks, in a charming way, some devastating questions. He is seen to be pro-Muslim, so he gets a good reception in Zenica. He is, as everybody knows, an ex-Royal Marine. The European Community Monitors here are led by Sir Martin Garrod, a former Major General Royal Marines. They spend an evening putting the world right. I was delighted to see him again. I must find out what tablets he is on. I look like Methusalah standing next to him.

It is Ramadan, and I have just been told a Sarajevo joke. What is the difference between a Muslim in Saudi and a Muslim in Sarajevo?

One fasts for Allah the other for UNHCR.

I did not laugh. Until on my own.

At the military briefing, we learn that Croat forces today drove the Bosnian Government forces away from the village of Santici. The front line is now back where it was two months ago. The only difference is that hundreds are dead. I also hear that a Royal Engineer sapper was shot in the boot whilst attempting to repair a water main in Novi Travnik. The non-infanteers are saying that the sniper thought he was an infantryman and was aiming for his brains.

The women are now placing boulders on the road to slow down convoys so that the men can rob them.

General Rose, who is sorting out BHC and achieving wonders in Sarajevo, is taking an interest in my campaign for Maglaj. This is good news and leads to a hectic but fruitless week. The Brit battalion mounts Operation Lawrence: a heavy escort from the Coldstream, a transport platoon from the Dutch/Belgian battalion, and UNHCR. The usual formula is two convoys, one for the Croats in Zepce and the other for Maglaj. We have all the usual embuggerance and then we arrive in Zepce where the trucks for Maglaj are inspected. This is done in such a casual way that I know we are not going to get in. I leave the convoy where it is and motor forward with just my own vehicle. Sure enough, the road is blocked with women and children stiffened out with some drunken men in uniform. They are very abusive. They again try to drag poor Kenan out of the vehicle. I get out

445

to try to reason with them. It is a waste of time, and it is degrading. A grandfather who is with his grandchildren squares up to me with his fists clenched and attempts to provoke me into a fight.

I am sorely tempted to lay him out but instead turn away. The crowd jeers. The grandfather pulls on my arm and draws his hand across his throat to signify that he would like to cut my throat. It is his moment of glory with his grandchildren. I get back in the vehicle and motor back to the convoy.

– *Turn around. Let's go back.* The military are openly critical of me.

– *Don't know why you brought us here. Nothing has changed since last time*—said one officer.

– *You are making a fool of us*—said another. I bit my tongue. It would not be right to vent my anger on the wrong group.

– *We are here because Maglaj has not been fed by convoy since October. They will know that we have tried today. That will help them to hold on.* I know I am right, but I also know I have not convinced them. A very dejected convoy returns to Zenica. I am reminded by a number of people that food and resources are scarce and we cannot waste them on personal quests. For the first time, I began to wonder if I had been here too long. Then I got my confidence back and realised that my detractors had not been here long enough.

The NATO ultimatum to the Serbs to pull back their weapons outside the total exclusion zone around Sarajevo plays havoc with the number of convoys. Few convoy leaders will risk being on the road. Those that do have to face a far more militant form of civil unrest at Opara and Lisac. A Dutch convoy has the misfortune to have one vehicle break down near Lisac. A mob strips it of its contents. The Brit escort fires shots into the air.

I am forced to suspend the local delivery of aid for the simple reason that I have no food in the warehouse.

I send desperate signals to Enda in Metkovic and he finds a convoy prepared to travel, but it is attacked and robbed by a violent crowd at Opara. This time there is a Bosnian police escort with it. They fire into the crowd. Now we have Croats firing on Bosnians and Bosnians firing on Bosnians. What a place, what a mess.

Peter Williams, who is as fed up as I am, decides on a head to head confrontation with the leaders of the Croat and the Bosnian authorities. He draws up a chronicle of all the hindrances, objections and incidents that have stopped the free and safe passage of humanitarian aid. Our first call is on the Croats. We are a large delegation. Peter, Sir Martin, Jay Carter, and me. They are Kordic, Blaskic, the Chief of Police Rajic, and the man representing the Mostar authorities, Marinko Bosnjak, whom I actually like.

Peter hits them hard, reading out the litany of sins. I went for cajoling and humour, Jay for straight, curt, common sense. We received an act of contrition and the immediate agreement for us to medevac two wounded from Stari Vitez. We came away at least feeling better. The Bosnian government troops and police are getting to grips with the banditry. We get eight convoys through with no trouble. But having psyched ourselves up to tackle both sides, we are not going to be robbed of the opportunity just because they improved. We call on Alagic. He gets the Muslim version of the chronicle. He is either tired or bored or disinterested. He listens and nods and smiles. He is a bey, a pasha, listening to a petition. Where his mind is, what he is thinking about, I do not know. We did not have the effect we should have had. In olden times, he would have had our heads off before we reached the courtyard door.

The reason for his indifference soon became apparent. Zagreb announced the signing of a cease fire between the Bosnian Government and the Bosnian Croat sides. It was a four-point agreement: a ceasefire, positioning of UNPROFOR troops at key points, withdrawing or placing under UNPROFOR control heavy weapons, and the establishment of a Joint Commission under the chairmanship of UNPROFOR.

It was to take effect in forty-eight hours' time. Alagic had no time to lose or waste. There were a fair number of scores to be settled and a fair few killings to take place in those remaining forty-eight hours. The first tangible sign of the peace was the unhindered arrival of twelve convoys. We were back in business. A couple of days later, another sign. The siege of tiny Stari Vitez was lifted. The worst of the sick were taken to hospital.

Poor Maglaj is still taking a hammering. I send another message to General Rose who has the whole of Bosnia to worry about. I hear back from BH command—*Be patient!* I also hear that the boys from Hereford are taking an active interest in the area.

February ends with a cease fire, a convoy route open, and with thirty-one per cent of needs delivered. My staff have worked their socks off. I hope that now that routes are open, I can get some of them away to the coast for a break. I am beginning to annoy the Zenica authorities. They are pestering my male staff. They want them in uniform. If only they knew how much war effort my boys have put in. They also do not like the composition of my staff. They would prefer me to employ only Muslims. Hence the most recent missive.

Dear Mr. Larry,
We would appreciate it very much if you could send us a list
of all your local staff for the purpose of our keeping a record of
your employees' nationality structure.
Signed: Minister Fuad Djidic

I whanged back by return.

Dear Sir,
All my local staff are Bosnians.
Signed: Mr. Larry

Doctor Djidic, who has a doctorate in Marxism, a qualification as useful as a comprehensive knowledge of the common diseases of the dodo, was not pleased with my reply. My staff were.

The reports coming out of Banja Luka are as horrendous as ever. Just because I am not there does not prevent me from reading the reports with anger at our impotence. I decide to go and talk to the Mayor Besim Spahic. I outlined to him the latest report and asked unofficially for his advice.

– *Would the Zenica authorities wish to help the Muslims in Banja Luka?*

If I could get them out, would Zenica offer them accommodation?

The mayor was not enthusiastic—*You will have to go and see Mr. Djidic. He is the Minister for Central Bosnia.* Not the answer I wished to hear but....

– *Dr. Djidic, I have come to ask your advice. I have not discussed this subject with my masters in Zagreb nor with my colleagues in Banja Luka, but could Zenica take any displaced from Banja Luka? If so, how many and how soon?*

I had to listen to the history lesson and then the diatribe—*If UN were stronger... If UNHCR were more aggressive...If the aggressor ...*

Eventually he told me that Zenica already had its fair share of displaced and was not prepared to take any more.

– *Look, if we UNHCR could provide more money, for refurbishment, for food. Read these reports.*

– *No, I am sorry.*

– *Thank you. I will not report our conversation to my masters. I was just after your advice. Thank you.*

The next morning, just after eleven, my phone rings. It is friends—*Have you or any of your staff listened to BiH radio?*

– *No, why?*

– *Mr. Djidic was on. He said that he had been visited by that well-known humanitarian aid worker Larry Hollingworth who has proved to be a hypocrite by attempting to persuade the authorities to ethnically cleanse Banja Luka.* I rang him up and thanked him *on behalf of the people of Banja Luka.*

My staff were very protective of my privacy. One evening I received a note.

Dear Larry,
I have been trying to reach you for a couple of days but your staff protect you far better than Mr. Clinton. Can you spare a couple of minutes for an old wounded compatriot?
Signed: Tony Birtley

It was marvellous to see him again. He told me how, after I had

left Srebrenica, he had still pursued the aerial bombers of the border villages. One fine day he had lingered too long, too far forward.
The Serb mortarman landed his bomb close enough to bite a sizable
chunk out of Tony's calf muscle. Two UN soldiers were also wounded. A helivac saved his leg—if not his life.

After such an incident, any sensible journalist would switch to fashion correspondent or religious affairs. Not Tony, the original ace
cameraman reporter. He was back limping around front lines, hob-
bling across checkpoints, filing the best stories. I briefed him about
the little Central Bosnian picture he briefed me on the big Bosnian
picture. We had a drink or two and he left... to the front.

I received a copy of a "report" from another old friend, the Serb
newspaper Glas Srpska:

*Who is UNHCR helping? It has become known through mili-
tary sources that the Moslem Special Army Unit 'Seven South'
is receiving, in the Tesanj region, special packages of weapons,
ammunition, and equipment by parachute. Messages sent in
cypher by the UNHCR's Larry Hollingworth specify the area
which is secured and guarantees that signals will be given to
the aircraft as to where to direct the parachutes.*

I sent a reply:

To the Editor of Glas Srpska,
*Reference your article 'To whom UNHCR helps.' Your article
accuses UNHCR and myself of giving assistance to military
elements in the Tesanj region.*
*It accuses me of holding conversations in cypher about special
packages which you speculate contain weapons, ammunition,
and equipment. This is libellous, scurrilous, blatantly untrue,
insulting, dangerous, and totally irresponsible. Air drops are
necessary in the Tesanj and Maglaj pocket because UNHCR
are not allowed free and regular access by road. If you gave
approval for road access there would be no need for air drops.
The contents of the air drops are closely inspected at Frankfurt. The inspection team consists of two Serbs, one Croat,*

and one Muslim. All were appointed by their own authorities. I have visited the Frankfurt base and can assure you that your two appointees are loyal, dedicated, and hardworking. Your accusation insults them and questions the choice of your authorities.

The air drops are expensive. If we must have them, they must be accurate. I regularly speak with the radio amateur of Tesanj and Maglaj in order to ensure the airdrops land in areas where they can be recovered. I never talk in cypher. I never talk about special stuff. There never is any special stuff.

I do attempt to disguise the location of the airdrop for two reasons. The first is to inform the authorities of the location without the public knowing, and the second for the hideous fact that when the air drop location is known, some sub-humans from the besieging forces fire on the air drop sites.

My dear editor, your newspaper regularly proves that the accuracy of the reports of some of your staff is not good. I trust that you personally will show some integrity and publish this letter.

I am still waiting.

We try Maglaj again. We fail again. Croats approve, no human barrier. But the Serbs refuse to let us up the road!

Boutros Boutros-Ghali discusses in New York the possibility of declaring Mostar, Vitez, and Maglaj safe areas. A bit late in the day for that.

The Bosnians in Maglaj have released the Croat prisoners. All out safe and sound. Dare I suggest another attempt. I do.

We hear that the main bridge over the Bosna in Maglaj has been destroyed. First reports blame Serb aircraft. This is disproved by NATO watchdogs in the sky. If not an aircraft, then blame a FROG missile. Whatever, the bridge is damaged but not down.

Tony Smith in Banja Luka tries a convoy to Maglaj from his end. It gets blocked in Teslic. We go into Zepce to await its arrival. It moves from Teslic to the top of the hill where the first Croat checkpoint used to be but is now a Serb post. I decide to get as close to it as

I can. I am with Vesna. We are followed by a press vehicle. We pass through Croat checkpoints with no trouble. We get quite close to the front line. We can see the convoy. I raise Tony on the radio. He is having a hard time.

– *Vesna, we will go forward as far as I can. Keep your eyes wide open—I do not want to cross inadvertently into Serb territory, OK?*

– *You are OK. Keep going.* It looks pretty isolated to me, the press are right on our tail, following blindly.

– *Vesna, are you sure we have not passed the last Croat checkpoint?*

– *Keep on going.*

– *Are you sure?*

– *Yes.* I can see no one. Ahead, the convoy is getting larger and closer.

– *Vesna are…* There is a sudden zip as a hail of bullets fly past the door of the vehicle.

– *Vesna, those bullets are from behind us.*

– *Yes stop. I think we are ahead of the front line.*

We get a second slightly longer zip. I stop and wait. I am certainly not getting out to step into another zip. A tall, blonde Croat soldier carrying his Kalashnikov very nonchalantly bangs on my door.

– *Get out.* I comply. He has already done the journalists—they are out and looking scared.

– *Where are you going?* the soldier asks.

– *To the front line.*

– *Theirs or ours?* he asks.

– *Yours.*

– *Ours is two hundred metres back there.*

– *I am terribly sorry. May we turn around?*

– *Yes.*

Back we go. Vesna loses her map reading licence. We returned to the main road and parked up. Tony is on the hill for two days. On his last day. I am waiting in a layby near Brankovici. I have regular contact with Tony and after each session I brief the press, the patient ones who have remained. I have approval from the Croats to go into Maglaj without a convoy. They tell me that I will have no difficulty with the Serbs. They will let me in without a convoy. The press are hoping that they will get in with me, with the convoy, or maybe without me and the convoy. They are furious and determined as they have all been told by their editors that Martin Dawes of the BBC has beaten them all to it. He is in and broadcasting loudly, graphically, and often.

I do not realise that my mini press briefings are a source of press amusement. They call the procedure "Waiting for Moses."

Whilst we wait, a strange event takes place. We are in Croat territory which, since the ceasefire, is now on the same side as the Bosnian Government forces. A car pulls up behind my vehicle. It has Serb markings. It is a Serb staff car. A man gets out of it and asks the bemused journalists if they know the whereabouts of Mr. Larry. They point to where I am and realise that the man is a Serb colonel.

It is Colonel Vojinovic, my old friend from Banja Luka. We hug.

– *Larry, I have heard that you are going to go into Maglaj today.*

– *I am going to try. I think I have approval.*

– *I have come as a friend to tell you not to try it. You will not make it. Please wait. I promise you will be there within ten days. With a convoy. But do not try today.* He saluted, got into the car, and left. He had come into enemy territory to give me a message.

I got onto the radio to Tony and the convoy. He was being moved. His attempt was over. I decided that in the light of the colonel's warning I had just received, so was mine. I returned to Zenica.

Two days later, two teams from Hereford were flown into Maglaj at speed. They were fired upon by SA 7 Missiles. A third team went in on foot. Amongst other tasks, they improved the accuracy of the air drops.

I was visited in my office by the Squadron Commander of the boys now in Maglaj. I briefed him on everything that I knew about Maglaj. He assured me that I would soon be in with a convoy.

– *If I helilift in any more of my men, are you prepared to go with them?* He did not need an answer, he saw the sparkle in my eyes.

– *OK, I will let you know then.* I was now really excited. But I heard nothing for more than a week.

Meanwhile, more excitement in a different direction.

Twenty Two

Close Call

I heard a buzz that a VIP was soon to arrive. No one would confirm who it was, but he or she was obviously very, very important, so much so that, whomsoever it was, was given a code name. I was intrigued.

I was even more intrigued when I received a message from Brigadier John Reith inviting me to dine with the code name. The dinner was to be in his headquarters in Split the following day. This left me with two options. The first, to motor to Sarajevo and try to get a flight to Split. This was the easiest but had that element of doubt. No airlift, no flights, no time to reach Split. Read about codename in the paper. The second, to motor myself to Split. This involved an early start but almost guaranteed me getting there. I asked my staff to prepare 333. Vesna was to accompany me. I packed the car with a change of clothes.

Vesna asked—*Where is your suit?*

– *My suit?*

– *Your Karadzic suit.*

– *I have given that up.*

–*Where is it?*

– *It is in the flat.*

– *Give me the keys.*

– *No. I don't need it.*

– *Why did you bring it to Bosnia?*

– *For special occasions.*

– *You are going all the way to Split to dine with a codeword. Do you know any occasion more special than that?*

– *Codename.*

– *Codename, codeword. Go and get the suit.* I went and got the suit.

Normally, I would travel to Split behind a convoy. It is easier. No map reading and there is the "safety in numbers" factor. But convoys are much slower than free running vehicles, so I decided to go it alone. The trip down was hot, dusty, sticky, and uneventful. In Split,

I went to the Brit headquarters where I was expected. A WRAC captain gave me the details about the dinner, the time, and the venue, but she said that she did not know who the codename was.

I booked into a local hotel and washed off the grime of the day. I changed into my lightweight suit. This was its second airing in almost two years. I felt strange in it. I wore a bow tie. This is a little game that I have with myself. When I left the army, I threw away the razor. When I joined UNHCR in the field, I determined to give up ties. However, thirty years of conforming make it difficult for me to be the only person without a tie on, hence the bow tie. It is there, but you can't see it, the beard obscures it!

The dinner was in the HQ senior dining room, a sort of combined WO's, Jo's, and officers' messes. When I got there, the early arrivals already had their first round into the bank. Everyone was looking smart. They were all wearing their codeword suits. Vesna was right. Over my glass of wine, I spoke to Andy Bearpark of ODA. He confirmed that his boss Linda Chalker was one of the guests.

The room filled with people, chatter, and excitement. Then the guests arrived. First through the door was Prime Minister John Major. I was near the door and was introduced to him. He very kindly said that he had seen me on the tele. We talked about the recent arrival of the second British battalion. Somewhat presumptuously, I thanked him for this extra support to the humanitarian effort. It was a great gesture by Britain, and as a Brit, I felt proud and pleased by it. Mr. Major seemed genuinely pleased with my comments.

He was then whisked away, and I saw Baroness Chalker. She was smashing; she came across and gave me a kiss and asked me how things were. Choosing her to head the ODA was a masterstroke by someone. She has the respect of everyone in the international humanitarian aid business. She is hands on and caring.

I next spoke to Mr. Rifkind, the Minister of Defence. I had seen him in Bosnia on a number of occasions, including the time at a private party in the house of the CO of the Coldstream Guards in Vitez when I asked him if he had ever wanted to be anything else other than a politician. He very gently reminded me that he was a successful lawyer and a Queen's Counsel!

The Minister left to higher planes and I joined the padre. He asked me if I had seen the seating plan for the dinner. I had not, so I scurried away to find that I was on the top table. A small intimate group of eight, including Mr. Akashi, the Special Representative of the Secretary General. I could not believe that I was so lucky and remain to this day in the debt of John Reith for this honour.

I had a great time. The PM began by saying that everything we said was to be in private and "off the record." I detected a little glance at me here. In two and a half hours we discussed many, many topics. I learned a lot. I asked the PM how important Lord Whitelaw had been to Margaret Thatcher; he thought that he had been very important. I asked him if he had a Willie Whitelaw. He said—*No*. I then asked him if he would have liked a Lord Whitelaw. He said—*Yes*. He also told me that his favourite writer at the moment is Joanna Trollope. He said that her characters fascinated him. My revelations are not up to the tabloid diaries, but I can say that I thoroughly enjoyed the evening and especially the company of Mr. Major. He was charming, easy-going, frank, and very patient with me.

The following morning, I left Split to return to Zenica but not by the route I had arrived. I wanted to visit Enda Savage, who ran the UN-HCR warehouse in Metkovic. Enda is an ex-Irish Army officer. He is very straight. A direct talker. A man you know where you stand with. He had not been happy with the number of damaged bags of flour arriving in Zenica. He suspected that some bags were damaged on arrival and that the contents found their way onto the black market. In the aid business, we are always conscious of criticism concerning the loss of vital aid. We know that the money is hard to come by, that what we need is expensive, that transportation of it is exorbitant, and especially that every grain, every gram, is vital. We are constantly asked about aid ending up on the black market. Journalists are always prepared to recount a story in which they purchased our aid at some stall or other. We operate, more often than not, in environments where the normal channels of law and order have broken down. We often have to deal with national and local authorities with priorities at variance with our own. Some aid does go adrift. Even in the best of supermarkets, in the most sophisticated of countries, "shrinkage" occurs. A percentage goes missing. The trick is to keep it as low as possible. We normally pride ourselves on very little shrinkage within our own ranks. The troubles normally begin once we have delivered it, once we have handed it over. As often as not, this is to local authorities.

Enda was suggesting that more bags were being "written off" in Zenica than should be. I had investigated at my end and discovered that broken bags of flour, in effect, damaged sacks, were not accepted as part of the account in Zenica. The contents were tipped into a large container, later to be re-bagged and issued. The system was not fool proof. Enda's account showed a loss. My account should show a gain. Worse still, the issue of the salvaged flour was haphazard and a little preferential. Enda was right to have pointed it out. I tightened up the procedures, moved a few staff on, and the system improved. I wanted to call in on him and discuss the way ahead.

I underestimated the journey. We left Split at eight. I intended filling up the vehicle with fuel early in the journey but forgot and very nearly got caught out. The coastal route is quite scenic. The views of the mountains on the left side and the Adriatic on the right are stupendous.

What detracts from the view is having to constantly keep one eye on the needle of the fuel gauge and another on the road ahead, searching for a fuel station. At the same time, keeping up an endless chat with Vesna, not wishing to let her know that I have been such a dunderhead as to have set off without fuel. Future tourists, fellow travellers, take my tip, fill up in Split. To the best of my knowledge, there are no petrol pumps between Split and Makarska, and you have to leave the main road to enter Makarska, where the pump is at the far end of town.

From Makarska I was a different man. The feeling reminded me of being a boy on the coach trip to see the lights at Blackpool, after the coach had pulled over and we were able to relieve ourselves. This anecdote was wasted on Vesna.

Metkovic did not seem to get any closer. I began to get slightly worried. From Metkovic to Zenica was at least six hours. The last two, through some notoriously dangerous Croat territory with a reputation for hijackings. I did not fancy being a lone runner, on a dodgy road, late at night, especially as my translator was female.

We eventually arrived at Metkovic to discover that Enda was in bed with the flu. To his great credit, he got up and came in to see me. We discussed warehouses and ways of tightening up our system. I suggested that Enda send to Zenica his second in command to look, check, and recommend. He agreed and it was done.

There are three main ways of getting into Zenica from Metkovic. I asked Enda's staff which way was the best. I was told that the only safe one was via Medugorje, Mostar (Croat side), Jablonica, Prozor, Gorni Vakuf, and Travnik. There was a snag. The route from Mostar to Jablonica was via a new mountain route. *The best views in Bosnia... for the passenger*—I was told by Enda's convoy controller, who advised that we stay overnight in Metkovic and follow a convoy the next day. He also told me he believed the new mountain route was sign posted, protected, and patrolled by the Spanish.

From their territory, we would pass into the hands of the newly arrived Malaysian battalion.

We all agreed that time was our enemy if we were to clear lawless Prozor before dark. I did not want to stay, but I was uneasy about going on.

We left Metkovic at about two thirty. It was a hot, hazy, sticky day. At Capljina, we made two attempts at finding the tiny Zvirovici road. In Medugorje, amazingly, we met at the side of the road Dr. Lana Oruc, the wife of Zlatan, my Sarajevo skin specialist driver. She was there with the charity Care. She told me that Zlatan was in East Mostar with a UNHCR vehicle carrying out a medevac. I would dearly have loved to see Zlatan, but we were late and we had no approval from the Croats to enter East Mostar.

Our trip through West Mostar brought back some memories for me of my time there. It caused Vesna great pain. It was the first time she had seen Mostar since the war began. It was an ancient city she knew well. Being a Sarajevo girl, she was used to destruction, but it made her silent and sad.

We found the road out of Mostar, with no thanks to the Spanish. There was not a single sign anywhere, and we were well on our way along a rough twisting track before we came upon one lone Spanish APC. We had passed a number of forks in the road and by good luck had managed to choose the right ones. The Spanish told us that all was well. Nothing had passed ahead of us. We were on the road on our own. At this stage, the terrain was dreadful—huge boulders and barren hills. We began to climb. Sure enough, the views became spectacular and the track narrow. How the truck drivers get their vehicles around some of the tight hairpin bends I do not know. I was not happy to look down. Fortunately, the drop was on the passenger side. I concentrated on hugging the side of the mountains.

At the peak of this mountain road, there was a checkpoint manned by ten or so Croats, heavily armed and in uniform. They were a friendly, happy bunch. I clearly remember thinking, we were only two, we had a vehicle they would like, and they would guess that we had money. They could easily have thrown us over the side, and no one would have been any the wiser. I very rarely had worrying thoughts, but on this day I did. As we talked to the soldiers, I could see the drop down from the side of the track. It was truly spectacular. This was the view they were talking about in Metkovic. The drop was sheer and hundreds of feet below was the reservoir which, in better times, provided Mostar with its water. The reservoir looked like a green moss framed in silver rocks. It also looked a hell of a long way down.

As we began the descent, my admiration for the convoy drivers increased. It was a hairy run with tight bends, fast descents, and no barriers. Lose control and you would dive down, down, deep into the reservoir. When we reached the bottom, we crossed the reservoir by the bridge which is not many miles north of Mostar. In two hours, we had advanced no more than twenty-four kilometres.

The Malaysian army was manning the bridge. I was as delighted to see them as they seemed to be to see my attractive colleague. They assured us that the road was safe between themselves and Jablonica. We moved on in a far more relaxed manner. I felt safe once again.

In Jablonica we called in on the UNPROFOR headquarters. The Malaysian colonel was polite but not welcoming. I asked him if his men were patrolling the road from Jablonica to Prozor; he told me that they were. He also told me that to the best of his knowledge, there had been no incidents on the road recently.

This next bit was, for me, the most dangerous stretch. We were tired. It was getting late. Once we set off, there was no turning back. The next friendly forces were the Brits in Gorni Vakuf.

The road from Jablonica to Prozor is tarmac, in a valley. There was no traffic on it, not even a Malaysian vehicle. It may be twenty or twenty-five kilometres. Nothing passed us; we passed nothing. We tried to radio Zenica. We had tried all afternoon with no success, but we were now that much closer. Nobody could hear us. We could hear other channels and lots of inconsequential chat. Good re-assuring stuff, if we knew that they could hear us. But no one was acknowledging our call.

It was early evening as we approached the outskirts of Prozor. Prozor is the Croat equivalent of Doboj, another cowboy town. Fiercely Croat, strongly HVO, and anti-UNPROFOR. Coming up from Jablonica, you do not have to go into the centre of the town. You enter the outskirts, then take a right turn onto the Gorni road.

At this turn, we saw the first vehicle we had seen for half an hour or more. It was a Land Cruiser with some HVO soldiers in it. There were a couple of other cars about, and we set off along the road. It is carved out of a steep sided valley with mountain ranges on both sides.

Immediately out of Prozor, the road twists and turns quite dramatically, and then there is a steady climb up to a café at a barren outpost called Makljen. In October and November of '92, I had stopped on a number of occasions at the café. This was before the Croats and the Muslims had torn at each other's throats. It had never been a friendly place. It always had just a few surly HVO soldiers in it. Certainly not a place to stop, on your own, or worse still, with a female translator.

461

As we approached the summit of the road and the cafe, I noticed that we had a vehicle behind us. Although I was going slowly, it made no attempt to overtake us. At the crest of the hill outside the café, it surged past us and then slowed. Vesna was quicker than me.

– *That is the Land Cruiser that we passed in Prozor*—she said with only a trace of fear in her voice. I told her to get on the radio, try every callsign we knew. The road out of Makljen is a very steep descent. There are initially few bends. The car ahead was going no faster than us. We were not wearing our flak jackets. I said to Vesna—*get the jackets from the back, try to put yours on, put mine behind me.* Flak jackets are very difficult to put on in the confines of a moving car.

She put both hers and mine on our seats behind us. She was still trying to raise a voice on the radio. I was watching the car ahead and was trying to lengthen the gap by slowing, but as I slowed, it slowed. I thought about a quick turnaround.

I had the space, but where do I go? To the "safety" of the café? With the car ahead, I at least knew how many we were up against. There were three of them. Also, as long as we were moving, we had as much of the initiative as they did. To the right of the road was the mountain, to the left it varied between a drop or the other mountain side. It was obvious to me that the driver ahead knew the road and knew when he was going to move. Sarajevo had taught me that when there is danger about, you sit up straight, with hands firmly on the wheel. It is a strange feeling. Every muscle is alert. You are aware of your toes and your fingers. You almost feel as if you are outside your own body. Somehow you can see your own face. Time does stand still. Adrenaline definitely flows. You can feel it coursing through your veins. I was waiting for him to make his move. Our lives may depend on my reaction to whatever he did.

Suddenly, we approached a twisty section. I could see in the distance a turning off to the right. We were in the deepest part of the valley, the most isolated section. As I followed him around the bends, he was able to dictate the distance between us. We were closing all the time. Then he moved. He indicated that he was pulling to the left and braked sharply. I went to the left as if to overtake him. He swerved into my path to head me off and tried to push my vehicle into the side of the road. I was now completely in command of myself. I swerved to the right. He did likewise. I swung the wheel to the left again, but he anticipated this, and once again my path was blocked. I switched to the right, to the open side of the road. He did the same, but his vehicle reacted more slowly. The front of my vehicle was centimetres from the rear of his. I was heading for the edge of the road. I saw the gap was closing. I accelerated. The front side of my vehicle was alongside the front passenger wing of his. The gap between him and me and me and the barrier was just enough to get my vehicle through. I could see his passenger—he was shouting to him. Despite the bend, I went like the wind. Foot hard down, great sweeps of the steering wheel. Our kit tumbled around in the back as the car swayed from side to side. I expected shots, I hoped that the flak jackets would stop them, but the bends presumably prevented them from aiming. They gave chase for only a few yards. We sped away. Vesna pointed out that in the distance we could see the village of Gorni. We hammered on until we arrived at the checkpoint at the bottom of the hill. There was a Brit APC. I stopped the car and a Coldstream Guards officer approached. I told him what had happened. He sent the APC back up the road as far as the café, but they saw no one.

On reflection, I should have gone with him. I knew what and who we were looking for. I motored on to the Brit camp. When we had parked, we got out of the car and hugged each other for a long time. No words, no tears.

We had time to motor on to Vitez, but we could not have made Zenica. We decided to stay in Gorni. We had had enough excitement for one day. The Brits gave us a meal. We then returned to the vehicle and unrolled our sleeping bags, where I remember saying—*The least that would have happened is that we would have lost the vehicle and our possessions.*

What thoughts went through Vesna's mind I do not know.

Twenty Three

Return

Back in the office. First call to Peter Williams in Britbatt.

– Any news on Maglaj?

– No firm news but lots of gossip. The Croat news agency Hina is quoting a UN source as saying that the siege is soon to be broken either with Serb consent as a result of Russian pressure, or by it being declared a safe area and occupied under NATO air cover, or through a cease fire and a total exclusion zone. He concluded with a twinkle—*We thought you may be the UN source.*

A little later in the day, I heard a rumour that General Petkovic, the Croat commander, my old friend, Brigadier Enver Hazihasanovic, and Alagic were in Zavidovici planning a joint HVO/BiH operation to relieve Maglaj.

The good news has to be counterbalanced. That seems to be the rule here. Corporal Barney Warburton, a bomb disposal expert from Llanbedr, was killed instantly whilst removing improvised mines outside Stari Vitez. He was a handsome, very smart, gentle giant of a soldier. He had met the Prime Minister the previous day. I think he is only the second British soldier to die here.

The news seesaws again. The British cavalry unit C Squadron Light Dragoons patrolling close to Maglaj have discovered that the Serbs have withdrawn from Ljesnica, the approach road to Maglaj. The way in is open. Peter rapidly resurrects "Op Lawrence." We are off. I take "signalling Serb" Vesna with me, who was with Ginge and I on the first successful attempt.

The Hon. Richard Margesson is in command, one of the most professional officers I have ever met. He is an outstanding commander. With him, everything is planned to the last detail. The mission is to be achieved without hesitation or deviation. In an idle moment, I discover his grandfather was MP for Salisbury and that his Australian wife is an airline pilot.

Commander Alagic is determined that he is going to be first into Maglaj and has made a deal with his newfound allies. When we arrive at Zepce we are delayed, held at the side of the road for almost an hour. During this period, Alagic leads a joint HVO/BiH convoy into the town. He sends me a message by radio—*Alagic first. UN second. – Where were you five months ago?*—I reply.

The convoy of ten vehicles driven by Dutch and Belgian drivers follows me as I follow the new Earl of Maglaj, Richard Margesson. There are no mines on the road, just SAS troopers. This is very different to my previous attempts. At the spot where Ginge and I did our little dance to the tune of machine gun fire, we stop the vehicle and Vesna and I pose for a photo.

As we entered the town, we saw more people than we ever had before. They were lining the streets, on the balconies, waving and cheering. Commander Alagic was basking in his success, his laden convoy parked at the side of the road. His drivers were receiving their accolades. We quietly overtook him and went directly to the warehouse and unloaded first. We sent two trucks up to Tesanj with a Hereford escort. So we relieved not only Maglaj but Tesanj and Maglaj on the same day.

Aida greeted us warmly. She looked as elegant as ever. At our meeting in the municipal hall, she was full of praise for the SAS.

The great joy of the day was the fact that Richard and his boys stayed in Maglaj. The siege was over. The Brits kept the road open. For the rest of the war, Maglaj is not an encircled pocket but a finger along which convoys can pass almost unhindered.

Vesna met up with the translator Barbara. Violetta had gone to Zepce. At the hospital we met our dentist director friend. She looked well and was overjoyed to see us. We attended a lunch in our honour, which must have used up the rations we had brought in. Music was played, songs were sung.

Whilst we were in Maglaj, General Rose was celebrating in Sarajevo with a football match in the stadium. Music was courtesy of the Band of the Coldstream Guards, resplendent in their red tunics. What a day.

On my return to the office, I am told of a new medevac heartache story. A young man in Bugojno was badly wounded in a mortar attack. He lost one eye, can only distinguish light in the other, and has also lost one hand. My medevac doc, Melisa, has worked hard for weeks to get him a sponsor nation. At last she succeeded. A hospital in Denmark is prepared to take him. There is a complication, we need to send a relative with him. His wife is the obvious choice. She loves him dearly and is marvellous with him, but she is now nine months pregnant. When Melisa began her search for a hospital, the girl was in her eighth month. Today, when we went to collect him, the helicopter crew refused the wife. Their action is understandable. They have a minimum crew and no facilities.

It is also a war zone. Furthermore, as they rightly point out, when we get the couple to Split for transfer to a commercial flight to Denmark, no airline is going to take her.

A decision was therefore made to postpone the medevac until after the birth of the baby. The girl was devastated. She fears that her husband will lose his place, that we will say that she cannot go with an infant. On this latter point she may be right. She will be going to look after and to support him, can she do this with a tiny baby? Will the baby be OK? Will Denmark take an extra person? Will the airlines take a few days old baby?

The team left with promises to return, with reassurances that all would be well. Sadly, they were not enough. Two days later, we hear that they have committed suicide. She lay alongside him and pulled the pin out of a hand grenade.

This news destroys us for the rest of the day. We all feel guilty. He was twenty-six, she twenty-three. So close to a new life. In her final moments of deepest despair, did she blame us?

The competition for local staff to get a job with the UN was always fierce. The salary was not fantastic, but it was money when none was about. Which made it very strange when Leyla in the office wanted to resign, leave Zenica, and go back home to Sarajevo.

– *Leyla, of course you can go. And I will help you get there safely. But why do you want to give up the money and the better guarantee of safety that there is here?*

– Larry, my father is blind. Before the war he knew his way around his favourite hangouts. He could go out on his own. During the war he has not been able to go anywhere; shelling, craters, tram wires down, rubbish everywhere, snipers; not the place for a blind man to walk. Well, now it has changed. I want to go back and hold his hand and guide him through the new routes. She returned to her father.

March ended with us having achieved seventy-five per cent of needs. The roads are full of convoys, the warehouses almost full of food.

But in Gorazde it is a different story. It looks as if the Serbs have decided to take it. They are three kilometres from the centre of the city and shelling it. So far, sixty-four dead and three hundred and one wounded. It is of course a UN safe area. Or, it would be if all those nations who, in the General Assembly, said "Aye" to safe areas had agreed to provide a contribution to the thirty-five thousand troops requested by the military men to make and keep the areas safe. NATO has issued a warning. If the Serbs do not stop their offensive, then they will bomb them.

General Mladic predictably calls NATO's bluff. This time, however, NATO plays its cards. NATO F-16's attack the Serbs attacking Gorazde. But the shelling continues. NATO replies with a second airstrike, this time with F-18's. Two sorties in two days. I must confess, I have no idea what the difference is between an F-16 and an F-18. Perhaps the Serbs do now.

General Rose is apparently preparing to reinforce Gorazde. I shall be intrigued to see how he is going to get the extra troops there. I can just see Mladic allowing extra troops in through his cordon.

The news gets worse. The Serbs have ignored the might of NATO. An SAS man is killed. Presumably, he was a forward air controller. The local press is gunning for General Rose. Perhaps, running around after cease fires, he has taken his eye off the ball.

The Brits lose a Sea Harrier over Gorazde. The Pilot bails out over Bosnian territory and is safe and well....but in Gorazde.

The next news we receive surprises and depresses me. The SAS and the pilot have been evacuated from Gorazde by helicopter. Leaving a handful of unarmed UNMOs and UNHCR left in there. Not a good move. Morale has plummeted. If it is not safe for the SAS, the finest, fittest troops in the world, then who the hell is it safe for? UN-HCR has Eddie O'Dwyer as head of office in Gorazde. A calm, brave Irishman. Visiting but now caught in Gorazde is Mary Mclaughlin, a UNHCR doctor, also Irish. They could not possibly have known what hell they would be caught up in. They send daily reports to UNHCR Zagreb, who send them on to us.

Their report for today is terse—*Hospital has taken many hits throughout the day. Everybody in basement. UNHCR building has taken direct machine gun fire. Water source in no man's land. Total dead 389. Total injured 1324.*

Two days later:

– *We are running out of words to describe what is going on. Eight children killed early this afternoon. Four under five.*

The next day:

– *Hospital has been targeted throughout the day by tanks, wire guided missiles, and indirect fire. Reportedly with the aim of destroying it. Director of the hospital reports it is impossible to function in the hospital anymore.*

A little later in the same day:

– *More precise info on attack on hospital. Four hospital staff seriously injured, seven injured. 107 patients admitted, 38 of them died. Staff under shock. Unable to continue working. Patients abandoned.*

They sent more than twenty daily messages. They survived. God alone knows how. Two poignant extracts to close their account.

From Eddie—*This is a terrible place for human beings right now.*

From Mary—*Only the dead are lucky here.*

Twenty Four

Homeward Bound

For me, time to pack up and go home. Time to go home for a break and for pastures new.

Mark is to hold the fort.

The staff, whom I would miss enormously, gave a great farewell barbecue party and a fantastic present, a huge hand-made model boat which I treasure. Father Stipo brought me a small hand-made table and a beautiful crocheted tablecloth to cover it, made for me by the nun. The Red Cross gave me an outstanding abstract painting by an artist I know very well.

It was a warm day. There was lots of booze, thanks to Britbatt; lots of food, thanks to my staff. The car-park was clear of vehicles. Someone had rigged up music. My memory is of burning coals, grey smoke, sizzling meat; dancing and singing; party dresses and perfume; wine, beer, cokes; kind words, swapping of addresses; intimate conversations, cuddles, kisses, lipstick stains; handshakes and hugs; speeches and tears.

My dear Bosnian friends, my dear friends in Bosnia. I was there long enough to be able to see what was going on. Long enough to know that I would never understand it. Long enough to see moments of tragedy and of happiness, to hear laughter and crying, to condemn and to praise. To do my job was a privilege. I thank all who gave me the chance.

Epilogue

I am not a gardener, but within hours of my return from anywhere I like to sit in mine with a glass of wine in my hand, and look at the colours, listen to the birds, and think. I try to put recent events into perspective. Bosnia will take a lot of time in the garden.

The question I am most often asked is whether being in Bosnia changed me: meeting a priest who delays and prevents the delivery of food to a starving community; meeting a doctor who delays and hinders the delivery of medicine to a clinic performing operations without anaesthetics; meeting senior military men who have ordered the mortaring and the shelling of villages, towns and cities crowded with civilians; seeing snipers carrying telescoped weapons through the streets on their way to their eyries to fulfil their murderous work. This has all changed me. What I wanted to see were priests demanding convoys for the innocent; doctors demanding the free, unhindered access of medicines; military men fighting in the battlefield with valour and honour; outraged civilians denouncing the men of violence.

Another questions I am often asked is if the United Nations did enough. It can only be the sum of its parts. Some nations did nothing, which I think is preferable to some other nations who voted for action and took none. Some nations voted for action and took action. I once said the architects in New York had drawn up plans for a house and provided materials for a shed. But the shed did save hundreds and hundreds of thousands of lives. Wise old Tony Land says it better—*Debit all those who die to the war, credit all those who live to the humanitarian effort.*

The question I ask myself is whether I could kill my neighbour. Do I understand the action of the Muslim father in Zavidovici, whose son was killed by Croats, who in retaliation murdered the Croat son of his next-door neighbour? Do I understand the action of the Muslim soldiers in besieged, starving Srebrenica who attacked Serb civilians on the outskirts of Bratunac? I understand, but I still condemn the action. I also ask myself whether I could forgive my neighbour. That is the question that will keep me in the garden for a long time.

472

Afterword

What have I done in the twenty-five years since I wrote the book? I have worked for Christian Aid in Kosovo, ITN in Rwanda, back to UNHCR where I worked in Georgia and Abkhazia, then off to Banda Aceh with the Humanitarian Dialogue Centre. Next was UNRWA in Palestine, ICRC in East Timor, back to UNHCR in Dagestan and Chechnya, then across to OCHA in Pakistan, the Coalition Provisional Authority in Baghdad, UN in Baghdad, and OCHA in Lebanon.

In each of these tours, I have had enough stories to fill more books, but instead, I moved into a parallel humanitarian world, teaching humanitarian professionals on a postgraduate course.

As I write this afterword, the world is in the throes of the coronavirus pandemic. Many of you will be serving in countries that have enough problems without this added one. As some populations are challenging their governments because of not enough ventilators, critical care beds, and testing kits, others live in areas with few hospitals, few doctors, and little if any sophisticated equipment—facing the challenge with great apprehension. Some of you will have had previous experience dealing with Ebola, SARS, or HIV, but Covid-19 is an especially frightening, heavyweight global-killer.

I live in the UK, and seven weeks ago, we had thirty-five Covid-19 related deaths. Today it is 31,855 and rising daily. I write from my home, where we are isolated in lockdown.

Seven weeks ago, many of my friends and colleagues were working in the humanitarian field in one of the forty-two countries in crises and disasters that challenge the world. Life would have been difficult enough—not enough funding, not enough resources. And along comes Covid-19! It appears slowly, and the sale of bats in an outdoor market initially takes the blame. A brave Chinese doctor raises the first warning flags. And the rest will be part of history.

Covid-19 is centre stage. There are global appeals for funding, schools are closed, work is stopped, and lockdown is imposed. There is a race to find a vaccine, new drugs are tried, old drugs are modified. Politicians do their best to hide their ignorance and bluster through daily briefings with charts and figures and theories and projections. In hourly media news briefings, mathematical models compete with medical experiences, and both occasionally challenge common sense. This deadly unseen virus overwhelms societies, rich and poor. For the severest infected, it degrades dignity in dying and in death. It robs relatives of close contact in final moments and mocks mourning and burials. It has brought the fear of death to many who thought it was so far away, causing short term economic crises for individuals and the prospect of a great depression for countries.

Meanwhile in war zones, in areas with drought and famine and well-established but unconquered diseases, life and death goes on. The pandemic is just another burden to be borne.

Funding follows where the searchlight shines. Hunger, homelessness, inadequate medical services will stay in the dark, but the struggle will continue. Humanitarian aid will get through. Aid workers, local and international, will be in the front lines, will beg for resources, will find humanitarian space, will negotiate with impartiality and neutrality and independence as they have always done. They will do what they are trained to do. The better trained they are, the better the service they give and the greater the results. And this is where my third career began.

In 1994, whilst serving in Dagestan, I was contacted by Lord David Owen who introduced me by phone to Dr. Kevin Cahill. They had both experienced directly and closely the humanitarian response to crises over a number of years, and they both felt there were too many amateurs working in the field. They had seen totally, or partially, unqualified, yet very goodhearted people responding to populations in need who were desperate and vulnerable and who wanted and deserved a highly professional response.

Lord Owen and Dr. Cahill were proposing to raise the standard of humanitarian field workers by instituting a professional qualification. I was invited to attend a meeting in London chaired by Lord Owen with a doctor from the Royal College of Surgeons in Ireland, who had extensive field experience. We decided to devise an intensive academic and professional course. In effect, a licence to operate. To be successful, the course needed to have as the core of its students humanitarians who had at least some field experience with which the course could build on. After discussions with a small team of like-minded professionals, we agreed we needed the course to be at university level: fully residential, where the participants could concentrate solely on the course and for it to last no more than four weeks, the maximum period anyone was likely to be released by their agencies. I discovered that for a post graduate diploma, most universities demanded two hundred hours of tuition. You can, with the right group, squeeze 200 hours tuition into a month. Four fifty-hour weeks! Pretty much the same schedule for anyone working in the field. Next was to decide on the content. We decided to cover every aspect of field work to produce a graduate with an all-round knowledge. The Royal College of Surgeons in Ireland took us under their wing and set us off.

We needed forty students from a wide variety of humanitarian backgrounds who were prepared to devote a whole month to attend a course which had no track record! This course was a leap in the dark for staff and students. If you are starting off on a new venture, you must rely on a lot of your friends to get it off the ground, and course, one was no exception. We pulled in friends, relatives, acquaintances, and a few strangers. I contributed my own son. It did him no harm, he now holds a senior post at the World Food Programme. The cohort included doctors, lawyers, a priest, and operators from all the aspects of aid work. Their ages ranged from twenty-three to fifty-three. The participants were magnificent; they knew it was course number one and, if it was a success, it would continue. If it failed, it would be the first and the last.

We worked amazingly long hours, and all learned an enormous amount—they about the humanitarian world and me about how to run a course. Our most sophisticated piece of equipment was an overhead projector. The students all passed, and only one did not go on to work in the aid world.

The second course was in New York, and we were hosted by the City

475

University of New York (CUNY), a city university with a massive 274,000 students and the appropriate motto: "The education of free people is the hope of humanity." We held the course in classrooms in the main CUNY campus building and were accommodated in what had been the Bellevue Nursing Training College—a dark, tired old building. There were some who worried that our students would spend so much time exploring the great city that their studies would suffer. These doubters were just not aware of the rigour and discipline within the course. We offered 200 hours, and we demanded 200 hours. We worked a five-and-a-half-day week. One of the highlights of the organised social scene was very appropriate—a boat ride out to the Statue of Liberty. Another was a musical evening at the American Irish club where Dr. Cahill was President. Both events have become part of the syllabus and tradition of the course. Dr. Cahill is still our mentor and principal fundraiser.

I learned very early on that maintaining interest and enthusiasm over one month of high-pressure lectures was not going to be easy. The age and experience span in the group was so wide. Furthermore, the aid world tends to collect a lot of free spirits, albeit highly motivated free spirits, some, maybe many, maybe most, thought the course would be lots of fun and carried out in the intense but easy-going atmosphere so common, so prevalent in the field. I had to make it very clear on day one that this was not a pick and choose course, the 200 hours were for each and every one of us. If you're a water expert, for sure you will probably know everything in the water lecture; your contribution will be to add field flavour, to add your stories to the lessons taught. This was the same message for our medics, our shelter kings, our lawyers, and all other specialists. It took a little getting used to and was a bit of a bumpy ride.

For almost all of our courses, we were exceedingly lucky to persuade Pamela Lupton Bowers to join us in the early part of the first week to lecture on teambuilding and leadership. She has the reputation of being the best trainer in the business. She originally knocked into shape the highflyers of commerce and industry, and now she devotes her time with the leaders of the UN, ICRC, IFRC etc.

She was very happy and available to shape all except two or three of our courses. She ran the second and the third day of each course: lectures, teamwork and group discussions. She taught, she observed, she listened, she provoked, and she praised. By Wednesday night, she knew their strengths, weaknesses, foibles, and ambitions. This made her highly suited for her concluding task of dividing the class into syndicates of eight. Each team was to include a cross-section of the class with the aim to act like a newly formed team in the field which would work together for the duration of the tour. Ahead of each syndicate lay the forming, the storming, the norming, and finally the performing. Over the years, no team has ever missed one of the stages!

Each of the syndicates is allocated a tutor from our small core of teaching staff. With one exception, all the tutors are former students of the course who, after leaving us, returned to highly successful tours in the field. They know the highs and the lows in the field and in the course. The one exception is Dr. Tony Land, who taught course one when he was serving at the time with UNHCR and who maintained close links with us. He took his doctorate whilst a Fellow at Fordham University and is now an Adjunct Professor responsible for our Masters courses.

We average forty students, and the more international staff there are, the happier we are. The largest course was held jointly with the University of Geneva in Switzerland. We had around seventy students. It was a nightmare to control. It was attended by Brendan Cahill, son of Dr. Kevin. Brendan was not put off. He joined us as Executive Director, and with his father, guided us into transferring from City University to Fordham University, now our alma mater—a superb fit. They have made us so welcome, while also contributing another motto appropriate to us: *Sapienta et Doctrina*—Wisdom and Learning.

An important aspect of every course is to emphasize the danger of the nature of the aid world. In addition to exposure to the challenges of the climate and the prevalence of disease, there is now an ever-increasing challenge to security from hostile forces. We have lectures on security, and wherever possible, we have a security day in the field. Lots of bangs, lots of shouting, disorientation, and physical discomfort. It is a tiring, exhausting, stressful day. It is a vital day. Four of our graduates have been taken hostage. All survived. All four said that the experience of our security day made the early hours of captivity easier.

An absolutely vital component of each course is to produce a course "family." From day one, we stress that the aim is to ensure that all pass the course. Sadly, it does not always happen, more often than not because of language or comprehension difficulties, but we have also had our share of misfits.

In recognition of the work that the participants put into the course, we try to make the graduation very special. We have formality and decorum, opening speeches, a distinguished principal guest who hands over the well-earned diploma, a speech from one of the participants, and then a closing speech from the Course Director. There is a mixture of joy and happiness and sadness and nostalgia as the students realise that the course is over—it's very touching. This will be the last time that they all stay together, each of them as part of this family. There are hugs and cuddles, tears and cheers.

But we encourage the extension of the family. Each course family is part of the greater family of past students. We have a strong alumni body and a very active alumni council. Keeping in touch is so easy these days with all the smartphone gadgets and apps. We ask each student to seek out other graduates of the course when they arrive in a new duty station.

I have tended to focus on the principal actors of the theatre of the IDHA—the teaching staff and the participant body—but I am very conscious of the vital role of the backstage crew. None more so than the course administrators. A small group of exceedingly bright and loyal women who have held each course together.

We have over three thousand graduates from more than one hundred countries.

We have created a family and one of my proudest achievements is to be one of the Godfathers of the course. I humbly dedicate this new

478

edition to all in the IDHA family.
My thanks to you all.

Now for me—back to social distancing.

Stay safe!

Author Biography

Larry Hollingworth is the Visiting Professor of Humanitarian Studies at the Institute of International Humanitarian Affairs (IIHA) and the Humanitarian Programs Director for the Center for International Humanitarian Cooperation (CIHC).

After serving as a British Army officer for thirty years, Mr. Hollingworth joined the United Nations High Commissioner for Refugees (UNHCR) and held assignments in Sudan, Ethiopia and Eritrea. He was appointed UNHCR Chief of Operations in Sarajevo during the siege of that city in the Balkan conflict. Mr. Hollingworth later served, for example, as Deputy Humanitarian Coordinator for the United Nations in Iraq, Lebanon, East Timor, Palestine, and Pakistan. For over twenty-five years and throughout the world and now online, Mr. Hollingworth has directed or taught in nearly every single CIHC and IIHA humanitarian training course.

He was awarded Commander of the British Empire (CBE) in 2002 and honored by the U.S. Department of State on the 60th Anniversary of the 1951 Convention Related to the Status of Refugees in 2011. Mr. Hollingworth is a frequent lecturer on relief and refugee topics at universities throughout the world and is a commentator on humanitarian issues for the BBC.